IBM WebSphere Portal 8: Web Experience Factory and the Cloud

Build a comprehensive web portal for your company with a complete coverage of all the project lifecycle stages

Chelis Camargo

Helmar Martens

[PACKT] enterprise
PUBLISHING
professional expertise distilled

BIRMINGHAM - MUMBAI

IBM WebSphere Portal 8: Web Experience Factory and the Cloud

First published: September 2012

Production Reference: 1180912

Published by Packt Publishing Ltd.
Livery Place
35 Livery Street
Birmingham B3 2PB, UK.

ISBN 978-1-84968-404-0

www.packtpub.com

Cover Image by David Gutierrez (bilbaorocker@yahoo.co.uk)

Credits

Authors
Chelis Camargo
Helmar Martens

Reviewers
Joey Bernal
Philip Cheshire
Mark Polly
Michael Witherspoon
Krishna

Acquisition Editor
Rukshana Khambatta

Development Editor
Susmita Panda

Technical Editor
Devdutt Kulkarni

Project Coordinator
Sai Gamare

Proofreader
Clyde Jenkins

Indexers
Tejal Soni
Rekha Nair

Graphics
Valentina D'silva
Manu Joseph

Production Coordinator
Prachali Bhiwandkar

Cover Work
Prachali Bhiwandkar

Foreword

When I joined IBM in early 2001, WebSphere Portal was little more than an idea. But some believed this was going to be the future of web technology. When WebSphere Portal v1 was released later in that same year, spending the time required to cobble together the components needed to make it run, was an exercise in patience and persistence. But it did run; and it got better, until eventually it evolved into the robust enterprise platform that is the focus of this book.

The emphasis on the word 'Enterprise' within the content of this book is no mistake. Portal projects within an organization are generally enterprise-level projects. Of course, there are smaller and more focused portal implementations that lean toward a specific value proposition; but generally, a portal's strength lies in integrating an organization's content, processes, and systems in new, productive ways. This allows the portal to provide one-stop access across the entire organization. These types of large projects can bring out the best and worst of a company's internal processes and systems. In some ways, they can be the most challenging projects on the planning board.

Why is that? A portal can provide an integration and aggregation point for all of your existing systems. This allows you to expose deep hidden knowledge and information, providing immediate potential benefit. However, this can also expose weaknesses in those systems, due to integration complexity, scalability, security issues, or other lurking problems. It can also force an organization to reevaluate the way it does business. Processes need to be documented, reviewed, or reinvented, if maximum benefit is to be gained by the effort.

This book is all about providing guidance, expert advice, and counsel to the reader, and is the culmination of years of knowledge and best practices in the industry. By bringing together their own extensive knowledge combined with the knowledge of other practitioners, consultants, developers, and customers and then distilling the good bits, Chelis and Helmar have provided a new look at the industry, which is both welcome and long overdue. One thing I love about this book is its appeal to many types of different readers.

The book begins with a focus on identifying and defining your project, giving business owners and project managers the tools and information they need, to make the right decisions from the start. It then provides an update on some of the latest approaches for delivering projects in the most efficient way possible, and with the quickest return on investment. These could save many project teams from having to learn some things the hard way.

Starting with *Chapter 7, Introduction to Web Experience Factory*, the book takes a more developer-focused turn, providing readers with advice and examples for building the application functionality a project requires. This includes guiding the developer into the world of the Web Experience Factory and teaching him/her how to use it effectively to deliver results. The chapters build the reader's knowledge level, to go quickly from building simple applications to more advanced capabilities, such as profiling users, and providing customized views for mobile devices. Finally, *Chapter 18, Portal Troubleshooting* and the next chapters will appeal to anyone focused on administration and management. This is especially important for those who are challenged with the goal of making an environment run efficiently and effectively.

While different areas of this book focus on the goals and responsibilities of different stakeholders within an organization, this does not imply that these sections within the book are mutually exclusive. In fact, it implies just the opposite; while some chapters have more technical details, others are more focused on the overall business experience, providing benefit to everyone involved in the project. I can attest to this from personal experience; in reviewing this book I have read it from cover to cover, and I have learned much, much more than what my feedback to the authors has provided.

We all know that technology moves in cycles, and I have found that the same is true for the technical community. Hard-won knowledge and best practices are learned, gathered, and shared until everyone seems to be well educated. Eventually, a new crop of customers and users emerge and technology evolves just enough that best practices, once thought to be old news, are new again. This knowledge is shared across the community and a new cycle of learning begins. In that light, this book will help all of us learn, review, and continue this cycle. In some ways, the knowledge in this book can be considered timeless. Some best practices of this nature really never go out of style, and this book is packed with them.

But more than that, Chelis and Helmar have opened up a whole new approach to both portal and non-portal projects for the reader. If you are still looking for what you will learn, consider the following key themes that are covered:

- Helping us learn about the capability and capacity of hosted solutions in the cloud
- Helping us to understand which reusable industry assets are readily available
- Providing instruction and guidance on how to use the latest tools for quickly delivering custom applications

Armed with this knowledge, portal solutions can be delivered to provide business value quicker and easier than ever before. The resulting applications can scale better, run cheaper, and be more easily managed than their predecessors. This in itself makes it more than worth the price of the book.

To the authors, I say "Thanks guys", and to the reader I simply say, "Enjoy!"

Joey Bernal
Chief Technology Officer, Element Blue, LLC
Former Chief Programmer – IBM Intelligent Operations Center

About the Authors

Chelis Camargo has over 25 years of experience in IT consulting. He is a self-taught technology enthusiast and patent-awarded performance SME.

With over 10 years of portal experience as a Senior Lead Architect, he has led many large-scale, cross-domain, business- critical portal efforts with multimillion budgets. From proposals to business analysis to delivery, he has managed relations from the top executive business to the very technical level. Chelis has worked for the IBM Portals practice, and consulted for many IBM software divisions and business partners.

In his free time, his interests range from artificial intelligence to robotics, astronomy, Tesla, and quantum physics. Occasionally, he plays some "rare" percussion instruments, such as Cuíca (or "kweeca") and Berimbau (or beÉ¾Ä©Ëˆbaw) . Above all, he enjoys spending quality time with his family, teaching, and playing with his son. More about him can be found on LinkedIn.

Helmar Martens holds a degree in Economics from Mackenzie Presbyterian University, located in Sao Paulo, Brazil.

Helmar has been working with WebSphere Portal and WEF (formerly WPF) since 2000, when he joined Bowstreet, the company which originally created WEF. Helmar has also worked for IBM in several capacities including that of Lead Support Engineer, Technical Sales Specialist, and IT Specialist.

As a Senior WEF Specialist and Portal Architect, Helmar has worked in projects for clients such as NASA, Citibank, New York City Department of Education, Swiss Reinsurance, and other customers in US, Europe, and Asia.

Currently, Helmar lives in Texas, where he enjoys a wonderful Texan social and cultural atmosphere.

I want to thank God for the blessing of writing this book, as well as for the gift of eternal life through his son, Jesus Christ.

I also want to thank my beloved wife, Simone Martens, who has been an inspiration and is my greatest motivator, not only to write this book, but above all, in life.

About the Reviewers

Joey Bernal is a Managing Partner and Chief Technology Officer of Element Blue, LLC, an award winning IBM business partner. Joey is a leader and veteran of IBM software and solutions, and was formally the Chief Programmer of IBM's Intelligent Operations Center (IOC). His extensive background in portal architecture, and development and enterprise application architecture was applied to leading the IOC design and development. Prior to that, Joey was a Technical Leader for the WebSphere Portal Software Services team for IBM. He has assisted in many technical areas, especially IBM cross-brand opportunities with WebSphere and WebSphere Portal solutions within an enterprise context.

He is the author of many popular books and articles including, Web 2.0 and Social Networking for the Enterprise, Application Architecture for WebSphere, and Programming Portlets. Joey has a B.Sc. in Computer Sciences from the University of Montana and is completing his Masters at Regis University.

Philip Cheshire is an Application Developer specializing in IBM WebSphere Portal technology. He has been working with the portal for over eight years, in the grocery and insurance industries. In addition to portal development, Philip also offers a wide range of consulting services related to Java and Android development. Learn more about Philip by visiting `http://philipcheshire.com/`.

Mark Polly, in the past 28 years of his experience in IT, has worked in roles such as Strategist, Technical Architect, and Developer in large companies (Eli Lilly, KeyBank, Progressive), and has been consulting for the past 15 years with Perficient. Mark is currently a Director in Perficient's Portal and Social Company Wide Practice. He primarily works on strategy engagements as they relate to portal, collaboration, and social technologies. Mark holds a Bachelor of Science degree in Computer Science from Purdue University, and a Master of Business Administration degree from Cleveland State University. His current company Perficient's work includes many different portal types and, vendors, and the integration to a variety of technologies, social capabilities, and mobile sites.

Mark was referenced in the book, *Lotus Notes Developer Toolbox: Tips for Rapid and Successful Deployment*, by Mark Elliott, which was published on October 10, 2006 at IBM Press. You can find more information about this book at http://www.ibmpressbooks.com/bookstore/product.asp?isbn=0132214482.

Mark has also written several articles for IBM developerWorks, which can be found at (http://www.ibm.com/developerworks/).

www.PacktPub.com

Support files, eBooks, discount offers, and more

You might want to visit www.PacktPub.com for support files and downloads related to your book.

Did you know that Packt offers eBook versions of every book published, with PDF and ePub files available? You can upgrade to the eBook version at www.PacktPub.com and as a print book customer, you are entitled to a discount on the eBook copy. Get in touch with us at service@packtpub.com for more details.

At www.PacktPub.com, you can also read a collection of free technical articles, sign up for a range of free newsletters and receive exclusive discounts and offers on Packt books and eBooks.

PACKTLIB

http://PacktLib.PacktPub.com

Do you need instant solutions to your IT questions? PacktLib is Packt's online digital book library. Here, you can access, read and search across Packt's entire library of books.

Why Subscribe?

- Fully searchable across every book published by Packt
- Copy and paste, print, and bookmark content
- On demand and accessible via web browser

Free Access for Packt account holders

If you have an account with Packt at www.PacktPub.com, you can use this to access PacktLib today and view nine entirely free books. Simply use your login credentials for immediate access.

Instant Updates on New Packt Books

Get notified! Find out when new books are published by following @PacktEnterprise on Twitter, or the *Packt Enterprise* Facebook page.

Table of Contents

Preface

IBM WebSphere® Portal is a cost-effective, scalable, and proven solution for the portal enterprise space. Given the depth and the breadth of WebSphere Portal and the challenges of developing a portal project, you need a book that covers all the nuances of the entire portal project lifecycle. This book accomplishes just that.

In this book, we cover topics that range from portal assessment, governance, and architecture, to design and development. These topics are covered not only within these traditional areas, but also within the cloud environment context. Keeping both contexts in mind, several chapters are dedicated to portal and portlet testing, troubleshooting, performance monitoring, best practices, and tuning. The cloud option is also analyzed and discussed for hosting, developing, and publishing portal applications.

We also cover **Web Experience Factory (WEF)** as the tool of choice for portlet development. We take you from the introduction to the development of advanced portlets in an intuitive and efficient manner. We cover not only common topics, such as builders, models, and user interface development, but also advanced topics, such as Dojo builders, Ajax techniques, and WEF performance.

Within the WEF space, we cover other topics, which have never been covered before by any other competing book. You will learn how to develop multichannel applications, including web mobile applications, and you will learn about the model types available for portlet development, including when and how to utilize them. We also present and discuss numerous aspects and facets of implementing a WEF project and what it takes to successfully deliver them.

The richness and the profundity of the topics combined with an intuitive and well-structured presentation of the chapters will provide you with all the information you need to master your skills with the IBM WebSphere Portal project lifecycle and Web Experience Factory.

What this book covers

Chapter 1, Portal Assessment, covers the initial assessment of a portal project to a proof of value or concept exercise. It looks at the cloud as a possible paradigm for portal applications. It ends up with a case study that leverages the IBM Toolbox and Portal Accelerator Banking template to illustrate it in a step-by-step way.

Chapter 2, Portal Governance: Adopting the Mantra of Business Performance through IT Execution, covers the importance of portal governance and the best practices aligned with management and processes, to support at the enterprise level. It looks at steps to formulate and implement a portal governance committee and its associated roles.

Chapter 3, Portal Requirements Engineering, covers requirements engineering in the context of application lifecycle management. It provides step-by-step guidelines for functional and nonfunctional lifecycles, from requirements gathering to validation.

Chapter 4, Portal Architecture: Analysis and Design, covers another iterative step in a development lifecycle. It is time to take the requirements and exercise architectural analysis and design for both the functional and nonfunctional aspects, as they are mapped to portal capabilities.

Chapter 5, Portal Golden and Cloud Architecture, covers the best practices in building portal environments for high availability, and delivering the operationalization of the business models. In the context of traditional and cloud-hosted environments. It also looks at the best practices of modeling for portal capacity planning and sizing.

Chapter 6, Portal Build, Deployment, and Release Management, covers the interdisciplinary aspect of build, deploy, and release management in the context of traditional and cloud environments. It covers best practices for build and release management, portal tools and provides a high-level step-by-step release process for WEF and WP.

Chapter 7, Introduction to Web Experience Factory, will introduce **Web Experience Factory (WEF)** along with its main concepts — model, builder, and profile. We also cover the concept of regeneration of WEF applications and the details of its development environment. We finish this chapter by demonstrating how to create a WEF project and how a portlet can be deployed to WebSphere Portal directly from the development environment.

Chapter 8, Service Layers, covers WEF features to support the service-oriented development pattern. We explain the Service Consumer/Provider development pattern, and at the same time, we discuss the list of builders available to implement such a pattern. We also develop two sample models to demonstrate the utilization of this approach.

Chapter 9, Invoking Web Service, shows you how to implement Service Provider models, which can access web services. We cover the powerful and versatile Web Service builder call in detail, and explain how you can build a Service Provider model, which retrieves data through a web service. We also cover the WEF mechanisms available to transform and manipulate response data. A sample model is developed to demonstrate the utilization of this builder.

Chapter 10, Building the Application User Interface, focuses on how WEF builds user interface models. We explain in detail how WEF builds the application user interface. We cover a multitude of UI development-related topics, such as the data-driven development approach, high-level and low-level builders, design pane, and the Rich Data Definition builder call. We also develop a sample model to demonstrate the utilization of the new and incredible Data Service User Interface builder call.

Chapter 11, The Dojo Builders and Ajax, takes you to a journey into the incredible world of Dojo and Ajax. We demonstrate how WEF uses these technologies to provide cutting-edge builders and techniques that will make your applications not only look like, but also behave like the latest Web 2.0 applications. We also explain the performance benefits associated with the utilization of Dojo Builder calls and Ajax techniques. Two sample models enable you to get hands-on experience with both Dojo and Ajax.

Chapter 12, WEF Profiling, covers one of the pillars of WEF technology — profiling. We explain what profiling is, how it works, and how you can take advantage of this powerful technology to provide variability to your application. In addition to covering a profile set and profile, we dissect the profile set editor and all of its elements and nuances. We finish this chapter by working on an extensive sample, which illustrates the richness of profiling, and the numerous manners in which it can enhance your application, addresses requirement challenges, and reduces development costs.

Chapter 13, Types of Models, identifies and discusses the different model types a developer can use in order to develop an efficient application. No other WEF book has ever presented this topic. We demonstrate why it is important to use different model types to develop an application. We then clearly define when and how each of the available model types can be efficiently used to develop reusable, well-organized, and well-structured applications.

Chapter 14, WEF and Mobile Web Applications, addresses the development of web applications not only for mobile devices, but also, above all, for multichannel applications. It analyzes the differences between the development of traditional and mobile web applications. This chapter presents the builders and the framework provided by WEF to develop multichannel applications. We also develop a sample application, which can be invoked from multiple devices, including mobile devices.

Chapter 15, How to Implement a Successful Portal Project with WEF, completes the WEF coverage in this book. We put together a rich set of observations and recommendations that should be followed by any portal project. These recommendations are the result of many years of experience working with WEF. We cover topics that range from the required skills to successfully implement a portal project with WEF, to the type of training and mentoring required, to the proper handling of source control all the way to the development of POCs and prototypes with WEF.

Chapter 16, Portlet and Portal Testing, covers some of the best practices in portal and portlet testing. The test-driven approach is discussed along with some of the techniques used for validating the compliance to a portal's functional and nonfunctional goals via testing.

Chapter 17, Portal and Portlet Performance Monitoring, covers the subject of monitoring, which allows one to measure the success of the portal based on the established criteria. Both business and technical monitoring are much needed capabilities to ensure the right visibility, which allows for the tracking of goals and KPIs. It also covers the tools and metrics to be used during this process.

Chapter 18, Portal Troubleshooting, covers the main approaches for classifying, isolating, and resolving portal problems via troubleshooting and problem determination. It also covers tooling and the best practices applied to troubleshooting.

Chapter 19, Portal, WEF, and Portlet Tuning, covers mature processes for tuning lifecycles and test cases. It covers aspects related to the response time, throughput, and bottleneck resolution. It gives real samples of common bottlenecks and how to tune them.

Chapter 20, Portal Post-production, covers post-production of the main areas of APM, training, impersonation, and the potential benefits of a cloud-based solution. It provides an insight into the continuing support and processes around portal maintenance after the first production deployment.

What you need for this book

This book is comprised of two complementing segments. One segment covers the numerous aspects of implementing an IBM WebSphere Portal project and all its nuances. The other segment addresses the development of portlets using Web Experience Factory.

For the segment related to portal projects, no prior knowledge or experience with the portal is required. Of course, you will benefit even more from reading this segment if you have been exposed to the portal technology.

Equally, for the WEF segment, no prior experience is required. However, if you have not been exposed to WEF development before, we recommend you read and complete a couple of introductory WEF tutorials to maximize your understanding of the material and the exercises we develop. The standard installation of WEF offers a couple of useful tutorials that can provide you with the initial foundation on WEF.

While portal knowledge is not required, some basic knowledge of IBM WebSphere Portal is desirable. This basic knowledge can then be leveraged and advanced towards understanding how WEF powerfully and cooperatively works with IBM WebSphere Portal.

For the WEF chapters, access to a running installation of IBM WebSphere Portal Version 7 is required. An instance of WEF should also be installed on the same machine along with WebSphere Portal. WEF 7.0.0 will suffice for all chapters except for *Chapter 14, WEF and Mobile Web Applications*. For this chapter, you need at least version 7.0.1.

Who this book is for

This book is for portal architects, specialists, developers, WEF architects, testers, project managers, and business owners as well. Because it covers business and technical aspects, it can be applicable to any portal business or technical stakeholder.

Conventions

In this book, you will find a number of styles of text that distinguish between different kinds of information. Here are some examples of these styles, and an explanation of their meaning.

Code words in text are shown as follows: " Move the `.war` files to portal and deploy portlets."

A block of code is set as follows:

```html
<html>
  <body>
    <form name="RTE_Form" method="post">
      <div name="PageTitle"
```

```
                 style="font:12pt Arial; font-weight:
                      bold;color: #336699;">
            </div><br>
              <table>
                <tr>
                  <td >
                    <div name="refreshMessageArea">
                      <span name="inputText_RTE"></span><br>
                      <div name="DjContainer">
                        <span name="messageEntry_TXT"></span>
                      </div>
                    </div>
                  </td>
                </tr>
              </table>
            <div style="padding:20px;">
              <span name="append_BTN" ></span>
              <span name="replace_BTN" ></span>
            </div>
        </form>
      </body>
    </html>
```

Any command-line input or output is written as follows:

```
../bin/releasebuilder.sh -inNew todays_release_dir/exported_
ExportRelease.xml

-inOld previous_release_dir/exported_ExportRelease.xml -out

todays_release_dir/Release.xml
```

New terms and **important words** are shown in bold. Words that you see on the screen, in menus or dialog boxes for example, appear in the text like this: "These include **Broker Services** view where the **Customer Vault**, **Account Info**, **Transfer Info**, **Vault Feature**, **Deposit**, and **Vault Loan** processes can be managed and operated on, as shown in the following screenshot."

[Warnings or important notes appear in a box like this.   ]

[Tips and tricks appear like this.   ]

Reader feedback

Feedback from our readers is always welcome. Let us know what you think about this book—what you liked or may have disliked. Reader feedback is important for us to develop titles that you really get the most out of.

To send us general feedback, simply send an e-mail to feedback@packtpub.com, and mention the book title through the subject of your message.

If there is a topic that you have expertise in and you are interested in either writing or contributing to a book, see our author guide on www.packtpub.com/authors.

Customer support

Now that you are the proud owner of a Packt book, we have a number of things to help you to get the most from your purchase.

Downloading the example code

You can download the example code files for all Packt books you have purchased from your account at http://www.PacktPub.com. If you purchased this book elsewhere, you can visit http://www.PacktPub.com/support and register to have the files e-mailed directly to you.

For WEF, we provide the finished code for all chapters that develop sample exercises. The instructions to install these models are defined in the file entitled Installation instructions for the finished sample code.txt. This file is also available for download from our support site, http://www.packtpub.com/support.

Errata

Although we have taken every care to ensure the accuracy of our content, mistakes do happen. If you find a mistake in one of our books—maybe a mistake in the text or the code—we would be grateful if you would report this to us. By doing so, you can save other readers from frustration and help us improve subsequent versions of this book. If you find any errata, please report them by visiting http://www.packtpub.com/support, selecting your book, clicking on the **errata submission form** link, and entering the details of your errata. Once your errata are verified, your submission will be accepted and the errata will be uploaded to our website, or added to any list of existing errata, under the Errata section of that title.

Piracy

Piracy of copyright material on the Internet is an ongoing problem across all media. At Packt, we take the protection of our copyright and licenses very seriously. If you come across any illegal copies of our works, in any form, on the Internet, please provide us with the location address or website name immediately so that we can pursue a remedy.

Please contact us at copyright@packtpub.com with a link to the suspected pirated material.

We appreciate your help in protecting our authors, and our ability to bring you valuable content.

Questions

You can contact us at questions@packtpub.com if you are having a problem with any aspect of the book, and we will do our best to address it.

1
Portal Assessment

This chapter covers the initial portal assessment leading to a **Proof of Value (POV)**, which needs to be executed for portal engagements at program and/or project levels. One of the main assessment goals is to capture the business drivers for choosing this technology and evaluate the business value to be added with a portal solution. The outcome of the business assessment is a current and future state gap analysis and subsequently a mapping of the business drivers to portal capabilities. The assessment covers business and technology aspects. It helps drive the next discussion of the need for portal governance, process, and organizational changes that a portal project can bring as a requirement to an enterprise moving to the portal paradigm. This chapter will provide orientation to get started with assessing and looking at options for a portal POV; and how the cloud plays an important role in the enablement. By the time we are done, we will have looked at the following topics:

- **IBM WebSphere Portal (WP), IBM Web Experience Factory (WEF),** and the cloud
- Cloud service models—SaaS/IaaS/PaaS
- A case study
- Cloud use cases applied

IBM WebSphere Portal (WP), IBM Web Experience Factory (WEF), and the cloud

Portals are single point of access for information, knowledge, business services, and transactions; providing aggregation and role-based access to **Business to Business (B2B)**, **Business to Consumer (B2C)**, **Business to Employee (B2E)**; along with vertical and horizontal domain support. Portals also allow for that data to be served on a variety of devices, anytime, anywhere. From an architectural viewpoint, a **portal** is an architectural pattern implemented and realized via a product with out-of-the-box integration potentials and capabilities. From a technology standpoint, the IBM WebSphere Portal is a J2EE application with its engine being compliant with portal-specific APIs, such as JSR 168, JSR 286, and WSRP. So what is the cloud and how can it help you with your WP and WEF related initiatives? Let's first start with some basic definitions.

Cloud is a delivery model that uses virtualization to build, provision, deploy, and enable environments, resources, and services. More precisely, its canonical definition according to the working definition of cloud computing published by the U.S. Government's **National Institute of Standards and Technology (NIST)** is as follows:

Cloud computing can be described as a model for enabling ubiquitous, convenient, on-demand network access to a shared pool of configurable computing resources (for example, networks, servers, storage, applications, and services) that can be rapidly provisioned, and released with minimal management effort or service provider interaction.

To complement it, IBM defines cloud computing as follows:

Cloud computing changes the way we think about technology. Cloud is a computing model providing web-based software, middleware, and computing resources on demand. By deploying technology as a service, you give users access only to the resources they need for a particular task. This prevents you from paying for idle computing resources. Cloud computing can also go beyond cost savings by allowing your users to access the latest software and infrastructure offerings to foster business innovation.

SaaS/IaaS/PaaS cloud engagement models

For almost every new technology and trend in business and technology initiatives, there are standards developed around it. Along with the Open Cloud Manifesto, there are some use cases for cloud computing defined in a white paper entitled *Cloud Computing Use Cases 2.0* pioneered by the Cloud Computing Use Case group. Let's now take a look at cloud NIST definitions as for the three major cloud service models. Because, whenever the cloud topic is involved, it is in the context of these services models, which are **Software as a Service (SaaS)**, **Platform as a Service (PaaS)**, and **Infrastructure as a Service (IaaS)**. Let's break them down and look at their defining characteristics:

- **SaaS**: SaaS is related to an application that is served and consumed over the wire, where the consumer itself has no control over the runnable software in terms of the operating system, network infrastructure, and hardware; so it is more like a black box for the consumer. The consumer only uses the service provided but does not control nor have knowledge of the behind-the-scenes mechanics.

- **PaaS**: PaaS is related to the consumer having a little bit of control over the hosting environment for the application it consumes and runs. So the platform can be an application framework; but still the consumer does not have any control over the hardware, network, storage, and operating system for that hosting environment.

- **IaaS**: IaaS is related to the consumer having control over the deployed resources as a whole in terms of storage, operating system, hardware in general, and in some cases even networking.

How WP and WEF in the cloud can help your initiative, and the value added will vary depending on what phase of the **Systems Development Life Cycle (SDLC)** you are addressing. Regardless, if you are planning a new infrastructure or portal migration, or a POV, the level of value the cloud brings can vary. However, the **return on investment (ROI)** can be achieved in all phases of the SDLC.

How are WP and WEF represented in the IBM business SmartCloud and Amazon Cloud? For those interested in the new cloud delivery model of provisioning portal development, integration, system test (user acceptance and performance), and production environments, the IBM SmartCloud has a plausible and viable solution. Based on the starting guide, we will walk you through the whole process. For the purposes and scope of this chapter, we will focus on the development environment only.

Getting started – case study

In this book, we will base all of our case study examples on a fictitious bank client named A2Z Bullion Bank that has, as a business driver, the need for modernization of its call center operations. Another major driver is the need to revamp and rebrand some of the banking operations via the consolidation and integration of a lot of application functionality, previously available in **Customer Information Control System (CICS)**. Even though this client belongs to the financial sector, all the examples in this book can be easily correlated and translated to several other industry domains.

At a high level, the A2Z Bullion Bank, which has been providing other commercial banks with Bullion Vault services, uses 3270 terminals for its offshore call center operations. It uses CICS and a relational backend for its many frontend applications, all of which need to be consolidated via Portal. So far, the bank had only interfaced with other bullion or central banks, but it is now opening its operations to other corporate broker consumers interested in Bullion Vault services. The Vault services allow users to store physical bullion metal bars (gold, platinum, palladium, and silver) in the Vaults. Transfers from fiat currencies and loans are also services aligned with Vault services. Furthermore, users can forecast and trend their future Vault performance based on future metal spot prices. The bank stakeholders have decided on the need to have a self-service consumer-oriented channel for this new activity.

The goal of the bank is to understand how portal and the cloud would be able to help in the modernization process to be able to gauge the value added and ROI.

Let's start with our case study and the **Business Value Assessment (BVA)**. IBM BVA is an IBM-driven methodology and should be applied with the help of IBM consultants and business partners. The generic steps of a portal BVA are cited and illustrated as follows:

1. One of the main goals of the assessment is to capture the business drivers for choosing this technology and evaluate the business value to be added with portal. The outcome of the business assessment is a current and future state gap analysis and subsequently a mapping of the business drivers and requirements to portal capabilities. The assessment covers business and technological aspects, and helps drive the next discussion of the need for portal governance, process, and organizational changes that a portal project can bring as a requirement to an organization new to portal. First, we cover in a workshop-like format with active interviewing of stakeholders per module target background, objectives, and defined approach. The output of these first items serves as an input to feed the next exercise. The business need and portal solution align together via the particular business and technical drivers and the current state of the business assessed. This initial portal assessment needs to be done for every portal engagement at a project and ideally at the program level. Next, we will cover the main steps in the BVA cycle—background, objective, and approach.

2. Business need and portal alignment.

3. A "Day-in-the-Life" demonstration.

4. Financial case.

5. Recommendations and next steps—POV.

Step 1 – background, objective, and approach

IBM consultants and partners have many ways to explore a BVA methodology. This direction was chosen because the BVA methodology can help to do the following:

- It aligns **Line of Business (LOB)** and IT management with a common and prioritized set of capabilities for your portal.

- It provides you with a vision of the portal when it's complete.

- It gives you a high-level cost and benefit analysis to define the value of a portal solution in financial terms. The corporate positioning helps to set the stage for defining the vision, the strategy, and the execution.

Step 2 – business need and portal alignment:

In order to get to the road map and future state, the IBM consultant and portal architect had to go over a few workshops to gather the required data.

Business value alignment

It starts with the million dollar question—"What should our organization do with a portal and workplace to solve their current pain points and address the need for the future and new business demands?" We will not go into any details of this approach in this book, but we will give you the pain points to make our lifecycle story complete and give you a frame of reference for your own portal initiatives. The following diagram will provide the high-level phases to get the portal off the ground. Any portal engagement would have to apply a similar level of analysis in order to realize the portal value.

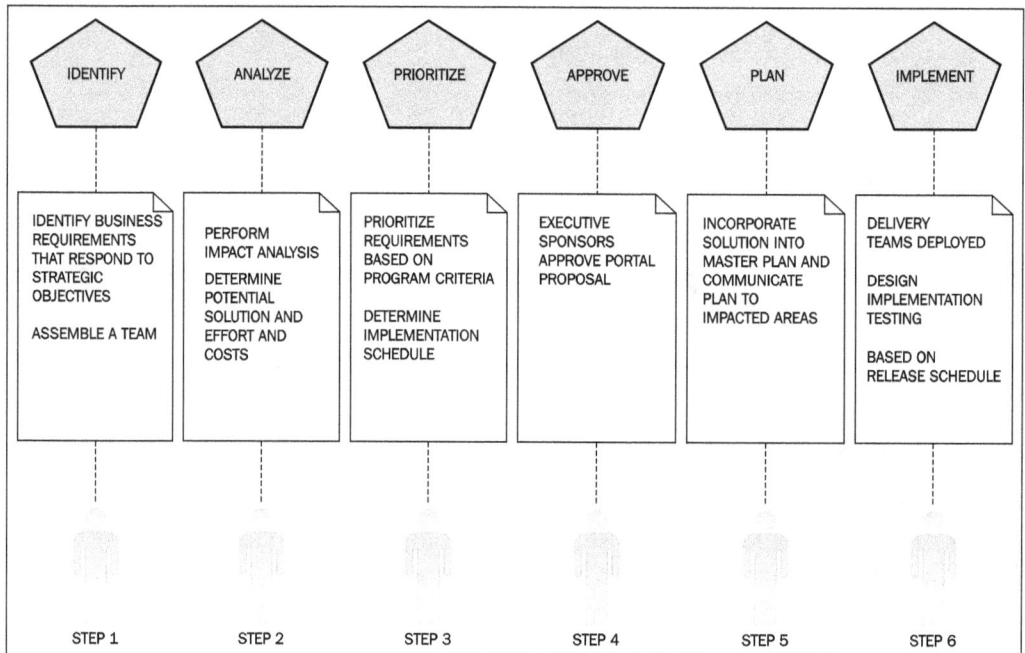

IDENTIFY	ANALYZE	PRIORITIZE	APPROVE	PLAN	IMPLEMENT
IDENTIFY BUSINESS REQUIREMENTS THAT RESPOND TO STRATEGIC OBJECTIVES ASSEMBLE A TEAM	PERFORM IMPACT ANALYSIS DETERMINE POTENTIAL SOLUTION AND EFFORT AND COSTS	PRIORITIZE REQUIREMENTS BASED ON PROGRAM CRITERIA DETERMINE IMPLEMENTATION SCHEDULE	EXECUTIVE SPONSORS APPROVE PORTAL PROPOSAL	INCORPORATE SOLUTION INTO MASTER PLAN AND COMMUNICATE PLAN TO IMPACTED AREAS	DELIVERY TEAMS DEPLOYED DESIGN IMPLEMENTATION TESTING BASED ON RELEASE SCHEDULE
STEP 1	STEP 2	STEP 3	STEP 4	STEP 5	STEP 6

Business drivers and current state

The A2Z Bank has funded a program with PMO support to facilitate the need for governance around the portal initiative. They are in the process of being educated on the value of having such infrastructure support around the new initiatives. They want to have a POV done quickly to show how the portal value can be added within a short time to market. The major business drivers were the need for modernization and the new line of business and self-service customer channel to support. A series of workshops was done with several lines of business stake holders to cover the preceding aspects.

Current state, future state, and a road map

One of the main focuses of capturing current state is to capture the current organization processes in place at the enterprise level and understand how they can be positioned to a future state and enterprise road map that has portal capabilities in its critical path. From there, a future state can be mapped out and a demonstration can be done at a more generic level with the "Day-in-the-Life" demonstration for vertical markets. Then a POV using stubbed data from real data and service models can be used to further illustrate and demonstrate quick business-driven development with the IBM SmartCloud, WP, and WEF patterns.

Current state – pain points and how portal capabilities can fill the gap

Once the workshop and interviews that focus on documenting current internal processes, governance maturity level, and so on are all done, there is a mapping to portal and cloud capabilities, along with the demand for fast application development and value to market. The outcome of this exercise will allow the value of portal to be illustrated and imagined. The next step is to map out the demonstration of financial case to the "prospects" executive sponsors.

The following list consists of a high-level road map potential with a few critical points identified and their recommended solution provided:

- According to the BVA, 70 percent of the A2Z IT budget goes into maintenance of current applications
- According to the BVA, 39 percent of A2Z bugs in the system are due to misconfiguration
- According to the BVA, 85 percent of its IT capacity sits idle
- According to the BVA, 49 percent of the A2Z enterprise applications are not integrated but working in large IT silos and without any governance oversight

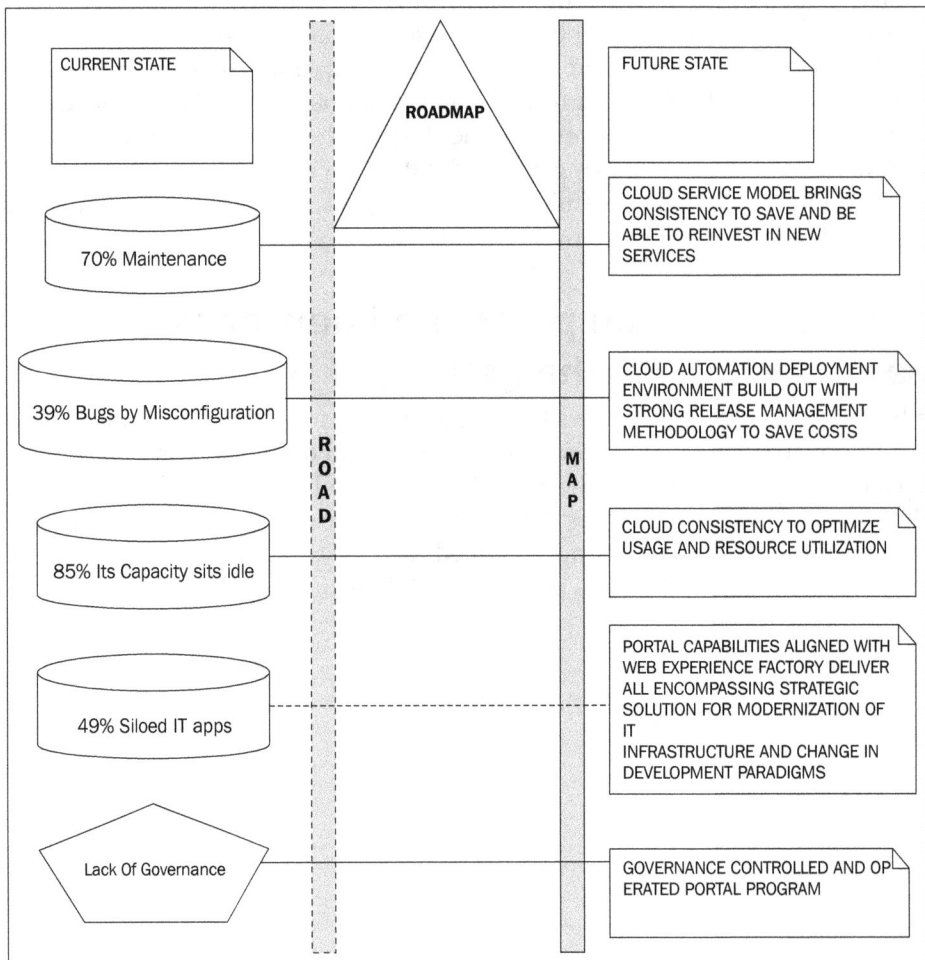

Step 3 – A "Day-in-the-Life" demonstration

In order to make the business case and demonstrate, some of the added value with portal and the cloud, a series of presentations were made available to top decision makers and stakeholders. These dynamic demonstrations are not just static PowerPoint presentations. They are full-fledged, interactive demonstrations presented via a web browser. It allows for stakeholders to relate to and anticipate that their business goals would be positively changed by portal capabilities. These are necessary steps in bringing the road map vision closer to the business case. Take your time to watch them and look at a sample that matches the industry domain for which you work. After these presentations were shown, that was a general consensus that the portal initiative would have A2Z Bullion Bank on the right road to the future. The next step was to create a financial case to show the financial gains of adopting both portal and the cloud as the new paradigms for A2Z Bullion Bank Infrastructure Technology.

Here are some links where you can read articles and watch videos, and learn more about the following topics:

- IBM Industry Toolboxes for WebSphere Portal at
  `http://www-01.ibm.com/software/websphere/portal/industry/`
- WebSphere Portal Web 2.0 for Banking at
  `http://www.youtube.com/watch?v=uR3FUl8Jqws`
- WebSphere Portal works for Banking – Part 1 at
  `http://www.youtube.com/watch?v=X4_vqk2qpCE&feature=related`
- WebSphere Portal works for Banking – Part 2 at
  `http://www.youtube.com/watch?v=jVsRaeFlU80&feature=related`

Step 4 – the financial case

IBM consultants, software sales experts, and business partners can help build a financial case for an enterprise. In this case, A2Z Bullion Bank utilized the services of an IBM business partner for most of its modernization efforts. The financial case was built and shown to the CFO and his teams, along with other important executive players, such as the CTO and his teams. The financial case is an important module in the BVA exercise, as it plays the role of the major decision-maker item in a value proposition. Besides the huge financial gains, this cloud-enabled portal initiative (with fast time to market value proposition as one of the main criterion) and major pain points with which the current IT infrastructure deals and struggles with, were going to be addressed.

Stakeholders also watched online banking, multichannel banking, and payment presentations, and were highly impressed with all the capabilities that portal could bring to the table as a way to allow A2Z Bank to move into the future.

Step 5 – recommendations and next steps—POV

The next steps were laid out and agreed upon.

A POV was approved by the stakeholders, and a full project schedule and resource support allocated and dedicated to make it come to fruition.

In our sample, we will perform the following steps:

1. Use a cloud provider to quickly provision the development environment dedicated to the POV.

2. Use the WP and WEF cloud patterns to expedite the development and integration phases along with IBM Industry Toolbox.

3. Use the feedback from the BVA to drive the use cases for the POV with the assistance of a portal architect and WEF specialist.

4. Have the scope and use cases for the POV, and implementation plan reviewed and approved before moving to implementation. In this case, the POV was going to be focused on the banking channel only using data mostly from the banking template, but add some customization, and serve as a functional development sandbox for portal-related development efforts.

With a POV funded and ordered to be delivered within a timeframe, the decision was made to use the IBM development and test cloud. After that, a private cloud would be used to jump-start the physical infrastructure for the entire portal initiative lifecycle.

A program-level road map was designed and agreed upon in the following circumstances:

1. Where first phase would transfer and/or integrate some of the foundational functionality into portal information architecture for both the banking channel and the call center. It would use the new IBM X150 DataPower appliance to mediate the data entry points and functional layers via SOA reference architecture; along with the Master Data Management reference architecture.

2. Second phase would deal with portal areas such as **Business Process Management (BPM)**, content management, **Single Sign-On (SSO)**, and custom search. The entire program would have strong governance, **Application Performance Management (APM)**, and business intelligence (via analytics) support. This initiative would take advantage of the cloud capabilities for its plan of business success via IT execution. Cloud patterns would be reused to expedite the environment build-out and time to market via IBM Workload Deployer (second phase BPM, SSO, search topics will be fully covered in the next edition).

Cloud use cases applied

The BVA covered a lot of ground and provided a road map for the future.

The generic outcome of the BVA concerning cloud-related aspects was that:

- IaaS would be adopted for this transformation effort (as a consumer) saving costs

- PaaS would be adopted for this transformation effort (as a consumer) saving costs

- SaaS would be a service model on which the bank would start capitalizing via its call center and self-service channels (as a cloud provider); thus generating profits

A decision was made to start the prototype effort using a cloud provider. Both the Amazon and IBM SmartCloud are great options, which provide both development and test micro images that can be easily and quickly deployed. They both offer the elasticity and standardization on top of virtualization and the value of central monitoring, and quick environment build-out is added along with the other advantages. In this chapter, we will share how to get started with both cloud providers. In the real world, one would choose one cloud provider, but for informational purposes, we will show both of them for the prototype and POV goals. Let's first start with IBM SmartCloud. This next section will demonstrate how to log in, choose, create, manage, and deploy both the portal run-time environments and the WEF development environment in IBM SmartCloud, Amazon Cloud, or on a standalone virtual image machine.

Cloud approach with IBM enterprise SmartCloud – initial high-level tasks

The following diagram illustrates the basic steps in getting your IBM Cloud up and running, and then using the banking template:

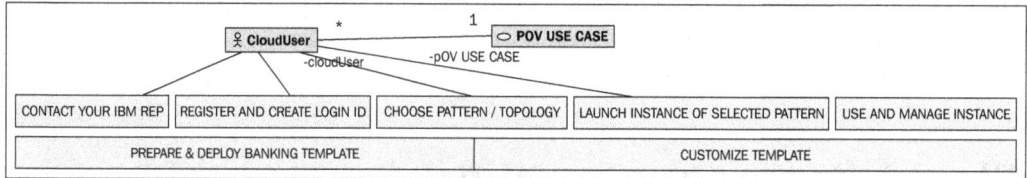

CloudUser			1	POV USE CASE

-cloudUser   -pOV USE CASE

CONTACT YOUR IBM REP	REGISTER AND CREATE LOGIN ID	CHOOSE PATTERN / TOPOLOGY	LAUNCH INSTANCE OF SELECTED PATTERN	USE AND MANAGE INSTANCE
PREPARE & DEPLOY BANKING TEMPLATE			CUSTOMIZE TEMPLATE	

To get your IBM Cloud up and running, perform the following steps:

1. Contact your IBM representative to set up an account, and order the SmartCloud plan and the capacity options for reserved, capped, or uncapped resources.

2. Register and create a login ID, and access the cloud.

3. We then choose a pattern topology based on the needs and scope of this environment. In this case, it will have WP, WEF, IHS. Initialize a new instance and add necessary topology artifacts (start and stop portal server – start and stop HTTP server). Start WEF and get your Hello portlet up and running. For further information on this step, please read the *IBM Smart Business Cloud getting started guide - WebSphere Portal V6.1.5* article located at http://www-10.lotus.com/ldd/portalwiki.nsf/dx/IBM_Smart_Business_Cloud_A_getting_started_guide.

4. Prepare and deploy the banking template and create necessary portal pages to host the portlets based on the wire frames identified and proposed during the BVA and implemented via services contract for the POV initiative.

5. Customize the template with the bank data model (captured, documented, and stub developed during the BVA) and the desired corporate branding. Prepare some stub data for the POV itself.

Cloud approach with Amazon Elastic Compute Cloud (EC2) – initial high-level tasks

The following diagram illustrates the basic steps in getting your Amazon EC2 Cloud up and running, and then using the banking template:

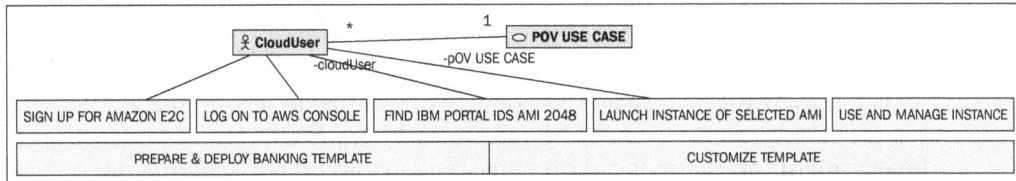

To get your Amazon EC2 Cloud up and running, perform the following steps:

1. Sign up for Amazon Service.

2. We register and create a login ID and log on to the console.

3. We then choose an AMI pattern topology based on the needs and scope of this environment. Go to `http://aws.amazon.com/amis/2048` for the standard development **Amazon Machine Image (AMI)** for portal.

4. Initialize a new instance and add necessary topology artifacts and launch it (start and stop portal server, start and stop HTTP server). Start WEF locally and get your Hello portlet up and running. For more information on how to boot and manage your portal image, please read *IBM Websphere Portal and Lotus WebSphere Content Management Amazon Machine Image Get Started Guide* located at `http://public.dhe.ibm.com/software/dw/cloud/wps-wcme/Get_Started_Lotus_AMI.pdf`.

5. Create a test project on WEF and download the WebSphere Portal Solution Installer. Consult the IBM WebSphere Portal Solution Installer – User Guide for any questions related to the Portal Solution Installer. Move the .war files to portal and deploy portlets and pages to the cloud (or to a standalone virtual machine from VMware). Smoke test the banking portlets' functionality.

> For a great advanced demonstration on how to manage Amazon images, please watch the multimedia presentation by Andrew Glover in the IBM developerWorks article — *Cloud computing with Amazon EC2*. It can be found at `http://www.ibm.com/developerworks/offers/lp/demos/summary/j-cloudamazonec2.html`.

6. Prepare and deploy the banking template and create necessary portal pages to host the portlets based on the wire frames identified and proposed during the BVA.

7. Customize the template with the bank data model (captured, documented, and stub developed during the BVA) and the desired corporate branding.

The next steps are common to either cloud provider. They are as follows:

1. Prepare the environment for the portlets using IBM Toolbox banking portlet. Follow this article and read the instructions on how to do so. In this case study, we use the IBM Toolbox banking portlets to jump-start the development for the financial domain. We look at the real banking data model and document it with the labor resources allocated to the POV.

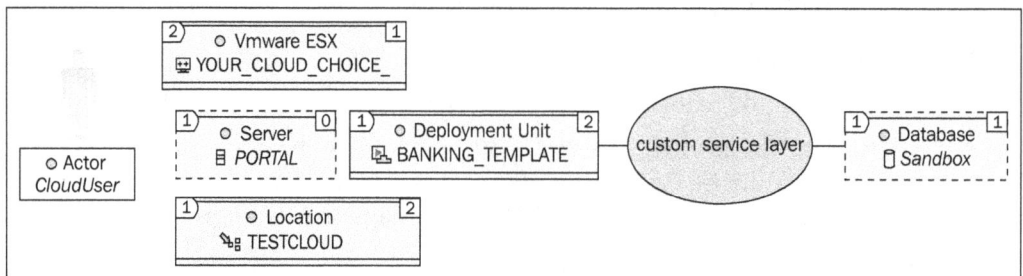

2. Prepare the environment (either cloud or a private standalone virtual machine mentioned in cloud vendor choice steps).

3. Configure the banking portlet database along with authentication, and run a verification test to make sure the containers are up and running with the expected container and application-level connectivity. Create a test project on WEF, and download the WebSphere Portal Solution Installer. Consult the IBM WebSphere Portal Solution Installer User Guide for any questions related to the Portal Solution Installer. Move the `.war` files to portal and deploy portlets and pages to the cloud (or to a standalone machine). Smoke test the banking portlets' functionality.

4. Prepare and deploy necessary custom test stub data. Create a custom data or stub a service layer and implement it for the POV. In case of A2Z Bank, a service layer was created to map to the data layer as part of the POV requirement to have a fully functional portal. In this case, the SQL provided to build the data model for the banking template was architecturally converted into web services definitions with the proper operations to the data layer, as part of the POV project scope. The following link provides the documented data model, which was converted into XML and then created as service interfaces:

   ```
   http://www-10.lotus.com/ldd/portalwiki.nsf/dx/Introduction_to_
   the_IBM_Banking_template_for_WebSphere_Portal_bnk_2.0.0
   ```

   These steps require the collaboration of a portal, service, and data architect.

Once your Portal sandbox environment is operational, (regardless of the cloud vendor or if you create a standalone virtual machine) and you have some stub data to play with, perform the following steps:

1. Configure and customize look and feel, and align it with corporate branding strategy.
2. Officially demonstrate and prove the value of WEF and WP aligned with a cloud.

After the POV was done and its success was acknowledged, the next steps were laid out for the full-blown portal initiative to be kicked off. It was decided that while the banking template would speed up time to market on the self-service channel, the Web Experience Factory would allow for fast development of custom code for the center effort. Both of them would benefit from the advantages of using a cloud service and delivery model.

Portal and Cloudonomics sense

We hope we have given the reader the tools to look into the various possible adoptions of cloud computing in relation to portal initiatives. There are ways to look into the pain versus gain and cost benefit of such claim that "cloud computing can be viewed as a means of reducing cost, increasing revenue, improving business agility, and enhancing the total customer experience". Joe Weinman from www.cloudonomics.com coined the term "Cloudonomics" and laid out 10 laws and formulae to contextualize the value created by cloud computing. They could be used to look at your own portal and gauge the benefits of cloud computing.

To simplify, let's look at first five ones that made the business case for A2Z portal in the cloud, and how the ROI is measured against these items as follows:

- **Law no. 1** — *Utility services cost less even though they cost more*: The "Value of Utility in the Cloud" (simulation) enables assessment of different provisioning intervals and their resulting costs in light of the demand function." That means a good cloud estimation model can show hybrid, shared, dedicated cloud patterns, and the overall cost benefit of outsourcing your cloud to a provider versus creating and managing your own enterprise cloud. Besides, this can take into account how the pay-per-use model (as opposed to just on demand) can help us build a financial case.

- **Law No. 2** — *On-demand trumps forecasting*: "The ability to provision capacity rapidly means that any unexpected demand can be serviced, and the revenue associated with it captured. The ability to rapidly deprovision capacity means that companies don't need to pay good money for nonproductive assets". So, if the portal utilization growth rate is linear versus exponential, the value of the cloud utility exercise can help us define the capacity provisioning approach based on the estimated or known growth patterns.

- **Law No. 3** — *The peak of the sum is never greater than the sum of the peaks*: Under this strategy, the total capacity deployed is the sum of these individual peaks. However, as clouds can reallocate resources across many enterprises with different peak periods, a cloud needs to deploy less capacity. So, let's say that in the banking domain (unlike tax businesses are concerned about April 15th, a retailer with Black Friday, a broadcaster with Super Bowl) due to the dynamic nature of its business, A2Z Bank used the cloud to manage the sum of the peaks and the peak of the sum, as metal and bullion markets vary on a daily basis on the different world markets.

- **Law No. 4** — *Aggregate demand is smoother than individual*: These two laws (3 and 4) are related in that value of aggregation and the value of resource pooling for peaks. They point out that economies of scale can apply cloud to its problems.

- **Law No. 5** — *Average unit costs are reduced by distributing fixed costs over more units of output*: So in other words, A2Z Bank took into consideration demand patterns for both new bullion banking business and call center operations when deciding on the benefits of cloud computing for its enterprise portal solution.

Infrastructure as a Service (IaaS) can be highly beneficial to portal applications for server, networking, data center, storage functionality, and the scalability. These are foundational and business critical infrastructures, which require the most flexibility to stay operational within the expected service-level agreements. There are, however, other business drivers as follows:

- Reduced capital expenditures and labor costs for portal and overall IT.

- Fast provisioning and deprovisioning of services to be exposed or consumed by portal.

- Elastic resource pooling as computing resources are pooled to serve multiple capabilities. It fosters dynamic allocation and entitlement of virtual and physical resources based on service-level agreements, as well as on changing demand.

- Superior service management with visibility, control, and automation across IT and business services. One of the main portal challenges is around having this visibility around portal services.

- A plethora of possible portal deployment choices over the cloud, behind the firewall or as an integrated service delivery platform make it even more appealing.

The fact of the matter is that portal is an entry point to content, data, information services; and its performance and availability directly depends on the availability of all the services associated to it. Furthermore, cloud computing as a technology paradigm is only viable because that technology offers many benefits to business organizations deploying business solutions as follows:

- Optimized development systems resources to keep portal developers productive. Portal development environments can become complex and expensive to create and maintain.

- Reduced capital and licensing expenses portal efforts. They can be as much as 50 to 75 percent due to the on-demand provisioning of virtualized test resources via a test cloud.

- Decreased portal operating and labor costs as much as 30 to 50 percent by automated provisioning and configuration of portal test environments. Portal application deployments and environment build-outs and configuration can be unique and prone to errors if not automated.

- Improved quality by reducing defects that result from faulty portal configurations as much as 15 to 30 percent.

Summary

In this chapter, we covered the main phases of an initial portal evaluation. We looked at how a BVA can be done to uncover the value added by portal and how a road map for the entire enterprise can be one of the outputs of the BVA exercise. We looked at how a prototype can be started leveraging cloud using development images from either Amazon EC2 or IBM SmartCloud. We saw how patterns are built to expedite the prototype environment and kick off the portal effort. In this case, this fully functional environment would be leveraged for future development purposes. We also looked at high level, how Portal accelerators and toolbox assets can expedite the realization of value for an enterprise moving to the Portal paradigm. Remember that team work is always the best solution. These efforts are implemented with the collaboration of all stakeholders involved in a technology transformation effort and the support of IBM software, services, and other subject matter experts.

2
Portal Governance: Adopting the Mantra of Business Performance through IT Execution

This chapter covers some foundational aspects and best practices for determining and implementing a portal governance strategy. Governance allows an enterprise to step a level above the technology stack and work with **Project Management Office (PMO)** to align with the business and IT processes. It defines a governing body with roles, responsibility, and accountability supporting the portal lifecycle and its operational aspects. As **portal** is, architecturally speaking, an integration pattern that can touch every single part of an organization, it requires new processes to be defined (or existing processes to be refined) around its lifecycle and mission. In this chapter, we will discuss the following topics:

- Social and technical evolution
- Five planning steps to governance
- Portal governance best practices
- Value interests

Social and technical evolution

Portals are web-based interfaces that comply with established standards for integrating, aggregating, collaborating, and personalizing structured and nonstructured data from a plethora of sources. There are many types of portals including collaborative, transactional, e-commerce **Business to Business (B2B)**, **Business to Employee (B2E)**, **Business to Consumer (B2C)** enablers serving procurement, self-service, sales, **customer relationship management (CRM)**, **Human Resources (HR)**, and many vertical and horizontal domains. Portal evolution has followed social evolution. First generation provided static content, while second generation was centered on collaboration and dynamic content; third generation focused on the full function, personalized, and single point of access for a domain available on many presentation devices, based on open standards and frameworks. Current generation is cloud-aware, while future generations will include artificial intelligence with highly interactive and intelligent voice portals with talking agents mediating data, people, and processes.

Based on the evolution of portal technology, it is safe to say that in the past, many portal initiatives could have succeeded without any governance at all. That is the past, when there were less complex integration and collaboration scenarios. Today, business communities from medium to large portal implementations see how crucial it is for the portal initiative to be aligned with the current IT governance maturity level within the organization. New processes, portal offices, and steering committees may need to be created in order to support the portal venture.

There are many contributing reasons to the failures in portal initiatives:

- Lack of governance
- Lack of vision or commitment from stakeholders
- Lack of product knowledge and proper quality skill set fail to understand how its capabilities can help the business achieve its goals
- Lack of a discipline that tailors for the needs of a portal initiative at the program level and the project level

Portal implementations need strong alignment with business processes as well as with involved **Lines of Business (LOBs)** via a precise, repeatable, and well-planned approach to bring strategic alignment and business execution together. In order to be successful, portal engagements need both governance and management to define and enforce new processes and engagement models needed to make a portal venture successful today. One crucial item is defining a vision that clearly states and supports a migration from current to future state based on the many business and technical drivers for this adoption. It is crucial to have both governance and management by contextualizing these two aspects.

This concept is well presented in the IBM book — *IBM IT Governance Approach Business: Performance Through It Execution* — authored by Lynn Mueller, Matthew Magee, Petr Marounek, and Andrew Phillipson.

> *"A governance process, as described earlier, is used to define the chains of responsibility, authority, and communication to empower people, as well as to define the measurement and control mechanisms to enable people to carry out their roles and responsibilities. Thus, a governance activity is intentionally designed to define organizational structures, decision rights, workflow, and authorization points to create a target workflow that optimally uses a business entity's resources in alignment with the goals and objectives of the business. A management process is the output from the governance process. Unlike a governance process, a management process implements the specific chain of responsibility, authority, and communication that empowers people to do their day-to-day jobs. The management process also implements appropriate measurement and control mechanisms that enable practitioners the freedom to carry out their roles and responsibilities without undo interruption by the executive team. These measurement and control mechanisms allow the executive team the ability to monitor the execution of both the governance and management processes remotely, as well as monitor the output quality of the management process in execution."*

Along these same lines, John Kotter presents eight steps in his book — *Leading Change* — that can be looked at here in the context of a portal venture and how it will bind to the existing governance-based processes and create new ones as needed.

This model may be a helpful reference for your portal governance solution team during a transformation effort. We will describe five of these steps along with the action items taken by the A2Z Bullion Bank leadership.

Five steps to governance

The five steps to governance are as follows:

1. Establish a sense of urgency.
2. Create the guiding coalition.
3. Develop a vision and planning strategy.
4. Communicate the changed vision.
5. Empower broad-based action.

Establish a sense of urgency

There are simple questions to start with, which can be linked to the complexity of pain points to be solved by the portal solution. The answers to these questions must be clear:

- Why are you doing this?
- What is the urgency?
- How is a portal solution solving the pain points?
- What is the impact of not having a portal?

These questions assist in determining how serious your organization is. If the urgency is not there, senior sponsorship enthusiasms and lack of proper attention will impact its course, because it will not be given the appropriate financial support, along with labor resources and genuine funding. In our case study, all the stakeholders shared the sense of urgency when presented with portal roadmap.

A2Z Bullion Bank action

The sense of urgency was established due to the potentially fatal duel between modernizing and transforming now, or risking to perish due to lack of agility to react to changing markets and demands. When businesses face transformation demands, they must be able to respond and adjust accordingly, or risk financial stability. Because of the acknowledgment and sense of awareness created during the assessment phase, sponsors were onboard and ready to act towards the common goal.

Create the guiding coalition

The next step is creating the coalition of the people, who will help make this change initiative happen and make it successful. Include a combination of key players with credibility with senior leadership from your management team, with IBM portal and governance experts on the subject, and those who are from within the larger organization. The key people will be the Portal Governance Change Steering Committee and the **Portal Center of Excellence (CoE)**.

A2Z Bullion Bank action

PMO office sponsored the creation of a Portal Steering Committee and implemented as a Portal Office was created to be aligned with the portal mission and the existing organizational processes for the enterprise. They would then be aligned with the CoE for ongoing business and IT lifecycle support.

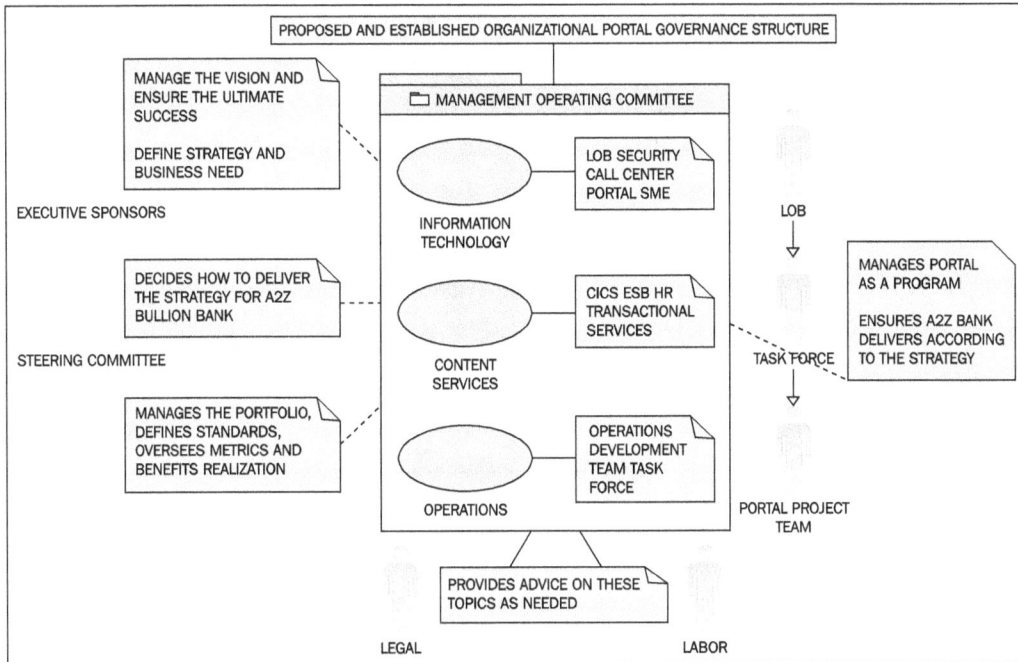

Develop a vision strategy

It includes establishing a clear portal vision and mission at the program level that is well articulated in how a portal solution will help to get from current state to future state. A Portal Program Office was launched under PMO to support the mission and strategy, and to be disseminated at the project level.

A2Z Bullion Bank action

A2Z used its PMO office to articulate the vision and strategy for portal for the organization. Along with the Portal Steering Committee and Portal Program Office under PMO, all the involved LOBs and their leadership were educated on the vision and strategy for the transformation initiative. The six steps were mapped for the implementation.

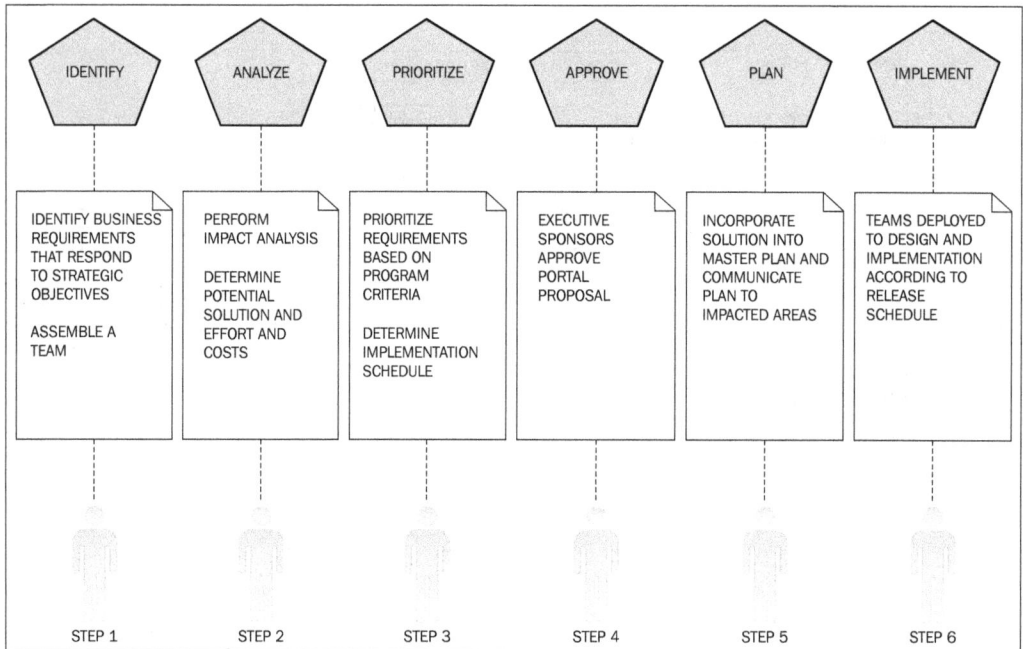

IDENTIFY	ANALYZE	PRIORITIZE	APPROVE	PLAN	IMPLEMENT
IDENTIFY BUSINESS REQUIREMENTS THAT RESPOND TO STRATEGIC OBJECTIVES ASSEMBLE A TEAM	PERFORM IMPACT ANALYSIS DETERMINE POTENTIAL SOLUTION AND EFFORT AND COSTS	PRIORITIZE REQUIREMENTS BASED ON PROGRAM CRITERIA DETERMINE IMPLEMENTATION SCHEDULE	EXECUTIVE SPONSORS APPROVE PORTAL PROPOSAL	INCORPORATE SOLUTION INTO MASTER PLAN AND COMMUNICATE PLAN TO IMPACTED AREAS	TEAMS DEPLOYED TO DESIGN AND IMPLEMENTATION ACCORDING TO RELEASE SCHEDULE
STEP 1	STEP 2	STEP 3	STEP 4	STEP 5	STEP 6

Communicate the changed vision

While articulating the vision via management meetings is a great start, but it is not enough unless this vision is consistently well communicated across the organization and various teams.

A2Z Bullion Bank action

A2Z sent out communication across the LOBs engaged in the portal venture. New internal literature, town hall meetings, and workshops were set up to communicate and further educate the entire enterprise on the newly established changed vision.

Empower broad-based action

Finally, in order for the portal transformation change along with governance to be successful, the right people need the right amount of empowerment and the mitigation tools to remove and bypass internal or external barriers.

A2Z Bullion Bank action

The Portal Steering Committee (later reconfigured to evolve into a portal center of excellence) was empowered to allow the portal decisions to be expedited with all the necessary input from the stakeholders. Governance established the processes that serve as a blueprint for management enforcement.

As part of the services engagement, the Enterprise Governance Implementation Strategy was also adopted in a way that it was aligned with the Portal Governance Strategy. The following diagram shows the high-level picture of drivers and entities for a governance model that was proposed. This is a whole echo system in itself. On one hand, we have business strategy, the information systems, and the technology stacks; the underlying elements that work in synergy with them are the architecture vision, the business and IT architectures, the opportunities, and potential solution to current pain points. On the other hand, we have linked elements, which constantly evolve and change according to business demands and social changes. They are directly intertwined with new and emerging business and technology opportunities.

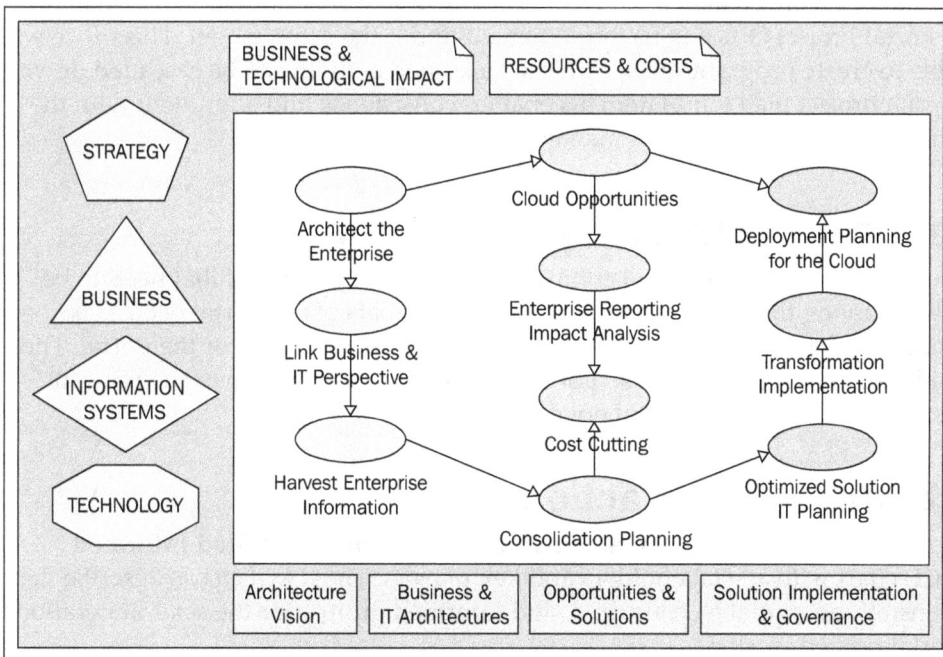

Portal governance—best practices

In the developerWorks article by Pradeep Behl on *Winning strategies for portal governance*, some foundational points on portal governance are laid out. We will use each point from it and explain how it was applied by describing which action was taken in our case study to meet that best practice criteria. This set of best practices can be adapted to your own portal initiative.

There are documented best practices, which every portal initiative should follow. In our case study, we used each point to initiate an action to engage LOBs and strategic planning of stakeholders.

Formulate a portal governance committee

Formulating a portal governance committee is vital for effective governance so that you can coordinate and manage the activities concerning the portal, enhance communication among the portal constituent teams, and build plans for the portal. The Portal Governance Committee (also referred to as the Portal Project Office) should be composed of representatives from key portal constituencies with a regular meeting schedule and well-defined processes and means of communication.

A2Z Bullion Bank action

We collaboratively created a partnership with the PMO of our bank to enable the new Portal Project Office to be implemented under the same model. This office will be able to create program-level artifacts, tasks, and activities to be cascaded down into each project plan template. This enables consistency and alignment with the methodology used and project management planning.

Obtain Executive Sponsorship

Often, there are competing and colliding priorities for the portal that need to be resolved among the portal teams. The long-term goals of the portal need to be defined, and key organizational resources need to be procured for the portal. These considerations often require a senior executive with oversight over the relevant departments for effective portal governance.

A2Z Bullion Bank action

We collaboratively created a **Responsible Accountable Consulted Informed (RACI)** chart with all stakeholders and key players. The RACI charts describe the responsible, accountable, consulted, and informed groups for the several iterations of portal-related work.

Establish a Portal Center of Excellence

Effective portal governance requires building competencies on a range of technologies for the portal. It also involves developing documentation and training materials on the portal operational procedures, and disseminating these materials to the various portal constituents. The Portal Center of Excellence helps to coalesce and drive these processes.

A2Z Bullion Bank action

We collaboratively created a Portal Center of Excellence. The most important aspect of this item was to make sure that the Center of Excellence served as a facilitator for portal decisions instead of a bottleneck. Corporate cultural tuning needs to be applied to a Center of Excellence. A CoE that is not founded on a rigid formula but instead on a flexible model to be adapted in a way which is both effective and productive.

Develop governance effectiveness metrics

The Portal Governance Committee should formulate a set of quantifiable metrics to measure the effectiveness of portal governance and use those metrics as a feedback loop to refine the portal governance effectiveness. Our action for each of the items was implemented and documented into current operational processes as follows:

- **Number and severity of portal problem reports**: Portal problem management, along with the operations group, adopted some automated tools via the IBM Support Assistant Platform to manage container defects with IBM. The Collaborative Application Lifecycle Management approach by IBM Rational was proposed to be utilized to tie the requirements and defects to artifacts, and owners to allow for a more fluid feedback loop based on reported problems. Support teams were scheduled to be trained in impersonation in order to better troubleshoot end user experience problems.

- **Portal usage statistics**: Portal analytics was planned to be applied in order to provide a detailed account of how portal is being used. A lifecycle strategy was aligned with the portal initiative to provide the necessary visibility to the portal sponsors and leadership.

- **Turnaround time to post new content:** The existing organizational processes for content management and data governance were expanded to be all inclusive and aligned with the portal initiative.

A2Z Bullion Bank action

Make sure the portal content is up-to-date and new processes are defined (based on need) to support the business needs and drivers for posting new content that is shared along with LOBs and based on the defined RACI chart at the CoE and portal office levels.

Time to develop and release new portal artifacts – A2Z Bullion Bank action

Web Experience Factory was chosen as the development tool for this initiative precisely due to its fast time-to-market capabilities. The cloud was chosen for the same reason—to increase time-to-market delivery of portal artifacts.

Adopt and adapt portal governance

The nature of the portal governance can change as the portal program evolves from inception to production. Moreover, after portal application first goes into production, the portal mission and usage could evolve continually, based on ongoing business needs. Therefore, portal governance is not static; to be effective, it also needs to evolve along with the changing nature of the enterprise portal.

A2Z Bullion Bank action

The review and validation cycles were scheduled to continue to evaluate the portal mission and its governance in order to combine a hybrid approach to its implementation. This approach is not too centralized to become a bottleneck; nor it is fully decentralized where achieving the governance mission is harder. Society evolves, so do corporations and the people that make them. This governance was set up to be adapting to ongoing enterprise change, instead of being a static entity with rigid rules, regulations, and processes. Once all involved parties were convinced of the crucial importance of governance, the necessary action steps were adopted. The acknowledgment that portal evolves, and governance is not a static concept, but rather evolves with all the other business and social economic aspects by which a business can be affected. In this particular case, a hybrid approach was adopted as the preferred one.

Adopting virtual portals – A2Z Bullion Bank action

A2Z bank decided to leverage virtual portals for the LOBs soon-to-be portal users and customers. Along with a custom look and feel, and navigation schemes, virtual portals would allow for a sharing of the same cloud infrastructure and other services and resources by all LOBs. Both the Call Center portal and the Core Banking portal would share the same backends and leverage virtual portal feature by attending to different user populations and saving on software license cost.

Typical portal processes based on governance best practices were also defined. Let's take a look at the processes themselves, their description, and the action taken by A2Z Bullion bank to implement them:

Process	Description	Action taken by A2Z Bullion Bank
Prioritization and release strategy	Introducing and prioritizing the new services and capabilities for the portal.	A program-level template for portal projects was created with the overall PMO-focused prioritization and release strategy.
Site brand management and user experience	Measuring and improving the quality of the experience of the site; including the introduction of personalization, portal logos, styles, and colors.	An enterprise-level branding with portal look and feel approaches (themes and skins) were to be developed for the target LOBs and end users.
Portal operations	Portal IT management including downtime, backups, and patches; maintenance; automation of troubleshooting; and problem management was anticipated..	The IBM SmartCloud was chosen to streamline, automate, and expedite some of the complexities around availability, failover, capacity, and portal
Portal development	Developing portal artifacts such as custom portlets and themes.	Public cloud for development and test. Virtual images or easy to use cloud patterns for POVs and private cloud for the production-level enterprise applications.

Process	Description	Action taken by A2Z Bullion Bank
Site taxonomy	Enhancing site map artifacts, such as pages and navigation schemes.	As part of the transformation effort as the information architecture Center of Excellence became a member of the Portal Steering Committee. New portal taxonomies would be done in according to governance processes and future-state goals for developing and maintaining, visual brand consistency, and navigational flow logic. Information architecture would enforce best practices against the new portal sites.
Content management	Defining creation, modification, and archival of content.	Along with site taxonomy, content management strategy was scheduled to start as part of phase two, but was designed to be aligned with site taxonomy strategy since phase one.

Typical portal roles

The following table explains the typical portal roles:

Portal roles	Focus areas: Creation and implementation of RACI chart	Action taken by A2Z Bullion Bank
Portal Center of Excellence	Creating competencies for the portal and disseminating them across the organization.	A Portal Center of Excellence was created for the ongoing effort along with organizing an RACI chart.
Portal Project Office	Tracking and coordinating activities around the portal impact areas.	A portal PMO branch was created for the ongoing effort along with organizing an RACI chart.
Portal project manager	Managing the day-to-day activities with the portal.	PMO aligned with governance to create a program manager role and some portal project manager roles.

Portal roles	Focus areas: Creation and implementation of RACI chart	Action taken by A2Z Bullion Bank
Portal administrators	Configuring and administering the portal resources.	A team of portal administrators resources to support the business releases for the self-service and call center efforts.
System administrators	Managing the IT infrastructure supporting the portal.	A team of system administrators resources to support the business releases for the self-service and call center efforts
Content managers	Publishing content and managing the content.	Business users would be trained in content creation for their LOBs.
Branding specialists	Designing and developing the portal UI graphics, UI consistency, navigation, and branding.	UI creators along with portal administrators are now focused on portal-oriented look and feel for each of the virtual portals attending the target LOBs.
Developers	Developing, testing, and releasing portal components, such as custom portlets and themes.	Utilizing Web Experience Factory to speed up development, and minimize coding.
Cloud testers	Testing functional and nonfunctional requirements in the testing and production of the cloud.	Creating the role of a cloud tester to test the functional and nonfunctional requirements against the test and production cloud-enabled environments.
Cloud designers	Designing service and deployment cloud patterns to be leveraged via the cloud.	Created the role for a cloud designer to allow patterns to be created and deployed to the cloud, utilizing IBM Workload Deployer.

The next table explains the portal metrics and portal governance metrics. These metrics can be used to tune the effectiveness of the portal governance processes. It is crucial for a portal initiative to have metrics that are agreed upon by the sponsors.

Portal governance metrics	Focus areas: portal stakeholders	Action taken by A2Z Bullion Bank
User problem reports	Frequency and severity of the user problem reports with the portal.	Analytical dashboards would allow technical and business leaderships to understand the types of problems and their frequency in terms of portal frequent reports that would be shared among the stakeholders and portal offices. Both initiatives would have automated portal support utilizing **IBM Support Assistant (ISA)** and other IBM tools for the operational teams assigned with user-reported problems.
User satisfaction surveys	Level of satisfaction with the portal in user surveys.	Both customer center and core banking transformation initiatives would use portal-based surveys to capture feedback from end users.
User population	Number of registered and online users and the rate of increase in the portal user population.	Both application performance metrics and portal analytics were funded as disciplines to support the future state of the portal initiative. They would be constantly monitored and validated against the nonfunctional requirements for these metrics.
Page and portlet hits	The number of page hits and portlet hits, which are particularly relevant if there is a portal personalization campaign.	Again the same application performance metrics for system metrics and portal analytics for user metrics were funded as disciplines to support the future state of the portal initiative. They would be constantly monitored and validated against the nonfunctional requirements for these metrics.

Portal governance metrics	Focus areas: portal stakeholders	Action taken by A2Z Bullion Bank
Commerce revenues	For e-commerce portals, the revenues derived from the portal and the rate of revenue growth.	Commerce revenue deriving from the portal initiative would be measured within six months after the portal is in production.
Content turnaround time	Time taken to approve and publish new content on the portal.	For the second phase of the portal, **web content manager** (**WCM**) was going to be used for content management.
Development turnaround time	Time taken to develop new custom portlet components and release them on the portal.	Rapid development via WEF and test and development cloud for fast environment build-out.

Value interests

Along with the governance infrastructure, the metrics given in the preceding table will align with the so called "value interests", which are briefly described as follows:

- **Return on investment (ROI)**: ROI is the first value interest. It would be realized via the cloud and via the benefits of virtualization, automation, and standardization. Portal capabilities would set ROI so as to set the stage for A2Z Bullion bank to be well positioned in today's bullion market and up-to-date in its technology and agility to market.

- **Enterprise architecture**: The enterprise architecture is the second value interest. Enterprise architecture strategy was going to be revamped to support the new business demands and computing paradigm.

- **Deliverable value**: The deliverable value is the third value interest. It was realized via the adoption of the cloud as a service and deployment model, via the adoption of portal and the WEF for fast value-to-market.

- **Operations**: The operations is the fourth value interest. Operations were streamlined and standardized via the cloud with its virtualization and standardization qualitites.

Summary

In this chapter, we looked how governance and management are two important aspects to ensure that the portal initiative is well-aligned with the business drivers and the organizational processes to support it. We looked at how PMO and Portal Offices can be established (or enhanced) to serve towards the overall business goal. We shared some vital steps that can be reused towards a portal governance regardless of the industry domain your portal serves. We provided some examples of how A2Z Bullion Bank dealt with and acted against each of the best practice steps. We finished the chapter showing how the ROI can be measured and realized during the lifecycle of a portal initiative. Portal initiatives need to be run by a strong governance, and this governance will now provide the foundation to enable the portal initiative to be successful.

3

Portal Requirements Engineering

This chapter covers the discipline of requirements engineering for portal. One of the most fundamental aspects of successful portal implementations is the functional and nonfunctional requirements gathering. The focus of this chapter is to help you understand how to best gather these requirements. Functional aspects, for example, which functionality set the portal needs to support based on existing or new business demands, and nonfunctional aspects, such as security, performance, availability, scalability, maintainability, trainability as well need to be well understood and prioritized by all **Lines of Business (LOBs)**, project, and program-level teams. Best practices will be presented in a step-by-step way. By the end of this chapter, we will have covered:

- The discipline of requirements and requirements as a discipline
- The step-by-step approach based on the best practices

    - List users, existing systems, and functional requirements
    - Derive actors and use cases to create the use case model
    - Inventory-large reusable assets
    - Identify delta use cases
    - Document nonfunctional requirements

The discipline of requirements and requirements as a discipline

Before getting into the requirements themselves, let's briefly talk about the need to have a strong tool and approach to manage these requirements, and create a traceability matrix and automated reporting for all functional and nonfunctional business and IT requirements. This would allow an easy flow of communication between business owners, business analysts, project managers, architects, specialists, and stakeholders involved in the development lifecycle. The system and customer requirements should be mapped to owners of those requirements and subsequently to the test cases, tests scripts, and any other artifacts, work item, or activity related to that requirement. Based on the best practices in requirements engineering and management for any development methodology, A2Z Bullion Bank decided to adopt the **Collaborative Application Lifecycle Management (CALM)** approach. It provides automation, traceability, and reporting needed to support this transformation effort. It would further enhance the business sponsors and management teams with a visibility via health dashboards for the overall portal program and portal projects combined efforts.

Interactive time – watch and learn

What is the collaborative application lifecycle management? Watch the IBM multimedia presentation at `http://www.youtube.com/watch?v=iDOofBh5FPQ`.

After watching the preceding video, the CALM approach should be understood. Think about how your project can benefit from these collaboratively integrated, proactive requirements management and traceability platform. A2Z bank decided to adopt CALM in order to support its upcoming portal projects for its obvious delivered value added. The following diagram depicts the requirements strategy for the A2Z bank program based on IBM Rational software stack.

The requirements management stack for the governance program is laid out in the following diagram as we highlight the top engines aligned with the governance and requirements management approach:

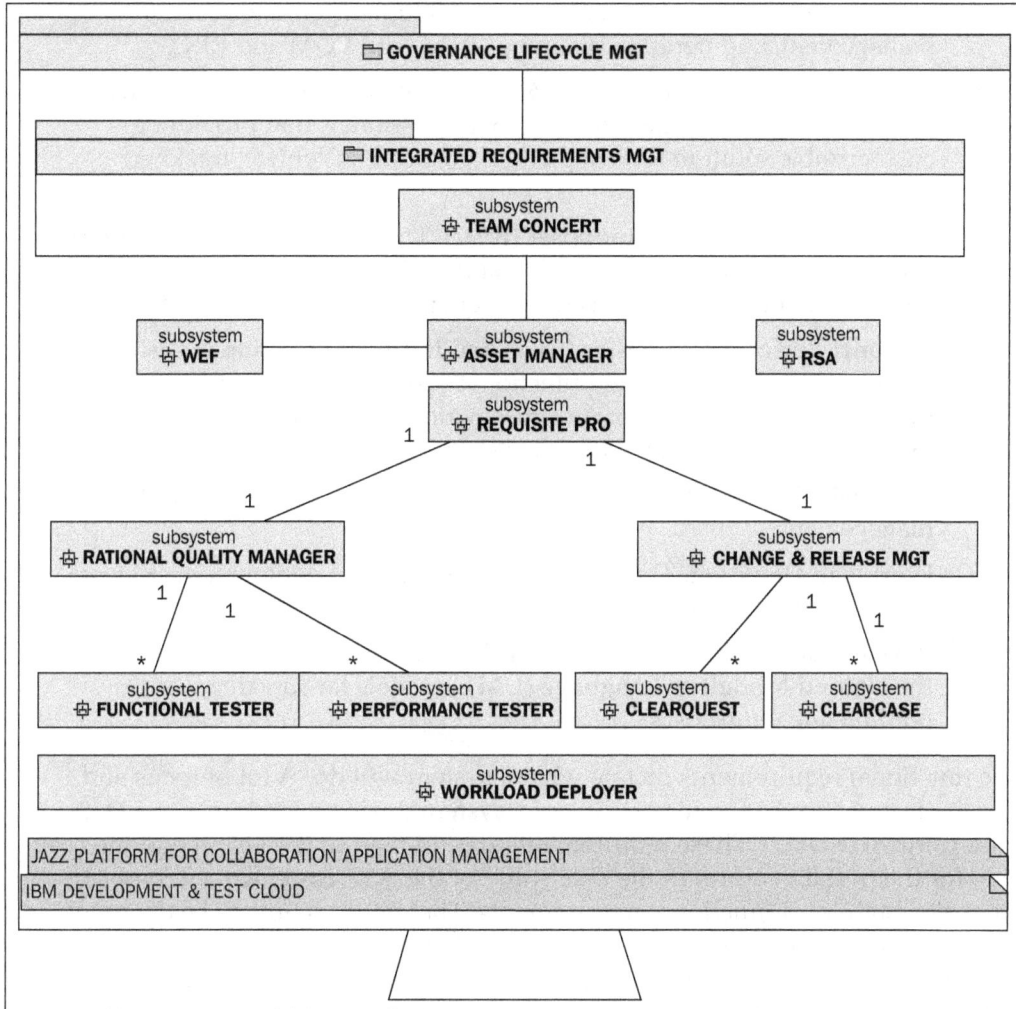

The following is the list explaining about the preceding diagram:

- **Rational Team Concert (RTC)**: This is a great collaborative work environment for developers, architects, and project managers with unified work item, source control and build management, process management, and iteration planning along with RQM and RRC.

- **Rational Quality Manager (RQM)**: This is an intuitive web-based test management environment for quality professionals that provides a customizable solution for test planning, workflow control, tracking, and reporting.

- **Rational Requirement Composer (RRC)**: This is a requirements definition solution with easy-to-use elicitation and definition capabilities that enable the refinement of business needs into unambiguous requirements.

- **Rational Performance Tester (RPT) and Rational Functional Tester (RFT)**: These execute the automated functional and load tests according to the functional and nonfunctional requirements synchronized with quality manager for integrated testing efforts.

- **Rational ClearQuest and ClearCase**: These align with change and release management.

- **Workload Deployer**: This provides the automated deployment strategy to the cloud.

- **Rational Software Architect (RSA)**: This allows architects to work with the **Unified Modeling Language** (UML) models for functional and nonfunctional purposes.

The functional requirements dictate what a system will do. A lot of focus and priority is given to the functional side of a system during a **Synchronous Data Link Control (SDLC)**. These requirements should map to the vision and the road map for the portal venture. In the case study of the A2Z bank, we will describe the major high-level functional requirements. The requirements to be documented for your portal project should cover both the IT drivers as well business drivers. Our premise is that you should never reinvent the wheel if it is not needed. The best practice guide to architecting portal solutions has laid out the foundational steps to capture the portal customer and system requirements — functional and nonfunctional — in a consistent and repeatable way. You can find it at http://www.redbooks.ibm.com/abstracts/redp4100.html?Open and http://www.redbooks.ibm.com/abstracts/sg247011.html?Open. A2Z bank leveraged these best practices and incorporated them into its portal efforts and related processes. Next, we will illustrate at a high level what was done for each of these steps.

List users, existing systems, and functional requirements

The functional requirements describe, define, and detail how a function, system, or component is supposed to behave based on a set of inputs and the expected outputs. In this case, we will list all the existing systems, users, and the functional requirements. This activity is lead mostly by business analysts or business architects with input from other documents and lines of business. When we follow the best practices, we need to go from the high-level description and system context diagram to the actors and the primary high-level business functions. We then take a look at the interactions and correlations between these actors and business functions. The first step in this identification process is to list the users and existing systems from these work products and to identify the major functionality required by the system. Next, we will list what A2Z bank discovered and documented for this step. We will start by defining the current (and then future state) system context diagram. In this context diagram, we have to list at a high level, the main systems, user interfaces, and actors that will be present in the functional flow.

For A2Z portal solution, we have:

- Human actors
  - **customer service representative (CSR)** operators
  - Business users (brokers)
  - Managers

- Systems actors:
  - **Interactive voice response (IVR)** systems
  - Legacy (existing systems) to be touched by the new portal initiative

The following is the system context diagram:

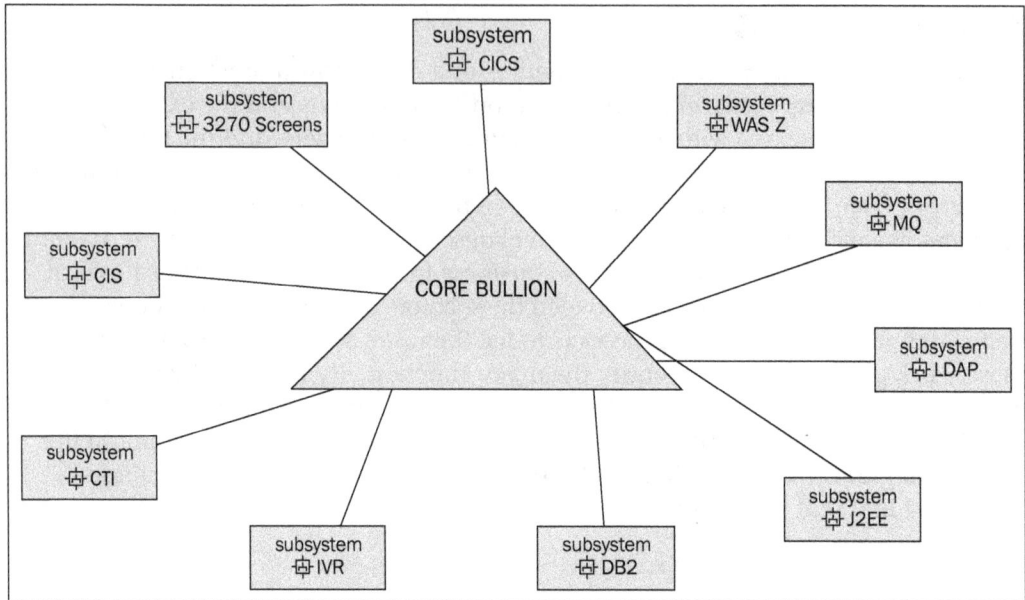

This system context diagram provides the high-level depiction of existing systems as follows:

- Telephony infrastructure with green screen frontend
- The **Customer Information Control System (CICS)** infrastructure for banking and a J2EE frontend
- **Customer Information System (CIS)** with J2EE frontend
- IVR Infrastructure with green screen frontend
- IBM mainframe infrastructure with IBM DB2 (for persistence) and IBM MQ and Broker (for queuing and pub/sub)

When the business and process analyst (and sometimes business architect) are familiar with portal capabilities, it is possible to write some lower-level requirements that map better to these capabilities, and for instance, require the need of component-level intercommunication within the GUI pages, which in the portal would map to inter-portlet communication. In theory, the requirements should be agnostic to the implementation and solution. However, in practice and in an agile approach, it is possible to be one step ahead and more granular towards the requirements rewriting to fit portal capabilities.

In our case, A2Z bank had two top requirements, each for the new business initiative. It had a clear requirement for the call center portal to have an integrated soft-phone interface into the portal application **graphical user interface** (**GUI**). This would allow CSRs to have a full view of a user and account information history via populated portal screens based on the information passed from the IVR and telephony systems. The main requirement for the self-service portal was to allow business and financial users to register and manage account, customer, and vault-level information, as well as vault transactional history and forecasting. Even though requirements were written for all phases of the portal initiative, here we will focus on the ones for the first phase only, excluding collaboration and the requirements related to **business process management** (**BPM**). The following is a summarized list of the main functional requirements using **call center** (**CC**) and **self service** (**SS**) to describe the business domain:

- **Incoming call (CC)**: The system shall allow a call in the telephony system to come into the graphical interface system and customer service representative operator via user interaction IVR system and soft-phone specifications

- **Legacy integration (CC/SS)**: The system shall allow integration of new GUI and services to integrate into legacy systems

- **Close call (CC)**: The system shall allow a CSR to close a call via the GUI and soft-phone specifications

- **CRUD customer vault (CC/SS)**: The system shall allow authorized users to create, read, update, and delete customer vault(s)

- **CRUD account (CC/SS)**: The system shall allow authorized users to create, read, update, and delete an account associated with customer vaults

- **Vault performance (SS)**: The system shall allow authorized users to view vault performance metrics

- **Configure vault settings (SS)**: The system shall allow authorized users to configure vault settings

- **New deposit (SS)**: The system shall allow authorized users to deposit into a vault customer

- **New customer vault (SS)**: The system shall allow authorized users to create a new customer vault

- **Loan process (CC/SS)**: The system shall allow authorized users to participate in the full lifecycle of the loan process

- **Transaction information (CC/SS)**: The system shall allow authorized users to view transaction information, vault transactions such as gold, silver, platinum, palladium, ETF
- **12-vault receipt (CC/SS)**: The system shall allow authorized users to view and print vault receipts
- **Checking savings/transfer and conversion (SS)**: The system shall allow authorized users to convert from fiat checking and savings into bullion vaults
- **Vault scheduling (SS)**: The system shall allow authorized users to schedule vault operations
- **Vault read (CC)**: The system shall allow authorized users to read vault contents
- **Vault forecasting (SS)**: The system shall allow authorized users to forecast vault performance based on current fixed operations
- **Customer vault history (CC/SS)**: The system shall allow authorized users to view customer vault's history
- **Last five customer vaults (CC/SS)**: The system shall allow authorized users to view last five customer vaults
- **Log in (CC/SS)** - The system shall allow authorized users to log in to the GUI system
- **Cloud integration (CC/SS)**: The system shall allow integration into a private, hybrid, or public cloud
- **Monitoring integration (CC/SS)**: The system shall allow for user and system monitoring integration
- **Global search (CC/SS)**: The system shall allow authorized users to perform a global search
- **Forms and notes (CC/SS)**: The system shall allow authorized users to fill out forms and write customer, vault, and loan or account-related notes
- **Loans**: The system shall allow authorized users to process loans based on the loan processing business rules and management workflow

Due to scope and space constraints, we will keep these requirement descriptions at a high level. In a portal project engagement, it is needed to capture and document them at their greatest details and minutia. Capturing the requirements at the right level of granularity allows a solid direction on what the design and development should be. This is a crucial step in a successful portal initiative. Creating a traceability of these requirements with the deliverables, artifacts, and owners is another step towards success.

Derive actors and use cases to create the use case model

Regardless of the adopted development methodology or deliverable work, there are sequence events and flows (from user to system and system to system) to be captured and documented via use cases or story boards. They provide the scenario under which actors will interact with the application based on the required functionality and expected results. In the following diagram, we will take a look at how A2Z Bank creates a use case model. Each use case is related to another use case based on the story or functionality required by the use case. For simplicity's sake, we will list on the left-hand side, the users such as customer service representatives, brokers, and managers, but we will focus mainly on the CSRs and broker roles in this chapter. Note that some roles would have manager roles, and the customization of the portal view will be done later with the role-based capabilities of profiling by **Web Experience Factory (WEF)**.

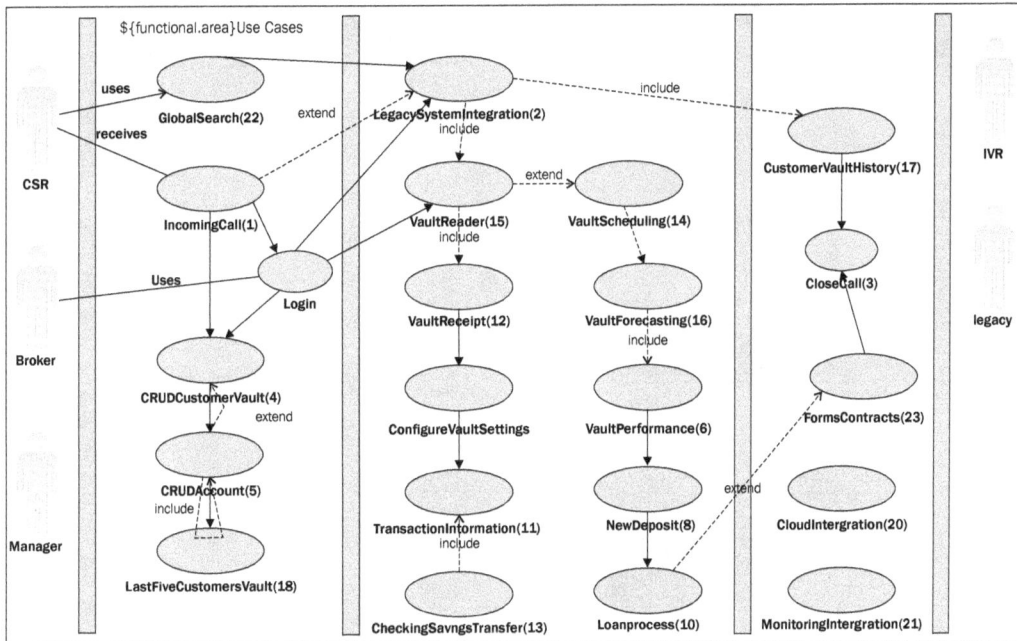

The preceding diagram shows the high-level description of the requirements via use case modeling.

Storyboard or wireframes

As part of capturing the functional requirements for portal, it is considered a best practice to create visual mock-ups of what the new system screen should look like, along with the action flow to be executed per user type or transaction type. The wire frame shows which pages should be created and how many portlets should be on each page. It further helps the next phase of analysis and design to map which portlet fields will map to service or data points.

Inventory-large reusable assets

The next concurrent step in this process is to create an inventory of reusable assets. The following component diagram provides a short functional description of existing systems with reusable assets for the presentation, control, domain, and resource via architectural elements and services:

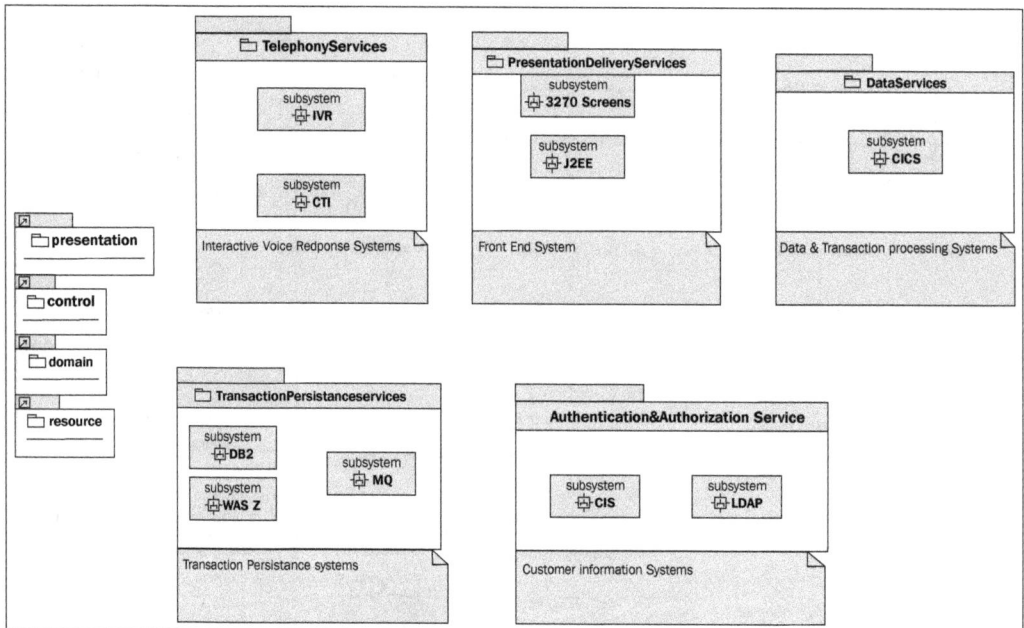

The following is the list of the assets documented for the A2Z bank effort:

- Telephony services via IVR and **computer telephony integration (CTI)**, that is call routing
- Presentation delivery services via 3270 screens and some J2EE

- Data services via CICS
- Transaction persistence services via WebSphere on z/OS via DB2, MQ
- Authentication and authorization services via CIS and LDAP

Identify delta use cases

Once we have the laid-out mainstream use cases and classified reusable assets, we will look at the delta use cases not covered by the reusable assets. Because of the phased approach, some of the functionality and related use cases (stories) are set for phase two.

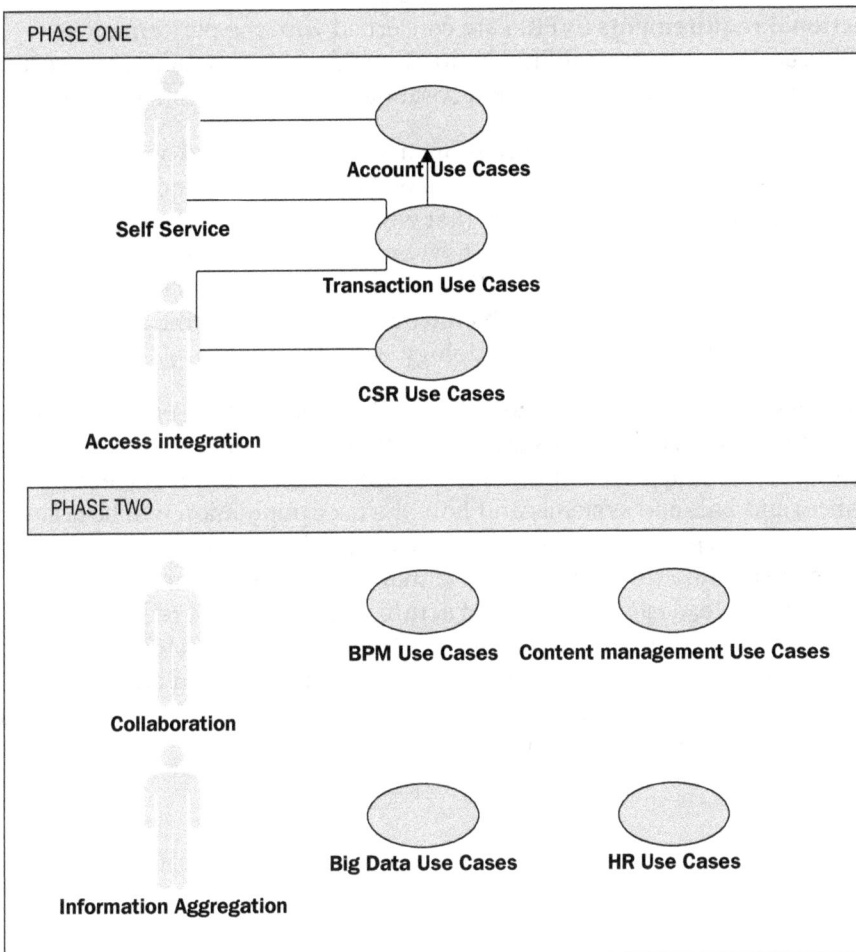

The following are the functionality and related use cases (stories) that are set for phase two:

- **HR use cases**: Enterprise-wide human resources
- **Big data use cases**: Big data for banking domains
- **BPM use cases**: Business process management for loan process
- **Cloud use cases**: Software, Infrastructure and Platform as a service

Document nonfunctional requirements

While the functional requirements are concerned with the behavior, the **nonfunctional requirements** (**NFRs**) are concerned with the performance, availability, accessibility, trainability, maintainability, supportability, and security of a system or component. It all serves as a baseline to judge the system at hand.

Due to the scope of this chapter, for nonfunctional customer and system requirements, we will focus on the performance-related NFRs, such as throughput, response time, capacity, and scalability first while other NFRs, such as security, trainability will be separate. Because of how critical the performance is for any portal initiative, the deserved focus will be given to it. Now, let's take a look at the performance-related requirements, which would be saved into the requirements tool as well as in other development methodology work products.

Performance starts on day one. Some of the key questions about performance-related portal nonfunctional requirements are related to the user concurrency, growth rate of the user population, capacity of frontend systems (security and reverse proxy servers for instance) and backend systems, and how the user population will be accessing the portal (device type and connection bandwidth). The degree of precision to which these items are captured will raise the potential to avoid common performance anti-patterns (at the code, design, and infrastructure levels) and ensure a successful portal experience. From day one, if you are the architect or project manager or portal lead for a portal initiative, make sure that the items in the next section are examined with the proper priority. At a high level, the following requirements were documented as a part of the nonfunctional requirements.

Portal call center channel

The following are some of the high-level nonfunctional requirements documented for the call center track of work:

- System shall support internationalization

- System shall support 400 concurrent users

- System shall support 2,000 total users

- System shall support GUI-based transactions, which have response time within a maximum of three seconds

- System shall support Single Sign-On in the existing systems

- System shall scale according to projected business growth of 5 percent a year

- System core components shall have a maximum response time of 500 milliseconds

- System shall operate according to 98 percent operation standards of availability

- System shall not allow anonymous users but only registered users

- System shall process 200,000 CSR transactions a day

Portal self-service (core banking) channel

Again, we will look at the following high-level nonfunctional requirements for the self-service track of work:

- System shall support 25,000 concurrent registered users

- System shall support 250,000 total users

- System shall allow self-service management of available services

- System shall support internationalization

- System shall support encrypted security

- System components shall have a maximum response time of three seconds

- System shall operate according to 99.9 percent operation standards of availability

- System shall not allow anonymous users but only registered users
- System shall process 500 million core business transactions a day
- System shall process core business transactions in a maximum of 500 milliseconds

Workload distribution

As the NFRs are gathered, it is important to document the workload distribution of all major business transactions. This matrix is created to understand normal utilization patterns versus peak and the 80/20 rule for these transaction volumetrics. This exercise provides an output parameter that serves as input for a performance modeling exercise. Along with the performance model, a full performance strategy is set for the entire program lifecycle. Creating a matrix is optional, but it allows for a better alignment of deliverable artifacts with the proposed strategy. It creates requirements traceability that links them all throughout the lifecycle of the initiative. The following is the list, at a high level, of some of the related deliverable work items:

- **Portal performance strategy**: This aligns with the cloud and business drivers.
- **Portal performance test plan**: This aligns with test plan approach for nonfunctional (and functional) testing.
- **Portal test environment**: This aligns with the cloud for fast environment build-out (same for other environments).
- **Portal performance test cases**: This aligns with use cases (same for functional). The test scripts are derived from these test cases.
- **Portal test data**: This aligns test data with the proper data governance to manage the lifecycle of test and development data.
- **Portal performance model**: This aligns with business input for workload distribution. It is used to model and forecast system resources utilization, and predict future performance behavior based on changing workloads.
- **Portal benchmarking**: This aligns with the monitoring requirement and plan to benchmark each business release to evaluate application performance and memory footprint.

Validate requirements with the customer

Once the requirements are finalized, there is an approval cycle (regardless of the development and project management methodology at hand), which allows approvers and reviewers (based on the RACI chart for this initiative) to validate and sign off on the documented requirements. Controlling the scope of requirements and changes is one fundamental aspect to allow portal initiatives to be successful. A phased approach that deploys strong change management policies aligned with great management and governance allows for a successful path to a portal initiative. Any business analyst, process analyst, developer, specialist, architect, project manager, and sponsor would know how a change in the requirements can affect a lot of the players and add risk to a portal initiative in achieving the target goals and return on investment as well as meeting deadlines.

Summary

This chapter started with the requirements approach that supports the requirements engineering efforts of a portal solution. We covered very high-level functional and nonfunctional business and IT requirements. Then we looked at major steps defined by portal architecture—best practices. We mapped out the requirements and the strategy for testing the requirements. We finished with the customer validation of the functional and nonfunctional requirements, which leads to the next iteration effort, that is, analysis and design, and implementation and monitoring of such requirements.

4
Portal Architecture: Analysis and Design

This chapter covers another iterative step in a development lifecycle. It is time to take a look at the requirements and exercise architectural analysis and design for both the functional and nonfunctional aspects, as they are mapped to portal capabilities. We will cover how to create a wireframe to understand information architecture of portal pages' navigational flow and also to map the **Portal Object Model (POM)** to service and data layer. We will also cover the macro view of aspects of portal's functional and nonfunctional architecture. By the end of this chapter, we should have looked at the following:

- Cloud architectural model
- Portal architectural decisions
- Portal information architecture
- Portal Object Model, service-oriented model, and data mappings
- Enterprise reference architecture
- Banking reference and portal application architecture
- Call center reference and portal application architecture
- Cloud as the fabric for resilient architecture
- Architecting for nonfunctional requirements

Cloud architectural model

Cloud architecture must define the capability set to support all the delivery models for that cloud, for instance, federated identity, orchestration of services to allow different service providers to collaborate and handle service interconnections, along with flows and mediations, and the expected workloads and data flow between services in the cloud. Unlike traditional environments, the capabilities delivered by the cloud architecture serves as a blueprint for the infrastructure implementation. Portal's functional and nonfunctional requirements can be mapped and realized using the cloud architecture for design, implementation, test, deployment for its actors, such as cloud services consumers, providers, and service developers. From an enterprise-architecture standpoint, ubiquitous networks access, location-independent resource pooling, rapid elasticity, and flexible pricing models are a few advantages of cloud-enabled architectures. A2Z Bullion Bank decided to utilize private cloud resources dedicated to the enterprise. These capabilities would lower the cost of delivering IT services via enhanced delivery models; making IT more responsive to and aligned with the business needs. In the next chapter, we will look more closely at portal gold and highly available architecture via the cloud.

Portal architectural decisions

Regardless of the adopted development methodology from an architectural perspective, it is must to document architectural decisions for the infrastructure and application domains. This document provides a rationale and justification as to decisions being made on architectural items and helps the team to have a clear vision of each item discussed. There is also the benefit of traceability to how and when the decision was made, and the respective reviewers and approvers. In the following table, we will point out the high-level architecture decisions' topics documented for A2Z Bullion Bank portal:

	High level	Low level
1	IBM WebSphere Portal and Mobile Capabilities	Utilize portlet-to-portlet and event-driven communication
2	IBM DataPower for **service-oriented architecture (SOA)** realization	Utilize **Session Initiation Protocol (SIP)** for telephony integration.
3	Utilize the cloud for agile infrastructure	Global and portlet session size decisions
4	Utilize WEF for agile development	**Portal Access Control (PAC)** (role-based authorization rules)

	High level	Low level
5	Reusable assets from the IBM toolbox and accelerators	Caching (page, portlet, cash access control, scope, and expiration)
6	DataPower and Broker for call routing	Portlet modes and views
7	Virtual portals	Ajax-related decisions
8	Forms and digital signatures	**Web Services for Remote Portlets (WSRP) decisions**
9	BPM	WEF builders
10	Single Sign-On	WEF models
11	Other decisions	Other decisions

Information architecture – wireframes and storyboards

Portals differ from pure J2EE applications in many ways from a component, engine, and API perspective, but one of them is the concept of many portlets on the same page, which is very unique in nature. One crucial deliverable in a portal engagement is the information architecture work, which produces a wireframe, or storyboard, of the role-based portal pages and their flows, actions, potential page wires, portlet-to-portlet communication, and associated services and data points to be consumed by the portlet. The wireframe has the mission to illustrate and allow information architects to work with Application and infrastructure architects in creating a traceability of the POM to SOA and data layers. The GUI design model describes the user navigation flow through the portlets and pages. The portlets and pages are described in a storyboard fashion, which depicts the user interface of the position, type, font, and style of the data elements and controls including the portlet skin and page theme.

We will start by looking at the high-level roles and views for each user role and its associated pages and portlets. At this point, the look and feel is not finalized, and the focus is on the content and data flow itself. Later, a portal theme specialist will refine the look and feel, based on usability requirements for the graphical user interface specifications according to corporate branding guidelines. In the following diagram, the roles such as executive, CSR, CSR manager, broker, and intranet user are represented:

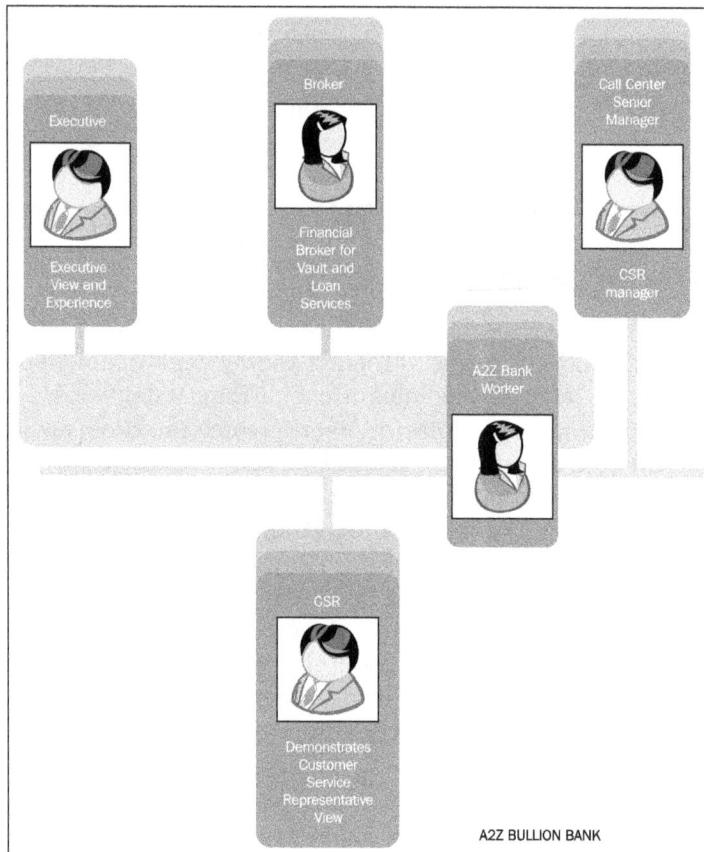

Note that each of them will have a different view of pages with different portlets that map to their organizational roles. The following images will depict each of these views based on their roles (or in WEF language, the profiling). Note that each user sees a different set of portlets. Let's see how the storyboard and wireframes assist in the analysis and design of a portal solution. First, we will look at some of the users and how they will experience this new application paradigm. Remember, most of them are coming from either a 3270 background (CSR and managers), while others have had some exposure to modern graphical user interfaces using J2EE as the frontend.

Let's first look at the executive user. In his/her portal experience, there are portlets providing dashboards for Business Performance, Forecasting, Business Intelligence, Analytics, and ROI metrics reporting. This user is really interested in seeing how the business is running and the key performance indicator metrics from an **Executive** view, as shown in the following screenshot:

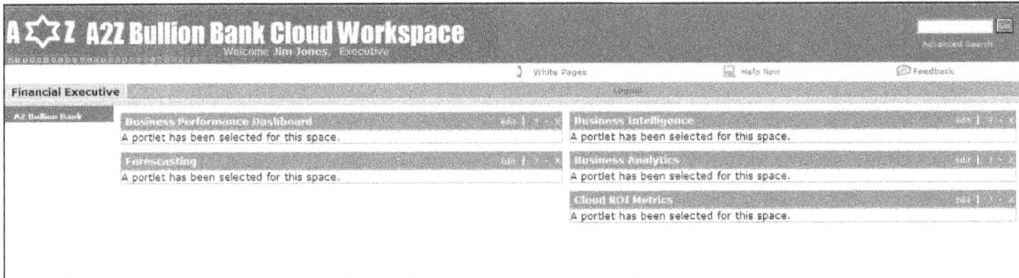

For a **CSR** view, another portal experience is presented where a softphone is integrated with the **Interactive Voice Response** (**IVR**) system and receives a call that allows the portal screen to be populated with the account or customer vault IDs the broker is authenticated to see. By requirements, the **SoftPhone** portlet will populate **Account Info, Customer Vault, Transaction Info**, and **5 Last Customer Vault**. It allows the CSR take a call (using a headset) that pops up on the portal page and populates the portlets with that account or customer information. It allows the CSR to be extra productive by having all the needed information on one screen. Eventually, as the second phase kicks off, the CSR will also have escalation and tasks-related portlets available for more functionality.

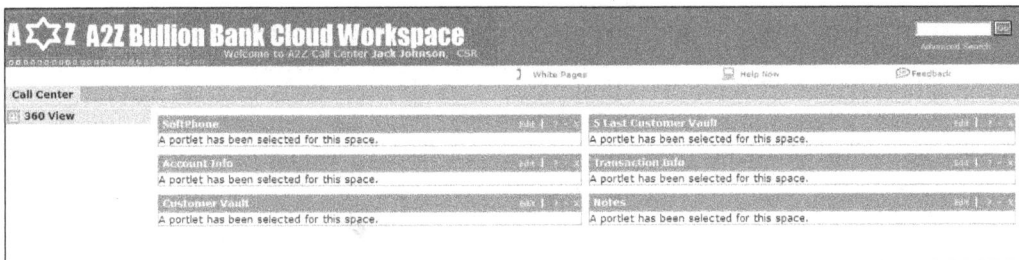

The CSR manager has a different portal experience based on his/her role. The following screenshot shows the portal page and functionality for **CSR Manager** where a **CSR Manager Task Portlet** is available for queue or call escalation; a total **CSR Average Call Time** is displayed in a portlet; additionally the CSR manager can assign queues to employees and view **Queue Performance** based on target business goals:

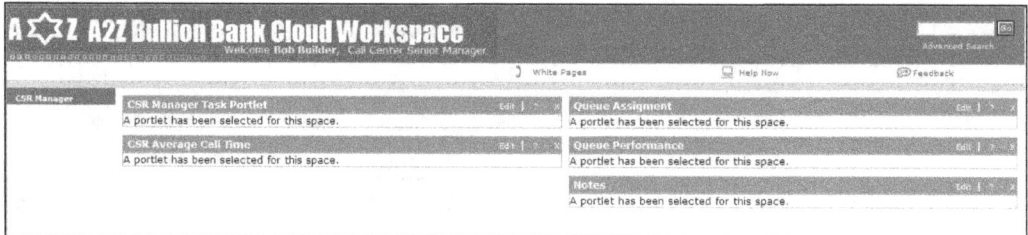

For the Financial Broker, yet another experience and functionality is presented. The broker has some different views into Bank Bullion services. These include **Broker Services** view where the **Customer Vault**, **Account Info**, **Transfer Info**, **Vault Feature**, **Deposit**, and **Vault Loan** processes can be managed and operated on, as shown in the following screenshot:

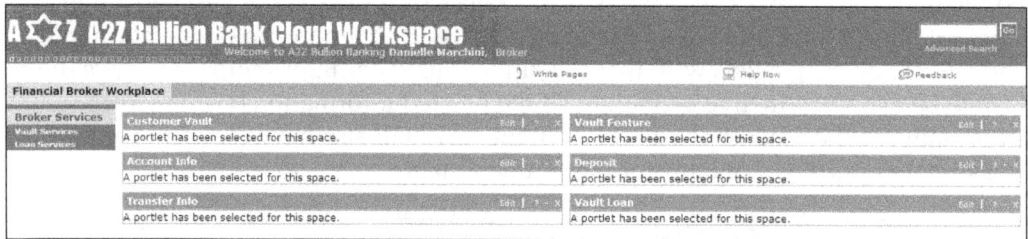

The **Vault Services** view, on the other hand, provides specific vault functionality and a view of **Vault Reader**, **Vault Performance**, **Vault Forecasting**, and **Vault Scheduling**. They all come from the functional requirements captured by the business and process analysts, and business architects.

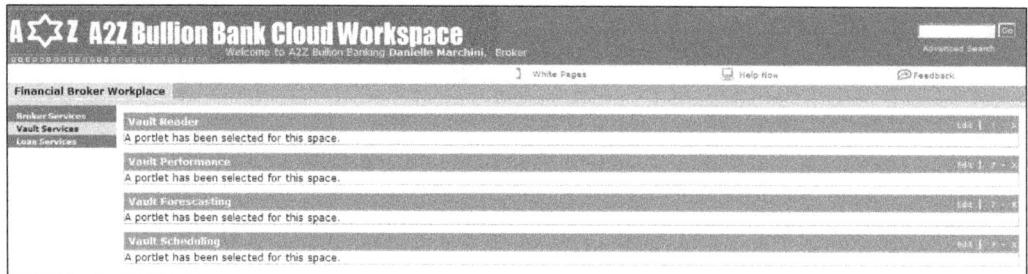

Yet another functionality set provided to the Financial Broker is the **Loan Services** view. This is where the broker can manage loans associated with vaults. This functionality as per Governance Mandate was scheduled for phase two. It will provide the broker with the load process allowing him/her to see a loan status, assess loan risk, and see associated tasks and loan processes through the **Loan Status**, **Loan Risk**, **Loan Task**, and **Loan Process** sections respectively, as shown in the following screenshot:

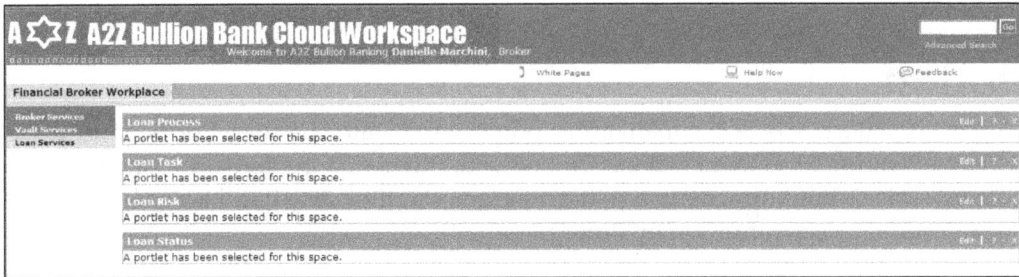

Another user is the administrative intranet user, who is neither a broker nor a customer service representative. Another view is provided to this role where only gold and silver Spot prices, and some news are displayed in the **Gold Spot**, **Silver Spot**, and **News** sections, as shown in the following screenshot:

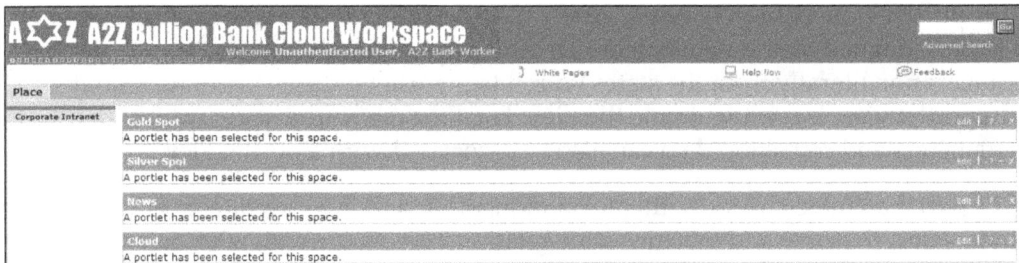

As the pages, portlets, and user flows are depicted, a portal architect, along with SOA and data architects will map out the POM to the SOA (and data) layer. Next step is to lay out each portlet field and map it to another element in the request-response and transaction flow. So, that is a mechanism to understand which service(s) or data point(s) is/are being invoked and consumed by the portlet. It also helps to understand and drive discussion on what needs to be kept in the portlet session and in the global session, as it allows for an end-to-end view of how the portlet invokes services and services invoke messages and data. This exercise must be done and documented for each flow and portlet component in your portal architecture.

A good way to implement this documenting process is via **Universal Modeling Language (UML)** modeling and **State Oriented Portlet Pattern (SOPP)** presented in IBM developerWorks article—*Architecting on demand solutions, Part 14: Build portlets using Rational Software Architect State Oriented Portlet Patterns* at `http://www.ibm.com/developerworks/ibm/library/i-odoebp14/` where each portlet transition (and view) is mapped to a state machine's state for a certain process. Let's take a quick look at the three main elements of this pattern as described by the pattern's authors.

Portlet

"A portlet pattern acts as the main entry point to the State Oriented Portlet Patterns. It allows binding of a state machine for use with other state patterns. As states are not available to bind directly to a pattern parameter, they also build a `<<States>>` enumeration for consumption by other patterns."

A2Z portal architects will use this pattern to map and bind to state machines defined for the banking and call center transaction processing documented by business and process analysts.

Portlet view

"The portlet view pattern is responsible for associating views and data to accompany a state as defined by a state machine. To bind a state, you should choose an enumeration literally from the states bound to a portlet pattern. The data bound to a portlet view is used to define the view bean for the bound state. Additional parameters and transition data can also be associated with a portlet view."

A2Z portal architects work with information, SOA, and WEF architects to understand the view and machine state relationship. Along with SOA and data architects, they map out the delta cases where additional transition data is associated with a portlet view and is not provided by the banking template, as well for the call center architecture design.

Transition data

"Transition data is used to define data for the application that exceeds the lifetime of the request. The generated view bean is created from the portlet view pattern and defines the navigational state for the portlet state. The transition data is used to define data that can be persisted between requests and can include storing data in session or portlet data."

A2Z portal architects work with SOA and data architects to understand the lifecycle of the portlet request, the end-to-end mapping to that business transaction flow, along with the session related for any data structure. It drives the discussion of what needs to be in the portlet session and in the global session, and what needs to be persisted elsewhere.

It is important to note that we utilized this pattern for documentation and not necessarily to generate or automate code via Eclipse transformation plugins. For code automation, we use the capabilities provided by IBM Web Experience Factory. In the following diagram, for illustrative purposes we have a state machine notation for the customer vault component. The states in the state machine map to the portlet views, request cycle, and functionality.

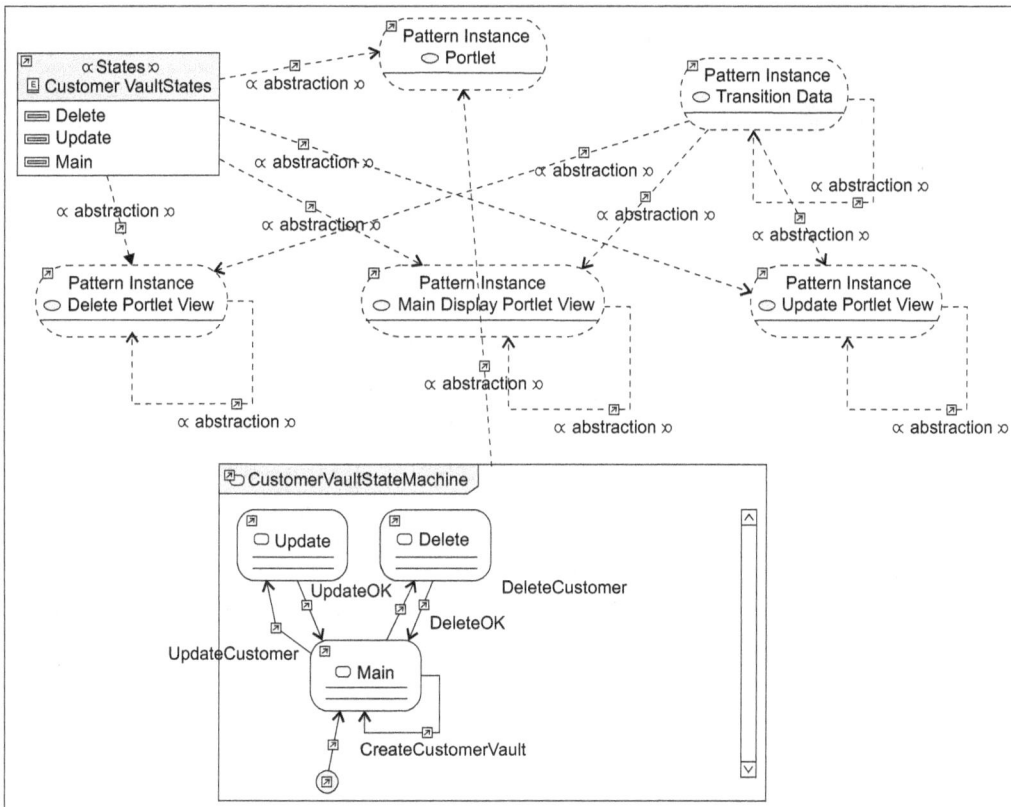

POM and service design conceptual overview

From that conceptual level, implementation designs are created via view points from the architectural layers and the project packages that are created to implement a logical functional architecture. The following diagram uses UML to describe this abstraction:

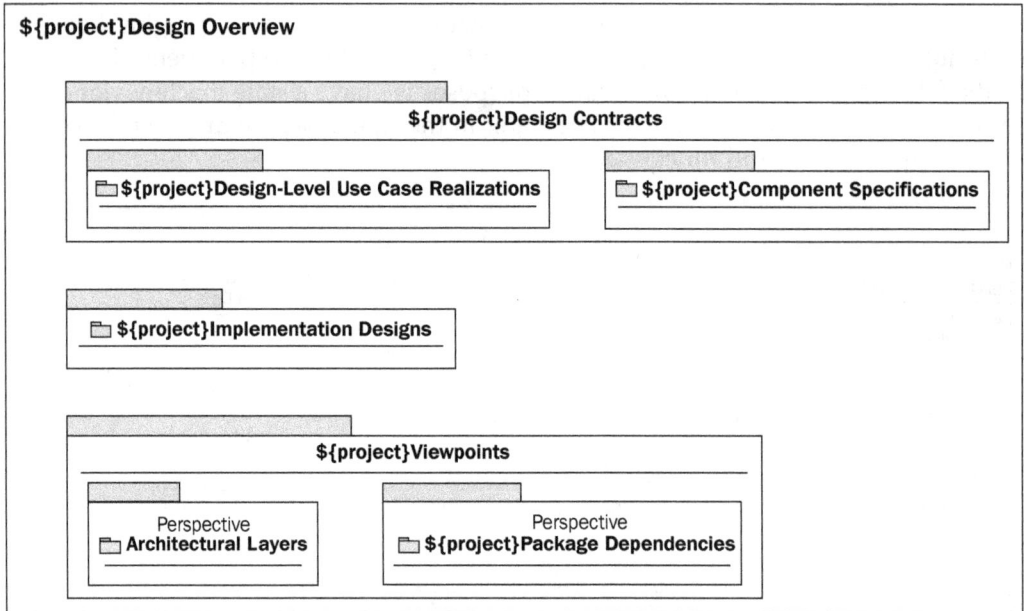

```
${project}Design Overview

    ${project}Design Contracts

       📁${project}Design-Level Use Case Realizations    📁${project}Component Specifications


    📁${project}Implementation Designs


    ${project}Viewpoints

       Perspective                     Perspective
       📁Architectural Layers          📁${project}Package Dependencies
```

Likewise, for each functional flow, a service design model is used to demonstrate the POM collaboration view, the SOA service view, and the data layer abstraction via the message view showing messages in and out of a service to the data layer. Depending on how complex the integration is or how phased out the implementation is structured, these can be built in different phases of the lifecycle of a portal program for the several projects under it.

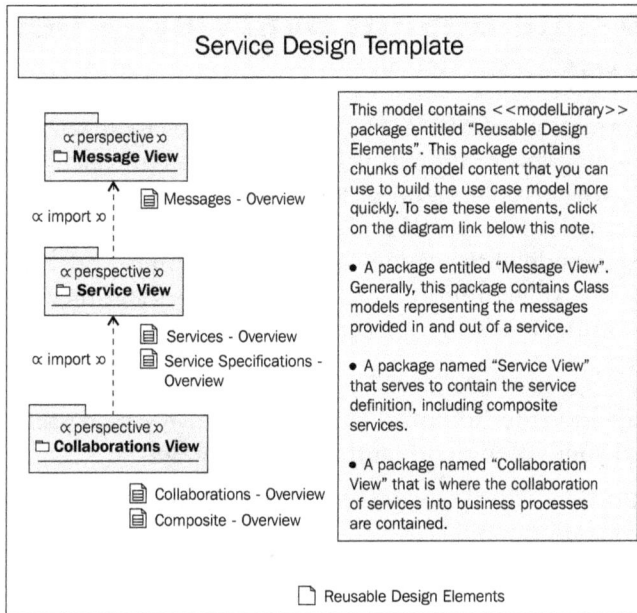

A more granular view of the service decomposition is another way to design for SOA. In this granular and low-level SOA design, the service is broken down into the different elements presented in the following diagram:

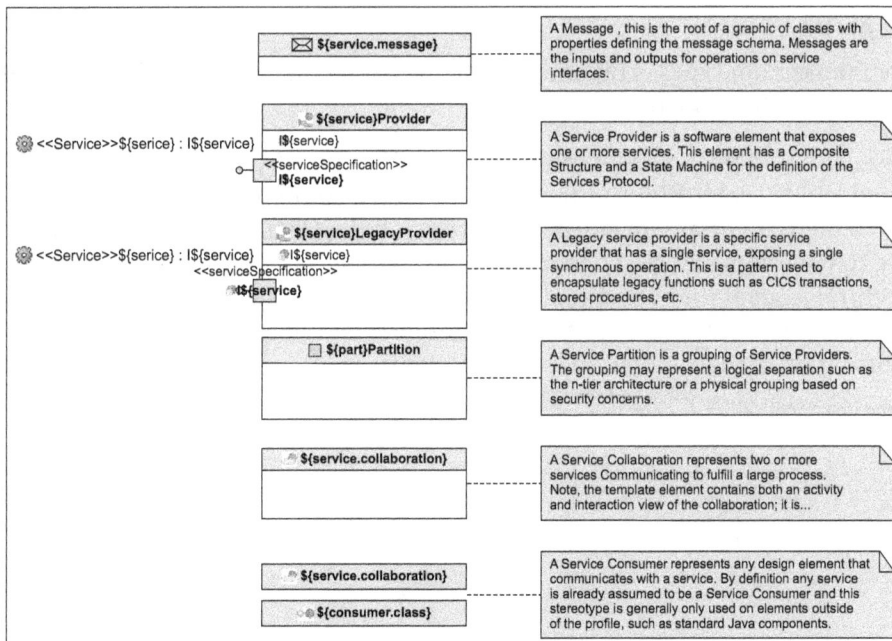

Service to data design overview – best practice artifacts

In complex transformation efforts, it is a best practice to create a traceability matrix and end-to-end view of the lifecycle of a business transaction. Due to the scope of this book, we can only mention some of the necessary understanding and documentation that will make portal and service-oriented architecture designs much simpler and agile. Outside of the canonical UML notation for providing knowledge via sequence, activity, collaboration, state nachine, class diagrams, the following are some of the potential artifacts for traceability of a portal-driven end-to-end transactional flow:

- **User group and roles to portal page**: This shows which user roles map to each portal pages along with authorization model

- **Pages to portlets**: This shows which screens contain which portlets along with authorization model

- **Portlets to service methods**: This shows which builder calls map to service methods

- **Portlets to services**: This shows how portlets map to services in SOA

- **Portlet calls**: This shows which portlet calls are made, the lifecycle and state machine of the data associated with the call, and used transactions

- **Call types to portal**: This shows which calls coming from telephony map to portal

- **Transaction types**: This shows which transaction types portal will process based on the functional domain

Likewise, any portlet-to-portlet communication (for **Java Specification Request (JSR)** and WSRP web APIs) and the many potential combinations (one to many – many to one) can be architecturally described in the UML notation. It is a best practice to have some level of documentation so that there is traceability from the architectural asset at the conceptual level to the implementation asset to be deployed to the cloud. At the abstraction level, we present a template for the portlet-to-portlet communication at the annotation level as follows:

<<interface>>
○ PropertyOut

type:target1, direction="out"

- Property
1

-Propertyout

<<component>> *
▣ Source end
- Source end

source end

1 -source end
1 -Portletinstance

<<Component>>
🖳 portlet

Name, ID

-PortletInstance
1

<<Component>>
🖳 PortletInstance
(Source)

Id

1 -PortletInstance

1 -source page

<<Component>>
🖳 Source Page

Name, ID

<<Component>>
🖳 WIRE

ID, User

1

<<interface>>
○ JSR286GlobalApplicationScope

0..1

-portletservice
<<interface>>
○ PortletService

<<elementsimport>>

<<interface>>
○ PropertyBrokerService

<<Pattern Instance>>
○ PortletView

Pattern Parameters
Session Facade
| state[1] : |
| Name[1] : |
| Kind [1] : o |
| Data [1] : Ⓒ |
| isMultiple [1] : |
| Transition Data [1..*] : |

<<Pattern Instance>>
○ Session Facade

Pattern Parameters
Session Facade
| Session Facade[1] : Ⓒ |
| Entity Bean[..*] : Ⓒ |

<<interface>>
○ PropertyIn

type:target, direction="in"

-target end

<<component>>
▣ Target End

-target end

-portletinstance(target)

<<Component>>
🖳 PortletInstance(Target)

Id

-portletinstance(target)

1 -portletinstance(target)

1 -target page

<<Component>>
🖳 Target Page

Name, ID

-para meter

<<interface>>
○ Parameter

<<interface>>
○ Action

Name

-action 1

-portlet 1

<<Component>>
🖳 Portlet

Name, Id

<<Pattern Instance>>
○ Portlet

Pattern Parameters
Portlet
| Portlet[1] : |
| States[1] : ≡ |

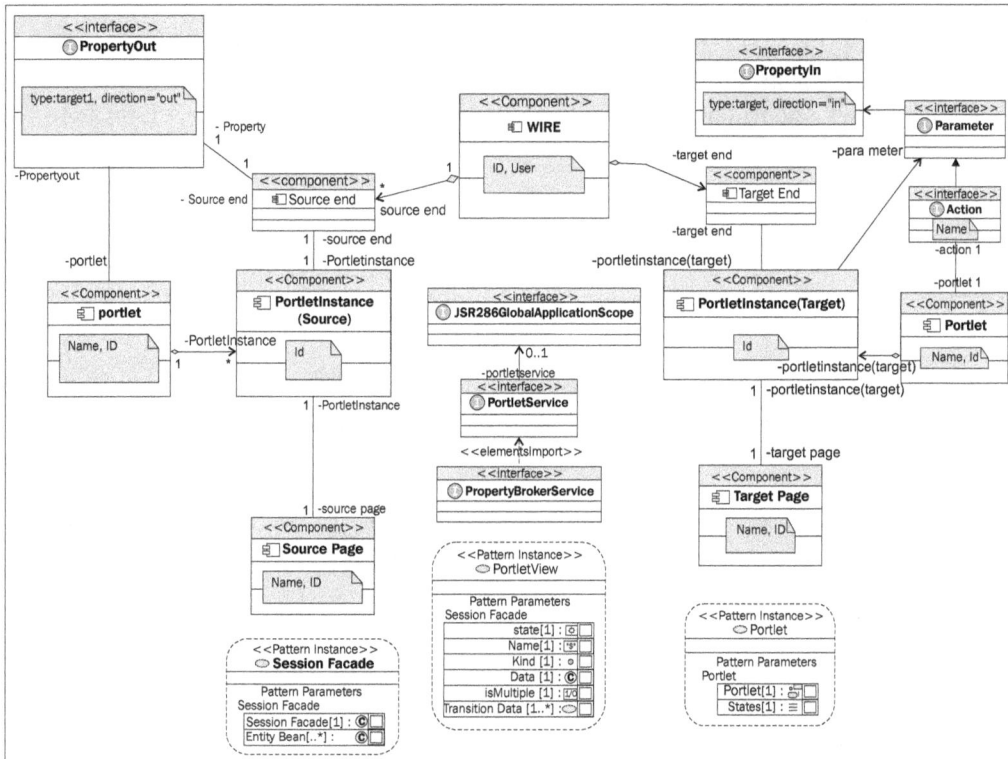

Enterprise reference architecture – simplifying complexity with DataPower and all handlers

There are many IBM Redbooks on DataPower that can assist architects to leverage the appliance concept and benefits to portal solutions. Please check the IBM Redbooks' website for further information.

A2Z steering committee and architecture board decided to utilize DataPower as the realization mechanism for SOA. Along with IBM Broker, **IBM Enterprise Service Bus (ESB)**, and **IBM WebSphere Process Server (WPS)**, it would provide the entire functionality stack and needed agility and interoperability. For now, let's first describe how the "all handlers" feature was used in the A2Z transformation effort.

At a high level, it takes input from and provides output to all data and protocol types, provides the necessary mediation engine, and the agility and advantages of low maintenance of an appliance. It drives operational costs, and architecturally speaking, allows one to virtually implement any conceptual flow. The X150 sits in the middle and the following diagram depicts the high-level UML notation:

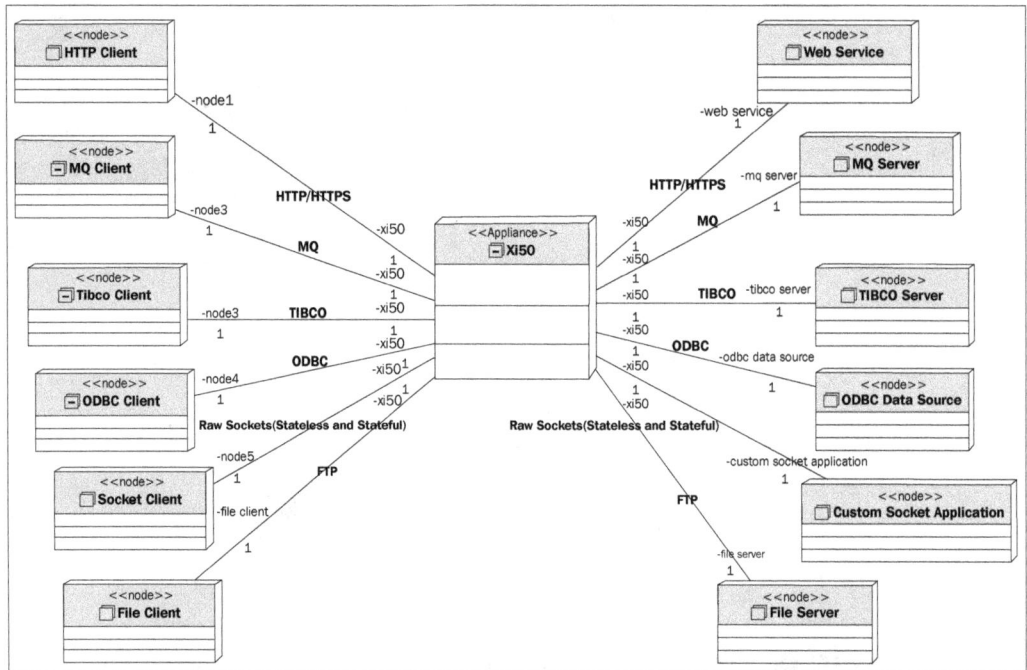

DataPower provides **high availability (HA)**, where incoming requests are load balanced via replicated appliances' instances. Portal itself also has gold architecture patterns for high availability (availability of 99 percent), which will be discussed in the next chapter.

A2Z architects also annotated a transformation view where the IBM DataPower appliance is the brain of the operation. The SOA realization via DataPower allows **Customer Information Control System (CICS)** legacy core banking systems to talk to distributed systems where WebSphere ESB, WPS for phase two. It also allows for the XML and non-XML clients to run requests via the appliance. The same SOA and integration architectural approach was used for both core banking and call center efforts with integrated authentication and authorization security architecture via **IBM Tivoli Access Manager (TAM)**.

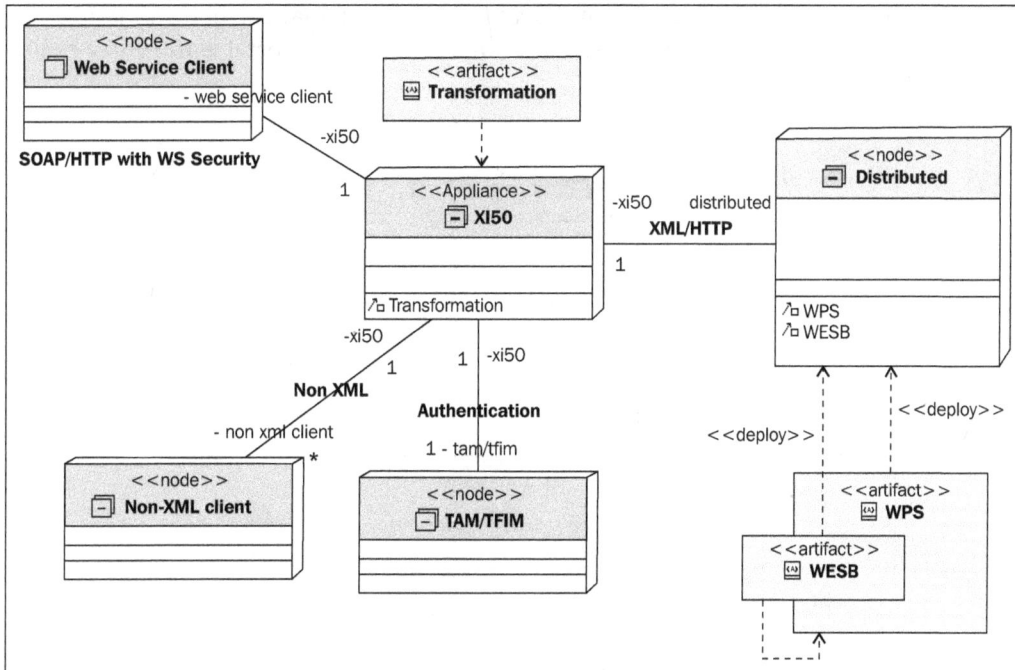

A2Z banking reference and portal application architecture

Let's now dive into the macro view of the logical application for A2Z banking core functionality. The following logical and deployment diagrams show the main structural nodes, which participate in a business transaction flow. WebSphere Portal is the entry point for the enterprise. It uses Tivoli Access Manager to implement Single Sign-On (on a limited scope for phase one). Portal interfaces with DataPower as the main brain for the mediating and transforming data (based on established business rules) in a way that all the complexity behind it is encapsulated from portal. Portal knows which services or processes to invoke, but it is agnostic to what is behind the scenes. CICS and WebSphere on z/OS keep the transactional and persistence data backbone; while WPS and ESB collaborate on the SOA and business process management stack; ESB maintains the services, and MQ and Broker facilitate Pub/Sub and other asynchronous functionalities.

The following logical and deployment diagram shows the main structural nodes, which participate in a business transaction flow. WebSphere Portal is the entry point for the enterprise.

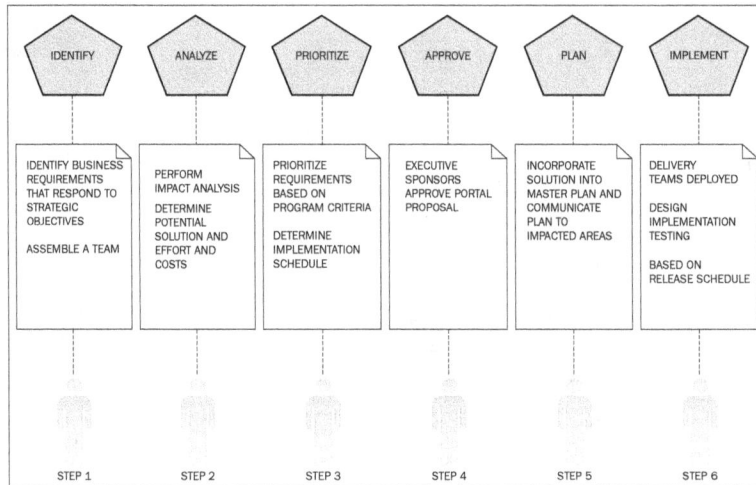

A2Z call center reference and portal application architecture

Let's now dive into the macro view of the logical application for A2Z call center functionality. Here, the main difference is in the incoming request from the telephony infrastructure. CTI, IVR, and WebSphere Voice collaborate to pass the call onto portal and allow the **Softphone** portlet to populate the portal screen for the CSR. Once the call is routed to portal, a queue is assigned to receive the call. The operator looks at its 360 view and is able to be highly productive. Portal is highly performance efficient in the cloud and delivers the expected value to A2Z modernization's effort.

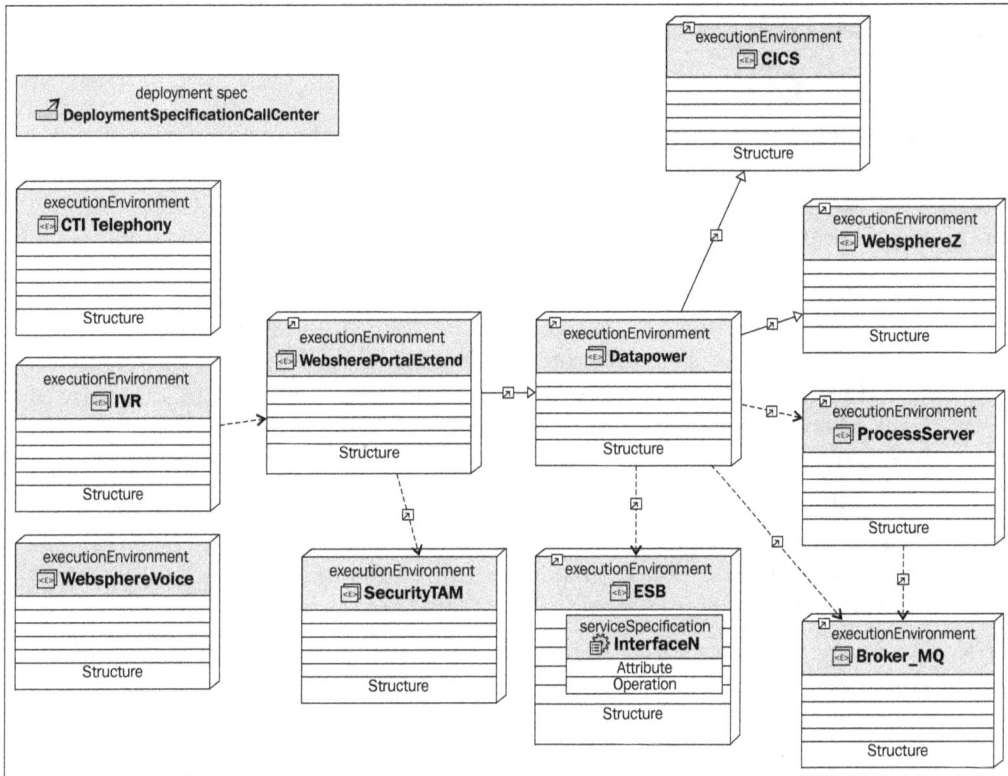

Cloud as the fabric for resilient architecture

A2Z Bullion Bank is headed in the right direction—this resilient cloud computing model helps to reduce the effort for capacity planning at an application level, as an application can just request resources from the cloud and get them in a matter of minutes based on dynamic demand. In a cloud-enabled portal environment, it is the data center manager's shared responsibility to predict resource requirements of all the portal-integrated applications and engines, and to order sufficient hardware ahead of time, independently of the input from application owners. The basis for capacity planning rests in monitoring existing usage patterns and keeping track over historical time periods so that long-term trends can be projected based on previous workload activity and self-adjusted without any knowledge of business plans. In the case of a new private cloud, it is still necessary to follow best practices in performance modeling to achieve a final cloud specification and footprint before elasticity and on-demand provisioning takes over.

Architecting for nonfunctional requirements

One major risk of system capacity is already mitigated by the fact that cloud was written as a requirement. This is not just a technology requirement, but a business-based enterprise direction. Let's take a quick look at some of the other nonfunctional requirements and how the architecture is aligned to solve them:

- **Aesthetics**: It is the aesthetic quality of the user interface. This requirement is architecturally fulfilled by the use of portal technology as the main presentation layer. The call center users are coming from a green screen world for user interface; while the bank users are coming from a mixture of both green screens and some J2EE frontends. Utilizing portal is a huge leap in interface enhancement.

- **Accessibility**: It is the ease with which different facets of the system are exercised. Both the Single Sign-On and the information architecture for this transformation effort make this requirement to be aligned with portal capabilities to deliver its goals.

- **Accuracy**: It is the accuracy of any calculations performed. Because of the risk associated with financial transactions, accuracy is must, and the DataPower appliance along with the existing infrastructure makes this requirement very achievable.

- **Availability**: The degree to which a system or component is operational and accessible when required for use is realized via the cloud. The cloud's elasticity provides the proper execution environment for highly available applications.

- **Consistency**: It is the consistent use of mechanisms employed in the user interface. This applies both within the system and with other systems. Again, this requirement is aligned with portal capabilities.

- **Efficiency**: It is the amount of resources used and the duration of such use in performing its function, for example CPU time, disk time, number of active threads at the high watermark level of usage. Knowing the efficiency should lead to a solid understanding of the overall system capacity. This is another requirement fulfilled by the use of a cloud-enabled execution environment.

- **Usability**: It is the ease with which a user can learn to operate, prepare inputs for, and interpret outputs of a system or component. Usability is a key portal capability, which is well aligned with this requirement and the business goals.

- **Mobility**: It is the ability to utilize a system on portable devices, such as PDAs, smart cell phones, laptops, and tablet PCs. This requirement is fulfilled by Portal Mobile Accelerator.

- **Performance**: Performance refers to the responsiveness of a system. It is the time required to respond to events, or the number of events processed in some interval of time. Performance qualities are often expressed by the number of transactions per unit of time, or by the amount of time it takes to complete a transaction. In portal applications, it also means user perceived and system response time. This requirement is supported by the chosen gold standard portal architecture, which is focused on getting best performance due to the fast-paced nature of banking and call center transactions.

- **Workload models**: The workload assessment is a crucial and vital ingredient for a cloud formula. It allows the cloud to be projected based on the workload average and peak characteristics for the business transactions and services hosted by and available via the cloud.

- **Reliability**: It is the ability of a system or component to perform its required functions under stated conditions for a specified period of time. One of the great combinations to fulfill this requirement, architecturally speaking, is the use of the cloud.

- **Recoverability**: It is the restoration of a system, program, database, or other system resource to a prior state following a failure or externally caused disaster; for example, the restoration of a database to a point at which processing can be resumed following a system failure.

- **Response time**: It is the time for the portal pages and portlets to provide a response (that is, elapsed time). Based on the nonfunctional requirements, portal pages and portlets got an expected response time for both call center and banking domains. The use of parallel rendering and other portal caching options, along with the elasticity of the cloud, will allow for this requirement to be realized. The test architecture will be focused on the target business goals and will also be done using the cloud. Rational Performance Tester was the chosen tool for testing the performance of this A2Z portal.

- **Security**: Cloud-suitable security model and **Single Sign-On (SSO)** are implemented along with corporate and IT guidelines and business requirements. We could write a whole book on the security implementation itself. Due to limited page constraints, we will fully cover it in another edition along with **Business Process Management (BPM)** and WSRP.

- **Throughput**: It is the capacity of a system to support a given flow of data and activity volume. Both domains captured the necessary throughput for the business transactions. Cloud monitoring will allow for a close look at how the requirement is being fulfilled.

Summary

In this chapter, we looked at architectural best practices for portal efforts. We started showing how to take customer requirements and map them to storyboards or wireframes. We then looked at how these wireframes or storyboards can assist in the mapping of the portal object model (portlet fields and objects) to an SOA and data model. We proceeded looking at service design conceptual view and some end-to-end traceability possibilities. We then looked at a high-level logical portal architecture view for both core banking and call center portal efforts. We finished with a brief discussion of nonfunctional aspects of portal implementations, which will take us to the next chapter. The next chapter will go over into portal gold architecture and reusable assets.

5
Portal Golden and Cloud Architecture

This chapter covers the best practices in building portal environments for high availability and delivering the operationalization of the business models. The portal golden topology for traditional and cloud environments is discussed in the context of the case study, and also to help guide portal implementations. Additionally, it gives best practices in sizing portal environments using performance modeling techniques and tools. By the end of this chapter, we should have looked at the following:

- Reusable architecture assets
- IBM Accelerators for IBM WebSphere Portal
- Cloud execution environment
- Highly available A2Z portal golden and SOA reference architecture
- Virtual portals, realms, and cluster partitioning
- Portal collaboration, pervasive, and voice architectures
- Portal security architecture
- Portal architecture and performance modeling
- Portal operational model and workload analysis
- IBM lab tools – mainframe and distributed
- Commercial tools – mainframe and distributed
- Cloud capacity planning – IBM SmartCloud Monthly Cost Estimator
- Cloud capacity planning – Amazon Monthly Calculator
- Test architecture and test data governance
- Architecture assessment and operational technical readiness review

Reusable architecture assets and IBM Portal Accelerators

Before we get into the A2Z Bank portal's physical and operational architectures that can be deployed to both traditional and cloud-enabled IT, let's take a look at some of the out-of-the-box assets delivered by IBM and other teams. They have created a plethora of different portal assets via IBM Toolbox, IBM Portal Accelerators, Lotus Portlet Catalog/Lotus Greenhouse, and IBM Content Templates Catalog, to name a few. Finding large reusable assets, both internal and external to the enterprise, is a mandatory step for all stakeholders involved in a portal initiative. The idea is to map requirements to existing portal assets that allow them to be architecturally extended, adjusted, and reusable to one's custom needs.

One of the great advantages of portal is to be able to integrate at the glass with other applications and data sources. The entire involved group benefits from reusability. As a portal architect, one wants to make sure that the design patterns needed to fulfill the requirements can be found and applied towards the desired logical and operational architecture.

As a portal specialist or developer, one wants to reduce the amount of coding for functionality already available. One wants to maximize his/her productivity by focusing on the custom logic, and not the portlet or application framework's barebone mechanics, so to speak. Time to value and market is of essence, and by carefully analyzing all these options, mapping and correlating them back to the context of your particular needs; one could save a lot of time while keeping quality. Understanding these assets allows one to take more holistic approach towards reusability. So, remember that whenever you are involved in a project as a solution architect, application architect, WEF or WP specialist, or developer, you want check out these resources and see how they deliver functionality needed for your own portal project.

For more detailed information on the assets themselves, please visit IBM's website for Portal Accelerators at http://www-01.ibm.com/software/websphere/portal/industry/.

IBM recorded interactive presentation on IBM Accelerators for WebSphere Portal, which can be seen at the link provided in our site for this chapter as follows:

http://download.boulder.ibm.com/ibmdl/pub/demos/on_demand/Streamed/IBM_Demo_Integrating_IBM_accelerators_for_WebSphere_Portal-1-Sep07.html?S=DL#IBM_Recorded_Demonstration.

We also recommend further reading the IBM e-book—*Exploring IBM Accelerators for WebSphere Portal* at `https://www14.software.ibm.com/webapp/iwm/web/signup.do?source=swg-Accelerators_ebook`.

For our case study with A2Z Bank, once these reusable assets are mapped to the overall enterprise architecture, we will move on to the portal architecture notation itself.

A2Z steering committee and governance along with IBM subject-matter experts helped to drive the reusability of large out-of-the-box assets. Program-level decisions made by the stakeholders for the portal program were in progress. The core banking transformation initiative, which was quickly jump-started via the **Business Value Assessment (BVA)** and **Proof of Value (POV)**, would architecturally utilize a combination of existing assets for the portal program and portal application project plans while still following the banking reference architecture. The banking reference architecture was utilized to guide the architectural realization of the banking transformation from a core system enterprise-wide perspective. For more information about the banking reference architecture adopted by A2Z Bullion Bank, please read the IBM developerWorks article "Modernizing Banking Core Systems"

> For more information about the banking reference architecture as a starting point, please read the IBM developerWorks article—*Modernizing banking core systems* by Scott Simmons at `http://www.ibm.com/developerworks/websphere/techjournal/0809_col_simmons/0809_col_simmons.html` and visit the IBM Worldwide Banking Center Of Excellence at `http://www-03.ibm.com/systems/services/bankingcoe/`.

For the call center initiative, it was decided that agile and custom rapid development would be fully done using the **IBM Web Experience Factory (WEF)**. No other assets were deemed useful for this particular domain, except for the call center reference architecture itself and the Mobile Accelerator. For more about the call center architecture, please see the white paper—*The Contact Center of the Future Paper* by Andrew Pritchard and Raj Mirchandani at `http://www-935.ibm.com/services/us/gbs/bus/pdf/the-contact-center-of-the-future.pdf`. The call center initiative, in collaboration and synchronization with the core banking transformation effort, used DataPower and IBM **Master Data Management (MDM)** reference architectures as foundational blueprint for this IT modernization endeavor. For more information about the MDM reference architecture itself, please read the IBM developerWorks article—*An introduction to the Master Data Management Reference Architecture* by Martin Oberhofer and Allen Dreibelbis at `http://www.ibm.com/developerworks/data/library/techarticle/dm-0804oberhofer/index.html`.

Now, returning to the portal-specific reusable assets and accelerators, let's see how they were mapped to the A2Z Bank's architecture. The following list illustrates all the core and prioritized reusable assets selected for the portal initiative in a phased approach:

- First business release
    - ◦ IBM Mobile Accelerator from the IBM Accelerator (both core banking and call center domains)
    - ◦ IBM Banking Template 2.0 for WebSphere Portal from IBM Toolbox (core banking domains)
- Second business release
    - ◦ IBM **Content Template Catalog (CTC)**
    - ◦ IBM BPM Accelerator
    - ◦ IBM Collaboration Accelerator
    - ◦ IBM Dashboard Accelerator

IBM Accelerators for IBM WebSphere Portal

These assets were created by IBM teams to make the 3D concept (design, development, and deployment) agile and conformant to best practices for the domains they address. According to the website literature, which can be found at `http://www-01.ibm.com/software/lotus/portal/value/`, "In order to expedite portal deployments and facilitate integration to existing IT assets, IBM created the concept of Portal Accelerators. IBM® accelerators for IBM WebSphere® Portal software are prepackaged offerings, comprised of various combinations of portlets, software, frameworks, and templates to address specific business requirements. IBM accelerators help speed time to value of web portal deployments by providing the flexibility to respond quickly to changes in market dynamics and business requirements from a common WebSphere Portal software foundation." A2Z Bullion Bank included the discovery in the BVA phase of the strategic project plan. Portal Accelerators were also utilized during the POV. The available accelerators are listed in the next sections, along with the actions taken by our portal team in our case study.

IBM Retail Banking Template for WebSphere Portal (v2.0)

This 2.0 release of the IBM Retail Banking Template runs on WebSphere Portal 7x and 8x. According to the literature and our experience, this template carries the best practices and the data model for banking operations. It can be integrated to provide rapid value, as it implements design patterns that are canonical to any online banking portal.

All the content, layouts, and portlets can be customized and configured to meet specific requirements. The template assets can be integrated with existing systems and content to provide an exceptional user experience for banking customers, bringing together technical capabilities and industry-thought leadership to deliver an exceptional web experience. For more information, please visit its website.

> The following demo provides an interactive view into the Banking Template capability from IBM Toolbox. Enjoy online banking, loan origination, mortgage processing, and retail banking at `http://www-01.ibm.com/software/websphere/portal/industry/banking/demos.html`.
>
> Additionally, this demo demonstrates the Banking Template at work at `http://www14.software.ibm.com/webapp/download/demo.jsp?id=WebSphere%20Portal%202.0%20for%20Banking%20Demo`.

A2Z Bank leveraged the template to provide accelerated value during both the POV phase as part of the BVA and for the first phase, and business release based on the roadmap and project plans. It took the template and customized it for its own newly modeled service layer. It leveraged the WEF for quick customization of the out-of-the-box portlets in order to deliver the expected value and return on investment. It also made development extra agile in a development cloud, which provided the operational runtime.

IBM Mobile Portal Accelerator

With this asset, portal code can be developed once and run over 8200 devices via an intelligent multichannel server that adapts portal content to mobile devices. More on building for pervasive devices (smart phones in particular) will be covered later. A2Z Bank decided to adopt the Mobile Portal Accelerator as part of its strategic and tactical project plans for the self-service portal business pattern. One of the requirements for the self-service interface was the ability to allow the end user to consume data from different devices. Major read-only functionality related to account status and investment information would be available via all devices. The choice was tactical, because it allowed the POV to be done in a very quick time to value. IBM SmartCloud comes equipped with the Mobile Portal Accelerator (for the Amazon Cloud, it can be added), making development and deployment incredibly faster processes. Aligned with the power of WEF to prototype what is needed quickly and a cloud-ready image with an operational version of it running, this was a win-win choice for all stakeholders involved.

Please visit the IBM Mobile Portal Accelerator information center for full product documentation and literature at `http://publib.boulder.ibm.com/infocenter/mpadoc/v7r0m0/index.jsp`.

IBM Dashboard Accelerator

Before issues become critical, it is essential to have the real-time visibility into your organization's **key performance indicators (KPIs)** via performance dashboards. A2Z Bullion Bank adopted IBM Dashboard Accelerator as a part of the strategic business monitoring and KPI tracking identified during the BVA iteration. They would allow a role-based interaction with the data for KPI tracking. For the self-service initiative, the CEO to the LOB vice presidents, executives, and managers broker end users' dashboards with their customer vaults, account, and transaction data charts. For the call center initiative, it would allow manager and other parties to look at their call center business goals and KPI via the dashboards.

IBM Collaboration Accelerator

Based on the established roadmap, A2Z Bank chose this accelerator for an incremental business release for the call center application that would run in parallel with the other portal initiatives under the same portal office and center of excellence umbrella. This would be the the call center v1.5, where floor supervisor, managers, and customer service representatives would communicate via instant messenger and calendar, and have their e-mail services all consolidated. Because of the scope of this book, we will leave this item for the next book that will deal with BPM, collaboration, search among, SSO, and WSRP, among other topics.

IBM Content Accelerator

Likewise, the Collaboration Accelerator, A2Z Bank chose this accelerator for an incremental business release for the call center application; only that would run in parallel with the other portal initiatives under the same portal office and center of excellence umbrella, based on the established roadmap. This would be the the call center v1.5, where floor supervisor, managers, and customer service representatives would have search-enabled and role-based access to manuals, policies, procedures, documentation, and human resources information around the call center operations.

Portlet Catalog and Lotus Greenhouse

Another portal resource for reusable assets is Portlet Catalog. It is basically an application store with portlets that can range from Google gadgets to mobile themes, portlets skins, to wizards, installers, and so on. There are many ways to look for something ready to be customized, tested, deployed, and used.

For the POV and the first release of the portal initiative for A2Z Bank, we used one set of portlets from the catalog and a set of accelerators for the subsequent portal release phases. For the first phase, e-banking portlets including the KPI banking portlets were chosen.

Please visit the Wikipedia site for the banking template for full description of data model, code, and other assets along with documentation at `http://www-10.lotus.com/ldd/portalwiki.nsf/xpViewCategories.xsp?lookupName=IBM%20Bganking%20template%20V2.0%20for%20WebSphere%20Portal`.

Cloud execution environment and architectural model for cloud computing – IBM cloud reference architecture

In the cloud environment, where there is virtualization, standardization, and automation to harvest the exponential business value, we have delivery modes with defined policies for ownership and control in the following:

- **Infrastructure as a Service (IaaS)**, which delivers the basic computing foundations, such as the operating system, storage, networking
- **Platform as a Service (PaaS)**, which delivers additional capabilities to the infrastructure, such as middleware, development tools, transaction, and database management
- **Software as a Service (SaaS)**, which delivers the applications and business processes to the business end users
- **Business Process as a Service (BPaaS)**, which delivers business processes and process portals to users and business applications

There are architectural decisions for the entire enterprise to be made for the cloud. How hybrid it should be is a question based on business and technology needs. Architectural decisions, for example, what should be public and private; what can be enterprise or vendor operated, to name a few, have to be made. In the case of A2Z Bank, there was a decision on moving all of the new initiative into a vendor-operated cloud model.

The major core banking data, operational model, and information-sensitive components were moved into a private and enterprise-operated cloud under single tenant model. All dedicated elastic resources were moved to A2Z Enterprise. For portal cloud infrastructure alone, it was decided to start with a vendor-operated model for development/test and production. That allowed the enterprise to learn about cloud managing their integration, staging (which was a replica of production), and UAT portal environments as depicted at a high level in the following diagram:

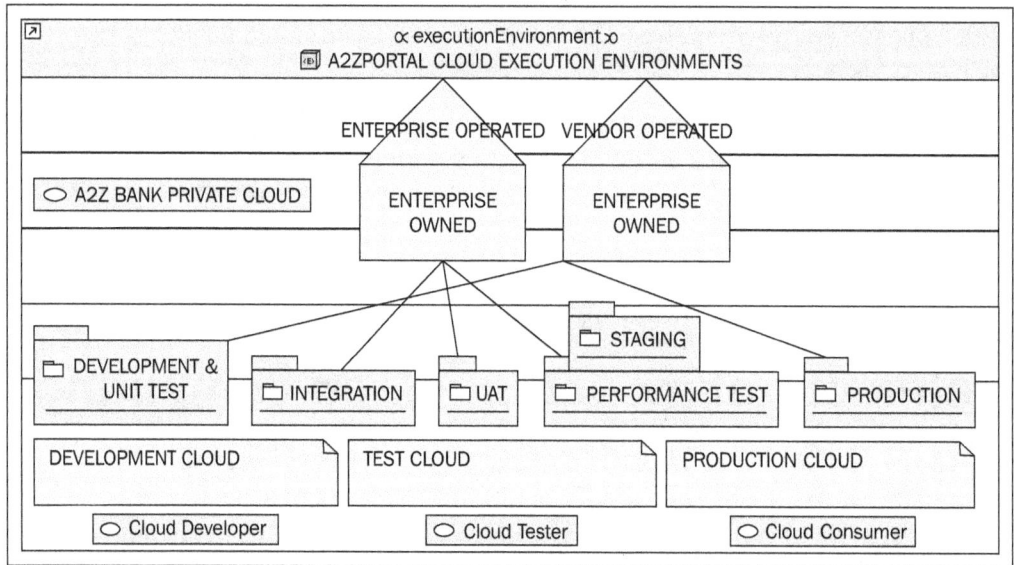

If we look at this cloud operational and engagement model, we can see that the A2Z portal production and test environments were implemented as enterprise owned, but vendor operated as private cloud. The advantage is that development environments are provisioned within minutes. Production also takes advantage of the cloud's elasticity, the on-demand flexibility based on user needs, while providing out-of-the-box virtual images templates with portal configuration patterns for high availability and gold (or platinum) **service-level agreement (SLA)** standards. On the integration, user acceptance, and staging environments, it was decided to have a private cloud that is entirely enterprise owned and operated. The integration and UAT environments were a more robust and clustered version of the development environment. The staging (performance) environment was a mimic of production. It allowed for the enterprise to rely on the vendor-operated cloud for test and production, while provided leverage in empowering the enterprise to learn and manage its own environments. This strategy also enabled the business to have another full secondary disaster recovery mechanism. The A2Z Bank had basically built flexibility for the future to look at the cost benefit of both enterprise-operated versus vendor-operated clouds.

Highly available portal golden and SOA reference architecture

Now, let's look at how A2Z Bank realized each layer, based on the architectural principles described by IBM SOA reference architecture and best practices. We always recommend looking at reference architecture and best practices to be reused in a business or technology development effort. The following diagram contextualizes the IBM layered SOA architecture to the A2Z portal architecture. On one hand, we have one to five layers of the service-oriented architecture. Portal sits on the presentation layer but also integrates into business processes, composite services, and enterprise components. Layer six relates to the integrated architecture at a high enterprise level. Layer seven relates to the **Quality of Service (QoS)**, the security management, and monitoring, meaning to some of the nonfunctional aspects of a layered architecture. Adding to the canonical IBM layered SOA architecture, A2Z Bank uses a set of principles (described after the following diagram) to serve as a foundation to the hybrid cloud model adopted by A2Z Bank:

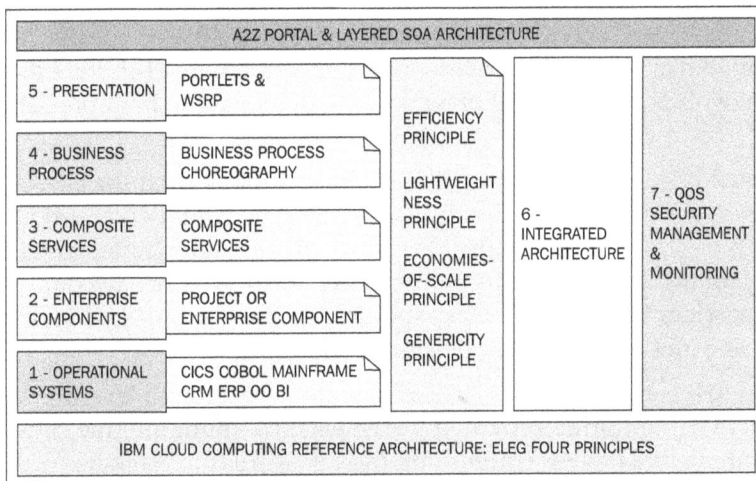

The following are the set of principles used by A2Z Bank. For more information on this, refer to the site at `http://www.ibm.com/developerworks/webservices/library/ws-soa-design1/`.

- **Layer 1**: It is the operational systems layer. In the case of A2Z Bank, it comprises of the CICS, CIS, and mainframe legacy application for core banking and the call center. This layer has applications with commonly named legacy systems, as well as other foundational business intelligence applications. They can be leveraged and integrated via service-oriented integration techniques.

- **Layer 2**: It is the enterprise components layer. In the case of A2Z Bank, this was realized into the modernization effort via MDM, and the IBM out-of-the-box templates, along with existing core applications. The enterprise components layer is tasked with providing functionality and maintaining the QoS of the exposed services. Service-level agreements are managed in this layer. Different lines of business make use of it.

- **Layer 3**: It is the services layer. A2Z Bank decided to expose its data layer via services. It uses services to map the banking template to the data layer. This is the layer where services are exposed, hosted, and discovered. This layer externalizes a subset of service interfaces in the form of service descriptions. They can be deployed in isolation or as a composite service.

- **Level 4**: It is the business process composition or choreography layer. As a part of releasing 2.0, A2Z Bank will utilize this layer for the process portal initiative, where business process management workflow tasks would be integrated into the portal via the task portlet. This is the layer where the choreography of business processes occurs. BPM is where portal plays a key role with the integration capabilities aligned with the BPaaS mode of delivery.

- **Layer 5**: It is the access or presentation layer. A2Z Bank utilizes WebSphere Portal to realize this SOA reference architecture while fulfilling its business goals. This is where portal plays a big role displaying both portlet and WSRP technologies.

- **Level 6**: It is the integration (ESB) layer. A2Z Bank used the best combination of integration capabilities with WebSphere ESB, DataPower, MDM, and MQ. This is the layer, which supports service orchestration; intelligent routing; protocol mediation; transformation mechanisms to message data, messages, and services based on these capabilities. ESB also represents a location agnostic mechanism for service integration.

- **Level 7**: It is the QoS layer. A2Z is in a great position to leverage the ongoing proactive monitoring provided by the elasticity built into the cloud. This is a fundamental layer for providing the capabilities to track nonfunctional metrics required to sensor, monitor, manage, and maintain QoS, such as security, performance, availability, and overall health of portal, SOA, and other layers in the cloud. It implements standards that proactively support QoS for a SOA portal gold standard for highly available architectures.

A common denominator set of principles taken from the IBM Cloud Computing Reference Architecture was applied to the A2Z portal and SOA reference architecture. Four principles were foundational for this architecture, as follows:

- **The Efficiency Principle**: This refers to the realization of the cloud elasticity and self-service, and focus is given to its efficiencies to shorten time to delivery and changes

- **The Lightweightness Principle**: This refers to support of lean service management processes and technologies

- **The Economies of Scale Principle**: This refers to identification and leveraging of commonalities in the service design itself

- **The Genericity Principle**: This refers to a common management platform

Let's now take a look at the A2Z Bullion Bank portal's operational and runtime architectures. The goal is to have no single point of failure in all the portal-specific execution environments. The presentation, content management, collaboration, security, pervasive, BPM, backend, and content tiers are properly clustered, load balanced, and replicated. Note that this is a production (potentially can be replicated as disaster recovery or performance) target operational topology. Lower environments, such as development, integration, and user acceptance can be used with shared or vertical topologies if they are being set up in traditional IT, and shared using cloud development resources. We will not get into details of what should be set up as active-active or active-passive, or session persistence and affinity, and overall details on elimination of any single point of failure including the network layer. However, careful architectural analysis should be done to clarify each detail of the operational architecture to make sure it meets the performance, availability, and scalability requirements.

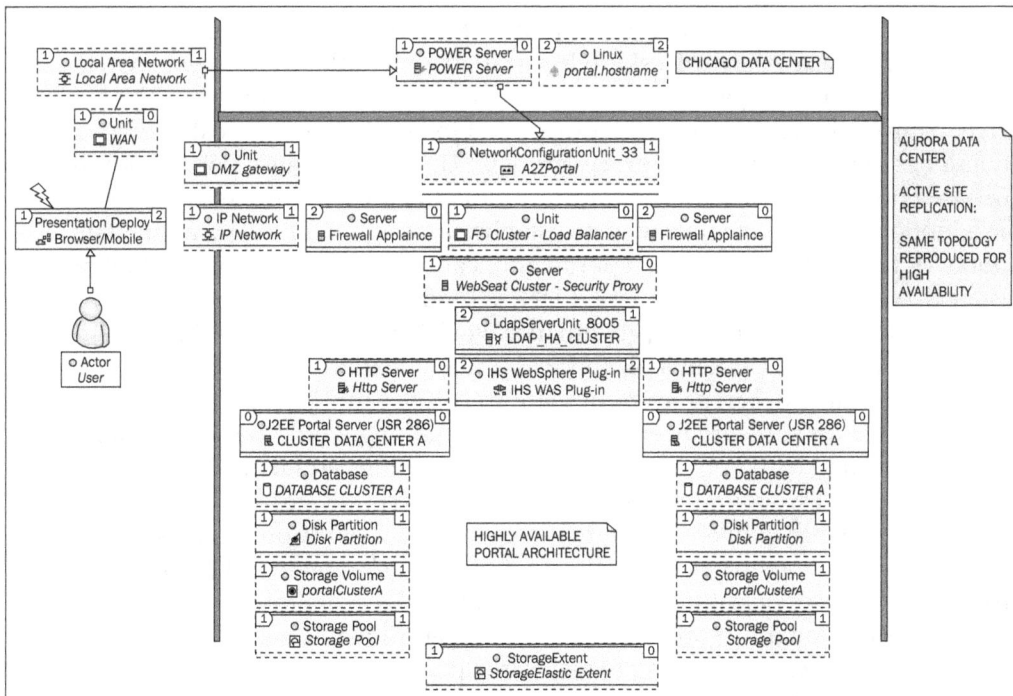

This is the canonical basic portal operational architecture, which for the sake of page space does not include the portal telephony, voice, BPM, full content management, search, and some other operational components that would make the complete portal solution ecosystem for the A2Z Bullion Bank. Likewise, they should be replicated for an end-to-end highly available architecture. The portal user comes in via a device, which is the desktop and in the case of brokers, smart phones, iPads and PDA(s). It is via a WAN, LAN, or Wireless that the connection is made to the network. Depending on whether the user is within the **demilitarized zone (DMZ)** or not, via a VPN remote connection or outside of the DMZ, it will hit the firewall layer, which will then forward the request to the IP sprayer and load balancer via HTTP server and the WebSphere plugin, which in turns passes to the security layer for portal authorization and authentication. Session affinity keeps the user bound to one side of the portal cluster. Databases are fully available and replicated with elastic storage and archiving mechanisms. Because this portal setup uses the virtual portal feature, users are also routed to content based on the virtual portal community to which they belong.

Virtual portals, realms, and cluster partitioning

As part of both portal application development efforts for the different lines of business (on the Call Center Desktop Integration and Banking Core systems), the use of virtual portal was a governance and enterprise-level-driven decision. The business driver behind this decision was the prospect of lowering the total cost of ownership on number of licenses paid per processor or CPU. This is because portal licenses are based on CPU cores activated. The technical and architectural reasons behind the adoption of virtual portals were to establish a design pattern and architectural option for future A2Z application portal application tenants. The same portal, when installed, would run on Blade 7, 64-bit UNIX, Linux, or AIX-based systems. Virtual portals as decided by the portal governance would be leveraged for the A2Z lines of business. Along with custom look and feel, and navigation schemes, virtual portals allow for attending different user populations on the same physical installs and saving the cost for software license. Cluster Partitioning would permit the portal users to be routed based on their LDAP-realm mappings and their lines of business. The virtual portal would allow the A2Z Bank brokers, CSRs, corporate users to have a unique experience, while taking advantage of cluster partitioning. This portioning allows administrators to have a single point of configuration for all portals, thus enabling better user distribution among the physical servers for the virtual portal user level. Additionally, it allows for easy reconfiguration of mini clusters of virtual portals on the fly without having to restart the portal server.

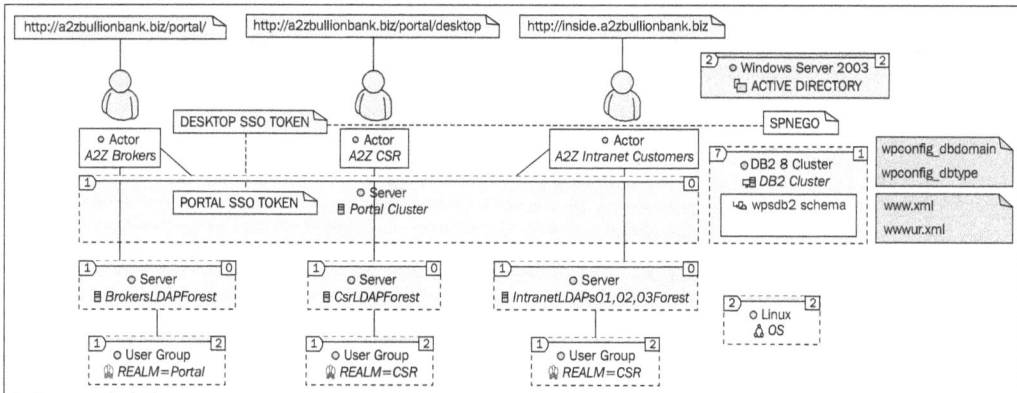

Portal collaboration, pervasive, and voice runtime architectures

As part of a nonfunctional requirement to make portal content available to other devices, a pervasive architecture was designed, and IBM Mobile Portal Accelerator was deployed to make this effort agile. The following diagram depicts a generic notation for the pervasive runtime pattern architecture for A2Z Bank portal along with the voice and collaboration components. It shows all the necessary components that will make the requirement to be realized and fulfilled via its implementation. In the voice infrastructure, we have three voice-related components, excluding the CTI telephony components. There is a Voice Server, a Unified Messaging for Voice Response, and the embedded component. This piece of the architecture allows for the CTI telephony infrastructure to route calls to the **Interactive Voice Response (IVR)** system and pass it on to portal's **SoftPhone** portlet on the portal screen.

The pervasive side of the architecture is comprised of the Translation Server, Everyplace Mobile Portal Enable, Everyplace Micro Environment, and the Connection Manager. It is beyond the scope of this chapter to describe how they interact, but when documenting dataflow via sequence or collaboration diagrams, a full step-by-step description of the dataflow and the **Session Initiation Protocol (SIP)** would be needed.

Finally, for the collaboration portion of the architecture, which would be mostly for the second business release of the A2Z portal, the combination of Lotus Domino Everyplace, Lotus EasySynch, and Sametime Everyplace would allow the pervasive and collaboration requirements to be realized as a whole.

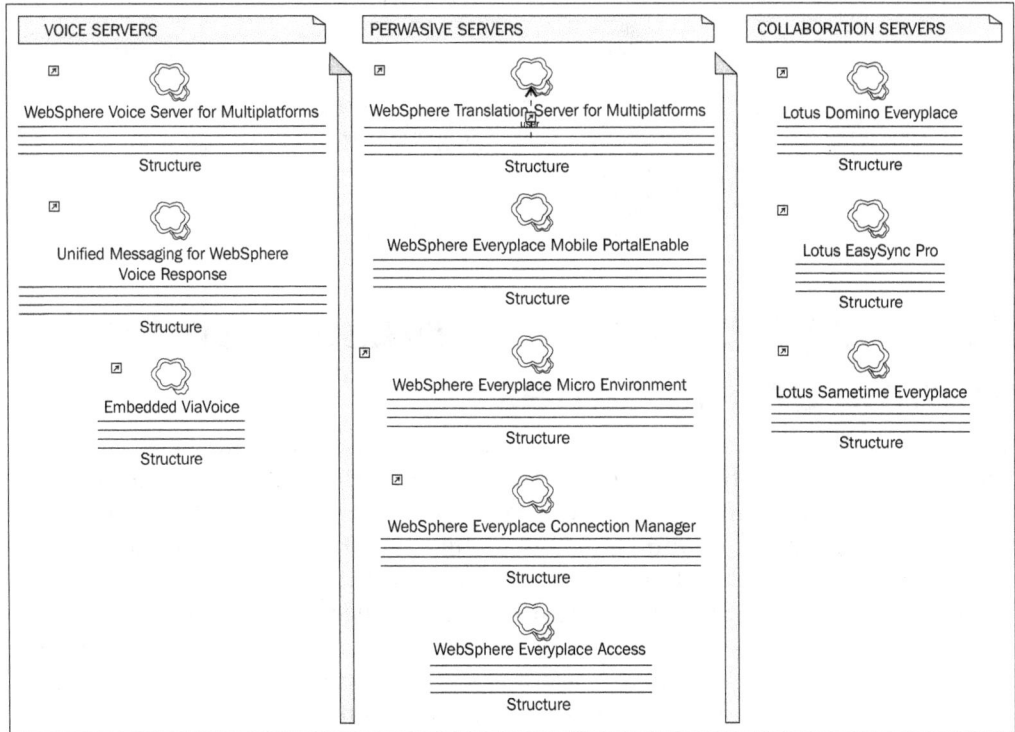

At a high level, and for the sake of scope, let's take a quick look at the dataflow and the main components invoked in the pervasive portal architecture.

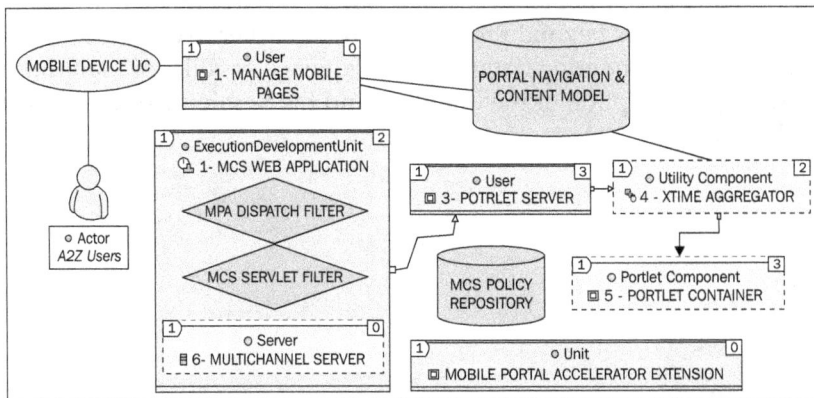

The following are the main components invoked in the pervasive portal architecture:

- A2Z portal administrators use the Manage Mobile Pages portlet to define the navigation for a mobile portal, based on the information architecture specifications for the Core Banking virtual portals. The navigation hierarchy defines nodes (pages, URLs, and portlets), and the optional extended properties specify device capability, type, and display requirements for each node. These nodes and properties are stored in the WebSphere® Portal mobile database.

- When the A2Z WebSphere Portal Server receives a request, the MPADispatchFilter forwards this request to the MCS web application. If the request is from a mobile device, the MCS web application prepares the request for processing and forwards it back to the portal servlet. If the request is from a PC device, the MCS web application forwards the request as it is, back to portal servlet.

- The A2Z portal servlet uses the supported clients table to determine which portal theme (aggregator) should handle the request. Mobile device requests are directed to the XDIME theme by the supported clients table.

- The A2Z portal XDIME aggregator queries the A2Z portal model to determine the navigation, as well as portlet availability, based on the user and extended properties of each node. If the request is for a portlet node, the request is passed to the portlet.

- If the A2Z portlet is an XDIME portlet, the portlet renders the content in XDIME and returns the content to the XDIME aggregator.

- Once the aggregated XDIME page is fetched by the MCS web application, MCS converts the XDIME content for the page to device-specific markup by using the appropriate policies in the MCS policy repository.

- Finally, the MCS web application returns the device-specific content for delivery to the MPADispatchFilter, which in turn delivers this markup to the mobile device.

Portal security architecture

In order to support the strategic goals for SSO for portal, a phased approach was set by the portal governance. For the overall security, user management, and associated capabilities, a full-blown security model was designed and implemented to serve the core banking, call center, and the enterprise as a whole. Both portal initiatives needed to have portal security integrated into the desktop for customer service representatives and brokers.

The requirement, in a nutshell, is that when the bank user would log on to his/her Windows-based machine, he/she should be immediately logged on to portal, avoiding re-entry of credentials. So, even though enterprise-wide, this SSO was scheduled for the second phase of the project, a desktop SSO realm and a portal SSO realm had to be created to deliver this first piece of functionality. For simplicity's sake, we will illustrate the runtime architecture for the security layer as follows:

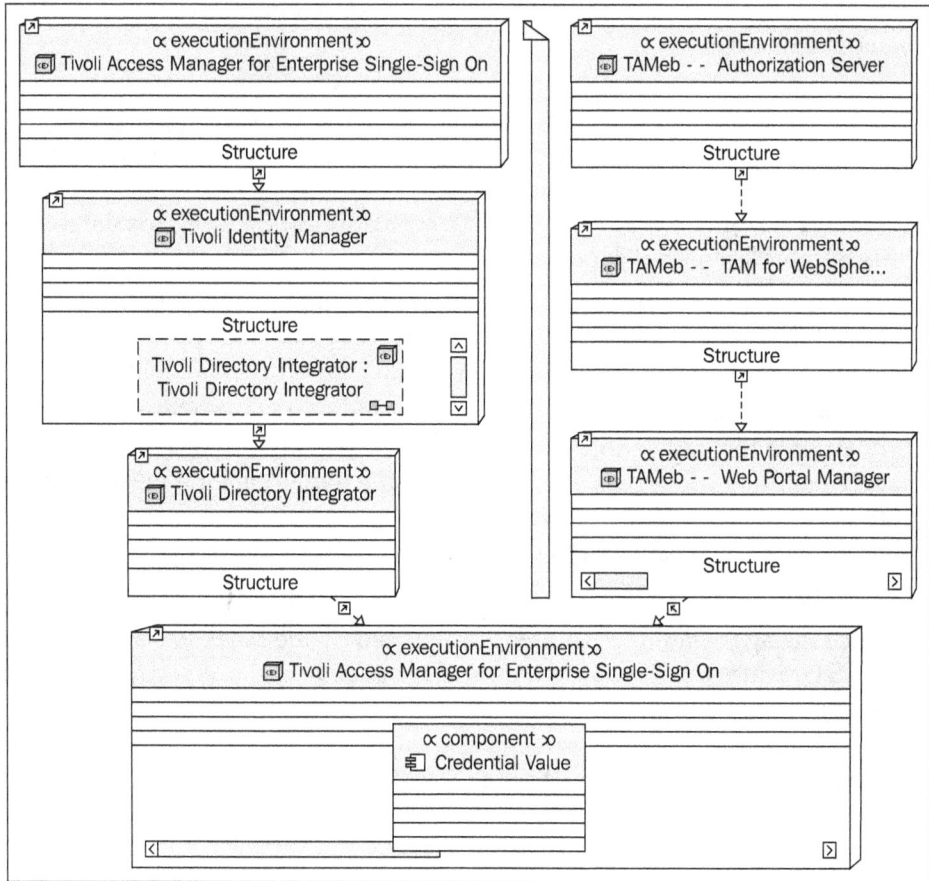

As we can see in the illustration shown in the preceding diagram, the Tivoli Access Manager works with Tivoli Identity Manager for the integrated access management propagation and credential provisioning control. Tivoli Directory Integrator, on the other hand, synchronizes credentials and active control lists, and keeps all the LDAPs and Active Directory changes in synchronization. TAM authorization, policy server, and Web Portal Manager components provide the rules engine and policy guidelines for the security integration and implementation into portal.

Single Sign-On (SSO) – patterns

There are several SSO patterns that can be used with WebSphere Portal and WebSEAL. They include Desktop SSO, Web SSO, Proxy SSO, Standard SSO, and so on. Portal security architects need to analyze requirements and map them to one or more of these patterns. In the case of A2Z Bank, the standard WebSEAL pattern with desktop, web, and portlet realms where basic authentication and HTTP header authentication are used within the SSO context. Both brokers and CSRs have Windows operating system on their desktops and have it integrated into portal SSO. As they log on to the operating system, they are also logged on to portal. For the Desktop realm, SPNEGO was used as the integration mechanism. Once the desktop realm is active, it passes the **Lightweight Third-Party Authentication (LTPA)** SSO token to both Web and portlet SSO realms. The Web SSO realm forwards SSO action to web servers, services, and portal applications. It includes basic authentication, HTTP header, forms, and LTPA token authentication. Then the portlet SSO realm manages SSO from the portal to content providers, but in the case of A2Z Bank first release, it was not a consideration. Portal server would be within the Web SSO realm and in the future state where content management was going to be added. The content provider would be within the portlet SSO realm. So, the portal would be responsible for authenticating with other content providers. As we are saving the credential vault topic for another edition of this book, it will suffice to say that credential vault architecture played an important role in the SSO effort. Portal junctions were created in WebSEAL to support the SSO realms. The main consideration for any portal security architect is to look at how the user identity reaches and is propagated:

- The A2Z Bank (CSR, broker, manager) user authenticates to WebSEAL via Desktop SSO integration to Windows login
- WebSEAL signs the user on to the portal using SSO techniques and the Web SSO realm
- The portal returns a redirect to the browser
- The browser follows the redirect to the data and content provider via WebSEAL
- WebSEAL utilizes standard SSO techniques to perform Single Sign-On to the content provider
- The content from the content provider is returned to the browser

Portal architecture and performance modeling – cloud and traditional paradigms

What drives the exercise of performance modeling is the combination of system and customer requirements along with the need to predict and control cost, size, and growth of runtime IT environments supporting business goals. The goal of performance modeling can vary, but essentially, one wants to predict which environment configuration would fit a target workload and vice versa. Performance models can be sophisticated and deliver other predictions on metrics from response time to throughput and utilization. Modeling also provides a "what-if" capability to simulate conditional scenarios for peak and mixed workload scenarios and other growth projections that affect IT sizing. There are capacity planning and performance modeling techniques for both traditional and cloud-enabled environments. They both need to be fed by nonfunctional requirements pertaining to performance, scalability, throughput, response time, and be contrasted against its target operational environment.

Due to the purpose of this book, we will focus on the portal solution performance architecture and not the entire enterprise. However, because portal is integration at the glass, all related systems and their service-level agreements would need the same rigorous approach to performance modeling and capacity management. Using the cloud as part of an architectural model does not mean that capacity planning should be abandoned. It does mean that the cloud offers the elasticity to scale and grow based on demand at a calculated cost. A2Z Bank utilized **Application Performance Management (APM)** to control capacity planning for the modernization effort. Along with governance, the APM, development and testing methodologies are necessary to encompass the required activities in a project plan template level. These activities in turn need to be supported by top-notch tools and a mature supporting process around this activity. After we talk about the operational model and workload analysis, we will briefly take a look at what is used to feed these tools and capacity planning methods Let's briefly take a look at some of them and how A2Z Bank portal project applied them.

Portal operational model and workload analysis

The workload analysis against the operational model allows a performance architect to define a maturity model for the lifecycle of a capacity planning effort. First, the volumetric of business transactions, applications, users, and network are determined via both nonfunctional requirements combined with the understanding of existing system and current state user and system metrics. Along with that, the projected usage patterns and growth rate can also be documented and used to feed the capacity planning and management effort. Once documented, a chosen methodology tool or approach can be used to look at the physical topologies and target workloads, and create models to represent that. Once the model is created, it can be populated with the business functions and projected transactional volumetric to be calibrated later with real performance test results or cloud monitoring results.

Normally, once a model is populated, it can then be calibrated with single execution's results (in case, there is executable code available to be tested and benchmarked against) or with the nonfunctional requirements' expectations themselves. Performance modeling is an iterative process. Take this item with a grain of salt, because environments (development, integration, staging, user acceptance, performance, production) differ in sizes based on their target users and budgets. Different business releases of portal applications or portal-integrated applications can change the dynamics of resource consumption. A maturity model-driven implementation methodology supported by a mature tool is recommended to be used within the performance modeling discipline.

Next, we will look at some of the tools that allow one to do performance modeling for the cloud, mainframe, or distributed traditional environments, but for now let's look at a generic workload model. The workload model should contain both business (concerned with user perspective of what is required of the system) and technical (translating those concerns into IT terms) volumetrics.

Once an approach to sizing has been determined, the next question is about how many environments are needed. In order to size for an environment, it is necessary to map out the number of environments and their respective configurations in terms of being single, vertical, or horizontal. Best practices in portal architecture dictate a development and unit test, an integration, a user acceptance, a staging (or disaster recovery), performance, and production.

IBM lab tools – mainframe and distributed

If your portal project uses IBM services and your enterprise does not have a solution and tooling around capacity management for both distributed and mainframe paradigms, IBM labs can be a starting point for unveiling the power and value of a sophisticated tool for performance modeling. The starting point for high-level (ballpark) sizing is with IBM Techline Sizing Labs. If your portal project has sizing needs, it is worth reaching out to the IBM Representative on the account and find out more about it. Apart from them, we will cite two options from two different labs that can be used to assist in these sizing efforts.

IBM zCP3000

zCP3000 is a highly recommended IBM internal tool, which provides an advanced modeling framework that only IBM technical sales specialists can execute on behalf of customers. It encapsulates all lessons learned and best practices around understanding the needs of a particular configuration and providing the hardware and logical mapping of which system would meet such criteria. The results and output include number of engines, the number of **logical partitions** (**LPARs**), the mixture of special engine types, the impact of n-way effect. It also takes into account mixed and alternate workload characteristics and a variety of other factors. All of this has been embedded in the mathematical model contained within zCP3000 algorithm Any project that uses z, zLinux, and mainframe can introduce the zCP3000 tool in the capacity planning and performance engineering methodology, in case there is not one already in place. We have used this tool with the assistant of the experts from the Washington Labs and it works well providing great value to the business.

IBM Automatic Model Building using InferENCE (AMBIENCE)

While ZCP3000 is a great IBM lab tool for the **z operating system** (**z/OS**) and mainframe-related systems, AMBIENCE is the a great research tool that can be used by an IBM consultant, architect, or specialist in sizing distributed systems. According to the Watson research site at `http://www.research.ibm.com/compsci/project_spotlight/performance/`, it is defined as an optimization-based inference technique to tackle this important yet highly challenging problem. It is formulated as a parameter estimation problem using a general Kelly-type queueing network. A general Kelly-type queueing network has the property that its stationary queue length distributions have a product form. This allows a clean, analytical formulation of the problem.

A typical on-demand system processes different types of requests from clients. The **Network Dispatcher** (**ND**) routs each request to one of the frontend servers following some dispatching policy. Some requests are also processed in the backend server. We consider the case where aggregate and end-to-end measurement data (that is, system throughput, utilization of the servers, and end-to-end response time) are available. Note that such data is typically much easier to obtain than model parameters, for example, service requirements. Each set of measurements in which the working environment (load, scripts, and so on) is constant is referred to as an experiment.

We have personally used this tool many times while under service engagements as consultants for portal projects, and highly recommend it in case IBM services are being provided for a portal infrastructure. If your portal implementation is targeted at a traditional environment which used distributed technology, it can benefit from the performance modeling capabilities of AMBIENCE.

Commercial solutions and tools – mainframe and distributed

In case one wishes to purchase a commercial tool and doesn't want be locked into a solution tied to services, there are great options out there to help an enterprise size for portal efforts. HyPerformix and BMC are two options worth mentioning. It is important to note they both support cloud, and traditional capacity planning and performance modeling.

For further information on BMC products, we recommend visiting the site at `http://www.bmc.com/products/product-listing/BMC-Capacity-Management-for-Mainframes.html`.

CA HyPerformix

The HyPerformix solution is designed to deliver business insight into IT operations. HyPerformix has trademarked predictive IT management, a combination of modeling technology and best practice methodology. The insight derived from predictive IT management allows IT to plan effectively, make informed investment decisions, minimize deployment risk, and configure applications and architecture for optimal service levels. HyPerformix has been used by us in our consulting career, and it is a phenomenal tool that gives you the complete set of functionality for a long term capacity management strategy. HyPerformix started focusing on the distributed market, but has added functionality for mainframe modeling as well. You can not only size the target environments but also price them at the same time. You can find more information on this at `http://www.ca.com/us/search/default.aspx?q=hyperformix&sk=ca.com`. For HyPerformix internal cloud campaign video produced by sparksight, visit `http://vimeo.com/17005490`.

BMC

BMC Capacity Trending Advisor is another great capacity management solution for both mainframe and distributed. You can have a look at the BMC demo at `http://www.bmc.com/products/demonstration/capacity-management-how-full-is-your-tank.html?intcmp=stb_capmgt_see`.

BMC Capacity Trending Advisor is a capacity trending tool that automates the forecasting process by providing an easy-to-use workflow that guides your decision making to ensure that IT resources are used enterprise-wide to their optimal potential. BMC is a mature company providing a diverse set of solutions in the capacity management space. BMC Capacity Trending Advisor, a new member of BMC Software's capacity management portfolio of products, is an enterprise-wide solution that facilitates the creation of capacity plans according to industry best practices. With ease-of-use as a fundamental design element, BMC Capacity Trending Advisor makes capacity trend analysis and forecasting readily accessible to a broad range of IT specialists. It is a matter of analytical decision making to choose between great solutions for your portal and enterprise-wide capacity management needs. Like HyPerformix, you can not only size the target environments but also price them at the same time. Cloud providers also provide the means to size and price cloud-enabled environments. We will look at them next.

Cloud capacity planning – IBM SmartCloud Monthly Cost Estimator

Next, we will describe for illustrative purposes only some of the interfaces provided for sizing and pricing a cloud with the IBM SmartCloud Cost Estimator. The first step is to select the software images or build them using the IBM Workload Deployer appliance or the IBM Image Construction and Composition Tool found on `https://www.ibm.com/developerworks/community/groups/service/html/communityview?communityUuid=18d10b14-e2c8-4780-bace-9af1fc463cc0`. You can then both load them on the cloud, or use out-of-the-box patterns and customize them based on your environment and topology needs. Each operational node can be mapped to the same cloud profile. In the case of A2Z Bullion Bank, telephony, portal, process, ESB, monitoring, mail, file among other servers were sized, priced, and provisioned. There are options as to the operating system as well as for **Pay As You Go (PAYG)** and **Bring Your Own License (BYOL)**. Hourly rates and monthly charges are show on the right-hand side under the **Hourly rate** and **Software monthly charges** columns respectively, as shown in the following screenshot:

Estimated total monthly charge (USA / USD): $ 13,244   🗓 Snapshot

Software images | Virtual machine instances | Persistent storage | Internet data transfer | Network access options | Premium support

First, select the software images you want to run from the 'Software image' drop-down menu. Think of each line as a server type. The list of images includes standalone operating systems and operating systems combined with additional software, in 32- and 64-bit versions. For each image, the image name indicates the charge option associated with the image. PAYG stands for 'Pay as you go' and implies by-the-hour charges. BYOL stands for 'Bring your own license', i.e. you are bringing a license that you have already paid for.

Description for your reference	Software image		Hourly rate	Software monthly charges
Load balancers	Red Hat Enterprise Linux 5.5 (64-bit) - all software charges included in the instance charge	⌄	Prepaid	Prepaid
Application servers	IBM WebSphere Portal Server and IBM Web Content Management Standard Edition V7.0.0.	⌄	Prepaid	Prepaid
Application servers	IBM WebSphere Portal Server and IBM Web Content Management Standard Edition V7.0.0.	⌄	$ 8.019	$ 9,366
NFS servers	Red Hat Enterprise Linux 5.5 (32-bit) - all software charges included in the instance charge	⌄	Prepaid	Prepaid
DB servers	IBM Informix Innovator-C Edition V11.7 for SUSE Linux Enterprise Server 11 SP1 (32-bit) - P	⌄	$ 0.000	$ 0
Mail servers	IBM Lotus Domino Utility Server for LotusLive V8.5.2.2 for Red Hat Enterprise Linux Server 5	⌄	$ 0.541	$ 632
ITCAM Monitoring	IBM Tivoli Monitoring 6.2.2 Fixpack 1 for SUSE Linux Enterprise Server 11.0 (32-bit) - with P	⌄	$ 0.000	$ 0
Telephony Server	SUSE Linux Enterprise Server 11 SP1 for x86 (64-bit) - all software charges included in the in	⌄	n/a	n/a
ESB server - DataPower	SUSE Linux Enterprise Server 11 SP1 for x86 (64-bit) - all software charges included in the in	⌄	n/a	n/a
BPM Servers	IBM WebSphere Application Server Base V7.0.0.11/V7.0.0.9 for SUSE Linux Enterprise Ser	⌄	Prepaid	Prepaid

Total monthly software charge $ 9,998

Start over   Next

The next step allows you to select the virtual machines' images and input the utilization patterns desired, based on nonfunctional requirements and service-level agreements. Additionally reserved capacity is another option to dedicate resources fully to a cloud segment. In the case of A2Z Bank, they had a new infrastructure managed by IBM and used this interface to start the provisioning of environments:

Estimated total monthly charge (USA / USD): $ 13,244   🗓 Snapshot

Software images | **Virtual machine instances** | Persistent storage | Internet data transfer | Network access options | Premium support

Select the virtual machine instances you want and indicate how much you intend to use them. For each line, the 'Instance type' drop-down menu lists the machine sizes supported by the image you selected on the previous tab. Once you have done that, consider a reserved capacity package, located further down the page.

Description from previous tab	Operating system	Instances	Instance type		Usage		Hours per month	Instance type hourly rate	Instance type monthly charges
Load balancers	SUSE Linux	2	32-bit Copper	⌄	100	%utilized/month ⌄	1,460	$ 0.095	$ 139
Application servers	SUSE Linux	6	32-bit Copper	⌄	80	%utilized/month ⌄	3,504	$ 0.095	$ 333
Application servers	SUSE Linux	2	32-bit Copper	⌄	80	%utilized/month ⌄	1,168	$ 0.095	$ 111
NFS servers	Red Hat Linux	2	64-bit Copper	⌄	100	%utilized/month ⌄	1,460	$ 0.300	$ 438
DB servers	SUSE Linux	2	32-bit Copper	⌄	100	%utilized/month ⌄	1,460	$ 0.095	$ 139
Mail servers	Red Hat Linux	2	32-bit Copper	⌄	80	%utilized/month ⌄	1,168	$ 0.125	$ 146
ITCAM Monitoring	SUSE Linux	1	32-bit Copper	⌄	100	%utilized/month ⌄	730	$ 0.095	$ 69
Telephony Server	SUSE Linux	2	64-bit Copper	⌄	50	%utilized/month ⌄	730	$ 0.270	$ 197
ESB server - DataPowe	SUSE Linux	2	64-bit Copper	⌄	100	%utilized/month ⌄	1,460	$ 0.270	$ 394
BPM Servers	SUSE Linux	2	32-bit Copper	⌄	80	%utilized/month ⌄	1,168	$ 0.095	$ 111
		23			29	85 %utilized/month	14,308	$ 0.145	$ 2,077
		Instance	Total number of		Average instance		Total	Instance	Total monthly

Start over   Previous   Next

Once the software images and virtual machine images are defined, the next step is persistent storage. Again, this will vary based on the target environment's purpose for the cloud at hand. If you are provisioning development or integration versus performance or production cloud, these values would be adjusted accordingly. The virtual images themselves come with a default configuration. Here, one can define extra storage blocks along with the expected utilization and service-level agreement patterns. Whatever values entered can be dynamically adjusted once the cloud is operational and monitoring is active; that can all be set in terms of elastic and autonomic policies.

IBM ▼

Estimated total monthly charge (USA / USD): $ 14,029   🔖 Snapshot

| Software images | Virtual machine instances | **Persistent storage** | Internet data transfer | Network access options | Premium support |

Select the blocks of persistent storage you want, if any, in addition to the storage that comes with the virtual machine instances you selected. Choose the number of blocks, their size, and how active you expect them to be. The activity level translates into an IO rate for the calculation.

| | | | | | Monthly rates | | Monthly charges | | |
Blocks	Block size	Activity estimate	IOs/sec per block	Million IOs per month	Storage per block	IOs per million	Storage	IOs*	Total monthly charges
2	2048 GB ▼	High ▼	90	473	$ 224.26	$ 0.11	$ 449	$ 52	$ 501
2	2048 GB ▼	Medium ▼	40	210	$ 224.26	$ 0.11	$ 449	$ 23	$ 472
0	2048 GB ▼	High ▼	0	0	$ 224.26	$ 0.11	$ 0	$ 0	$ 0
0	2048 GB ▼	High ▼	0	0	$ 224.26	$ 0.11	$ 0	$ 0	$ 0
0	2048 GB ▼	High ▼	0	0	$ 224.26	$ 0.11	$ 0	$ 0	$ 0
4	8,192			683			$ 897	$ 75	$ 972
Block total	GB in total			Million IOs per month			Blocks subtotal	IO subtotal	Total monthly charges

Provide an estimate of the average number of private images you expect to have in your private image catalog and the number of times you expect to save images to the catalog during a month. In addition, please estimate the average size of your private images (cloud average is about 15 GB).

| Private images | | | | | Monthly rates | | Monthly charges | | |
Average number	Save operations	Average size (GB)	Avg. storage used (GB)	Million 'save' IOs per month	Per GB per month	IOs per million	Storage	IOs*	Total monthly charges

↩ Start over   ◀ Previous   ▶ Next

The next step in the pricing exercise is the data transfer patterns. An estimation of the amount of data to be transferred should be used. If a performance model was developed, the results of the model estimations can be inserted here.

Estimated total monthly charge (USA / USD): $ 14,029   📄 Snapshot

| Software images | Virtual machine instances | Persistent storage | **Internet data transfer** | Network access options | Premium support |

Provide an estimate of the amount of data you expect to exchange between the internet and the virtual machine instances you selected. Usually, only one or two of your server types handle most of the data transfers. You may want to start with them.

Data transfer in	20	GB / month ▾
Data transfer out	5	TB / month ▾

Total   5,140   GB transferred per month (total of inbound plus outbound)

	Rate per GB	GB	Total monthly charges
First 10 TB per month	$ 0.15	5,140	$ 771
Next 40 TB (10 TB to 50 TB) per month	$ 0.11	0	$ 0
Next 100 TB (50 TB to 150 TB) per month	$ 0.09	0	$ 0
All additional above 150 TB per month	$ 0.08	0	$ 0
	$ 0.15	5,140	$771
	Average rate	Total GB	Total monthly charge

The above charges for Internet data transfer apply after September 30, 2011. Until then, no charge for Internet data transfer.

⊙ Start over   ⊕ Previous   ⊕ Next

The next step is to define the network parameters by defining values for number of IPs and VPN access. Then one can decide on the level of support and look at the final price tag for a new cloud infrastructure.

Estimated total monthly charge (USA / USD): $ 14,029   📄 Snapshot

| Software images | Virtual machine instances | Persistent storage | Internet data transfer | **Network access options** | Premium support |

You can choose to make each virtual machine instance accessible either directly from the Internet or through a Virtual Private Network connection.

Direct internet access

A publicly accessible IP address is required for each instance that is directly accessible from the Internet. When an instance is provisioned, you can choose to allocate a static IP address that you have reserved or let the provisioning system dynamically allocate a random IP address. There is no charge for dynamically allocated IP addresses. Suggest you consider reserving one or two IP addresses per server that you use regularly.

	Hourly rate	Total monthly charge
Average number of IP addresses reserved per month: 28	$ 0.01	

Virtual private network access

You can choose to isolate instances on a Virtual Private Network to which only you have access. To do that, you need to order a Virtual Private Network service and provision the instances to that network. Each Virtual Private Network (VPN gateway/virtual LAN combination) is restricted to a single IBM SmartCloud delivery center (site), so you may want to specify more than one. You do not need to reserve or pay for IP addresses on your cloud VPN.

	Monthly rate	Total monthly charge
Number of Virtual Private Networks (maximum one per IBM SmartCloud delivery center): 0	$ 300	

In addition to the monthly charge, there is a one-time setup charge of $ 1,000.00 per Virtual Private Network service.

⊙ Start over   ⊕ Previous   ⊕ Next

Finally, cost and charges are presented based on the given cloud configuration. As these price tags will vary based on the environment and other attributes and parameters, we will not even show them here. But remember how valuable this interface is in giving you a price tag as soon as you define and specify the operational architecture.

Cloud capacity planning – Amazon Monthly Calculator

Likewise, Amazon Cloud users also have access to a cloud calculator. **Amazon Elastic Compute Cloud (Amazon EC2)** is a web service that provides resizable compute capacity in the cloud. It is designed to make web-scale computing easier for developers and stakeholders in general. Amazon EC2's simple web service interface allows you to obtain and configure capacity with minimal friction. It provides you with complete control of your computing resources and lets you run on Amazon's proven computing environment. Amazon EC2 reduces the time required to obtain and boot new server instances to minutes, allowing you to scale capacity quickly, both up and down, as your computing requirements change. Amazon EC2 changes the economics of computing by allowing you to pay only for capacity that you actually use. Amazon EC2 provides developers the tools to build failure-resilient applications and isolate themselves from common failure scenarios. The Amazon Cloud provides users with an interface for sizing as well pricing clouds. For illustrative purposes only, we will look at the Amazon Cloud calculator, the main interface for sizing and pricing, based on the virtual images:

Test architecture and test data governance

Both the test architecture and test data governance disciplines offer a great opportunity to work collaboratively on the same testing strategy. As portal depends on many other systems, test architecture aligned with governance for data and IT allows all the potential bottlenecks to be tested holistically. The test architecture needs to be set early and be consistent with the overall functional and nonfunctional goals and technologies available.

Aligned with other types of governance, data governance defines the processes for selection, extraction automation, messaging, and reusability for test data. Having a repeatable set of test data sets the tone for the right level of reliability test data sets must provide. As portal is an integration point for many multiple data sources, it is crucial that all these sources have the same level of rigor with test data governance and systematic repeatable processes for automation of extraction, messaging, and reusability of test data. A portal test architect needs to look at the requirements and understand which points in the portal architecture need to be reset for cached data, queues, dropping tables, or other aspects of the dataflow that make that test data unique and reusable.

Architecture assessment and operational technical readiness review

An important move on any architecture is the final review cycle, where an assessment is done by senior **subject-matter experts** (**SMEs**). IBM business partners and software group for Lotus and WebSphere services can assist in this task. The final review would certify the operational architecture and provide another SME-based approval and blessing. This approval cycle is normally tied to the development methodology and governance cycles.

Summary

This chapter looked at some of the reusable architectural templates that can help a portal project to take off. We looked at how A2Z Bank plans on using them. Then, we moved on to the reference architectures to show how golden portal, portal pervasive, and security portal architectural blocks are architecturally described. We moved on to workload analysis and sizing questions as capacity management and performance modeling go hand in hand. We looked at some of the options to size and price portal environments via traditional physical deployments or the cloud.

6
Portal Build, Deployment, and Release Management

This chapter covers the best practices in portal build, deployment, release, and configuration management. Portal code needs to be built, packaged, deployed, and promoted from one environment to the other. In the case of A2Z Bank, portal code goes from development workstations to the cloud development environment, to system test, integration test, staging, and performance before it goes live into the cloud production. Because of the complexity of portal applications, there needs to be a mature, repeatable, and more automated process around deployment and release coordination of portal artifacts. Aside from building and deploying of portal applications, another part of the portal administration is to provision new portal clusters and maintain them, along with business releases hosted by the portal infrastructure. We will briefly look at them as well. By the end of this chapter, we would have looked at the following:

- Build, deployment, and release management
- Best practices and Jazz
- Portal tools
- WEF and WP – high-level release steps
- Portlet deployment
- Portlet themes and skins
- Portal resources management via policies
- Publishing to the Amazon Cloud
- Cloud-enabled portal provisioning

Portal build, deployment, and release management

Now, we will cover building a business case for portal build and deploy automation via the Rational Value Estimator. Every portal project plan contains tasks to design, develop, and deploy artifacts belonging to the portal project. We know that portlets are a part of portlet application(s), which comprise portal as vertical for employees, customers, and partners. A portal application contains one or more portlets packaged together. There are other dependent components that go into the portal deployment. They all need to be properly changed, propagated, and synchronized based on the target environment and the business release versioning. There are at least two major aspects of portal release management as follows:

- Management of different business releases within the same environment
- Management of the business releases from environment to environment

Before we jump into the portal build and release lifecycle, let's start by looking at some basic definitions and see how they apply to the portal release management lifecycle:

- **Build**: This is the process of aggregating code artifacts, resolving dependencies, providing compilation of sources, and packing into a deployable unit. For portal, there is the local build on the WEF development environment. Then there is the server build, where the WEF Specialist checks the code into the code management system, builds master extracts from version control and builds a deployable unity.

- **Deployment**: This is the process of installing the deployable unit (an application or an operational unit).

- **Release management**: This is the discipline that defines the process of building and releasing software to make it available to others in a consistent way.

- **Release**: This is a complete set of portal configuration, which encompasses content, code, and dependent and shared artifacts. This complete set is deployed and tested for functionality and performance at a point in time. It is then certified and declared ready to be moved to the next environment in the release cycle.

- **Staging**: This is the process of building, deploying, and testing a final business release in an environment other than production, with the intention of deploying that release to production. This environment is sometimes named performance, staging, preproduction, and so on.

For each of these topics, there are available tools to implement and manage them. Let's see which ones A2Z Bank has decided to use for the portal and transformation effort. For source code repository, A2Z Bank decided to go with IBM Rational ClearCase. This choice was part of the **Collaborative Application Lifecycle Management (CALM)** approach. The **IBM Rational Automation Framework for WebSphere (RAFW)** was decided by Portal Governance Board. For portlet deployment, out-of-the-box portal tools and interfaces, such as XMLAccess and ReleaseBuilder, were adopted to be invoked within the automation framework. For overall release management and to assist with the build and deploy automation effort, Rational Build Forge, along with RAFW, were adopted. A build and deploy process varies depending on the target deployment unit for the asset, the build complexities, the dependencies, how documented the process is, and how automated the implementation is. In the case of the A2Z portlet objects, it encompasses the steps to create the portlet objects from the A2Z ClearCase version control system; push them to the portal server cluster; register them with the portal administration console; and place them on the target page. At first, each step is scripted and performed manually with the commands and sequence recorded, to be automated later using combination of the Ant scripts and XMLAccess to move it to the target platform. The XMLAccess scripts can register portlets with the WebSphere Portal administration console, place them on a portal page, and assign access rights to the portlet objects. All these steps would then be wrapped around Build Forge and RAFW for consistency, repeatability, labor savings, and quality control.

Click and learn

IBM has created an interactive value estimator for both Build Forge and Rational Automation Framework for WebSphere, which can be seen at `https://www14.software.ibm.com/iwm/web/cc/flash2/swg-rtl_bfve/en/us/Tool.htm`.

Best practices and Jazz-enabled staging

Before we get into the portal specifics, let's talk about best practices for build and release management as a whole. Ideally, build and deployment processes must be:

- Automated so that it is repeatable and consistent, and depends less on manual work and human intervention
- Operated based on policies for the management of environment specific properties, which should be saved in separate policies files, independent of scripts
- Remotely deployable into multiple environments
- Capable of automated rollback process after unsuccessful deployments

- User-defined processes
  - ° A2Z Bank had geographically distributed teams of portal architects, developers, specialists, project managers, LOB customers, and other project participants. All of them required real-time knowledge of both call center and core banking project's status, issues, and risks. Jazz Platform helped A2Z Bank to accomplish this by providing an automated user-defined processes, generating project metrics and providing global access to dashboards at the individual, team, LOB, or portfolio levels.
  - ° There is no single formula for a portal deployment, as it needs to be adaptive to the existing tools and processes in the IT enterprise. By allowing the team members to develop routines and processes around their shared responsibility towards a common deliverable (such as a portlet or the service consumed by the portlet), the process support is adaptive and allows teams to set rules for features such as automation, or tracking and status reporting.
- Collaborative in context

With the Jazz framework enabled, one is able to share one's current status to the whole team. For instance, A2Z team members working on shared deliverables were able to see on what each others were working. They could also see via dashboards what relationships and dependencies of other's works do to their own portal or core artifacts.

In the case of a defect, where a test or something else that needs to be reproduced, WEF development workspaces of team members working on the same artifacts could be shared and consumed remotely in a synchronized way. This is fundamentally important when you have remote groups sharing development responsibilities.

Portal tools

Managing portal environments is a challenging task, which is considerably more challenging than pure J2EE applications running purely on application servers. Portal environment management involves different tools, additional interfaces, and different approaches based on the type of deployable content that is to be deployed, such as portlets, themes, skins, syndicated content, and related artifacts. A few pages would not help one to have a deeper understanding of what these tools and interfaces bring to the table. We highly recommend further reading in the format of the "Managing Portal Environments Wiki" provided on our site in the PDF format.

The best way to manage portal environments is by understanding how each tool fits the build and deploy lifecycle and overall release workflow. Understanding when to use XMLAccess and ReleaseBuilder is a must. Automation should be everybody's goal, but the reality is that unfortunately there is still a lot of manual and error-prone work being done for portal management. The key is to build all deployment scripts manually, test them but eventually wrap them around an automated workflow. The more complex and large a portal effort is, the more there is a need for a systematic and automated release management approach. Let's describe the arsenal you have at your disposal to make the automated happy path happen.

XMLAccess

This is a command line client interface for XML configuration management also named XMLAccess. It connects to portal locally and remotely using an HTTP connection. XMLAccess is also used to perform a complete portal configuration transfer or parts of a configuration, install additional resources, and perform other documented and undocumented administrative tasks in a consistent way. There is an ACL requirement to have at least a manager role on the virtual resource for XMLAccess or be in a security administrator role on the virtual portal resource. The XML configuration interface requires authentication at the command line, or when scripts are automated; these credentials need to be passed as arguments.

For a great XMLAccess FAQs, please visit `http://www-10.lotus.com/ldd/portalwiki.nsf/dx/XMLAccess_Frequently_Asked_Questions`.

In totality:

- The XML configuration interface is a batch processing interface for portal configuration updates and other related tasks, where XML format is the standard output and input file format for requests and responses.

- It lets one export an entire portal configuration or portions of a portal configuration to an XML file. Portal administrators are able to recreate the exported configuration from such a file onto another portal cluster or standalone instance. It can be used to export requests, update requests, and export-orphaned-data requests.

- The XML configuration interface can be accessed using a command-line tool or through administrative portlets.

- An XML request can handle different types of content. Based on the content type, portal administrators and automated frameworks are able to create, modify, delete, and export portal application resources.

There are a few limitations to be kept in mind and mitigated, as follows:

- It can populate the content of virtual portals but cannot generate them
- It cannot be used to make configuration changes in WebSphere Application Server, for example, security configuration or data source definition
- It can't copy the portlet WAR files or theme files from one portal system to another; these tasks need to be automated via another framework
- It has limited features for the JCR and community domains. It is mostly utilized on customization and release domains
- It can't change custom properties utilized by portal runtime services
- It can't set portal states nor windows
- It can't execute direct SQL statements on the portal database.

> The XML configuration schema can be found in the WebSphere Portal Information Center at http://infolib.lotus.com/ resources/portal/7.0.0/doc/en_us/pt700abd001/ html-wrapper.html#adxmlabt.

As an example, for a first full release, a simple syntax is used:

```
[release builder cmd] -inOld FullA2ZRelease0.xml -inNew FullA2ZRelease1.
xml -out A2ZRelease1.xml
```

ReleaseBuilder

ReleaseBuilder is another tool within the portal server tool set. It executes comparisons on XMLAccess files inspecting their deltas and determines differences. In the context of A2Z Bank for instance, it runs a comparison between two release exports and produces a new file that can be utilized to synchronize environments. Behind the scenes, the tool keeps two list arrays—one representing the old release (which after the first release would be active in the production cloud) and one for the new release in the development cloud. It will match each resource using object IDs for URL mapping context, themes, skins, markup, virtual resources, content node, credential segments, wsrp producer, and web apps. The result of the matching algorithm is a new file that contains only important changes. In totality:

- ReleaseBuilder is directly related to XMLAccess but does not depend on XMLAccess to operate as an interface. When it generates a file, (a release) XMLAccess needs to be used to import the generated file into the target portal.

- It is designed to compare changes and subsequent exports created from the same portal host. It exports the delta between these exports in a process known as "building a release".

- ReleaseBuilder writes to its own `systemOut.log` file and does not write to the Portal's `systemOut.log` file, as for example the XMLAccess tool does.

As sample syntax:

```
releasebuilder.sh -inOld A2ZRelease_1.xml -inNew A2ZRelease_1_1.xml -out
A2ZRevision_1_1.xml
```

Site management tool

Yet another option to manage portal resources is the site management tool. It is basically a Resource Manager portlet, which is an administrative out-of-the-box portlet that allows portal administrators to perform site management functions. One needs to add a "Source" server and a "Target" server using the Resource Manager portlet.

Due to the scope of this book, we will not go into any details here but refer to it as a way to manage page-level resources; but this has many limitations, such as not publishing items that a page can reference, such as permissions or **access-level control lists** (**ACLs**), composite applications, personalized portlet preferences, URL mappings, cross-page wires, the `.portlet` or `.war` files, to name a few. It will definitely grow into a much better option with the support of the Jacl scripts as new portal server versions become available.

Subsequent releases

For subsequent releases there is another portal tool mentioned previously — ReleaseBuilder, which provides the much needed functionality of comparing deltas between releases. It creates a new file — `xmlaccess`, friendly to be used to synchronize environments. That is precisely what is needed to create incremental releases in the several portal environments, as new releases of portal business applications become available for deployment and test.

Release scenarios

Defining the release scenario upfront helps to keep the strategy aligned with the deliverables and processes that need to be in place to support the release scenario. The article we have mentioned about in the next paragraph was written for Portal 6x, but its strategies can be version agnostic.

The developerWoks article—*IBM WebSphere Portal Version 6.0 staging scenarios using ReleaseBuilder* by Matthias Kubik and Torsten Hoffman can be found at http://www.ibm.com/developerworks/websphere/library/techarticles/0712_kubik/0712_kubik.html.

Portal scripting

Another interface to manage and execute tasks on the portal server is the portal scripting interface. It is easy to be learned and used by advanced users. It allows for a powerful combination with other flavors of script interfaces such as Jython and Jacl.. Please check the information center for further syntax on this portal scripting interface.

Manual steps prior to using ReleaseBuilder

As noted in the WebSphere Portal Information Center (available as a PDF in our official site, with over 4000 pages), there are ways to prepare your portal environment for the ReleaseBuilder tool. One required deliverable is a checklist of the portal artifacts, along with global settings and property files. These policies, property files, and other independent artifacts need to be initially manually synchronized between the portal clusters in the execution of a release process to move a portal business release from staging to production. The following scenario describes a summarized version of a release scenario. It lists the three major portal deployment tools and their functions. It also shows some user roles that are involved in a portal deployment process. It further maps which containers (application server, database, filesystems, and so on) map to which portal artifact and deployment tool interface:

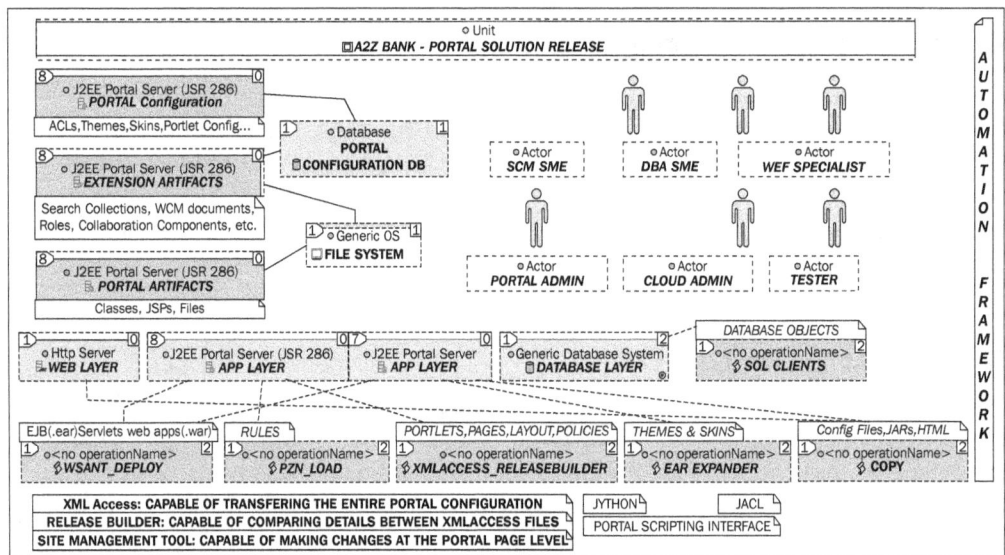

There are portal artifacts (classes, files, JSPs), extension artifacts (search collections, WCM documents), portal configuration, user and release data in a database. There are tools to manage different types of artifacts at the different layers and for different tasks within the build and release management. Tools and interfaces vary from XMLAccess interface to Ant, WS script, Ear Expander to Jacl and Jython. Actors vary from source and release management, WEF specialists, DBAs, portal and cloud administrators and testers. There are a lot roles and responsibilities, tools and interfaces, and steps to be architected, designed, scripted, tested, and automated. As A2Z decided to utilize automation framework, all these steps to be described ahead are eventually wrapped around Build Forge, Rational Automation Framework for WebSphere, and IBM Workload Deployer. These items would merit a book on these subjects alone. So, for now let's take a look at some deployment and release management options adopted by A2Z Bank.

WEF and WP environment – high-level release steps

To recap, the A2Z portal is successfully installed on the internally managed integration system. The A2Z development portal systems are available on the development cloud. We carefully followed best practices from the information center. Let's first look at the high-level task flow for the portal build and deploy. Then we can look how a more granular task flow can be documented, implemented, and automated. At a high level, there is a process flow for the release management of portal artifacts that has four steps to be followed. First, the source environment needs to be prepared; secondly, the release needs to be built; thirdly, the target environment needs to be prepared, and finally the business release needs to be imported into the target environment.

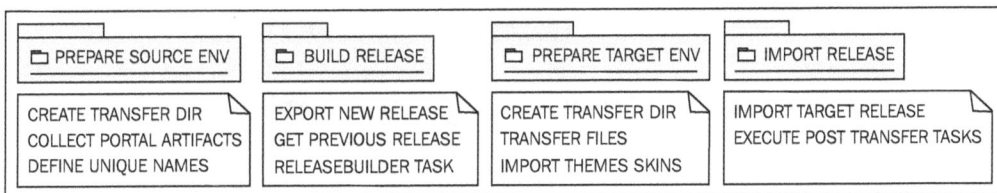

The following are the high-level release steps:

1. Export the A2Z source portal configuration using the XMLAccess commands.

2. Bundle the supporting files from the source A2Z portal.

3. Transfer the bundled files to the target A2Z portal.

4. Distribute the supporting files to the correct locations on the target A2Z portal.

5. Update the configuration of the target A2Z portal using the XMLAccess tool.

6. Execute the post-transfer activities.

Step 1 – Initial release – preparing the source environment

It is a best practice to prepare your source environment as well. So **staging**, as we have seen, is the term used to promote code from one environment to another. Both source and target environments need to be prepared for the deployment process and execution to be successful. It entails the following:

- Setting up a transfer directory under `wp_root` with current date in the `mmddyyyy` format

- Assigning custom unique names to pages, portlets, themes, and skins based on defined naming convention for the portal artifacts

- Collecting and placing supporting artifacts and files, such as themes, skins, WARs into the transfer directory

Step 2 – building the release

Once the source machine is prepared, it is time to export the release by running ReleaseBuilder. The XMLAccess files should also be stored in the version control system. It is never recommend running ReleaseBuilder tasks on the production machine. The task is executed with the following command:

```
../bin/releasebuilder.sh -inNew todays_release_dir/exported_
ExportRelease.xml

-inOld previous_release_dir/exported_ExportRelease.xml -out

todays_release_dir/Release.xml
```

Remember that XMLAccess can be used to create a full export of the portal site.

Step 3 – preparing the target environment

It is now time to prepare the target environment by:

- Creating a `transfer` directory and moving the entire `transfer` directory over

- Copying the WAR files to the target server under `InstallableApps`.

- Using `Release1.xml` to modify all URL tags to point to `InstallableApps` directory instead of the `deployed` or `archive` directory
- Deploying themes and skins

Step 4 – importing the release

Next is the task to run the `Import.sh` command on the `Release1.xml` file, as follows:

```
../Import.sh A2ZRelease1.xml
```

Step 5 – post-transfer actions

In a clustered environment, it is necessary to synchronize all the nodes after deployment and activation on updated portlet code. Under the `portal_server_root` directory, the following task will activate:

```
./WPSconfig.sh activate-portlets
```

The roles depicted in the following diagram show how portal roles map to the deployment tasks.

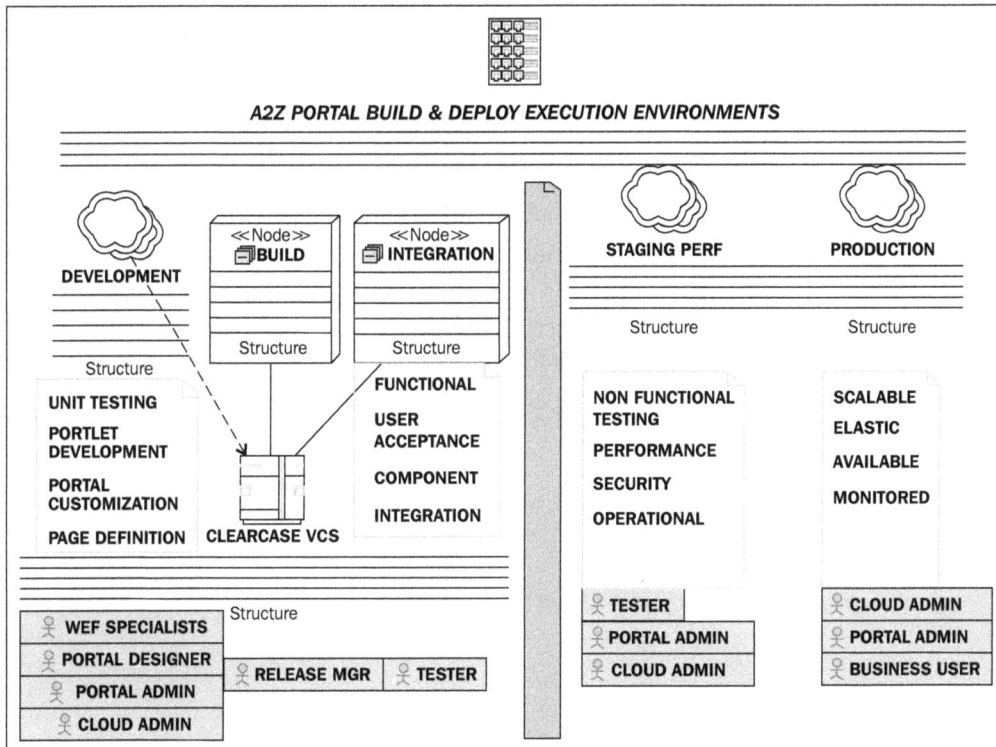

The following table explains about roles and their deployment tasks shown in the preceding diagram:

Portal roles	Deployment tasks
WEF specialist	• Develops portlets and portlet applications in WEF and executes unit tests of portlets and portlet applications in WEF Designer • Remotely publishes portlets and portlet applications on A2Z cloud development system • Checks portlets and portlet applications into the A2Z **version control system** (**VCS**), ClearCase • Generates portal artifacts on the development system • Executes unit tests of portal artifacts on the development system • Checks portal artifacts into the IBM ClearCase version control
Portal designer	• Customizes portal look and feel and generates artifacts (Themes, Skins, Screens, and Help pages) on the cloud development system • Executes unit tests of portal look and feel artifacts on a development system • Checks portal look and feel artifacts into IBM ClearCase version control project branch
Portal administrator	• Selects available and portal artifacts for use • Selects available portlets and portal artifacts into the VCS • Checks out all artifacts from IBM ClearCase version control project branch • Installs artifacts onto the cloud development system (content master)

Portal roles	Deployment tasks
Portal and cloud administrator	• Configures WebSphere Portal on the integration system. This includes global portal settings and other configurations, for example property file entries.
	• Produces documentation on global settings and configurations, for example, a description file, into IBM ClearCase version control project branch.
	• Generates the WebSphere Portal solution configuration including content hierarchy, page layouts, and portlet configurations, on the development system.
	• Exports release configuration (`export-release-only`) from content master using the XML configuration interface. Export the content topology as well as all portlets.
	• Delivers the portal solution release configuration into IBM ClearCase version control project branch.
Release manager	• Places the version artifacts and configurations as a portal solution release in the IBM ClearCase version control project branch
	• Checks out all artifacts for the portal solution release from the IBM ClearCase version control project branch
	• Installs the artifacts to the integration system
	• Checks out all configurations for the portal solution release from the IBM ClearCase version control project branch
	• Imports configurations into the integration system using the XML configuration interface
	• Notifies the portal operator about the availability of the initial portal solution release
Development team/test team	Performs integration tests of the release on the integration system
Cloud designer and operator	Deploys the certified release into the production cloud

Note that during this entire process, there are dashboards allowing for visualization and reporting real time, as they are integrated via the Jazz platform.

Building a portlet WAR for production

The WEF tool builds porlet WARs for production in the Java Portlet Standard 1.0 (JSR 168) and Java Portlet Standard 2.0 (JSR 286). In the case of A2Z Bank, they are all 286. The following are some steps followed by WEF specialist to build the WAR file:

1. In **Project Explorer** with WebSphere Experience Factory Designer, right-click on the **A2Z** project.

2. Choose **Export | WebSphere Experience Factory Portlet WAR**.

3. From the **Build Portlet WAR** dialog box, choose **Java Portlet Standard 2.0 (JSR 286)**.

4. Choose the file path where the WAR will be saved and click on **Finish**.

Later, the portal administrators still need to move the WAR file to the next A2Z Bank portal server cluster environment and publish the project.

In order to add JARs to the build, they performed the following steps.

They added the target JAR files as external libraries in the WebSphere Experience Factory plugin lib directory and in the WEF's lib directory. The following are the steps that they repeated to add an external library to the project Java build path in their WEF Designer environment:

1. In the WEF IDE, right-click on your **WebSphere Experience Factory** project and click on **Properties**.

2. In the **Properties** dialog box for the project, click on **Java Build Path**.

3. Click on **Libraries** and **Add External JARs**.

4. In the **JAR Selection** dialog box, specify the JARs to add.

5. Click on **OK** in the **JAR Selection** dialog box and click on **OK** in the **Properties** dialog box for your project.

Various WEF operations are configured by properties files, which can found in a project WEB-INF/config directory. For a POV, default settings for all properties can be accepted. But if you need to change a property setting for a real project, do so in only one file, the override.properties file. Properties placed in this file override equivalent properties in any other properties file. Properties files include the following:

- bowstreet.properties
- cluster.properties
- logging.properties
- override.properties
- server.properties

Other system-wide properties, such as the machine name and other properties, can be accessed by using the `system.getProperty` method. By default, changes to WebSphere Experience Factory properties files in a running WAR are not recognized until the WAR is restarted. To have property file changes take effect while the WAR is running, set the following property in the `override.properties` file and start the WAR:

```
bowstreet.properties.enableObserverThreads=true
```

If this property is set to `true`, several observer threads are kicked off when the application server starts the WAR. This allows updates to the properties file in the running WAR to be recognized by WebSphere Experience Factory.

Excluding files from a published WAR

WEF provides a couple ways to exclude one or more project files from a published WAR. This feature can be useful when you want to exclude development-related files, from the published WAR that is targeting a higher environment, for example production. These mechanisms are as follows:

- Artifacts placed with the `**/nodeploy/**` directory are not included in the WAR file
- Artifacts listed in the `.excludeFromServer` file are not included in the WAR file

Using the .excludeFromServer file

WEF WAR publishing scripts, along with application server scripts, should take this file into account when creating and publishing a WAR file. Each line in the `.excludeFromServer` file specifies a file that you want to exclude from the output WAR. File paths are relative to the project. The contents of a typical `.excludeFromServer` file look as—`WEB-INF/classes/nls/test/mymodel. properties samples/datapage/first_datapage.xml`.

A master version of the `.excludeFromServer` file is located in `C:\Program Files\ install-dir\FeatureSets\Web-App_X.XX.X\Tools\antScripts\public\`.

A version of `.excludeFromServer` file is located at the top level of each project created.

Global exclude across all projects

A2Z WEF specialists made changes to the master version of the `.excludeFromServer` file at the location specified previously, so their changes manifested in every project generated. When WEF specialists wanted to exclude a particular WebSphere Experience Factory-generated artifacts from every project, they listed the artifact in the master `.excludeFromServer` file.

Exclude on a project-by-project basis

Another common scenario is to exclude artifacts on a project-by-project basis. In this case, you work with the `.excludeFromServer` file located at the top level of a project. However, once you add artifacts to be excluded to the file, you must rebuild and/or regenerate the WAR so that your changes are picked up. This is necessary because the WAR created when you initially built the project did not exclude any artifacts. When somebody adds excludes to this file once the project is already created, these artifacts are no longer copied to the output, but they are already in the output as a result of the original publish operation. In order to delete the excluded files from the production WAR server, A2Z specialists must refresh/rebuild the WAR file to pick up their exclusions.

Using the **/nodeploy** directory

WEF comes with internal Ant scripts utilized to create WAR files that accept the pattern—`**/nodeploy/**`. Thus, one can create one or any number of `/nodeploy/` directories at any specified location within a project and place in these directories project artifacts that are not supposed to be included in the published WAR. When the WAR is built by the Ant scripts, the contents of the `/nodeploy/` directories will be excluded from the build process.

Publishing to the JSR 286 portal container

As A2Z WEF specialists were generating and customizing portlets under the requirement specifications, the JSR 168 and JSR 286 portlet containers that ship with WebSphere Portal Server to run standalone portlets were the target environment runtime. The A2Z WEF and WP cloud and administration specialists performed the following steps to set up their portlet container:

1. They edited their project's `.deployment/excludes/portletwar.excludes` file and removed references to `jdom.jar`. (When the production WAR is already installed to the server, `jdom.jar` can be added to the published application and restarted).

2. They exported the portlet WAR for A2Z project.

3. They logged on to the WebSphere Application Server Console Deployment Manager and installed the portlet WAR. They provided a context name and accepted all the defaults. It was published to server1, because WebSphere Portal security prevents the `WebSphere_Portal` instance from being a viable choice.

4. When the web application finished installing, they selected **Manage Applications** and the **A2Z** application. In the **Detail Properties** section, they clicked on **Class loading** and updated detection. Next, they verified that the WAR class loader policy was set to Class loader for each WAR file in the application. In the **Modules** section, they clicked on **Manage Modules**, in the WebSphere Experience Factory module and changed the class loader order setting so that class loader was first.

5. They then saved the master configuration.

6. They started the web application in the WebSphere Application Server Console Deployment Manager console.

7. They opened WEF and ran the model.

8. They manually entered the URL—`http://a2zportal:port/context_name/ portlet_name` into browser, where host and port utilized the same value provided while creating a WAS configuration that is targeting server1. For `context_name`, they utilized the same value provided while installing the portlet WAR from WAS. For `portlet_name`, they entered the value used for the portlet name input in the Portlet Adapter builder. The model is ready to be loaded.

Portlet deployment

The more you are familiar with the portal server, the more you will realize that there are different options for the deployment of portal applications. Portlets can be deployed as standard EAR through the deployment manager administrative console, using the GUI or via the wsadmin scripting interface. This allows for the cluster to notify each node of the deployment and allows portlets to be combined with different EAR-level resources such as EJBs, web services, or other web modules. This pre-deployed application must be updated via the EAR file in the WebSphere Application Server and the WAR file in portal using the XML configuration interface. There are some restrictions such as cross-updates of a pre-deployed EAR file with WAR are not possible yet under documented tasks. The other common way to deploy a portlet is to install it on the primary node of a portal cluster using the portal administration scripting languages such as Jacl; via GUI, or via XMLAccess interface.

Let's now look at some of the component artifacts part of the portlet deployment, their properties, and description, as shown in the following table:

Component	Property	A2Z action description
Portal server runtime	Portal system configuration	All documented entries for portal server property files that can change the portal server's behavior such as requesting object IDs or Parallel Portlet Rendering
Portal server runtime	Performance-related settings	All documented entries for portal server property files, not including settings related to environment scaling and elasticity
Portal statistics	Statistics log settings	Documented logs along with correlational ability to see transactional flow via log activity of several systems participants in a portal transaction
Portlet services	Service configuration	A2Z portal services created for the banking and call center efforts
Custom login commands	Login command	Custom login created for the Single Sign-On realms and desktop integration for both core banking and call center users
Custom credential vault adaptors	Vault adaptors	Custom A2Z SSO configuration for desktop SSO integration and web integration
Custom credentials	Credential implementations	A2Z custom SSO and ACL configuration for brokers, agents, and corporate users
JAAS login modules	Custom modules	A2Z custom SSO modules
Custom components	Custom component property files	A2Z custom components for MDM, EBS, telephony stacks
J2EE artifacts	Any IBM WebSphere Application Server configurations	Some custom WebSphere Application Server configuration for **Session Initiation Protocol (SIP)**
Custom User Registry	**Custom User Registry (CUR)** implementation	Custom User Registry for SSO and extra user attributes
External security manager	Externalized portal entitlements	A2Z TAM and WebSEAL configurations
User directory	User profiles, groups	A2Z corporate LDAP configuration

Component	Property	A2Z action description
Personalization	Personalization rules and campaigns	A2Z broker and marketing team personalization customizations
Policies	Policy files	A2Z custom policy via XML configuration files and theme policies

Checklist for portal artifacts

It is a best practice to have a list of all portal artifacts, which must be manually deployed (at least initially until automation is fully in place) to each cluster or system involved in the staging to production process. The documentation for the installation of each artifact should also be captured. Let's take a look at some of these artifacts:

Artifact	Type
Portlets	WAR files
Themes	JSPs, images, HTML, CSS, WAR, and so on
Skins	JSPs and images
Portal screens	JSPs and images
Portlet services	Java libraries
J2EE artifacts	EAR files, Java libraries
Custom User Registry	Java libraries
Credential vault adaptors	Java libraries
Custom credentials	Java libraries
JAAS login modules	Java libraries

Checklist for WEF-related JARs

The following table lists the JARs written to the project folder—`WEB-INF/clientLibs`. They should also be included in the build and release:

Filename	Description
`builderui.jar`	Contains the builder coordinator and UI support classes for the builders, in case you want to create your own
`j2ee.jar`	J2EE interface APIs (not implementation) for compiling generated Java classes against servlet APIs, EJB APIs, and similar artifacts
`portlet.jar`	Portlet API JAR (interface classes only, not implementation) for compiling Java classes against the ones that reference the Java Portlet Standard 1.0 APIs (JSR 168) and Java Portlet Standard 2.0 APIs (JSR 286)

In addition, the project directory — `WebContent/factory/classes` contains a JAR file (`BowTree.jar`) for the IBM WebSphere Application Server Portlet Tree applet. This JAR can be deleted if applications do not use the Tree builder.

web.xml processing and templates

We have modified the `web.xml` file and templates to customize feature sets and set properties to update servlet definitions and mappings. This modification was automated with an Ant script wrapped by Build Forge and Rational Automation Framework to facilitate new applications' publication.

web.xml template files

The following `web.xml` template files are used in IBM WebSphere Experience Factory:

- `portlet.standard.web.xml`: Used for Java Standard Portlets
- `standalone.web.xml`: Used for standalone applications (non portlets)

These files are stored in the `WebContent\WEB-INF\bin\deployment` folder. This provides the project with the capability for unique user editing of the template for the project and for multiple targets (standalone and portal) from a single project. These files are included in the publishing archive during the publishing process. The `standalone.web.xml` file is saved under the `WebContent\WEB-INF\bin\deployment` folder. This also allows for project-unique user edits of the template for the project and for multiple targets (local and remote) from a single project. These files are all included in the archive during the publishing process.

The WEB-INF\web.xml file

The `WEB-INF\web.xml` file is the copy of `web.xml` that is in place under the project's `WEB-INF` directory. This `web.xml` is a copy of one of the templates built at project creation. For instance, a copy of the `standalone.web.xml` template is built at project creation time and saved as `web.xml`. The template that is utilized will always depend on the specific project server configuration mappings.

> Do not edit the in-place `web.xml` directly, but edit a template instead.

web.xml processing at project creation and publishing

Depending on which function you are trying to perform, WebSphere Experience Factory processes the web.xml file in different manners as follows:

- By creating a new project, a new version of the web.xml file is created from the proper template.
- By upgrading a project, the current web.xml file and its template are backed up, saved, and a new template is generated.
- By publishing a project, a new web.xml file is created from this template. When changes are made to the web.xml template, there is a need to merge them from the template backup into the new template and republish to generate the updated web.xml file.

When publishing the project, or if the user requests a publishing action, you have to do the following:

- If this is to be a development WAR publishing request:
  - Update web.xml with application context
  - Add to the web archive
- If this is to be a production WAR export request:
  - Bundle the specific web.xml in the production WAR

Other things that impact web.xml

Look at the following Ant task:

```
addaservlet utility
```

This is a custom Ant task that is provided for adding a servlet to web.xml. It just adds a servlet definition and mapping to a named web.xml file.

Themes and skins deployment

Since WebSphere Portal Version 6.1, themes and skins can be packaged in their own WAR file, which can be installed, deleted, and changed via the XMLAccess scripts. A2Z decided to use this feature, and bundle their theme and skins deployment with the other portlets.

Portal resources management via policies

As of Version 6.1, IBM WebSphere Portal resources can be managed by policies. Policies are collections of settings that determine how different classes of users will perform functions on portal resources. This is ideal for sites with large user populations, where these management tasks would be otherwise much more time-consuming without these policies. User groups, pages themes, client types, caches, and composite applications are sample target resources that can be managed by policies.

Publishing to a remote AMI instance on the Amazon Cloud

If you recall, WEF and portal development cloud were chosen as the development paradigms for the A2Z portal. A2Z portal application developers and specialists generate and customize their portlets on their local WEF unit test environment and load them to the development cloud for further development with the other integrated components, such as global security. They are expected to move their portlet application from their local systems to a remote development cloud, an **Amazon Machine Image** (**AMI**) instance. With the image used during the POV as a template and others provisioned within minutes, A2Z portal and cloud administrators instructed WEF specialists to perform the following steps to publish their portlet application to the remote AMI instance:

1. They edited their local systems hosts file and mapped the AMI public and internal host names in their hosts file (usually located at `C:\WINDOWS\system32\drivers\etc\hosts` or `/etc/hosts`). For instance:

   ```
   192.168.200.100 ee1-123-456-789-123.computer.amazonaws.com ip-
       11-123-456-789-ee1.internal
   ```

2. They opened the `SOAP_CONNECTOR_ADDRESS` and the `WC_defaulthost` ports on your AMI instance using the ElasticFox extension for the Firefox browser for instance, or used PuTTY as some prefer. Once logged on to the cloud, they found the settings for that environment. From the IBM WebSphere Application Server console, select **Servers** | **Application Servers** | **WebSphere_Portal**; and in the right-hand side column, select **Ports**.

Cloud-enabled environment provisioning, deployment, and release management with IBM Workload Deployer

You can find a great IBM-published white paper entitled—*A Study on reducing labor costs through the use of IBM Workload Deployer* (Formally known as IBM WebSphere CloudBurst) at `ftp://public.dhe.ibm.com/common/ssi/ecm/en/wsw14161usen/WSW14161USEN.PDF`.

In this paper, a formula that uses the calculations based on labor and server provisioning lifecycle, which goes from setup and deployment to troubleshooting and maintenance to retirement. It looks at the current labor model for servers using "total hardware labor hours" with the "number of physical servers". It adds these two to total software stack labor hours and the number of software images to come up with the total labor hour costs for a given period. It shows that the benefits of virtualization, standardization, and automation can reduce the operational labor costs to 80 percent in the cloud and non-cloud environments over manual deployment.

> **Watch and learn**
>
> You can watch a video—*Using IBM WebSphere CloudBurst Environment Profiles* (Renamed as IBM Workload Deployer) at `http://www.youtube.com/watch?v=YUgxkF2VzNk&feature=related`.
>
> You can also watch a video—*Provisioning WebSphere Portal* at `http://www.youtube.com/watch?v=wKJsloglE0E`.

We would like to demonstrate how a cloud environment can be managed by the IBM Workload Deployer, as it relates to portal instances and cluster provisioning. Due to the scope of this chapter, we will leave this subject for our next book edition, which should also cover BPM, SSO, and some other topics. However, enjoy the presentation and think about including automation in your own portal project; it always pays off.

Summary

We started looking at some of the portal-related artifacts and tools. We also looked at some of the build and deploy tasks. We mentioned about some fundamental strategies for portal configuration, content, and release data propagation through portal environments and release promotion. We finished off looking at how to publish the final release to the Amazon Cloud.

7
Introduction to Web Experience Factory

In this chapter, we will introduce **Web Experience Factory (WEF)** as a rapid application development tool. Although we have already mentioned WEF in the previous chapters, here is where we will be focusing on WEF's capability to build portal applications to run on IBM WebSphere Portal.

The following are the topics about which you will be learning:

- Benefits of Web Experience Factory
- Models
- Builders
- Profiling
- WEF Designer
- Software automation
- Application regeneration

What is Web Experience Factory?

Web Experience Factory is a rapid application development tool, which applies software automation technology to construct applications. By using WEF, developers can quickly create single applications that can be deployed to a variety of platforms, such as IBM WebSphere Application Server and IBM WebSphere Portal Server, which in turn can serve your application to standard browsers, mobile phones, tablets, and so on.

Web Experience Factory is the new product derived from the former **WebSphere Portlet Factory (WPF)** product. In addition to creating portal applications, WEF always had the capability of creating exceptional web applications. In fact, the initial product developed by Bowstreet, the company which originally created WPF, was meant to create web applications, way before the dawn of portal technologies.

As the software automation technology developed by Bowstreet could easily be adapted to produce portal applications, it was then tailored for the portal market. This same adaptability is now expanded to enable WEF to target different platforms and multiple devices.

Key benefits of using Web Experience Factory for portlet development

While WEF has the capability of targeting several platforms, we will be focusing on IBM WebSphere Portal applications.

The following are a few benefits of WEF for the portal space:

- Significantly improves productivity
- Makes portal application development easier
- Contains numerous components (builders) to facilitate portal application development
- Insulates the developer from the complexity of the low-level development tasks
- Automatically handles the deployment and redeployment of the portal project (WAR file) to the portal
- Reduces portal development costs

The development environment

Before we discuss key components of WEF, let's take a look at the development environment.

From a development environment perspective, WEF is a plugin that is installed into either Eclipse or IBM Rational Application Developer for Websphere. As a plugin, it uses all the standard features from these development environments at the same time that it provides its own perspective and views to enable the development of portlets with WEF.

Let's explore the WEF development perspective in Eclipse. The WEF development environment is commonly referred to as the **designer**. While we explore this perspective, you will read about new WEF-specific terms. In this section, we will neither define nor discuss them, but don't worry. Later on in this chapter, you will learn all about these new WEF terms.

The following screenshot shows the WEF perspective with its various views and panes:

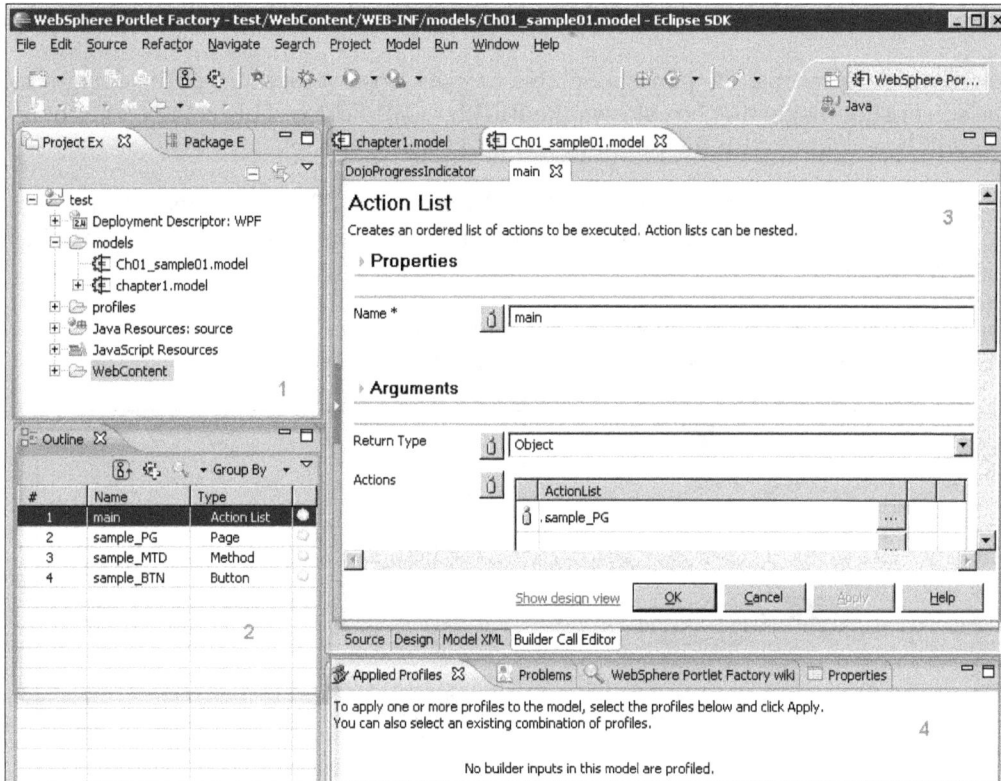

The top-left pane, identified by number 1, shows the **Project Explorer** tab. In this pane you can navigate to the WEF project, which has a structure similar to a JEE project. WEF adds a few extra folders to host the WEF-specific files. Box 1 also contains a tab to access the **Package Explorer** view. The **Package Explorer** view enables you to navigate the several directories containing the .jar files. These views can be arranged in different ways within this Eclipse perspective.

The area identified by number 2 shows the **Outline** view. This view holds the builder call list. This view also holds two important icons. The first one is the "Regeneration" button. This is the first icon from left to right, immediately above the builder call table header. Honestly, we do not know what the graphical image of this icon is supposed to convey. Some people say it looks like a candlelight, others say it looks like a chess pawn. We even heard people referring to this icon as the "Fisher-Price" icon, because it looks like the Fisher-Price children's toy.

The button right next to the Regeneration button is the button to access the **Builder** palette. From the **Builder** palette, you can select all builders available in WEF.

Box number 3 presents the panes available to work on several areas of the designer. The screenshot inside this box shows the **Builder Call Editor**. This is the area where you will be working with the builders you add to your model.

Lastly, box number 4 displays the **Applied Profiles** view. This view displays content only when the open model contains profile-enabled inputs, which is not the case in this screenshot.

The following screenshot shows the right-hand side pane, which contains four tabs—**Source**, **Design**, **Model XML**, and **Builder Call Editor**.

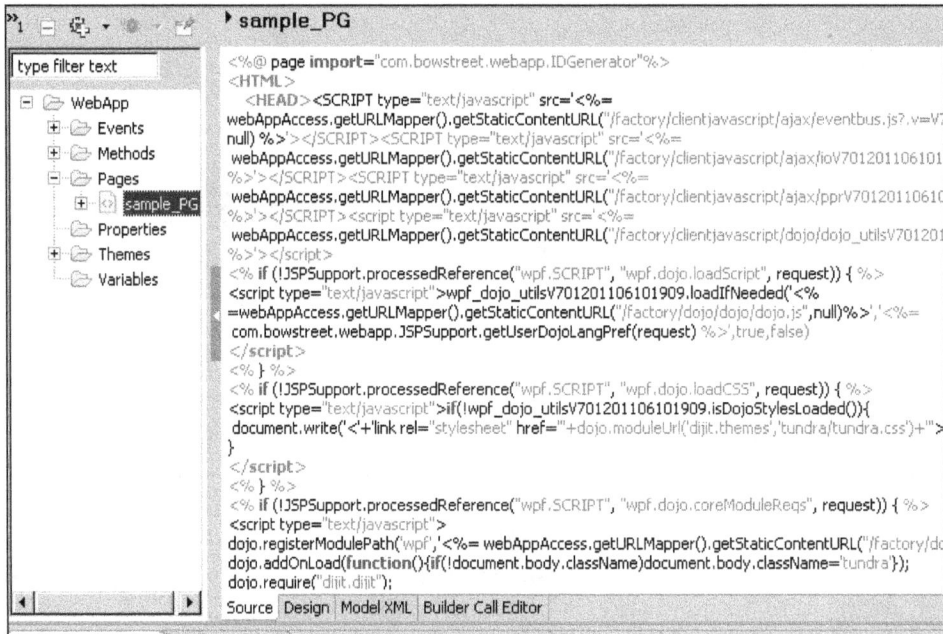

The preceding screenshot shows the content displayed when you select the first tab from the right-hand side pane, the **Source** tab. The **Source** tab exposes two panes. The left-hand side pane contains the WebApp tree, and the right-hand side pane contains the source code for elements selected from the WebApp tree.

Although it is not our intention to define the WEF elements in this section, it is important to make an exception to explain to you what the WebApp tree is. The WebApp tree is a graphical representation of your application. This tree represents an abstract object identified as WebApp object. As you add builders to your models or modify them, these builders add or modify elements in this WebApp object. You cannot modify this object directly except through builders.

The preceding screenshot shows the source code for the selected element in the WebApp tree. The code shows what WEF has written and the code to be compiled.

The following screenshot shows the **Design** pane. The **Design** pane displays the user interface elements placed on a page either directly or as they are created by builders. It enables you to have a good sense of what you are building from a UI perspective.

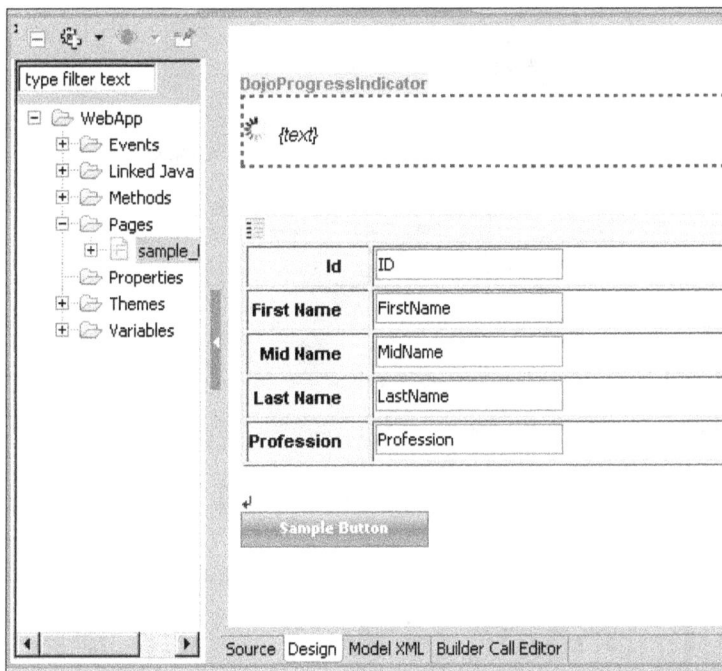

The following screenshot shows the content of a model represented as an XML structure in the **Model XML** tab. The highlighted area in the right-hand side pane shows the XML representation of the **sample_PG** builder, which has been selected in the WebApp tree.

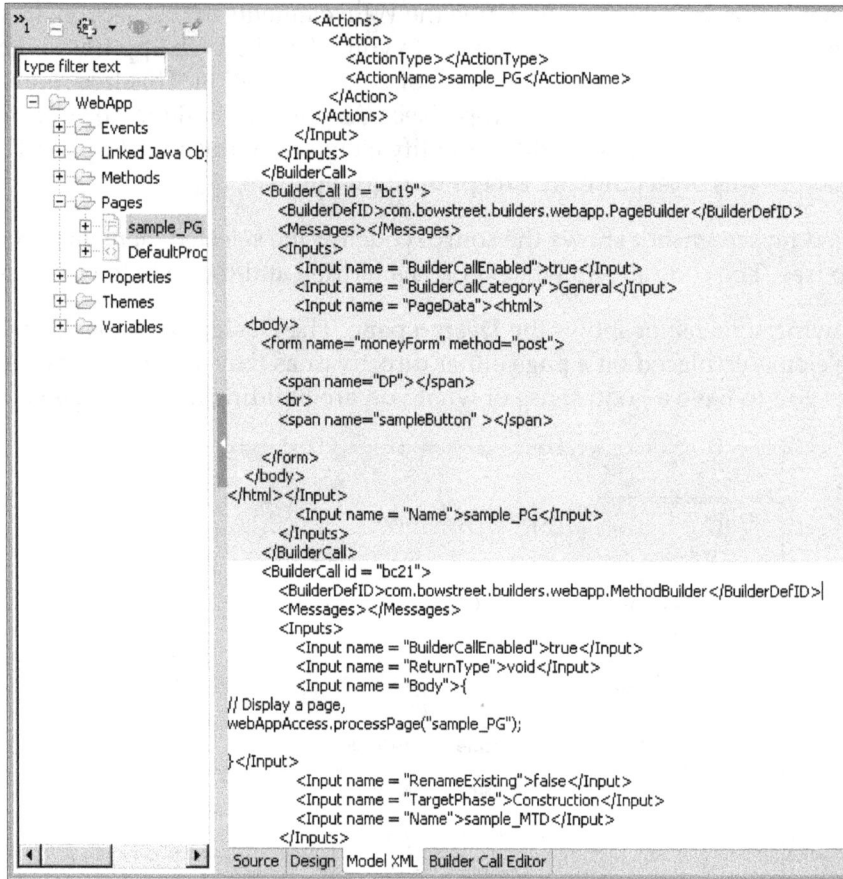

We will discuss the next tab, **Builder Call Editor**, when we address builders in the next section.

Key components of WEF—builders, models, and profiles

Builders, models, and profiles comprise the key components of WEF. These three components work together to enable software automation through WEF. Here, we will explain and discuss in details what they are and what they do.

Builders

Builders are at the core of WEF technology.

There have been many definitions for builders. Our favorite is the one that defines builders as "software components, which encapsulate design patterns".

Let's look at the paradigm of software development as it maps to software patterns. Ultimately, everything a developer does in terms of software development can be defined as **patterns**. There are well-known patterns, simple and complex patterns, well-documented patterns, and patterns that have never been documented. Even simple, tiny code snippets can be mapped to patterns.

Builders are the components that capture these countless patterns in a standard way, and present them to developers in an easy, common, and user-friendly interface. This way, developers can use and reuse these patterns to accomplish their tasks.

Builders enable developers to put together these encapsulated patterns in a meaningful fashion in such a way that they become full-fledged applications, which address business needs. In this sense, developers can focus more on quickly and efficiently building the business solutions instead of focusing on low-level, complex, and time consuming development activities.

Through the builder technology, senior and experienced developers at the IBM labs can identify, capture, and code these countless patterns into reusable components. When you are using builders, you are using code that has not only been developed by a group, which has already put a lot of thought and effort into the development task, but also a component, which has been extensively tested by IBM. Here, we will refer to the IBM example, because they are the makers of WEF—but overall, any developer can create builders.

Simple and complex builders

The same way that development activities can range from very simple to very complex tasks, builders can also range from very simple to very complex.

Simple builders can perform tasks such as placing an attribute on a tag, highlighting a row of a table, or creating a simple link. Equally, there are complex builders, which perform complex and extensive tasks. These builders can save WEF developers' days worth of work, troubleshooting, and aggravation. For instance, there are builders for accessing, retrieving, and transforming data from backend systems, builders to create tables, form, and hundreds of others.

The face of builders

The following screenshot shows a **Button** builder in the **Builder Editor** pane:

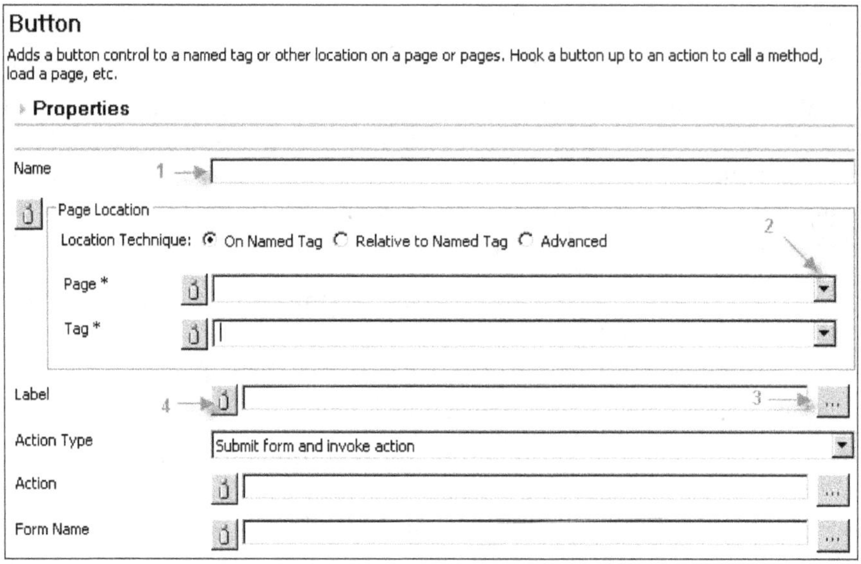

All builders have a common interface, which enables developers to provide builder input values. The builder input values define several aspects concerning how the application code will be generated by this builder. Through the **Builder Editor** pane, developers define how a builder will contribute to the process of creating your application, be it a portlet, a web application, or a widget.

Any builder contains required and optional builder inputs. The required inputs are identified with an asterisk symbol (*) in front of their names. For instance, the preceding screenshot representing the **Button** builder shows two required inputs—**Page** and **Tag**.

As you can see through the preceding screenshot, builder input values can be provided through several ways. The following table describes the items identified by the numbered labels:

Label number	Description	Function
1	Free form inputs	Enables developer to type in any appropriate value.
2	Drop-down controls	Enables developer to select values from a predefined list, which is populated based on the context of the input. This type of input is dynamically populated with possible influence from other builder inputs, other builders in the same model, or even other aspects of the current WEF project.
3	Picker controls	This type of control enables users to make a selection from multiple source types, such as variables, action list builders, methods defined in the current model, public methods defined in java classes and exposed through the Linked Java Class builder, and so on. The values selected through the picker controls can be evaluated at runtime.
4	Profiling assignment button	This button enables developers to profile-enable the value for this input. In another words, through this button, developers indicate that the value for this input will come from a profile to be evaluated at regeneration time.

Through these controls, builders contribute to make the modeling process faster at the same time it reduces errors, because only valid options and within the proper context are presented.

Builders are also adaptive. Inputs, controls, and builder sections are either presented, hidden, or modified depending upon the resulting context that is being automatically built by the builder. This capability not only guides the developers to make the right choices, but it also helps developers become more productive.

Builder artifacts

We have already mentioned that builders either add artifacts to or modify existing artifacts in the WebApp abstract object. In this section, we will show you an instance of these actions. In order to demonstrate this, we will not walk you through a sample. Rather, we will show you this process through a few screenshots from a model.

Here, we will simulate the action of adding a button to a portlet page.

In WEF, it is common to start portlet development with a plain HTML page, which contains mostly placeholder tags. These placeholders, usually represented by the names of **span** or **div** tags, indicate locations where code will be added by the properly selected builders. The expression "code will be added" can be quite encompassing. Builders can create simple HTML code, JavaScript code, stylesheet values, XML schemas, Java code, and so on. In this case, we mean to say that builders have the capability of creating any code required to carry on the task or tasks for which they have been designed.

In our example, we will start with a plain and simple HTML page, which is added to a model either through a Page builder or an Imported Page builder.

Our sample page contains the following HTML content:

Name *	🛈 sample_PG

Page Contents (HTML) *	🛈 `<html>`
	`  <body>`
	`    <form name="moneyForm" method="post">`
	
	`      <span name="sampleButton" ></span>`
	
	`    </form>`
	`  </body>`
	`</html>`

Now, let's use a **Button** builder to add a button artifact to this `sample_PG` page, more specifically to the **sampleButton span** tag. Assume that this button performs some action through a Method builder (Java Method), which in turn returns the same page.

The following screenshot shows what the builder will look like after we provide all the inputs we will describe ahead:

Button

Adds a button control to a named tag or other location on a page or pages. Hook a but
method, load a page, etc.

▸ **Properties**

Name	sample_BTN
🛈 Page Location	
Location Technique:	⊙ On Named Tag ○ Relative to Named Tag ○ Advanced
Page *	🛈 sample_PG
Tag *	🛈 sampleButton
Label	🛈 Sample Button
Action Type	Link to an action
Action	🛈 sample_MTD

Let's discuss the builder inputs we have provided in the preceding screenshot. The first input we provide to this builder is the builder name. Although this input is not required, you should always name your builders. Some naming convention should be used for naming your builders. If you do not name your builders, WEF will name them for you.

The following table shows same sample names, which adds an underscore followed by two or three letters to indentify the builder type:

Builder type	Builder name
Button	search_BTN
Link	details_LNK
Page	search_PG
Data Page	searchCriteria_DP
Variable	searchInputs_VAR
Imported Model	results_IM
Model Container	customer_MC

There are several schools of thoughts regarding naming convention. Some scholars like to debate in favor of one or another. Regardless of the naming convention you adopt, you need to make sure that the same convention is followed by the entire development team.

The next inputs relate to the location where the content created by this builder will be placed. For User Interface builders, you need to specify which page will be targeted. You also need to specify, within that page, the tag with which this builder will be associated. Besides specifying a tag based on the name, you can also use the other location techniques to define this location.

In our simple example, we will be selecting the **sample_PG** page. If you were working on a sample, and if you would click on the drop-down control, you would see that only the available pages would be displayed as options from which you could choose. When a page is not selected, the tag input does not display any value. That is because the builders know how to present only valid options based on the inputs you have previously provided.

For this example, we will select **sample_PG** for page input. After doing so, the **Tag** input is populated with all the HTML tags available on this page. We selected the **sampleButton** tag. This means that the content to be created on this page will be placed at the same location where this tag currently exists. It replaces the **span** tag type, but it preserves the other attributes, which make sense for the builder being currently added.

Another input is the label value to be displayed. Once again, here you can type in a value, you can select a value from the picker, or you can specify a value to be provided by a profile. In this sample, we have typed in **Sample Button**.

For the **Button** builder, you need to define the action to be performed when the button is clicked. Here also, the builder presents only the valid actions from which we can select one. We have selected, **Link to an action**.

For the **Action** input, we select **sample_MTD**. This is the mentioned method, which performs some action and returns the same page.

Now that the input values to this **Button** builder have been provided, we will inspect the content created by this builder.

Inspecting content created by builders

The builder call list has a small gray arrow icon in front of each builder type. By clicking on this icon, you cause the designer to show the content and artifacts created by the selected builder:

#	Name	Type
1	main	Action List
2	samplePage	Page
3	sampleMethod	Method
4	sample_BTN	Button

By clicking on the highlighted link, the designer displays the WebApp tree in its right-hand side pane. By expanding the **Pages** node, you can see that one of the nodes is **sample_BTN**, which is our button. By clicking on this element, the **Source** pane displays the sample page with which we started. If necessary, click on the **Source** tab at the bottom of the page to expose the source pane.

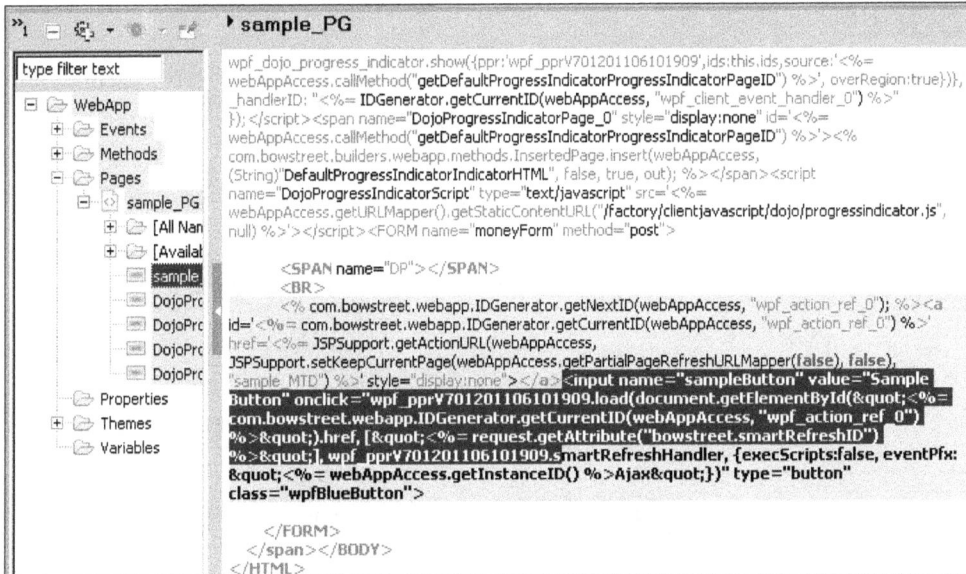

Once the WebApp tree is shown, by clicking on the **sample_BTN** element, the right-hand side pane highlights the content created by the Button builder we have added.

Let's compare the code shown in the preceding screenshot against the original code shown by the screenshot depicturing the Sample Page builder. Please refer to the screenshot that shows a Sample Page builder named **sample_PG**. This screenshot shows that the **sample_PG** builder contains simple HTML tags defined in the **Page Contents (HTML)** input. By comparing these two screenshots, the first difference we notice is that after adding the Button builder, our initial simple HTML page became a JSP page, as denoted by the numerous JSP notations on this page.

We can also notice that the initial **sampleButton span** tag has been replaced by an input tag of the **button** type. This tag includes an `onClick` JavaScript event. The code for this JavaScript event is provided by JSP scriptlet created by the Button builder.

As we learned in this section, builders add diverse content to the WebApp abstract object. They can add artifacts such as JSP pages, JavaScript code, Java classes, and so on, or they can modify content already created by other builders. In summary, builders add or modify any content or artifacts in order to carry on their purpose according to the design pattern they represent.

Models

Another important element of WEF is the Model component. Model is a container for builder calls. The builder call list is maintained in an XML file with a `.model` extension. The builder call list represents the list of builders added to a model.

The **Outline** view of the WEF perspective displays the list of builders that have been added to a model.

The following screenshot displays the list of builder calls contained in a sample model:

To see what a builder call looks like inside the model, you can click on the gray arrow icon in front of the builder type and inspect it in the **Model XML** tab.

For instance, let's look at the Button builder call inside the sample model we described in the previous section.

```xml
<BuilderCall id = "bc24">
    <BuilderDefID>com.bowstreet.builders.webapp.ButtonBuilder</BuilderDefID>
    <Messages></Messages>
    <Inputs>
        <Input name = "BuilderCallEnabled">true</Input>
        <Input name = "ShowAdvancedPostActionBehaviors">false</Input>
        <Input name = "PostActionBehavior">Default</Input>
        <Input name = "DefaultRefreshPageLocation">false</Input>
        <Input name = "ExecuteEmbeddedScripts">false</Input>
        <Input name = "IncludeEmbeddedCSS">false</Input>
        <Input name = "RenderOuterPage">false</Input>
        <Input name = "BreakContainment">false</Input>
        <Input name = "PreservePage">false</Input>
        <Input name = "HTMLAttributes">
            <HTMLAttributes>
                <class></class>
                <style></style>|
            </HTMLAttributes>
        </Input>
        <Input name = "ActionType">link</Input>
        <Input name = "ActionTypeUI">MODEL_LINK</Input>
        <Input name = "IsModelAction">true</Input>
        <Input name = "EarlyArgumentEvaluation">true</Input>
        <Input name = "PageLocation">
            <SimplePageLocation>
                <Page>sample_PG</Page>
                <NameSearch>sampleButton</NameSearch>
            </SimplePageLocation>
        </Input>
        <Input name = "Label">Sample Button</Input>
        <Input name = "Action">sample_MTD</Input>
        <Input name = "ActionURL">sampleMethod</Input>
        <Input name = "Name">sample_BTN</Input>
    </Inputs>
</BuilderCall>
```

The preceding image represents a builder call the way it is stored in the model file. This builder call is one of the XML elements found in the **BuilderCallList** node, which in turn is child of the **Model** node. Extra information is also added at the end of this file.

This XML model file contains the input names and the values for each builder you have added to this model. WEF operates on this information and the set of instructions contained in these XML elements, to build your application by invoking a process known as **generation** or **regeneration** to actually build the executable version of your application, be it a portlet, a web application, or a widget. We will discuss more on regeneration at the end of this chapter.

It is important to notice that models contain only the builder call list, not the builders themselves. Although the terms — builder call and builder are used interchangeably most of the times, technically they are different. Builder call can be defined as an entry in your model, which identifies the builder by the Builder call ID, and then provides inputs to that builder. Builders are the elements or components that actually perform the tasks of interacting with the WebApp object. These elements are the builder definition file (an XML file) and a Java Class. A builder can optionally have a coordinator class. This class coordinates the behavior of the builder interface you interact with through the **Builder Editor**.

Modeling

Unlike traditional development process utilizing pure Java, JSP, JavaScript coding, WEF enables developers to model their application. By modeling, WEF users actually define the instructions of how the tool will build the final intended application. The time-consuming, complex, and tedious coding and testing tasks have already been done by the creators of the builders. It is now left to the WEF developer to select the right builders and provide the right inputs to these builders in order to build the application.

In this sense, WEF developers are actually modelers. A modeler works with a certain level of abstraction by not writing or interacting directly with the executable code. This is not to say that WEF developers do not have to understand or write some Java or eventually JavaScript code. It means that, when some code writing is necessary, the amount and complexity of this code is reduced as WEF does the bulk of the coding for you.

There are many advantages to the modeling approach. Besides the fact that it significantly speeds the development process, it also manages changes to the underlying code, without requiring you to deal with low-level coding. You only change the instructions that generate your application. WEF handles all the intricacies and dependencies for you.

In the software development lifecycle, requests to change requirements and functionality after implementation are very common. It is given that your application will change after you have coded it. So, be proactive by utilizing a tool, which efficiently and expeditiously handles these changes. WEF has been built with the right mechanism to graciously handle change request scenarios. That is because changing the instructions to build the code is much faster and easier than changing the code itself.

Code generation versus software automation

While software has been vastly utilized to automate an infinite number of processes in countless domains, very little has been done to facilitate and improve software automation itself. Prior to being a tool for building portlets, WEF exploits the quite dormant paradigm of software automation.

It is beyond the scope of this book to discuss software automation in details, but it is suffice to say that builders, profiles, and the regeneration engine enable the automation of the process of creating software. In the particular case of WEF, the automation process targets web applications and portlets, but it keeps on expanding to other domains, such as widgets and mobile phones.

WEF is not a code generation tool. While code generation tools utilize a static process mostly based on templates, WEF implements software automation to achieve not only high productivity but also variability.

Profiles

In the development world, the word profile can signify many things. From the WEF perspective, profile represents a means to provide variability to an application. WEF also enables profiles or profile entries to be exposed to external users. In this way, external users can modify predefined aspects of the application without assistance from development or redeployment of the application.

The externalized elements are the builder input values. By externalizing the builder input values, line of business, administrators, and even users can change these values causing WEF to serve a new flavor of their application.

Profile names, profile entry names, which map to the builder inputs, and their respective values are initially stored in an XML file with a .pset extention. This is part of your project and is deployed with your project. Once it is deployed, it can be stored in other persistence mechanisms, for example a database.

WEF provides an interface to enable developers to create profile, define entries and their initial values, as well as define the mechanism that will select which profile to use at runtime. By selecting a profile, all the entry values associated with that profile will be applied to your application, providing an unlimited level of variability.

Variability can be driven by personalization, configuration, LDAP attributes, roles, or it can even be explicitly set through the Java methods.

The following screenshot shows the **Manage Profile** tab of Profile Manager. The Profile Manager enables you to manage every aspect related to profile sets. The top portion of this screenshot lists the three profiles available in this profile set. The bottom part of this screenshot shows the profile entries and their respective values for the selected profile:

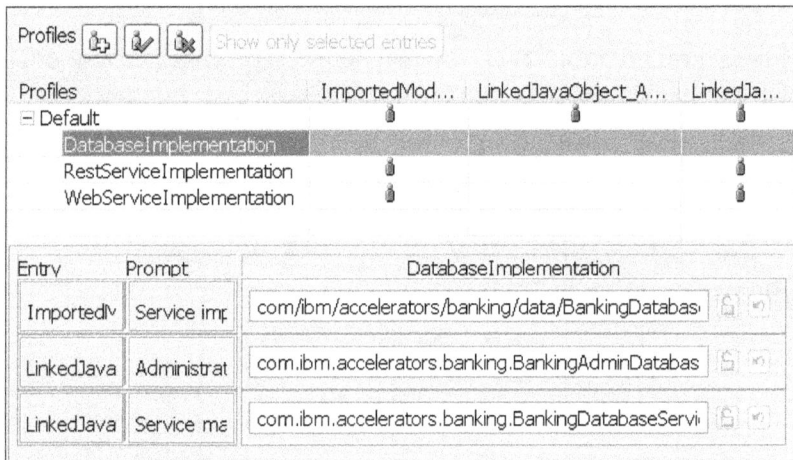

We will cover profiles and profiling in more details in *Chapter 12, WEF Profiling,* which is dedicated to it.

Regeneration engine

Now that you have learned about builders, models, and profiling, we can discuss the component that uses these elements to create your application, the regeneration engine.

We believe that, besides builders with its profiling capability, regeneration process is what sets WEF apart from any other rapid application development tool or code generators for this matter.

Sometimes, regeneration engine is also called **generation engine**. This is a small detail, but generation happens only the first time when your application is constructed by WEF. Regeneration takes place every time after that. So, one should think that it makes more sense to call this process regeneration instead of generation. Hence, we refer to it in this book as **regeneration engine**.

The **regeneration** process is the process by which the component of WEF known as regeneration engine constructs the representation of you application. In order to perform this task, the regeneration engine goes through the list of all builder calls in the model; looks at their input values that might be coming from the several sources we have provided, including a profile and their relationships; and then constructs the WebApp abstract object. The regeneration engine is responsible for making the call to the actual builders, in the proper order, passing in the right and the latest input values for those builders.

The following diagram demonstrates the regeneration process where models and profiles are used to generate instances of WebApps:

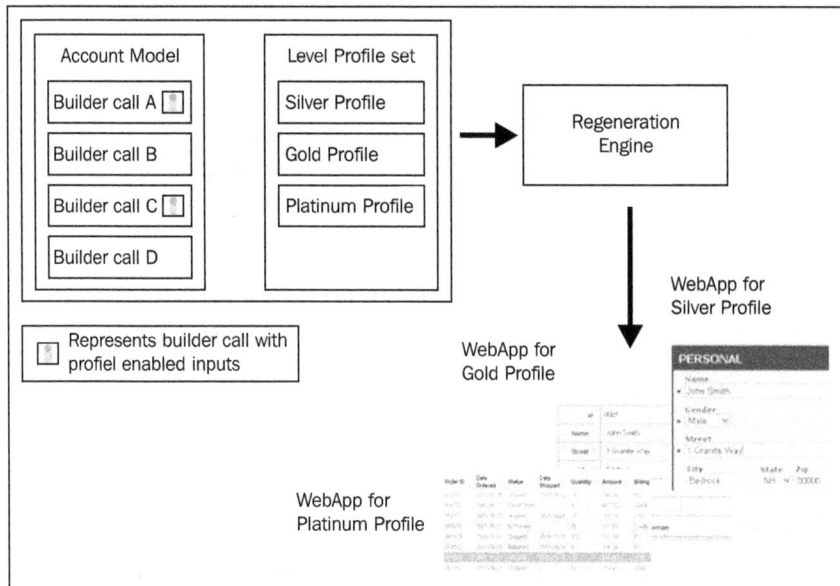

As we have already seen, builders can reference actions or artifacts created by other builders or even external components. The regeneration engine has the intelligence and the ability to understand and interpret these relationships and build a representation of all these complexities. As builders are added or removed from the model, their inputs and relationships change and the regeneration engine re-executes to make sure that the representation of your application maintains its functionality and integrity.

Regeneration happens both at design time as well as at runtime.

Creating a WEF project

If you do not have access to an instance of Web Experiece Factory, you can download an evaluation copy from IBM site. The following is the link: `http://www.ibm.com/developerworks/downloads/ws/wpf/`.

This trial version is valid for a period of 60 days. Please notice that the current version available for download is Version 8. In this book, we have covered Version 7.0, because Version 8 was not available at the time we started writing this book.

In order to create your portlets, first you need to create your WEF project either in Eclipse or in **Rational Application Developer (RAD)**. The process is the same whether in Eclipse or RAD. As we are using Eclipse, let's walk though the process of creating a WEF project in Eclipse.

Before you start your project, you should have your IBM WebSphere Portal Server up and running. We will instruct WEF to deploy the portlets we created in this project directly to the portal server. Perform the following steps:

1. Open your Eclipse. By default, it should open on the WEF perspective. The currently open perspective is indicated in the top-right side. If the WEF perspective is not currently open, then from the top menu, select **Window | Open Perspective | Other | WebSphere Portlet Factory**.

2. From the top menu, select **File | New | WebSphere Portlet Factory**. The **Create WebSphere Portlet Factory Project** window will open.

3. For **Project name** type **A2Z**. Leave **Use default location** checked and uncheck **Create default folders**.

The following screenshot shows the first screen for creating your project:

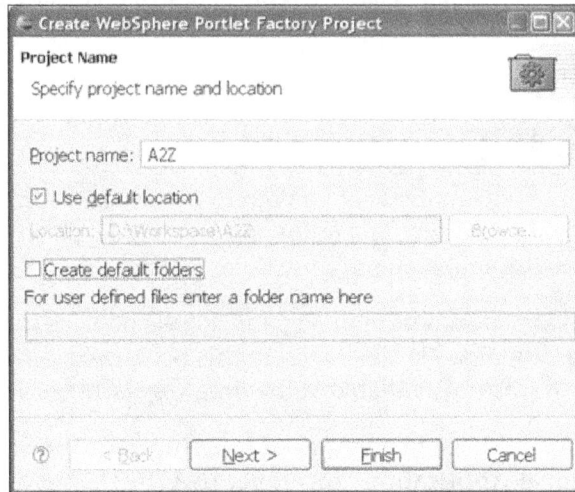

4. Click on **Next**. The next window, entitled — **Feature Set page**, enables you to select feature sets you would like to add to this project. By default, **Dojo Extension – 1.x** is checked. Leave it checked and click on **Next**.

5. The next window, entitled — **Server Configuration**, enables you to define a server configuration. If you do not have one for your portal, let's create one:

   ° Click on the **Create Server Configuration...** button. The **Create Server Configuration** window is displayed. This window contains a list of supported servers.

   ° We will be using Portal Server 7.0. So, you should select **IBM WebSphere Application Server** and **Portal Server 7.x**. Click on **OK**. The **Edit Server Configuration** window is displayed where you can provide information about your server.

   ° The following screenshot shows the **Edit Server Configuration** window, which is presented once you select the type of server for which you want to create a configuration.

Configuration Name	IBM_WebSphere_Application_Server_and_Portal_Server_7.x
Description	Develop and test portlets on IBM WebSphere Portal 7.x, web applications on IBM WebSphere Application Server 7.x and widgets on IBM Lotus Mashups 2.0.
Server Type	IBM WebSphere Application Server and Portal Server 7.x

Server Configuration Details

These settings are used for creating the files that are used in publishing. The Designer can automatically publish the project if the appropriate credentials are provided. The user will be prompted to publish the application when the project is created or any of the development WAR files are built.

Server Host	localhost	
SOAP Connector Port	10025	Detect
Portlet API	○ Java Portlet Standard 1.0 ◉ Java Portlet Standard 2.0	
User Name	wpsadmin	
Password	********	
Create Test Portal Page	Single Page	▼

Test connection

> WEF ships with a version of **WebSphere Application Server Community Edition Server** (**WAS CE**). WAS CE is installed by default when you install WEF. If you do not want to install WAS CE, then you need to perform a custom install and disable the installation of WAS CE.
>
> If you run the default install, then you also have the opportunity to deploy your projects to WAS CE.

° You can test the SOAP connector port, by clicking on the **Detect** button.

> Port numbers are assigned when the portal server is installed, and they may vary from system to system. For Windows systems, during installation Portal Install scans for available ports starting at port number 10000.

° For **Portlet API**, select **Java Portlet Standard 2.0**. This equates to JSR 286 standards.

° Provide the portal credentials and perform a test to make sure that both the SOAP port number and the credentials are correct.

- ° For the **Create Test Portal Page** option, select **Single Page**. This is a nifty option available on WEF 7.x, which creates a portal page in the portal. When you create your portlet, it then automatically places your portlet on that page. This page will have the same name as your current project.

- ° Once you confirm the information you have provided is correct, click on the **OK** button.

6. This will bring you back to the **Server Configuration** window. Click on **OK** in this window. A dialog box will inquire if you want to publish your project. Click on **Yes**.

WEF should display a message indicating that your project has been successfully published. Your WEF project contains all the artifacts required for you to develop your application. It also includes all the supporting files for any feature set you might have selected.

The steps you have completed in the preceding section will cause your project to be published to the installed servers.

> The development WAR file will be published to the WebSphere Application Server. This WAR file is used for testing purpose, because it enables you to run your models from the designer.
> The portlet WAR file will be published to the WebSphere Portal Server.

Creating your first Portlet

Now that you have created your project, we will create your first model, which will also be a portlet. Perform the following steps for doing so:

1. In the designer, make sure the **Project Explorer** tab is open in the top-left pane. Right-click your project, and select **New | WebSphere Portlet Factory Model**.

2. Choose **A2Z** from the **WebSphere Portlet Factory Model** window, and click on **Next**. A new page is displayed.

3. From this new page, you can select from a list of different starter models. Please select **Simple "Hello World" Model**.

The following screenshot shows the **Select Model** window with **Simple "Hello World" Model**:

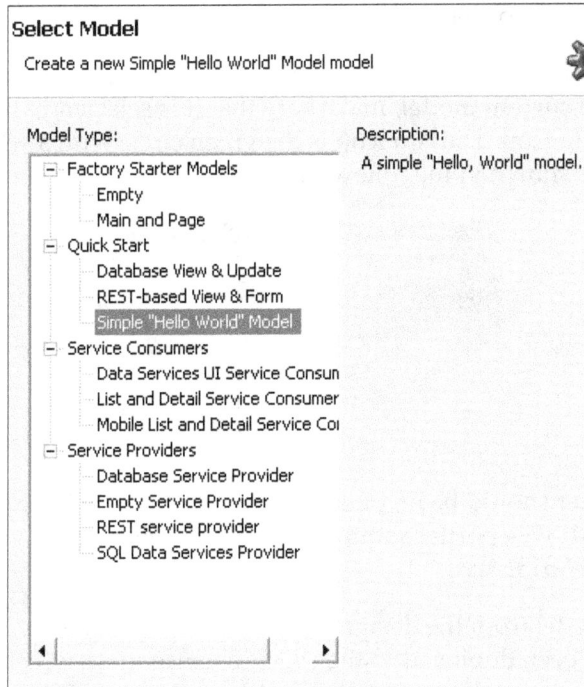

```
Select Model
Create a new Simple "Hello World" Model model

Model Type:                              Description:
  ⊟ Factory Starter Models               A simple "Hello, World" model.
      Empty
      Main and Page
  ⊟ Quick Start
      Database View & Update
      REST-based View & Form
      Simple "Hello World" Model
  ⊟ Service Consumers
      Data Services UI Service Consun
      List and Detail Service Consumer
      Mobile List and Detail Service Con
  ⊟ Service Providers
      Database Service Provider
      Empty Service Provider
      REST service provider
      SQL Data Services Provider
```

4. Click on **Next**. In the **Basic Information** window, leave the **Deploy this model as a portlet** checkbox selected. Click on **Next**.

5. In the next step, enter **HelloWorld** for **Name*** (No spaces). For **Portlet Title**, enter **Hello World** (with a space). Click on **Next**.

6. On the **display information** page, for **Entry Type** select **Just a line of text**. For **Text**, enter **Another Hello World!**. Click on **Next**.

7. In the **Save New Model** window, enter **HelloWorld** (no space). Yes, you had already provided the model name in a previous step, and now you have to provide the same information again. Well…Click on **Finish**.

You will see that WEF creates a new model with four builders for you. The first builder is the Portlet Adapter, which transforms your regular model into a JSR 286 portlet.

Executing your portlet from the designer

Now that you have a portlet, let's run this portlet from the designer. This is how you could quickly test your portlet.

By default, your designer should have a run configuration, which has been created by WEF. To run the current model, make sure that it is selected in the designer. Then click on the run icon. The run icon is the green circle with a white arrow inside pointing to right, as shown in the following screenshot:

Your default browser should be invoked, and the portlet you have just created should be displayed. This portlet should display the only page in your portlet with its **Another Hello World!** text.

When you run a model from the designer as instructed previously, you are running the project that has been deployed to the WAS instance upon which portal is running. In fact, your model is running as a web application. WEF refers to this action as running your model standalone. When your project is created, WEF adds several supporting files, which enables this project to be executed from your WAS server. These helping files are included only in the development WAR file. When you build your portlet WAR file, these files are exluded.

Deploying your portlet

Lastly, let's deploy your portlet to the portal and access it in the portal.

Your portlet WAR has already been deployed to portal. However, as you added a new portlet to your project, you need to publish your project again. This will cause the `portlet.xml` file to be rebuilt and include your newly created portlet.

Right-click on your **A2Z** project and select **Publish Application...** From the new window, make sure that the deployment configuration you have created is selected, then click on **OK**. It should take a minute or so to rebuild and redeploy your portlet WAR.

Now let's move to the portal side. WEF does a great job behind the scenes to make the task of testing your portlets in the portal much easier. As you recall, when you created you project, you have specified in one of the inputs that you wanted WEF to create a page for you in the portal. Now that you have created your portlet, WEF automatically places this portlet on that page for you. So, all you need to do to access your portlet is to log in to portal, and click on your page. Once you log in to your portal, you should see a page named A2Z. Click on this page. This page should contain your **Hello World** Portlet.

Congratulations! You have just built and accessed your first portlet built with WEF.

Summary

In this chapter, we have seen that WEF is a powerful software automation tool. Its software automation capability has been geared towards the creation of not only portlets, but also web applications, widgets, and even delivering these applications to mobile devices. This software automation capability not only enables great productivity gains, but also insulates developers from the complexity of writing low-level code.

As we saw, WEF has numerous features and builders that make the development of portlet applications much faster.

We also looked at the core components of WEF—builders, models, and profiles. With the topics we have covered here, you now have a good foundation to start thinking as a WEF developer or modeler. In the next chapter, we will apply all the concepts we have learned here to build our portlets.

8
Service Layers

In this chapter, we will discuss Web Experience Factory's ability to segregate responsibilities into distinct layers. Here, we will identify and discuss how models can be tailored to perform specific tasks which decouples data access and retrieval from the **user interface (UI)** presentation tasks.

You will learn about the following concepts:

- The Service Consumer and Service Provider patterns in WEF
- Service builders
- Service models
- UI models
- Support for testing services

While you learn about the preceding concepts, you will also build two models to help you understand these WEF concepts and builders.

The Service Consumer and Service Provider patterns in WEF

The provider/consumer pattern is implemented through the usage of specialized models. As we saw in *Chapter 7, Introduction to Web Experience Factory*, models are comprised of builders. This being the case, by adding specific builders to a model, we can clearly define the tasks to be performed by these models. For instance, if we add UI-related builders such as Data Page, Link, Input Control, and so on to a model, it makes sense that this model will be responsible for handling the display and input of data. On the other hand, if we add builders such as Service Definition, Service Operation, Web Service Call, and other such builders, it makes sense that these models will be entirely responsible for data access and data manipulation.

The models responsible for data access and data manipulation play the role of **Service Providers**, and the ones responsible for the UI presentation are **Service Consumers**.

The following diagram shows the Service Consumer and Service Provider patterns in WEF:

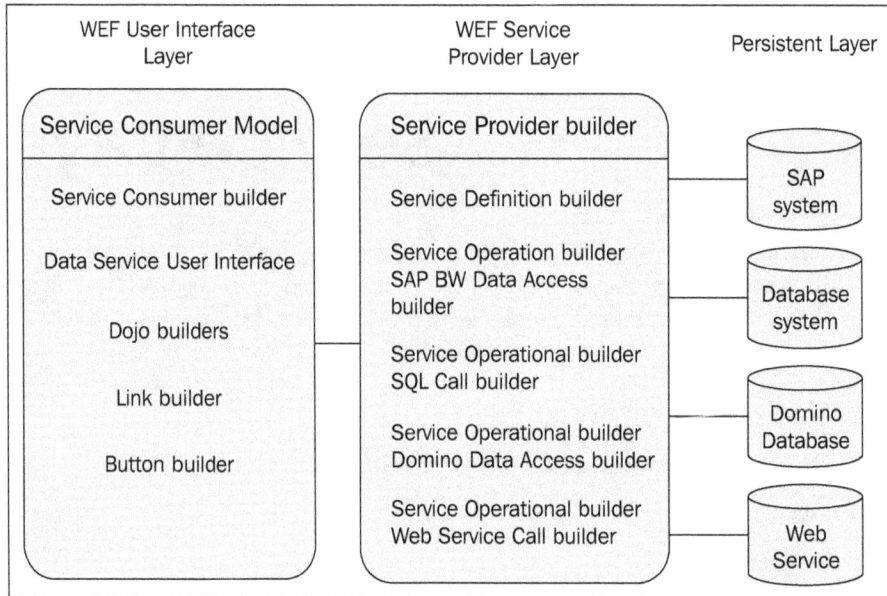

It is important to notice that although the pattern depicted in the preceding diagram is implemented just like that in many portal projects, depending on the magnitude of the project, there could be an Enterprise Service Bus between the Service Provider layer and the Persistence layer.

In addition to that, a mediation layer could be added here, too. This mediation layer would implement the business logic, business rules, processes, and so on.

When ESB is present, then inevitably data transformation to reuse existing services will happen. This brings the question of where would that transformation happen, before or after ESB? Both approaches have pros and cons. Before getting into heated discussion between the service and the portal teams, performance tests should be conducted to capture the data to help decide for one or another approach.

The following diagram depicts the communication between the different layers when the infrastructure architecture incorporates a mediation layer:

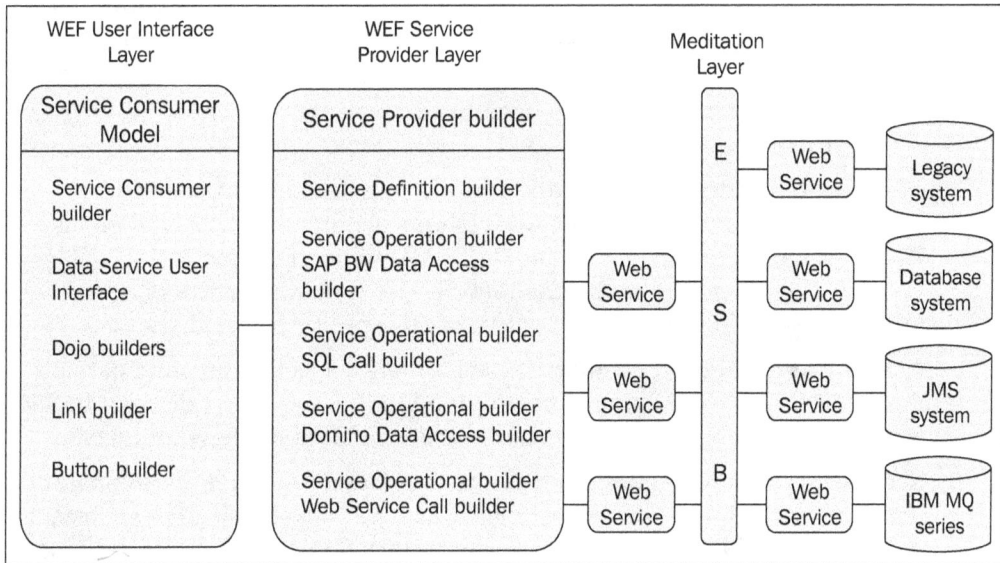

Service builders

Let's take a look at the builders that enable the **service-oriented architecture** (SOA) implementation and communication between the provider and the consumer layers.

The following screenshot shows the list of available service builders:

There are basically four types of builders a WEF modeler would add to a Service Provider model in order to implement a service operation:

1. **Service Definition builder**: The Service Definition builder is the builder that makes a model behave like a Service Provider model. This means that this builder adds the required support to expose the operations in this model via WSDL to other models. You need to add just one Service Definition per provider model.

2. **Integration builder**: The integration builders are builders specialized in connecting directly to one of the sources representing the backend systems. Such builders include SQL Call builder, SAP builder, Domino builder, PeopleSoft builder, and so on. The Web Service Call builder would be included in this category, although it is agonistic of any specific backend system.

3. **Action List or Method builder**: These builders act as the implementation for the service. The input value to be provided to the Action to call input in the Service Operation builder refers to the action created by these builders.

4. **Service Operation builder**: The Service Operation builder adds an operation, which most likely invokes one of the supported backend systems such as database, SAP, Domino, and so on. The Service Operation builder can also invoke an Action List or a Method builder as specified in the preceding point. You can add as many Service Operation builders to a model as necessary.

With the four builder types listed previously, you would have a complete Service Provider model, although it is very likely that a provider model will have other builders such as a Linked Java Object builder, possibly XML Transformer builders, and other similar builders to support the mediation between UI and the backend system.

Now let's look at the Service Consumer side. The data retrieved and manipulated by the provider needs to be consumed by another model. This other model needs to have a builder named **Service Consumer**. The Service Consumer builder will scan your project for provider models and make the public operations of those models available to your consumer model.

While it seems that this pattern adds overhead to your development effort, this is the recommended approach to develop portlets with WEF. Technically, there is nothing that keeps a UI model from accessing backend data directly, but that would be a bad practice, as your models would quickly become unmanageable.

Creating a service model

Let's walk through the creation of a service model so that you can put in practice the concepts we have discussed so far.

Open WEF designer and open the project you have created in the previous chapter.

In order to enable you to create this sample model without having to install or connect to any backend system, we will create a sample data to demonstrate the usage of the service builders.

It is a good practice to group Service Provider and Service Consumer models within their own folder. Let's do just that. Perform the following steps:

1. Under the **models** directory, create another folder named **chapter08**.
2. Inside this folder, create two more folders. Name them as **data** and **ui**.
3. Right-click on the **data** folder, and select **New**.
4. From the pop-up menu, select **WebSphere Portlet Factory Model**.
5. Select the project you have created, and click on **Next**.
6. From the **Select Model** window, select **Empty**.
7. Name this model as **investorsPr**.
8. Click on **Finish**.

There are a few starter models available here, but we are not going to select any of these. We want to work through a sample from the beginning.

When you click on **Finish**, the designer opens your model and presents a blank outline view.

Let's select our first service builder call and add it to our sample model. Open the builder palette by clicking on its icon as shown in the following screenshot:

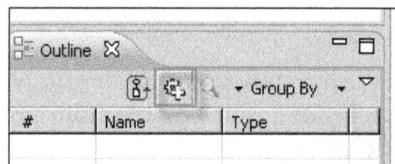

From the **Builder Picker** dialog box, select **Services** from the **Category Name** panel. From the **Builder** panel, select **Service Definition**. Click on **OK**.

The **Service Definition** interface opens on the **Builder Call Editor** tab.

Let's provide the inputs to this builder call. We will explain the meaning of these builders right after we provide the inputs. Enter the following inputs:

- **Service Name**: investor_SD
- **Make Service Public**: Checked

- **Generate WSDL**: Unchecked
- **Service State**
  - ○ **Maintain State**: **Stateless** (Fresh model instance for each call)
- **Testing Support**
  - ○ **Add Testing Support**: Checked
  - ○ **Generate Main**: Checked

- Click on **OK** and save you model

> It is important to adopt a naming convention in any project. WEF is not different from any other software project. While a formal naming convention should be established and maintained through documentation, for our project, we will append "_" (underscore) followed by the builder name initials after the builder call name that we provide.

Explaining the Service Definition builder inputs

Let's explain the most important builder inputs we have provided for this Service Definition builder:

- **Service Name**: This is the name, which will be listed in the Service Consumer models.

- **Make Service Public**: This input indicates that we want this model to expose the services we add here.

- **Maintain State**: This input defines whether you want this model to maintain state or not. From a memory consumption perspective, stateless models are more efficient, although they need to be instantiated each time you invoke them.

- **Logical Operations**: WEF version 7 adds a nice feature to the old Service Definition builder, **Logical Operations**. Through **Logical Operations**, you can define operations that will be picked up by other builders on the Service Consumer side. One of the builders graced with such capability is Data Service User Interface. This builder will be able to do much more for you on the UI front with the information you provide here. In fact, this builder will be able to build an entire **Create, Read, Update, Delete (CRUD)** application for you by extracting the information from this section.

For now, we are not going to provide any input to this section. We will revisit it after we create our sample operation.

Creating sample data for the Service Provider model

In order to develop our Service Provider sample model, we need to access some data. More specifically, our sample model will emulate the retrieval of a list of investors. In a commercial-grade project, we would be accessing some type of backend system such as a relational database, SAP, a Domino database, or even web services.

For our sample provider model, we will not be accessing any backend system. So, in order to emulate the retrieval of a list of investors, we will create an XML variable. This XML variable will be returned when our service operation is invoked.

Let's create a small list of investors for our Bullion Bank. This will be an XML data type, for which we will create an XML schema later.

Add a Variable builder to your current model. To find a builder in the **Builder Picker** dialog box easily, you can type the builder name for which you are looking. Type in the string variable at the search input field of the builder palette.

Once you select the Variable builder, type in the following inputs:

- **Name**: investors_VAR
- **Type**: XML
- **Initial Value**: Enter the following code snippet:

```
<Investors>
    <investor>
        <ID>001</ID>
        <FirstName>James</FirstName>
        <LastName>Smith</LastName>
        <type>Gold</type>
    </investor>
    <investor>
        <ID>003</ID>
        <FirstName>Peter</FirstName>
        <LastName>Claptrik</LastName>
        <type>Silver</type>
    </investor>
    <investor>
        <ID>002</ID>
```

```
            <FirstName>Susan</FirstName>
            <LastName>Rica</LastName>
            <type>Platinum</type>
        </investor>
    <Investors>
```

Click on **OK**, and save your model.

The variable we have created in the preceding section is not a schema-typed XML variable. The Service Operation builder needs to operate on schema-typed XML Variables. So, in order to define a type for our variable, we will create an XML schema type. We then use the type defined in this schema to define our XML variable type.

WEF provides a nice builder named Simple Schema Generator. This builder creates an XML schema based on a sample XML variable. As we already have our XML variable, let's use the Simple Schema Generator builder to create an XML schema based on the structure of our variable.

Add a Simple Schema Generator builder to your model and add the following inputs:

- **Name: investor_SCH**
- **Sample Data: investors_VAR**
- **Modify Variable**: Checked
- **URI: http://a2z.bullionbank.com/investors**

For the **URI** input, please make sure you completely replace the existing default URI with the input value supplied in the preceding list.

Once you click on **OK**, you can inspect this bulder call's content by selecting this builder in the **Builder Call** list and selecting the **Source** tab.

Explanation about Simple Schema Generator builder inputs

When you check **Modify Variable**, the variable you have selected here will be converted to the type you have specified in this builder.

Emulating the data retrieval

Now that we have data and a schema-typed variable, we can create a mechanism to emulate the retrieval of such data to be served by the Service Operation builder.

Let's add an Action List builder to our model. The Action List builder is a handy builder, which performs a set of actions defined in its **Action List** section.

Open an Action List builder and provide the following inputs.

- **Name**: retrieveInvestors_AL
- **Return Type**: IXml
- **XML Type**: investor_SCH/Investors
- **Actions**: Return!${Variables/investors_VAR/Investors}

To provide the XML type and the actions in the Action List builder, do not type in any of the values. Instead, use the pickers provided by this builder. By utilizing the picker, you not only speed up the development of your model, but you also reduce the possibility of errors. The picker is accessible through the button with the three dots label.

The following screenshot shows the selection of the **Investors** type for the XML Type input. The **Choose Variable Type** dialog box is accessed by clicking on the button with the three dots at the end of the **XML Type** input box:

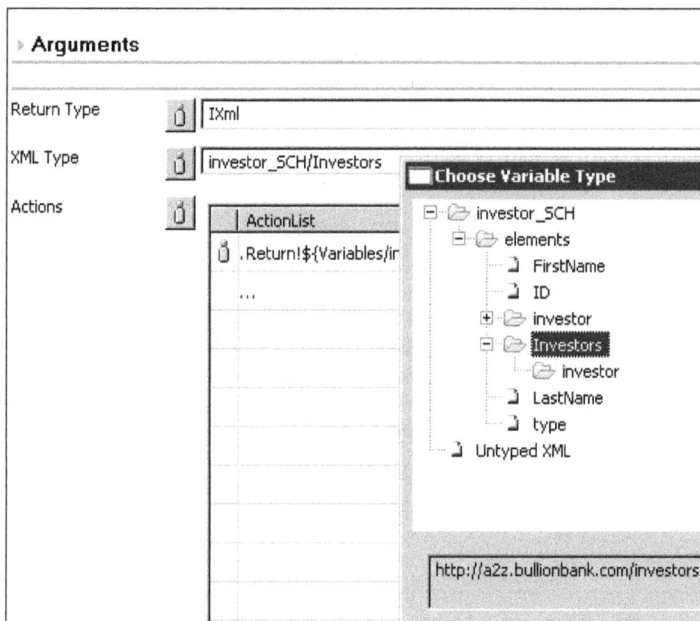

To select the action item in the **ActionList** box, also select the picker. The following steps show how to select the return value for this Action List builder:

1. Click on the button with the three dots inside the **ActionList** box to open the **Select Action** dialog box.
2. Expand the **Special** node

3. Select **Return**.
4. The **Set Return Value** dialog box is displayed.
5. Click on the **picker** button for the **Source** input.
6. This will open another dialog box entitled **Choose Reference**.
7. Expand the **Variables** node.
8. Expand **investors_VAR**.
9. Select **Investors**.
10. Click on **OK** in the last two dialog boxes.
11. Click on **OK** in this Action List builder, and save your model.

The following screenshot shows the dialog boxes described in the preceding steps:

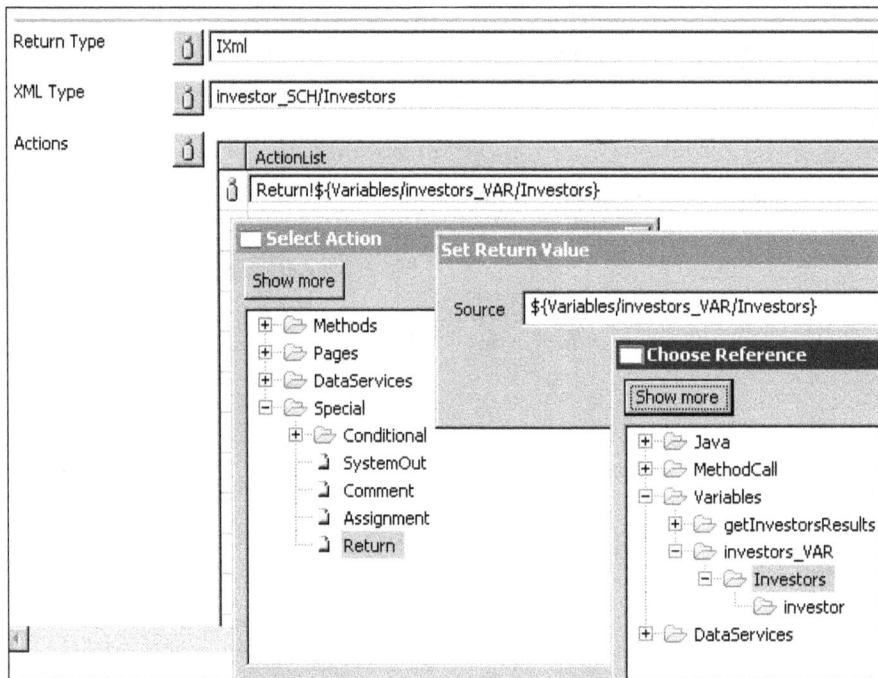

Always select your builder inputs through pickers when they are available. This not only reduces errors, but it is one more means by which WEF makes developers more productive.

Your Action List builder should look like the one depicted in the following screenshot:

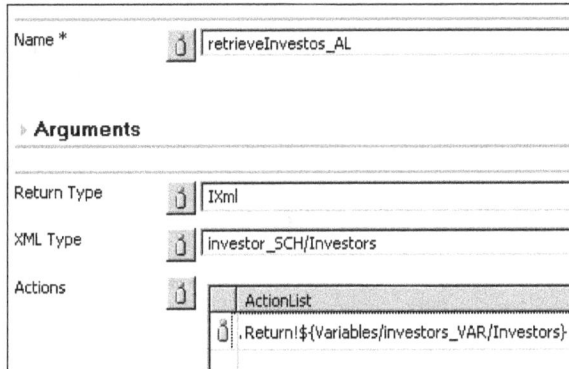

Name *	ⓘ	retrieveInvestos_AL

▸ Arguments

Return Type	ⓘ	IXml
XML Type	ⓘ	investor_SCH/Investors
Actions	ⓘ	ActionList
	ⓘ	.Return!${Variables/investors_VAR/Investors}

You certainly know where we are going with this approach. If you think we are going to invoke this action list to return data to our service operation, you are absolutely right. To prove you are right, our next step is to add the Service Operation builder to our provider model.

Creating a service operation

Lastly, in our simple Service Provider sample model, we will add a Service Operation builder call to define that the data will expose an operation to other models interested in consuming the operations defined here.

Open the builder palette and select the **Service Operation** builder. Notice that this builder has several sections as follows:

- **Service Operation Properties**
- **Operation Inputs**
- **Operation Results**
- **Result Caching**
- **Additional Processing**
- **Context Variables**
- **Paging Options**
- **Optional Schema Settings**

As you can see, the Service Operation builder is a very rich builder with great capabilities. Let's dissect some of these sections:

- **Service Operation Properties**: The most important input here is the **Action To Call** input. This is the action to be invoked when the Service Consumer model calls this operation.

- **Operation Inputs**: Two things happen here. Primarily, the source for the input structure for this operation is identified, if one exists. Secondly, it defines how the inputs to the **Action To Call** method or **Data Service** will be handled.

- **Operations Results**: Similar to **Operation Inputs**, you need to specify the source for result structure and how the result is handled once **Action To Call** is invoked.

- **Additional Processing**: You can specify an action to be invoked both before and after **Action To Call** is invoked. Here you have the opportunity to do further processing either to better prepare the inputs passed in from the consumer and prior to actually calling the action.

  You also have the opportunity to manipulate the result before returning control back to the regular flow. It is recommended that this extra processing should be done through a Java class accessible via a **Linked Java Object (LJO)** builder.

- **Context Variables**: Data transfer between the consumer and provider complies with an XML schema structure. If you want to pass extra data that is not part of the schema, then you can define context variables. The defined context variables will enable you to pass on this extra data, which very likely will be accessed from a pre-execution or post-execution method.

Now that we have a good understanding of the capabilities of the Service Operation builder, let's provide the inputs to this builder to conclude our simple sample:

- **Data Service: investor_SD**
- **Operation Name: getInvestors**
- **Action To Call: retrieveInvestors_AL**
- **Input Structure Handling: No inputs**
- **Result Structure Handling: Use structure from called action**
- **Result Field Mapping: Automatic**

Your Service Operation builder should look like the following screenshot:

Data Service *	investor_SD
Operation Name *	getInvestors
Action To Call *	retrieveInvestos_AL
Operation Description	

Operation Inputs

Specify the input structure for the generated service operation, and assign the inputs for the called action.

Input Structure Handling	○ Use structure from called action ○ Specify input schema ● No inputs

Operation Results

Specify the result structure for the generated service operation, and assign the result values.

Result Structure Handling	● Use structure from called action ○ Specify result schema ○ No results
Result Description	
Result Field Mapping	● Automatic ○ Specify result values

Click on **OK** and save your model.

Testing the Service Provider models

WEF provides a versatile way of testing your provider models. It would be very time consuming if we had to create UI to handle both inputs and outputs in order to test our operations. Well, that is where software automation comes handy again to increase developer's productivity.

At this point, WEF has captured all the information necessary to build a test interface to provide the service inputs as well as to display the service results.

When you added the Service Definition builder, one of the inputs you have provided was **Add Testing Support**. By simply checking this text box causes WEF to create numerous artifacts to enable you to run this model standalone from the designer.

Let's run the model and see the result. Click on the **Run active model** icon. Make sure your portal server is running if portal is what you have defined in your server configuration.

You should see a page entitled **Operations For Service "investor_SD"**. On this page, there is a link for **getInvestors**. Click on this link to invoke this service. You will see that the service is invoked and the results of your service are shown in a nicely formatted table. If this operation took any input, WEF would present you with an input page to capture these inputs.

Revisiting the Logical Operations

Now that you have defined your service operation, we can open the Service Definition builder again to provide the logical operations we would like to expose to UI builders.

Open the Service Definition builder and expand the **Logical Operations** section. Let's communicate to the UI builders that our getInvestors operation retrieves a list of investors. Click on the intersection of the **Retrieve List** row and the **Operation Name** column. This cell should present a drop-down element and it should contain the **getInvestors Operation** as the only option. Please select this option.

Click on **OK,** and save this model.

Invoking the Service Provider model from the Service Consumer model

Now that we have tested our Service Provider model, we are going to move to the UI model. We will access the data provided by the provider. In the WEF terminology, the UI models are identified as Service Consumers. The consumer name is probably due to two reasons — The UI model needs to add a Service Consumer builder to its builder call list and this UI model also consumes data provided by the provider. It is true that the consumer also sends data to the provider, but Service Consumer is a good name for this builder.

Let's create another model to perform the consumer role. Perform the following steps:

1. Open the **models** directory and open **chapter08** folder.
2. Right-click on the **ui** folder and select **New**.
3. From the pop-up menu, select **WebSphere Portlet Factory Model**.
4. Select the project you have been working on and click on **Next**.
5. From the **Select Model** window, select **Empty**.
6. Name this model **investorsCs**.
7. Click on **Finish**.

Now let's add our first builder to this model. Perform the following steps:

1. Open the builder palette by clicking on its icon.

2. In the **Builder Picker** dialog box, type **Service Consumer** in the search bar type.

3. Select the **Service Consumer** from the context search.

4. This should cause the builder panel to display the **Service Consumer** builder.

5. Select it and click on **OK**.

Let's provide the following inputs for this builder:

- **Name**: investor_SC
- **Provider Model**: chapter08/data/investorPr
- **Add All Provider Operations**: Checked
- **User Request-Scoped input variables**: Checked
- **User Request-Scoped result variables**: Unchecked

Let's take a look at two sections of this builder — **Performance Options** and **Context Variable**.

- **Performance Options**: These values are not checked by default but most of the times you will want to check them. As a WEF developer, you should always be aware of features and techniques to make your application as efficient as possible; at the same time, it should not consume unnecessary memory. The caching option should be part of a caching strategy you develop after thorough analyses of your application, users, groups, how the application will be used, and so on. You should not cache values without understanding how these items impact your application concerning caching.

- **Context Variables**: As you recall, we discussed about context variables when you were being introduced to the Service Definition builder. On the consumer side, this is how you would connect any context variables you would define there.

Click on **OK** on this builder call.

Now let's add another builder not only to take care of the data display, but also to invoke the data itself. WEF version 7 has numerous great enhancements and new builders. The next builder we will see deserves special note among them. The Data Service User Interface builder is a pretty neat builder that does a ton of work for you, the developer.

When you created your Service Provider model, in the Service Definition builder, one of the inputs you provided was the input for the logical operations. The Data Service User Interface builder will inspect the Service Definition builder to create the artifacts you need to display your data and to interact with the operations in the provider.

Add the Data Service User Interface builder to your UI model.

Provide the following inputs:

- **Name**: **investor_DSU**
- **Data Service**: **investor_SC**
- **Choose Pages/Operations**: Check **List Page**
- **Use Theme**: Checked

On **List Page Settings**, leave the default values.

Click on **OK** in this builder, save your model, and run it.

Great! The following screenshot shows what you should see in your browser:

1 - 3 of 3		Page 1		Previous	Next
Id	First Name	Last Name	Type		
001	James	Smith	Gold		
002	Peter	Claptrik	Silver		
002	Susan	Pali	Platinum		
Show: 5 | 10 | 20 | 50 | 100 | **All** items		Jump to page 1 of 1		Previous	Next

You can play with this page. You can see that WEF has added several capabilities to this page, including Dojo capabilities. Besides paging, WEF has added the ability to resize the columns as well as to reorder them in the table.

As you saw, WEF enabled you to retrieve data from the backend (provider) and display the result of this data on the UI quickly. WEF did a lot of work for you. If we were to build more operations, such as add, update, delete, and so on, WEF would have taken care of that as well for you. Now that you have created the two models, it would be even easier and faster to add the other operations.

Summary

In this chapter, we presented and discussed the Service Consumer – Service Provider paradigm implemented by WEF. In Version 7, WEF has greatly enhanced and strengthened the builders, which support this paradigm. Implementing the Service Consumer/Provider pattern makes the development of applications utilizing WEF not only easier but also well organized.

In addition to the features we have seen on this simple example, WEF offers many other service builders, which enable developers to work separately on the same application. This way, while certain developers focus on the backend side of the applications retrieving and manipulating data, UI developers can work on the UI with stub data and well-defined operations without interfering with the work being done in the backend.

9
Invoking Web Services

In the previous chapter, we introduced the concepts of the Service Consumer and Service Provider layers. We are sure that the topics we covered in the Service Provider section left you wanting to learn more, especially about the capabilities of WEF to access and manipulate backend data. Good for you, because this is exactly what we will cover in this chapter.

We dedicate this entire chapter to working with the Web Service Call builder as well as all the related builders and techniques that you will find in a commercial grade WEF project accessing data and business logic through web services. So, we go beyond the basics of simply describing the Web Service Call builder.

You will learn about the following concepts:

- Portal projects leveraging web services
- The Web Service Call builder
- Web service inputs from other builders
- Data transformation and manipulation of service response
- Transform builders
- IXml Java interface

To help you better understand the Web Service Call builder and how it relates to other builders in the Service Provider model, we will create a sample model as we progress throughout this chapter.

Portal projects leveraging web services

Before diving into the technical details of web services in your models, we find it important to provide some background information about what happens before the WEF development team gets to the point where they will be consuming the defined web services.

The implementation of a **service-oriented architecture (SOA)** has become standard throughout most enterprises. As such, web services are an integral part of any SOA project.

In order to successfully deliver a project involving such architecture, a tight coordination between all the technology stacks is a must.

As we have seen in chapters four and five, in analysis and architectural design; portal SOA and WEF architects worked together on the specifications and integration of the SOA layer with the portal layer.

In this brief section, we will focus on the existing relationship between the WEF development team and the other teams directly involved in the delivery of our Portal Solution. As the creation and maintenance of web services is handled by the Services team, it makes sense that we work directly with them to identify the required service operations and their XML schemas, both for requests and responses.

Prior to discussing with the Services team, the WEF architect would have already identified the data elements required to build the portlets. The WEF architect would also have grouped these data elements together in a manner that makes sense from the navigation flow perspective.

Once the WEF architect identifies the data elements that will be required to develop the portlets, the architect would work closely with the Services team to convey such elements to them. The Services team would then try to identify existing services that have already been developed or work with them to define new services.

Once the Services team has identified the required service operations, they would then make available a **Web Services Description Language (WSDL)**, which contains the service operations to be used in our development.

Upon availability of the concrete WSDL, the WEF development team can start the development of their Service Provider models.

The Web Service Call builder

Let's take a look at the Web Service Call builder.

The Web Service Call builder inputs vary depending upon the web service type you are invoking. The web services can be pure SOAP services or WSDL-based SOAP services.

In our example, we will work with a WSDL-based SOAP service. For this type of service, the Web Service Call builder presents the following sections to capture inputs:

- **Properties**
- **General** (This section is not labeled in the builder)
- **Request Parameters**
- **Request SOAP Headers**
- **Service Information**
- **WS-Security**
- **Advanced**

The **Properties** section is common to all builders. Besides that, this builder has an unmanned section identified as **General**. This section captures the builder name and the WSDL URL.

> **Web Service Multiple Operations**: WEF offers another builder to enable you to invoke web service. The Web Service Multiple Operations builder. While the Web Service Call builder enables you to specify one operation per builder, the Multiple Operations builder enables you to invoke all the operations described in a WSDL. In addition to offering the features available in the regular Web Service Call builder, it also offers the features available in both the Service Definition and the Service Operation builders.

Let's examine the content of these different sections. Please keep in mind that in order to expose all these sections and all their applicable inputs, you need to provide a valid WSDL in the WSDL URL input and click on the **Fetch WSDL** button. In the next section, we will work together to create and access a WSDL from our sample model.

General

In this section, you enter the builder call name as well as the WSDL URL. It is also possible to point to a local file WSDL.

> To improve regeneration performance, import the WSDL into your project and point to this file from the Builder input.

Request Parameters

Once you provide a valid WSDL and click on the **Refresh/fetch WSDL** button, the input fields for the other sections of this builder are automatically filled out. In this section, you can choose the operation you want to invoke. If the selected operation takes inputs, then the operation input fields will be displayed. If you desire so, here you can indicate that you want WEF to create the input variable to be populated before you invoke the service.

Request SOAP Header

If the operation you have selected requires a SOAP header, then WEF automatically displays this field. Unfortunately, this header variable is not exposed in the WebApp tree, and you cannot select it through the **Choose Reference** dialog box.

> You should create a method to populate a variable of the XML schema type defined for the SOAP header request. This will give you more flexibility to provide this input.

Service Information

This section is informational only. It does not contain any inputs. It displays information about the current service.

WS-Security

This section provides the required inputs to apply security to web services as defined by the OASIS WS-Security specification. While the WS-Security specification covers all aspects of security, this section makes provision only to its authentication aspect. Two signature formats are provided here—LTPA binary token and Username token. The LTPA binary token relates to the custom-defined token signature model. If you check the Username token input, then you are presented with further inputs related to this authentication model.

If you are exchanging SOAP messages between trusted peers, you do not need to implement security at all. If this is a valid alternative to your SOAP communication, this approach should be favored as it reduces complexity and improves performance.

Advanced

The inputs exposed in the **Advanced** section enable you to provide a variety of common inputs such as overrides to the existing service, additional SOAP headers if required, basic authentication information, and so on.

The override inputs are very handy, especially when you are doing testing with mock services and need to point to different services.

Web service inputs from other builders

Now that we have given you some background information and described the input sections of a Web Service Call builder, we can look at the builders normally used in a Service Provider model, which invokes a web service.

As you have observed on the Web Service Call input sections we have previously described, this builder offers a significant number of inputs. Because of that, you should consider using a set of builders to provide these inputs through indirect reference. This will add clarity and elegance to your model.

In this regard, it is important for you to define a pattern to be implemented by every service provider and every call to the service operations.

The following are some areas where other builders can help:

- Assigning header request inputs
- Assigning service input values
- Creating XML schemas
- Manipulating the response values

We will cover and discuss these areas as we build our example model.

Sample model

You, being such a great developer or modeler, must be eager to work on a sample to put in practice everything you have read so far. So, let's stop talking and start modeling.

While the model we describe here is available for download, you are encouraged to create your own model so that you can gain more experience with the tool. This model can be downloaded from `http://www.packtpub.com/support`. The file is named as `Chapter 9 Complete Models.zip`.

Before you can start with your example, you will need a WSDL document. We will not type the WSDL in here because it would take more than two pages to hold it. You can download it from `http://www.packtpub.com/support`. The file is named `Investor.wsdl`.

This sample WSDL contains one single operation named `getInvestors`. This operation takes one input named `VAULT_TYPE`. It also requires a request header.

It returns an element of the `INVESTORS` type. This element is comprised of a collection of elements of the `INVESTORS` type. A fault element of the `FaultDetail` type is also returned. As you can see, although our sample WSDL is simple, it is also quite complete.

Let's copy this WSDL to a directory in our project. This is a practice recommended not just for this sample, but even for your real projects. Under the `WEB-INF` directory, create a folder named `wsdl`. Under this folder, create another folder named `wsdl`. Copy the downloaded WSDL into this folder.

In accordance to what we have described in the *Web service inputs from other builders* section, the following screenshot shows what our model is going to look like concerning the builder calls. The following screenshot shows a list of builder calls for invoking a web service:

#	Name	Type
⊟ 1	Get Investos Operation	Comment
	investors_SD	Service Definition
	getInvestors_WSC	Web Service Call
	getInvestorsInput_VAR	Variable
	rqHeader_VAR	Variable
	populateRqHeader_AL	Action List
	getInverstos_AL	Action List
	getInvestors_SO	Service Operation
⊟ 9	Data	Comment
	investorsResponse_VAR	Variable

Let's create our Service Provider model to access our web service. Perform the following steps:

1. Open the A2Z WEF project, and then create a new empty model named `investorsPr`. This model should be created in the `models\chapter09\data` directory. This path can be specified in the **Save New Model** dialog box under the **Enter** or **Select the folder** input field.

2. Add the first builder to this model. This is going to be a Service Definition builder. Provide the following inputs:

   ◦ **Name: investors_SD**

   ◦ **Make Service Public**: Checked

3. Expand the **Testing Support** section, and provide the following inputs:

   ◦ **Add Testing Support**: Checked

   ◦ **Generate Main**: Checked

4. Click on **OK**.

5. Now add a Web Service Call builder to your model. Provide the following inputs:

   ◦ **Name: getInvestors_WSC**

   ◦ **WSDL URL: /WEB-INF/wsdl/Investor.wsdl**

6. Click on the **Refresh/fetch WSDL** button.

7. Once the WSDL is fetched by this builder, it should automatically populate both the **Request Parameters** and the **Service Information** sections.

8. For the **Request Parameters** section, please provide the following inputs:

   ◦ **Operation: 1: getInvestors - SOAP-document**

   ◦ **AutoCreate Input Vars**: Checked

   ◦ By checking AutoCreate Input Vars, WEF will populate the **RequestParameter (VaultInput)** field. This is a temporary step just so WEF can create all the artifacts related to the Web Service Call builder. We will modify this value soon.

9. Click on the **Apply** button.

Now let's take a little break from this builder and leverage the artifacts created by it so that we can create other elements we need for our model.

As we have mentioned previously, we need to add some builders, which will help us develop a clean, efficient, and maintainable model. The first of such builders will be a variable to provide the service input. By doing so, you will be able to provide this variable for the **RequestParameter** input instead of requesting that WEF should create it for you.

So, let's create this variable. Perform the following steps:

1. Add a Variable builder to your model.

2. Name it as getInvestorsInput_VAR.

3. For type, click on the picker button. In the **Choose Variable Type** dialog box, expand **getInvestors_WSC_WSDLSchema_2**.

4. Expand the **elements** node and select **VaultInput**.

The following screenshot shows the selection described in step 3:

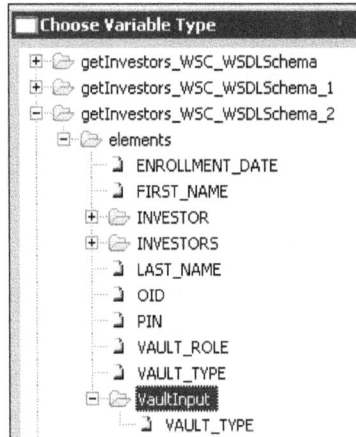

The value for the type input should be getInvestors_WSC_WSDLSchema_2/ VaultInput.

Continue working on the same Variable builder, and perform the following steps:

1. Click on **Create Sample Data**.

2. The initial value area should get populated.

3. Change this variable to provide a meaningful input.

4. Delete the string value, and type in **GOLD** for the **VAULT_TYPE**.

5. Click on **OK** and save your model.

For the sake of simplicity, our service takes only one single input. However, you would better appreciate this extra step if you are dealing with a more complex input.

As our service requires a header request, we will use the same approach to create a variable to take care of this task for us.

Add another Variable builder to your model and perform the following steps to provide the proper inputs to this variable:

1. Name it as rqHeader_VAR.

2. For type, click on the picker button.

3. In the **Choose Variable Type** dialog box, expand the **getInvestors_WSC_WSDLSchema_1**.

4. Expand the **types** node and select **rqHeader**.

   The value for the type input field should be `getInvestors_WSC_WSDLSche-ma_1/RqHeader`.

5. Click on the **Create Sample Data** button. Update the elements with the following code snippet:

```
<RqHeader
   xmlns="http://A2Z.bullionbank.com
   /2012/investors/WebService/Customers/header">
   <DateAndTimeStamp>2012-07-04T12:34:00.000</DateAndTimeStamp>
   <UUID>740925</UUID>
   <ESBUUID>AI867</ESBUUID>
   <ServiceName>Investors_WS</ServiceName>
   <OperationName>getInvestors</OperationName>
   <isStateful>YES</isStateful>
   <isLongRunning>NO</isLongRunning>
   <KeyFieldID>1200</KeyFieldID>
</RqHeader>
```

6. Click on **OK**.

Now, let's revisit our Web Service Call builder.

1. Open this builder and locate the **RequestParameter (VaultInput)** input field. Use the picker to select **getInvestorsInput_VAR**. This field should have the **${Variables/getInvestorsInput_VAR}** value. This means that, before invoking this web service, we will populate this variable with the input passed in from the UI model.

2. Our next step is to address Request SOAP Header. Here, we will take a slightly different approach. Instead of supplying a variable, we will supply the return of a method call. This is a common practice when populating header request, because you need to capture numerous values from different sources. This process would likely be done in a Java method. However, to keep things simple, here we will use an Action List builder to perform this task for us. So, add an Action List builder to your model. Name it as `populateRqHeader_AL`. The other inputs should be set as follows:

   ◦ **Return Type: IXml**

   ◦ **XML type: getInvestors_WSC_WSDLSchema_1/RqHeader**

   ◦ **Actions: Return!${Variables/rqHeader_VAR/RqHeader}**

   Next, we have given further instructions to provide the return type.

3. Use the picker to select **Special**, then select **Return**.

4. Click on the picker button again.

5. Select **Variables**.

6. Select **rqHeader_VAR**.

7. Select **rqHeader**.

8. Click on **OK**.

Now that we have our method, we can return to our Web Service Call builder and provide the value for the **rqHeader(rqHeader)** input value. This input is located under the **Request SOAP Headers** section of the Web Service Call builder. Perform the following steps:

1. Click on the picker to select the Method Call you just created.

2. Click on the picker **Method Call**.

3. Select **populateRqHeader_AL**.

Your input should look like **${MethodCall/populateRqHeader_AL}**.

For now, we are done with our Service Call builder. The following screenshot shows what your Web Service Call builder should look like so far. It shows the inputs for the Web Service Call builder:

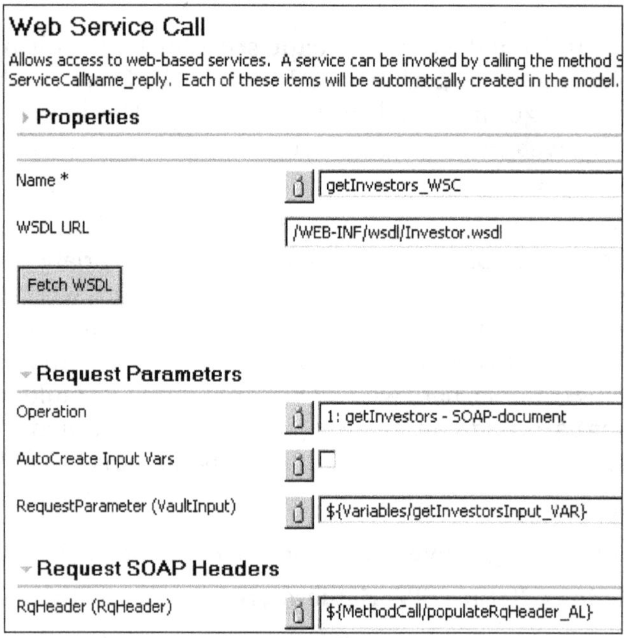

Click on **OK**, and save your model.

Now we are ready to create a method, which will actually invoke your web service. Prior to invoking the web service though, we need to populate both the input variable and the header variable so that the service operation can supply the proper input to the web service operation. Perform the following steps to do so:

1. Add an Action List builder to your model.
2. Name it as **getInvestors_AL**.
3. Expand the **Arguments** section and add one argument named **VAULT_TYPE**.
4. For type, select **String**, which you should select from the drop-down menu.
5. For return type, select **IXml**.
6. For type, pick **getInvestors_WSC_WSDLSchema_2/INVESTORS**.

In the **ActionList** window, we are going to perform the actions already described. The following screenshot shows the statements you should provide. Use the picker in each line to select the statements shown in the following screenshot:

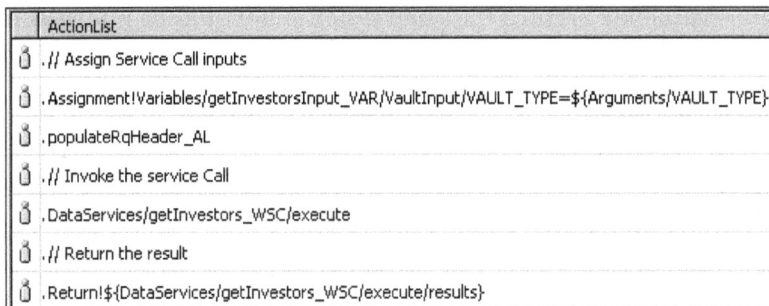

ActionList
.// Assign Service Call inputs
.Assignment!Variables/getInvestorsInput_VAR/VaultInput/VAULT_TYPE=${Arguments/VAULT_TYPE}
.populateRqHeader_AL
.// Invoke the service Call
.DataServices/getInvestors_WSC/execute
.// Return the result
.Return!${DataServices/getInvestors_WSC/execute/results}

To perform both, the variable assignment and selecting the return value, please remember that you need to open the Special node in the **Select Action** dialog box. Click on **OK** on this Action List builder, and save this model.

Lastly, let's add a Service Operation builder so that you can invoke this operation from a UI model.

Add a Service Operation builder, and supply the following inputs:

- **Data Service: investors_SD**
- **Operation Name: getInvestors_SO**
- **Action to Call: getInvestors_AL**

- **Input Structure Handling**: Use Structure from called action
- **Input Field Mapping**: Automatic
- **Result Structure Handling**: Use Structure from called action
- **Result Field Mapping**: Automatic

This should suffice. Click on **OK**. Save your model.

Great! You are ready to run your model and get data from your web service.

Oh no! Hold on! I just realized that this service is not running on any server. Hummmm… this is a big problem.

Ok, let's find a work-around to this problem. What if we create a variable that enables us to simulate the call to our web service? Yes, that should work. I recall seeing an input in the Web Service Call which points to a dummy result. Open the **Advanced** section of the Web Service Call builder. Scroll down and locate the **Dummy/Stub** result input. Perfect. You just found the solution to our problem. This input works in such a way that if a value is provided here, WEF does not make a call to the specified web service. Instead, it returns the value provide in this field.

So, let's create a variable to return the same result that would be returned if we were making the request from a real server.

Add a Variable builder and supply the following inputs:

- **Name**: investorsResponse_VAR
- **Type**: getInvestors_WSC_WSDLSchema_2/INVESTORS
- **Initial value**: Add the following XML content to your variable:

```
<INVESTORS
    xmlns="http://A2Z.bullionbank.com/
    2012/investors/WebService/Customers">
  <INVESTOR>
    <OID>223344559</OID>
    <ENROLLMENT_DATE>03/29/2012</ENROLLMENT_DATE>
    <FIRST_NAME>Bill</FIRST_NAME>
    <LAST_NAME>Clarck</LAST_NAME>
    <PIN>thePin@83</PIN>
    <VAULT_ROLE>GOLD</VAULT_ROLE>
  </INVESTOR>
  <INVESTOR>
    <OID>121314159</OID>
    <ENROLLMENT_DATE>02/20/2011</ENROLLMENT_DATE>
```

```
        <FIRST_NAME>Warren</FIRST_NAME>
        <LAST_NAME>Smith</LAST_NAME>
        <PIN>i4GotIt</PIN>
        <VAULT_ROLE>GOLD</VAULT_ROLE>
    </INVESTOR>
    <INVESTOR>
        <OID>213141519</OID>
        <ENROLLMENT_DATE>01/29/2011</ENROLLMENT_DATE>
        <FIRST_NAME>Kim</FIRST_NAME>
        <LAST_NAME>Stones</LAST_NAME>
        <PIN>cyberGold</PIN>
        <VAULT_ROLE>GOLD</VAULT_ROLE>
    </INVESTOR>
</INVESTORS>
```

The content of this variable is what will be returned when we invoke our service.

Because this variable is not part of the code, we should separate it from the other builders. Add a Comment builder to your model by right-clicking on the variable you just created and selecting **Insert Comment**. Name it as **Data**. Click on **OK**, and save your model.

Perfect! Now we are ready to test our model and invoke our web service.

As you recall, when you added the Service Definition builder, you checked the **Add Testing Support** input. This is a great feature, which WEF provides to enable you to test your service without having to create a UI for that.

Run your model. WEF should display a page entitled **Operations for Service investors_SD**. It should contain only one link because we have only one service operation. Click on this link. WEF presents a form with an input for Vault Type. This is the input to our web service. Although all the records we have created contain **GOLD** as **VAULT_TYPE**, we will always get the same data regardless the input we provide here. So, type **GOLD** for input. WEF should present the table as shown in the following screenshot:

Oid	Enrollment Date	First Name	Last Name	Pin	Vault Role
223344559	03/29/2012	Bill	Clark	thePin@83	GOLD
121314159	02/20/2011	Warren	Smith	i4GotIt	GOLD
213141519	01/29/2011	Kim	Stones	cyberGold	GOLD

Back

Dummy variables – The utilization of a dummy variable as we have described here might be seen as a solution not feasible to be used in a real project. However, this is a technique that can save you a lot of time when you are in the initial phase of the development of your Provider model. As development evolves, you probably would use a tool to provide mock response until you are ready to switch to the real service.

Handling SOAP fault exception – As you notice, our WSDL contains a type for the SOAP fault. In a real project, we would first check the value of the SOAP fault element. If it contains a value, then we would not process the response and would handle the exception gracefully.

Data transformation and manipulation of service response

One of the benefits of a SOA architecture is reusability of services. This means that services designed for one purpose can be reused for other different purposes. Consider the example of a service designed to return list of sales representatives for a given region. This service can be invoked by a portlet, which displays this list to prospect customers. At the same time, HR might use this same service to perform HR-related activities on the sales representatives records.

In the preceding example, if the service originally designed to supply data to the prospect customers portlet can also be used by the HR portlet, then the company can save valuable resources by reusing this service.

While in theory, service reusability is the best thing since the discovery of sliced bread; in reality, it is all common that in order to reuse services throughout projects some adjustments are required.

This adjustment will vary in complexity depending upon how close the existing service meets the requirements for the new consumer. Sometimes you need to convert a response from one XML schema type to another. Sometimes you need to modify the values or apply some business logic before displaying the result.

In order to perform this adjustment or data transformation, WEF provides two means — the transformation builders and the IXml Java interface.

Such data transformation would happen on the Service Provider models. In the sample, we have created an Action List, which returns the response. In the event, a response needs to be manipulated, then such action would take place before returning this data. This transformation would be either by adding transform builders to your model or by making a call to a Linked Java Object, which would use the WEF IXml API to perform this task.

Once transformation is done, the Action List builder would then return the response according to a defined XML schema type.

The transform builders

As the response of a SOAP request is returned in the XML data format, it makes sense to continue using this format throughout the models and all the way through the UI. In doing so, you have a standard way of manipulating data, be it in the provider or in the consumer models.

Due to the paradigm of reusability of services, it is not uncommon to retrieve data from web services, which do not meet 100 percent of the UI requirements. That is, the format of the XML result does not fit the format the UI builders are expecting. Sometimes you need to remove a few fields from this result; in other occasions you might need to modify or merge fields. In summary, some transformation of the web service response might be required.

WEF provides a set of builders to perform such transformation. They are conveniently named Data Transformation builders. These builders provide a quick means of performing the required transformation without the need for coding. The utilization of such builders can accelerate the delivery of your portlets as well as reduce complexity of your code. In fact, you should favor the utilization of these builders as opposed to using the IXml API to perform such transformation. Please refer to the next section to learn more about the IXml API.

These builders can perform activities such as sorting, merging, aggregating, and so on.

The list of the available transform builders is as follows:

- Transform Aggregate
- Transform Combine
- Transform Filter
- Transform Group

- Transform Map
- Transform Merge
- Transform Modify
- Transform Sort

IXml Java interface

Another means to transform XML data in WEF is through the usage of the defined IXml Java interface. This interface would be used in a Java class which would be linked into your model through the usage of a Linked Java Object.

While this interface is simple and easy to use, it is powerful enough to give you the means to perform any data manipulation you need on your response.

We will not cover this topic in this chapter, but you should be aware that this interface is available to you through a Java Class.

Summary

In this chapter, you learned about the Web Service Call builder, its inputs, and how to use it in a Service Provider model.

In addition to the specific details about the Web Service Call builder, we also had the opportunity to discuss about other project-related aspects concerning how WEF fits inside the implementation of a SOA architecture in an enterprise.

We demonstrated the utilization of the Web Service Call builder in a sample model. Besides that, we described how other builders can be used in conjunction with this builder to create a clean and easily maintainable model.

10
Building the Application User Interface

In the previous chapter, you worked close to the services to retrieve and make data available for consumption by the **user interface** (**UI**). As we have seen before, in WEF jargon, the UI is also referred to as the **Service Consumer** layer.

In this chapter, we switch our attention to the UI. We will discuss and demonstrate how WEF can offer tremendous productivity gains while building the application user interface for your portlets. We will look into some techniques to build the UI employing high-level builders.

In this chapter, we will cover the following topics:

- Choosing the right builders to create the UI
- Understanding how WEF builds UI
- Data-driven development approach
- High-level versus low-level builders
- Data Services User Interface builder
- Design pane
- Rich Data Definition builder
- Theme UI builder
- Modifier builders
- Base page in high-level builders
- HTML templates

As you can see from the preceding list, we have a lot to cover in this chapter. In fact, given the richness of WEF UI builders and techniques for building UI, only one chapter is not nearly enough to cover all the nuances of UI-related development. However, we are confident that at the end of this chapter, you will have a good understanding of UI development with WEF.

Choosing the right builders to create the UI

One common question that comes up often when we teach WEF, relates to the task of identifying the right builders to add to a model. The question is—"How do I choose the right builder to add to my model?" This is a fair question. After all, WEF contains more than 160 builders. Let's try to answer this question together.

> The decision regarding which builders to select in your model is not different from any other development framework where developers need to learn the API or available development tools.

To identify the right builders to use in your models, we suggest that you adopt a top-bottom task-oriented approach and match the tasks to builder categories.

Within this approach, we identify the high-level tasks our application needs to perform. These tasks could then be organized into a **task hierarchy**.

Once you identify the tasks to be performed, start at the top-level task, and try to identify the builder category that would contain matching builders to carry on this task.

For instance, if you want to create a Service Provider model to access a database and perform several database operations, you certainly would look into the **Services** category to choose the top-level builders for the task of creating your Service model.

You would then select a Service Definition builder and a Service Operation builder as two top-level builders. You then would move to the next task of identifying the SQL Call builders to be added to your model. For this task, it would make sense to look into the SQL category of builders. From this list, you would then select the builder that performs the initial and topmost task of accessing the database. Once the top-level builder is added to your model, you would then add other builders that perform the low-level tasks identified on your task hierarchy.

The following table briefly demonstrates how this approach can be implemented. The numbered items represent high-level tasks, which map to builder categories.

All defined tasks		Builder category	Builder
1	Create a Service Provider model.	Services	
	Add a Service Definition builder.		Service Definition
2	Interact with the database.	SQL	
	Connect to the database.		SQL Data Source
	Query the database.		SQL Call
	Implement transaction.		SQL Transaction
3	Transform or merge result sets.	Schemas and variables, data transformation	
	Create xsd schema for data structure.		Schema
	Apply transformation.		Transform Merge
4	Expose result as a Service Operation.	Services	
	Add Service Operation.		Service Operation

The following screenshot shows how **Builder Picker** can help in the process of identifying possible builders by category. In this example, the **Services** category has been selected to list all the service-related builders:

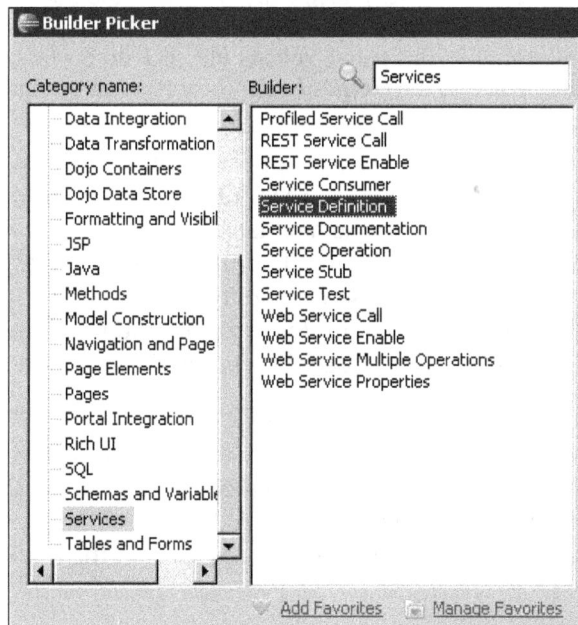

This same top-bottom task-oriented approach can be applied to any other WEF model development activity, including the UI development. What is the top-level task that needs to be performed first in order to develop a UI? In terms of portlet development, everything starts with a page. You might argue that the page itself does not perform any task. That is true, but pages hold all the UI builders in your model. So, this is your starting point.

Now that we have identified the starting point, we should look at **Builder Picker** to see if there is a category that groups together Page builders. Let's explore this together. Open the designer and then open any model residing in your WEF project. Now click on the **Builder Picker** icon. Look at the list at the left-hand side panel of this dialog. There you find a **Pages** category. So, select the **Pages** category. As we are referring to pages, you will notice three page-related builders, namely, **Page**, **Inserted Page**, and **Imported Page**.

Now that we have narrowed our quick exploration to three builders, which one should we choose? Here is where we tell you that you should never be afraid of accessing the help documentation when you are uncertain about your options. The **Builder Picker** dialog box has added a handy panel where it displays a description about the highlighted builder. By reading the help text in this dialog, you will notice that only two builders would fit for this initial top-level task. That would be either the Page or the Imported Page builder.

> The **Related Topics** panel, which is part of the **Builder Picker** dialog box, contains three links. After reading the provided description in this panel, you should click on the first two links to access the **Help Info** panel for the selected builder.

To keep the focus on the discussion of our approach, let's select the **Imported Page** to be added to our model. Now you need to identify the next builders to be added to this page. That is when you move to the next task in the task hierarchy. Which one is the next task? Is it the task of displaying data from the backend? Is it the task of building an input form? Or is it the task of displaying charts? Whatever the next task is, you need to identify the matching builder category and select the top-level builder from that category. This action would be followed by the selection of other low-level builders associated with this category.

In summary, you should create a task hierarchy for the activities you want to perform followed by the identification of the category of builders that match such tasks. Select from that category the top-level builder that will get you started, and use the low-level builders within that category to carry on the low-level tasks.

Understanding how WEF builds UI

We know you are eager to start building the user interface for your portlet. But before we demonstrate how to do so through our examples, we need to cover a few important concepts.

We have already mentioned that WEF offers tremendous productivity gains when building the user interface for your portlets. Let's understand how this is accomplished.

Data-driven development approach

The fastest way to build UI pages and even an entire application is by taking advantage of the data-driven approach implemented by WEF. This approach can be noticed not only in the Service Consumer layer, but also in the Service Provider layer. In the Service Provider layer, WEF inspects backend objects to build numerous artifacts. In this process, the main artifacts created by WEF are the XML schemas.

In the UI layer, WEF uses these XML schemas and other data definition elements to build a representation of the UI it needs to create. This representation includes information about a plethora of elements, such as HTML controls and their attributes, labels, tables, validation rules, layout, error message information, and so on.

In the end, the information extracted from the XML schemas, combined with the inputs provided to related builders, are used to build all the elements required to create a JSP page as well as the Java code and the JavaScript code to support this user interface.

The task of building the JSP page with all its required elements and supporting code is performed by a section of WEF known as **Page Automation Engine**. Page Automation Engine builds the data-related portions of your pages.

Modifying the content created by WEF

Upon creation of your page, the generated JSP pages might have a layout or a behavior that does not match exactly what you intend to build. There are two major approaches you can implement to modify content created by WEF. The first one is by using the Modifier and Enhancer builders. The second one is by modifying the HTML code that WEF relies on to build pages and the application.

Modification through builders and the Design pane

To address this issue, WEF offers a combination of features, which are used after the application is created by WEF.

Some of these features include a set of builders to enable you to modify or enhance the content created by WEF. As you would expect, these builders are conveniently named as **Modifier builders**. In *Chapter 7, Introduction to Web Experience Factory*, you read that builders either add elements to the WebApp tree or modify existing ones. Well, these Modifier builders are a fine example of this mechanism.

Another powerful feature available to modify an application is through the design view. Through the design view, WEF automatically adds and modifies builders, which act on content created by other builders. We will cover these features in the sample model we will build in this chapter.

The following screenshot shows how a page can be enhanced by utilizing two Modifier builders. The form in the left-hand side is created using only the first four builders. The form in the right-hand side is enhanced by adding a Data Field Settings builder and a Display Manager builder. Notice that the enhancements include not only changes to the layout by creating a two-column display and headers, but also the formatting of the input fields such as the currency, date, and check box types:

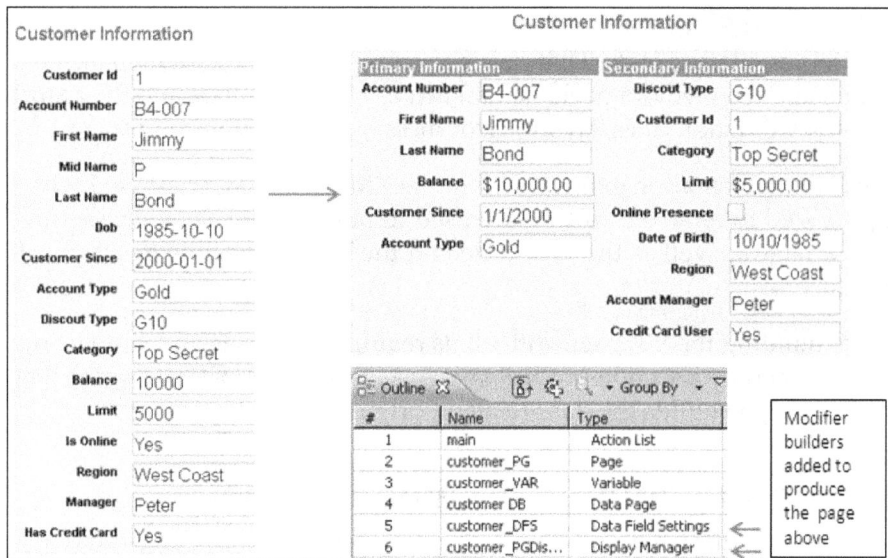

Modification through the HTML code

WEF also enables developers to modify the HTML code to create the desired layout of the pages. For the high-level builders, developer can modify the base pages used by these builders. We will discuss high-level and low-level builders in the next section.

In addition to modifying the base page, you can also modify the HTML template. This approach is less intuitive and requires knowledge of the inner works of HTML templates. You will learn more about HTML templates later, although we will not cover it in detail, because we would need at least one more chapter to cover this topic.

Another mechanism that can be grouped within this **HTML Code Modification** category is a technique by which developers export from the designer HTML elements created by WPF, modify such elements, and then WEF reimports them into the model. We will not be able to cover this technique here.

High-level and low-level builders

Throughout this chapter, you will read references to high-level and low-level builders. This is an abstract concept. Although this concept is widely used in the WEF literature, we have not seen a formal definition for this concept.

So, as an abstract concept, let's derive a definition from the context by which this concept is used, as well as from the knowledge of how builders are created.

Let's start with the low-level builders. **Low-level builders** can be identified as builders that perform very specific tasks—a single unit of work. As a result, they impact only a fragment of your model.

A good example of a low-level builder is the Attribute Setter builder. The whole purpose of the existence of this builder is to set a value for an HTML attribute. We are not implying that this is not a noble and useful task to be performed in the grand schema of building portlets. We recognize that there is greatness in performing such a task, but this builder does not do anything beyond that. Anyway, let's move to high-level builders.

At a first analysis, **high-level builders** can be defined as builders that perform a large number of aggregated tasks in your model. However, if we scratch the surface and look into the technical aspects of certain builders and how they are created, we will see that many builders are created by incorporating and encapsulating functionality from other builder.

Two fine examples of such builders are the Data Service User Interface builder, and the View & Form builder. These builders construct a significant number of features in a model. Behind the scenes, high-level builders invoke other low-level builders to perform an orchestrated work of higher magnitude.

Comparatively, there are many other builders in between the lowest-level builder and the highest-level builder. Take the example of a Data Page builder. You can build all the functionality of a page and everything a Data Page builder creates by using low-level builders. Data Page incorporates all these low-level builders. In this sense, Data Page is a high-level builder compared to the other low-level builders it incorporates. However, the View & Form builder is a higher-level builder when compared to Data Page, because View & Form builder incorporates a Data Page builder call.

The SQL Data Services builder is another example of a high-level builder. This builder encapsulates the functionality of builders such as SQL Data Source, SQL Statement, and the powerful SQL Transform to XML.

> It is an IBM recommendation, captured through WEF best practices articles that, whenever possible, WEF developers should favor a high-level builder in detriment of low-level builders.

The preceding note is a nice transition into our next topic and the creation of our sample model.

Data Service User Interface builder

With WEF, it is possible to create an entire data-driven application with just a few builders. In fact, if we consider the UI segment of the application only, then one single builder can display a result set and a single record from this result set as well as enable you to update, create, and delete records. In addition to performing this operation, this single builder can even take care of pagination and navigation between pages. All these tasks can be performed by the **Data Services User Interface** (**DSUI**) builder alone.

Let's develop an application using this builder. However, before we work with the DSUI builder, we need to create and make available the data we will be exposing in the UI.

Creating a simple database Service Provider model

Let's create a simple Service Provider model to produce the data we need for the UI.

Although we will not spend much time in this section, you still will have the opportunity to see some pretty interesting actions performed by WEF.

1. Before you start this sample, please make sure that your portal server is up and running.

2. Open Eclipse or RAD, and then open the A2Z WEF project we have been using.

3. Before we can do any coding, we need to create a simple XML file to be used by WEF to create a SQL Table for us. Let's create a folder to hold this file. Create a folder named A2Z under WEB-INF. Inside this folder create another folder named xml.

4. Now, you can either download or create this file. If you download it, place it in the folder you just created. The file can be downloaded from http://www.packtpub.com/support. The file is named InvestorsForDB.xml

5. If you want to create this XML file, also do so in the folder we mentioned in the preceding section. Name it as InvestosForDB.xml. The content of this file is as follows:

```xml
<?xml version="1.0" encoding="UTF-8"?>
<INVESTORS xmlns="http://A2Z.com/BullionBank/DB">
    <INVESTOR>
        <OID>01</OID>
        <ENROLMENT_DATE>2011-01-01</ENROLMENT_DATE>
        <FIRST_NAME>Kris</FIRST_NAME>
        <LAST_NAME>Kramer</LAST_NAME>
        <PHONE>305-123-1212</PHONE>
        <PIN>zt1213</PIN>
        <VAULT_ROLE>Gold</VAULT_ROLE>
    </INVESTOR>
    <INVESTOR>
        <OID>02</OID>
        <ENROLMENT_DATE>2011-01-02</ENROLMENT_DATE>
        <FIRST_NAME>Paul</FIRST_NAME>
        <LAST_NAME>Walker</LAST_NAME>
        <PIN>1312al</PIN>
        <PHONE>508-123-5566</PHONE>
        <VAULT_ROLE>Silver</VAULT_ROLE>
    </INVESTOR>
    <INVESTOR>
        <OID>03</OID>
        <ENROLMENT_DATE>2011-01-02</ENROLMENT_DATE>
        <FIRST_NAME>Karla</FIRST_NAME>
        <LAST_NAME>Jones</LAST_NAME>
        <PIN>yu23to</PIN>
        <PHONE>469-111-5467</PHONE>
```

```
        <VAULT_ROLE>Silver</VAULT_ROLE>
    </INVESTOR>
    <INVESTOR>
        <OID>04</OID>
        <ENROLMENT_DATE>2011-01-03</ENROLMENT_DATE>
        <FIRST_NAME>Mary</FIRST_NAME>
        <LAST_NAME>Smith</LAST_NAME>
        <PIN>aa49jk</PIN>
        <PHONE>469-111-5467</PHONE>
        <VAULT_ROLE>Silver</VAULT_ROLE>
    </INVESTOR>
</INVESTORS>
```

This file will be used to create our database table.

6. Create a new empty model named DBInvestorsPr. This model should be created in the models\chapter10\data directory. This path can be specified in the **Save New Model** dialog box under the **Enter** or **Select the Folder** input field.

7. Once the model opens, access the **Outline** panel. In this panel, click on the icon to open the **Builder Picker** dialog box. From the **Category Name** panel, click on the **SQL** category. From the **Builder** panel, select **SQL Table Create**.

8. For builder name, enter **Investors_STC** in the **Name** field.

9. Click on the **Fetch DataSource Names** button. This action should expose all the data sources already configured in your portal server. Click on the drop-down button of the **SQL DataSource** input field. One of the data source names should read **jdbc/CloudscapeForWPF**. Select the **jdbc/CloudscapeForWPF** entry.

10. If this is the first time you are accessing this data source, the Designer will display a message indicating that this is a create-on-demand data source. If that is the case in your system, then click on **Yes**. In doing so, WEF will create this Cloudscape data source on your local portal server. Once again, you need to make sure your portal server is up and running before starting this exercise.

The following screenshot shows the dialog box that might be displayed if you do not have this data source in your server:

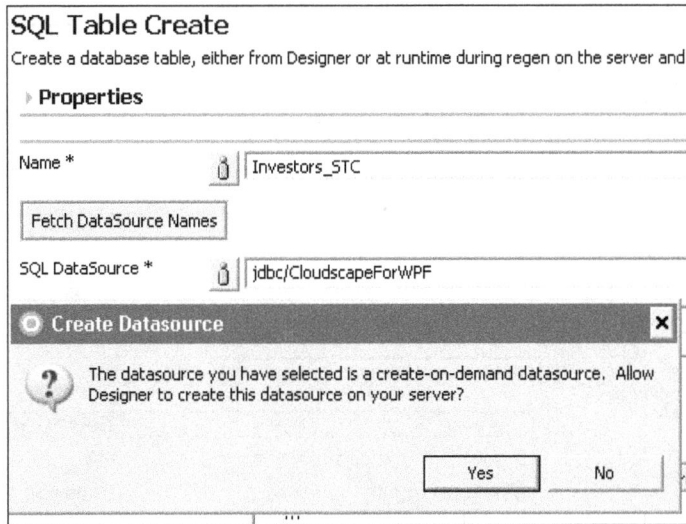

1. Supply the following inputs to this builder:
   ○ **Table Name: Investors_A2Z**
   ○ **Import Data**: Use the picker to select **/WEB-INF/A2Z/ InvestorsForDB.xml** (If the **Choose File** dialog box does not show the A2Z or the xml folder you have just created, you can type in the path to the xml file; will find it.)

2. Click on **Scan Import Data**. This will cause WEF to import the data you have provided in the XML file and display them in the **Table Columns** area. You need to make one small change in this table. Locate the **PHONE** row and set its type to **String**.

3. Enter **OID** in the **Primary Key** input field.

4. Click on the **Create Table** button. You will receive a message stating that the table has been created.

5. Expand the **Advance** section of this builder and check **Enable Testing Support**.

The following screenshot shows what your SQL Create Table builder should look like:

Name *		Investors_STC
Fetch DataSource Names		
SQL DataSource *		jdbc/CloudscapeForWPF
Table Name *		Investors_A2Z
Import Data		/WEB-INF/A2Z/InvestosForDB.xml
Scan Import Data		
Create Primary Key		□
Primary Key *		OID ▼
Table Columns *		

	Name	Type	Source Element
	.OID	Integer	OID
	.ENROLLMENT_DATE	String	ENROLLMENT_DATE
	.FIRST_NAME	String	FIRST_NAME
	.LAST_NAME	String	LAST_NAME
	.PHONE	String ▼	PHONE
	.PIN	String	PIN
	.VAULT_ROLE	String	VAULT_ROLE

1. Click on **OK** and save your model. You are ready to test your model.

2. Run your SQL Provider model by clicking on the green circle with a white arrow inside.

This **Service Test** page is not new to you. You have seen it in the previous chapter. The difference is that now you have five operations as opposed to only one operation in the previous chapter. Click on **listInvestors_STC**. You are going to see the list of investors residing in your database. Play with the other operations.

As you have seen, WEF performs a pretty amazing job by quickly creating all the required artifacts to create this provider model.

Now that we have a Service Provider model that can provide us with data to expose in the UI, we can move to the UI layer to perform the UI-related tasks.

Service builders: We did not add any of the service builders
to our service provider model. The features of these builders are
still required to expose our DBInvestorsPr model as a Service
Provider model. Under the covers, WEF takes care of adding the
required support so that all the operations are made available to
a consumer model. This is done by the SQL Table Create builder,
which under the hood includes many other builders.

Working with the Data Services User Interface builder

DSUI builder is such a powerful and feature-rich builder that we will provide an
overview of this builder and its main input sections before we start building our
sample model.

Data Services User Interface overview

DSUI is a high-level builder that creates a full data-driven application for you.
It is quite impressive, the amount of work performed by this builder. It is a true
testament to software automation and to rapid application development.

DSUI builder looks at all service operations exposed by the Service Consumer
builder and creates all the artifacts necessary to build the UI application. This
includes pages, methods, events, variables, and much more. Most of these features
are implemented by other low-level builders, which are incorporated into the DSUI
builder. Some of these builders include Theme, Data Page, Paging Assistant, Link,
Text Input, Button, Dojo Enhanced Table Modifier, Event, and many other builders.

The following sections describe this builder and a brief explanation about a few of
its inputs.

General

In this section, you select the Service Provider model, as well as the pages you want
this builder to create.

By checking the individual listed pages/operations, DSUI will create all the related
artifacts in your model. This includes pages, HTML and Ajax controls, JSP and Java
code necessary to invoke the services, display data, handle the page layout, and
navigation of your portlet.

The pages available in the **Choose Pages/Operations** input, depend upon the
definition and availability of the service operations from your Service Provider model.

List Page Settings

This section of the builder enables you to control all the aspects related to **List Page** if you have selected this option in the **Choose Pages/Operations** input. Aspects such as paging, number of rows per page, whether you want to have the rows highlighted or not when you move the cursor over a row, whether you want to have columns for update or delete, and other options.

This section has an input to define even if you want to enable resizing and change the order of columns in your list. This is a pretty cool Ajax feature , which can be implemented in your model without requiring you to write one single line of Ajax code.

Settings for the Create and Update Page

This section is available only if you check **Update Page** and **Create Page** in the **Choose Pages/Operations** input. Here you define the action to be executed after you click on the respective buttons to either create or update a record in your table.

Page-to-Page Navigation

This enables you to control how navigation between pages will be implemented. You can specify whether you want page navigation to be implemented by this builder or not. In addition to that, you can specify if you want to display the buttons on an individual basis.

Label Translation Settings

Here, you have the ability to specify the user facing texts to be used by the application. This includes not only the labels for the controls, but also the table headers and the field labels. You can either use a resource bundle where you define the text entries and its corresponding values for each locale and language, or you can directly type these values in the builder input table.

Run time localization is also provided. This feature enables your application to read the localization settings defined in the browser and automatically selects the corresponding resource bundle for the identified locale.

Building the Data Services User Interface sample model

It is time for us to work on our User Interface model. Create a new empty model, and name it as DBInvestors. This model should be created in the models\chapter10\ui directory, in the same A2Z project.

Once your model is created, please switch to the **Outline** view.

Add a Service Consumer builder to this model. Name it as `Investor_SC`. For the **Provider Model** input, use the picker to select **Chapter10/Data/DB_InvestorPr**. Leave **Add All Provider Operations** input checked. Click on **OK** and save your model.

Now, we are going to add a second builder to our UI model. Add a Data Services User Interface builder to this model. You can search for this builder by entering **Data Services** in the search input box of the **Builder Picker** dialog box.

Provide the following inputs:

General

- **Name**: Investor_DSUI
- **Data Service**: Investor_SC
- **Choose Page/Operations**: Select **all pages**
- **Use Theme**: Checked

List Page Settings

- **Paged Data Display**: Checked
- **Rows per Page**: 5
- **Enable Client-side Column resize and reorder**: Checked
- **Enable Row Highlighting**: Checked
- **Make Column a Link to Details Page**: Checked
- **Choose which Column**: Select OID
- **List Page to Update Page**: No Navigation to Update Page
- **Add Delete Column on List Page**: No Delete Column

Settings for the Create and Update Page

- **Action After Update Operation**: Go to Details Page for that record
- **Action After Create Operation**: Return to the previous page

Page to Page Navigation

- **Control All Navigation buttons**: Include all the navigation buttons

Label Translation Settings

You can leave all the inputs to its default values in this section. Just inspect the key/text table in this section to be familiar with what WEF is giving you in terms of user facing texts.

We are done with this builder. Click on **OK,** and save your model.

Let's run this model to take a look at the application created by WEF. Run your model by clicking on the green circle with a white arrow inside it.

You should be able to see the list page as shown in the following screenshot:

1 - 4 of 4		Page 1				Previous	Next
Oid	Enrollment Date	First Name	Last Name	Phone	Pin	Vault Role
1	2011-01-01	Kris	Kramer	305-123-1212	zt1213	Gold
2	2011-01-02	Paul	Walker	508-123-5566	1312al	Silver
3	2011-01-02	Karla	Jones	469-111-5467	yu23to	Silver
4	2011-01-03	Mary	Smith	469-111-5467	aa49jk	Silver

Show: 5 | 10 | 20 | 50 | 100 | **All** items   Jump to page [1] of 1   Previous | Next

Create

Let's explore all the features generated by WEF in this page.

Paging

In your DSUI builder, you specified that you wanted paging support in the **List Page Settings** section. As a result, WEF added the top and bottom portion of the application with paging information.

At the top of the table, it displays the current counter for the initial record, last record, and total number of records. It also displays the page the application is at and the previous and next links. The link is disabled because we have only four records, which is one record short of the number of records per page you have specified in your builder.

At the bottom part of the page, you see the result set navigation links. You also see a **Jump to page** input text box. WEF has not only built it for you, but also provided even data validation for this field. Confirm that you cannot type any letter in this field.

Another interesting aspect of the DSUI builder is that, if you decide to change the number of records per page, all you need to do is to open the DSUI builder and enter the new value in the **Rows per Page** input field, save the application, and the software automation capability of WEF will take care of everything for you. Try it now. Change the current value of this input field from **5** to **2**. Click on **OK** in the DSUI builder, save the model, and run it again to see the changes. See how the previous and next result set navigation links are enabled now.

Table

The table you just created also contains some neat features. Let's start by the row highlighting. Move the cursor over the rows. As you can see the rows change to a dark blue as a consequence of the mouse over action. Once again, with the builder technology, all it takes is one check mark to incorporate this feature to the application.

You also noticed that the **OID** column is a link. Click on this link. It takes you to the record detail page. Click the **Back** button to return to the list page.

Now, here is something pretty cool. Click and hold on the header of the **Pin** column and drag it to the left in front of the **Phone** column. Now release the mouse. As you noticed, the **Pin** column moved to the new position. You just saw your application performing a nice Dojo implementation without having to write one single line of Dojo code.

Update

To see the update feature, click on one of the links. On the **view record** page, click on the **Edit** button. Modify this record and click on **Submit**. You should see the changes on the **record detail** page.

Play with the application so that you get familiar with everything that WEF has generated for you.

Modifying the generated application

Well, WEF did a pretty good job by building a ton of features for us. However, as you further explore the resulting application, you will notice that there are a few things that need to be enhanced, which brings up a great question—"How can you modify the generated application?" You might want to change the application in several ways: you might want to change the layout of the page, or you might want to change the field display, validation, formatting, and so on.

You might also want to change the navigation flow or intercept a form submit action. WEF provides several means by which you can perform such modifications. They are as follows:

- Use the Design panel
- Use the Rich Data Definition builder
- Modify the UI theme
- Add Modifier builders
- Modify the CSS file
- Modify the base pages used by high-level builders
- Modify the HTML templates
- Export and modify the HTML fragments from a model

As you can see, WEF offers several options to enable you to modify, enhance, and adjust your application to your need or likeness. In fact, there are so many options that we will not be able to cover all of them in this chapter.

The preceding list is organized in such a way that the options at the beginning of the list are more common and easier to use. The ones towards the end of the list are more involving and more time consuming.

It is also important to notice that some of these modifications are performed through the designer and modify the application after it is generated. Points one to four from our list in the preceding section are in this category. Points five to seven relate to modifications that you make prior to the generation of the application. As such, you do not work in the user interface design view.

Point eight is a category apart and represents a mix of working through the Designer and the HTML code.

Design panel

The **Design** panel contains a multitude of features that enable you to easily and quickly modify the generated application. The following screenshot shows what the user interface design panel looks like:

To access this panel, click on the **Investor_DSUI** builder, and then click on the **Design** tab at the bottom of the right-hand side panel. By default, neither the palette icon nor the properties are shown.

In order to show the palette icon, in the right-hand side of the panel, you need to click on the little left pointing arrow at the top and rightmost edge of the panel. In order to display content in the **Properties** view, you need to select an item in the **Design** panel. Click on the **First Name** cell to have the **Properties** view populated.

Let's examine these panes. The top part of the UI Designer contains three panes. The left pane shows a graphical representation of the JSP pages, which have been created by the DSUI builder given the operations we have provided. Make sure you click on the **Pages** tab in this pane. Click on each page image to update the **Design** central pane with the graphical representation and layout of the HTML controls, which compose the selected page.

The central panel graphically displays the page elements. WEF has built them using the information from several sources, such as the base HTML pages, HTML template, UI theme, and the action of the Page Automation Engine. You can notice that the pages contain several placeholders marking the location where WEF will build its content. In addition to that, you can notice that the elements are grouped by a concept that the Page Automation Engine identifies as containers.

The rightmost pane is reserved for the cool palette of elements. Well, this is not a vivid or creative name for this palette, but that is how it is identified in the WEF world.

In previous versions of WEF, the current **Builder Picker** dialog box was called **Builder Palette**. The palette of elements groups different builders that can be dragged and dropped into the **Design** pane. You can drop these builders onto specific placeholders or regions in the **Design** pane. When this action is performed, WEF opens the corresponding **Builder Editor** as a dialog.

Lastly, at the bottom part of the designer, you can see the **Properties** view. This view displays input fields related to the selected element at the **Design** pane.

Let's get back to our sample model and use the designer pane to perform modifications on our model. If you refer back to the list page which displays the list of records, you will see that we are displaying the pin number from each investor. Let's hide this column.

Open the designer and then your DBInvestor model. Now click on the **Investor_ DSUI** builder. At the top of the right-hand side pane, click on the **Pages** tab. Select the first page icon, which should be **Investor_DSUIList**. In the center pane at the top, click on the **Design** tab. Now click on the cell representing the **Pin** column. The **Properties** view in the bottom panel shows the field inputs available for this type of element. In this **Properties** view, notice that the first input defines **Page Scope**. Here you define if the inputs you are supplying are to be applied to all pages or only to the page you have selected. For our current example, select **Current Page**. Go ahead and change the **Hide** input to **Hide Always**.

Click on **Apply** in this same view. You will notice that WEF automatically adds a Data Field Settings builder to your model. Save your model and run it. Inspect and confirm that the **Pin** field is no longer displayed on the list page, but make sure that the other pages have not been affected.

The same task you just performed can be performed through another interface. To do so, right-click on a column name in the **Design** pane. Select **Data Field Settings,** and then you can select **Hide** from the available options.

Let's make another modification. Go back to the **Design** view on the same **List Page**. Click on the **OID** cell. In the **Properties** pane at the bottom, for **Page Scope** select **Current Page**. Then change the **Sort** input to **On**, and the **Field Type** input to **Integer**. Click on **Apply**, save the model, and run it again. Notice that now you can sort the rows both in ascending or descending order.

Rich Data Definition builder

Rich Data Definition, also referred to as **RDD**, is a builder that provides means to enrich the definition of the data on which Page Automation Engine operates. RDD is always associated to an XML schema. Any page which references such schema will contain all the definitions made by this RDD.

It is important to notice that RDD does not modify the schema itself; it only provides enhanced information to the Page Automation Engine while it is building the target page.

RDD had a more prominent role in previous versions of WEF. Starting at version 7.0, new builders, for example, **Data Field Settings** are providing more and more features and some of them overlap with RDD and even other Modifier builders. However; I would not say that the best days of RDD are behind it. RDD still can provide valuable services, especially if you define your modifications through the file instead of using the RDD builder interface.

Ok, let's see how this builder works. Let's switch to the **Update** page of our application so that we can work with an input form. Please open the **Investor_DSUI** builder and access the **Design** pane if it is not already open. Click on the **Investor_DSUIUpdate** page in the left-hand side panel. In the central pane, you should see a graphical representation demonstrating the labels, input fields, buttons, and other placeholders from the **Update** page.

Open the **Builder Picker** and type **Rich** in the search input. The second option in the suggested list is **Rich Data Definition**. Select it, and Click on **OK** in this dialog box.

Provide the following inputs:

- **Schema: Investor_SCInvestors_STCUpdateInputs**
- **Data Definition Type: Specify Data Definitions in Builder UI**
- **Base Data Definition File: /WEB-INF/factory/data_definitions/ dojo_base_datadef.xml**

- **Reorder Elements**: Checked
- **Container Element: Investors_STCUpdateInputs**

All the preceding values should be automatically filled out for you when you select the schema. You only need to change the dojo_base_datadef.xml file.

Right now the **Fields** table should show the **OID** field at the bottom of the list. If that is the case, move it to the top of the list. You can either use the up arrow or you can drag-and-drop it to the top. Notice that this task can also be performed through the **Design** pane.

Now, let's change the **OID** field to make it read-only. After all, we do not want to enable users to modify the primary key when they update a record.

In the **Fields** table, click on the **OID** row. The right-hand side panel should be updated to reflect the settings for this field. Check the **Read Only** check box.

Next, we will change the password field so that the application does not show clear text for the **Pin** field. Click on the **PIN** row. On the right-hand side panel, for **Base Data Definition**, select **base_Password**.

Lastly, we will add a dojo calendar picker for the **Enrolment Date** field. Go ahead and click on the **ENROLMENT_DATE** row. On the right-hand side panel, for **Base Data Definition**, select **base_date**.

Click on **OK**, save the model, and run it again.

Click on record number four, and then click on the **Edit** button on the **View** page. The **Update** page should display **OID** as a read-only field and the **Pin** input field should no longer display the real values. If you type in any value in the **Pin** field, the characters will not be displayed as a clear text. Lastly, if you click on the **Enrollment Date** field, the application will display a calendar picker from which you can select a date.

Your **Update** page should look like the following screenshot:

Oid	4
Enrolment Date	1/3/2011
First Name	Mary
Last Name	Smith
Phone	469-111-5467
Pin	●●●●●●
Vault Role	Platinum

Cancel   Submit

Theme builder

Through themes, you can specify CSS files, HTML templates, HTML base files to be used in your model as well as other features, such as Smart Refresh, Progress Indicator, and so on.

Data Page and other high-level builders such as View & Form and our familiar DSUI builder enable you to add theme information to your model. This is accomplished by pointing to a project-level theme file.

For instance, the **General** section of our DSUI builder contains a **Use Theme** input. By default it is checked, which means it uses the theme information that has been specified in a file provided by WEF.

To inspect this file, click on the **Project Explorer** tab and navigate to the **WebContent\WEB-INF\factory\themes** folder. In this folder, you will find four files. Open the first one—**blue_WPF7.uitheme**. As you can see, this file contains instructions that influence several aspects of your model, not only in terms of style, but also layout and features.

It is not difficult to see how themes can help you in the task of modifying the presentation of your application.

In addition to checking or unchecking the **Use Theme** input on the builders we mentioned here, WEF makes available a Theme builder, which can be added to your model. By using this builder, you can overwrite the default project theme as well style elements. If you use the Theme builder, it should precede any other builder that creates pages in your model.

Modifier builders

WEF provides a set of builders identified as **Modifier builders**. Their list is as follows:

- Data Column Modifier
- Data Field Modifier
- Data Hierarchy Modifier
- Dojo Enhanced Table Modifier

As the name implies, Modifier builders modify content added by other builders to your application, or more specifically to the WebApp object.

The first three builders in the preceding list modify content created and managed by the Page Automation Engine. The Dojo Enhanced Table Modifier adds Dojo capabilities to a regular HTML table, and enables you to configure the related settings.

Starting at version 7, WEF provides other builders that do not contain the Modifier adjective in their name, but they do enable you to modify or enhance the content created by Page Automation Engine. A few of these builders are already built into the high-level builders, for example, DSUI.

Except for the Dojo Enhanced Table Modifier, it is fair to say that the other Modifier builders have lost their glamor. Aside from backward compatibility, these builders do not provide more than what the new builders provide.

Modify the base pages used by high-level builders

Another way, in which you can modify content created by WEF is by modifying the base pages used to construct the JSP pages of your application. High-level builders such as View & Form, DSUI, which render data-driven content, use base pages as a starting point. These base pages contain common placeholder tags to identify where WEF should place the content it creates. Therefore, by modifying these base pages, you have the opportunity to influence the construction process and drive the outcome of your final JSP pages.

Let's investigate the base pages used by the DSUI builder. These pages are located in the `WebContent\factory\pages\dsui` folder. Switch to your **Project Explorer** view, and open this folder.

You will notice that there are eight pages in this folder. These are the pages used by the DSUI builder to construct the JSP pages. Now, it might be that not all pages are used in your model. The DSUI builder will add pages only for the pages/operations you have selected in your model.

Open the **list_page.html** page. You should see the content, as shown in the following screenshot:

```
<body>
  <div class="dsui_full_width vf_view_container"
  name="vf_view_container">
    <div class="vf_header" name="vf_header"></div>
    <div class="vf_search_section">
      <span name="search_section"></span>
    </div>
    <div class="vf_view_list" name="vf_view_list">
    <form name="view_form" method="POST">
      <div name="data_placed_here"></div>
      <div class="paging"><span name="paging_buttons">
      </span></div>
      <div class="vf_buttons" name="vf_buttons">
          <span name="back_button"></span>
          <span name="update_button"></span>
          <span name="search_button"></span>
          <span name="extra_button1"></span>
          <span name="extra_button2"></span>
      </div>
      <div class="vf_create_button">
        <span name="create_button"></span>
      </div>
    </form>
    <div class="vf_footer" name="vf_footer"></div>
  </div>
  </div>
</body>
```

You may notice that this page is comprised mostly of **div** and **span** tags.

We can easily infer and associate a few tags with content to be created by the Page Automation Engine. For instance, about the middle of the page, there is a **div** tag named **data_placed_here**. If you guessed that the table, which holds the list data, goes here, you are 100 percent right.

Also, notice the tag named **vf_header** at the beginning of the page as well as the **vf_footer** tag. It is also easy to infer the content they will hold.

> The **list_page.html** page contains various tags, the names of which are preceded by **vf_**, for View & Form. That is because this base page is reusing many of the tags originally defined in the View & Form base page.

Now, if you want to modify elements in this base page, you would not do so in it. It is advisable that you create a new page and copy the contents of this page into your new page.

Once you have created a new page, you now need to instruct the builder you are using to point to your newly created page and not the default page used by WEF.

For the DSUI builder, the page to be used as a base page is defined in the UI theme file. So, you would need to add a Theme builder to your model and use one of the techniques available to point to your base page file. One technique you can use is to create a new theme file through the Theme builder. Be aware that the default UI theme files are comprised of a chain of base UI theme files. For instance, the base list page for the DSUI builder is defined in `wpfbase.uitheme` located in the `WEB-INF\factory\themes` folder. The `wpfbase.uitheme` files is extended by the `blue.uitheme` file, which in turn is extended by the `blue_WPF7.uitheme` file.

It is important to emphasize that you should not rename any of the tags defined in the base files. If you do so, your DSUI builder will not work properly.

Now, let's get back to the modifications you can do to a base page. Basically, you can add new tags or relocate existing tags within a page. It is very unlikely that you would remove existing tags as you can control elements you do not want to display from the builder. In addition to that, leaving unused span tags on a page should not have any negative impact on the rendering of the page.

For the add action, a good example would be the need for a tag to indicate the location for an image and/or a header text. Such tags could be added right above the `vf_view_container` div tag. Another example in this same category would be the action of adding a new tag to display disclaimer note at the bottom of the page. Such tag could be added immediately above the body closing tag.

Concerning moving tags, let's refer to another page for a better example. Please open the `details.html` page in the same `dsui` folder. In the middle of this page, you will find a `div` tag named `vf_buttons`. At this current position, these buttons are displayed right below the area where the details about a record are shown. If you want to move these buttons so that they are shown above the record area, then you should move the entire block represented by the `div` tag so that it will be located above the `vf_fields` div tag.

Remember that once you modify and save a base page, you need to click on **Apply** or **OK** button of the builder that is using that page so that its new content can be read by the builder.

HTML Templates in WEF

HTML templates in WEF are anything but what you would traditionally think of templates.

Whenever someone reads about HTML templates related to a Web design tool, they quickly associate it with code fragments to be used as base or a starting point for creating HTML pages.

In the WEF world, **HTML template** is an HTML page containing powerful set of instructions to the Page Automation Engine. These instructions define how to build a final JSP page in your model. In that sense, the information placed on an HTML template page needs to have meaningful value to the Page Automation Engine. It needs to understand how Page Automation will build a page based on such instructions.

The following screenshot shows an excerpt of an HTML template:

```html
<table class="displayPageTable" cellpadding="3"
    cellspacing="1" name="OuterTable">
 <HTMLWRAPPER name="PageContentsContainer">
  <HTMLWRAPPER name="DisplayGroupWrapper">
    <HTMLWRAPPER name="LabelContainer">
    <tr name="DisplayGroupLabel">
      <td colspan="2" height="25"
      class="sectionLabelCell" nowrap>
      <span name="LabelText" class="sectionLabel">
      Section Label
      </span></td>
    </tr>
    </HTMLWRAPPER>
    <HTMLWRAPPER name="GroupContainer">
      <HTMLWRAPPER name="DisplayGroup">
        <!-- Begin: Data display fields -->
        <HTMLWRAPPER name="DataContainer">
          <tr name="DisplayField" class="DisplayFieldRow">
            <td class="labelCell" align="right" valign="top" nowrap>
               
            <span name="FieldLabel" class="label">
            Field Label
            </span></td>
            <td width="100%" class="outputDataCell" valign="top">
            <span name="FieldElement" class="outputData">
            Field Value
            </span></td>
          </tr>
        </HTMLWRAPPER>
        <!-- End: Data display fields -->
      </HTMLWRAPPER>
    </HTMLWRAPPER>
  </HTMLWRAPPER>
  <!-- End: DisplayGroupWrapper -->
```

Some developers find HTML templates over-complex and counter-intuitive. Whether this is true or not, whoever takes up on the challenge of building or modifying HTML templates in WEF does need to have a thorough and comprehensive understanding of how its instructions are interpreted and manipulated by the Page Automation Engine.

At the same time that HTML templates are complex, they are also potent means by which developers can modify and enhance the application built by WEF.

The default HTML template contains section responsible for building list tables, record view, and forms for given data structures defined by schemas or other data definition means.

Builders such as Data Page, View & Form, DSUI all use HTML templates. You can reference them either directly through the builder or through the UI theme files. The default HTML templates used by WEF are located in the `WebContent\factory\ html_template` folder. You can open and inspect the `gridtable.html` file. This template is extensively used by the high-level builders.

In contrast to the Modifer builders and other builders, which modify the application or page after it is constructed into the WebApp object, HTML template influences the process before and during the creation of the WebApp object.

Summary

In this chapter, you learned how to build the user interface portion of your application.

You worked with the Data Service User Interface builder to quickly construct an entire application.

We also showed you how to modify and enhance an application created by WEF.

Concerning the ability to modify your application, we looked at the options provided by specialized builders as well as the HTML code modification option represented by modifying base pages and the HTML templates.

11
The Dojo Builders and Ajax

In this chapter, we will look into the Dojo capabilities and the Ajax techniques available through WEF.

In the previous chapter, you have already seen how WEF utilizes Dojo to accomplish many common tasks, for example, displaying tabular data. In fact, most of the high-level builders make extensive usage of the Dojo framework.

A few of the topics we will cover in this chapter are as follows:

- What is Dojo and Ajax
- The benefits of using Dojo and Ajax in portal development
- The Dojo and Ajax related builders
- **Dojo Rich Text Editor (RTE)** sample model
- Dojo Tree sample model

This chapter starts with some concepts about Dojo, Ajax, and how they work in portal. However, the majority of this chapter will be spent working on two sample models to demonstrate how models can take advantage of these technologies.

What is Dojo and Ajax

It is impossible to talk about Dojo without making reference to Ajax. Before we define and discuss these technologies, let's briefly investigate the challenges encountered by web applications as well as portal applications.

The problem

Dynamic web applications heavily rely on the Application Server to maintain a user session. The interaction with the user and consequently the session maintenance is performed through the processing of request and response objects leading to the rendering of a full web page. This process needs to be done synchronously.

Throughout the session life of a web application, there can be many requests to return the same page, but with small changes. This brings us to the core of the problem. Even for the smallest changes, traditional web applications require a full page reload.

Concerning Portal, this limitation is even more problematic because in order to respond to changes to update the content of one portlet, all the portlets on a page need to go through the render and action phases. This page reload action can consume valuable Portal Server resources.

The solution

Enter Ajax and Dojo. **Ajax** stands for **Asynchronous JavaScript and XML**. Dojo is a toolkit or framework based on open source JavaScript library. Please refer to the Dojo Foundation site for further information (`http://dojofoundation.org/projects/dojo`) and the Dojo Toolkit site (`http://dojotoolkit.org/`).

Ajax techniques and the Dojo framework can provide an efficient solution, which reduces the workload on servers at the same time that it enhances the user experience. In short, this is accomplished primarily through the ability to make asynchronous requests to the server to avoid a full page refresh. By not requiring full page refresh, web applications can refresh only specific regions of the page.

The benefits of using Dojo and Ajax in portal development

As far as IBM WebSphere Portal Server is concerned, Ajax provides numerous techniques that are extensively used by portal to manage users interactions with portlets. For instance, by the utilization of Ajax, a portal page does not need to build and include the **Portlet Menu** option when rendering such page. By asynchronous calls, the menu can be requested on demand, making the portal page aggregation process lighter and consequently making the rendering of the page faster.

Concerning portlet development, developers can leverage both Ajax techniques and the Dojo framework to create rich portlets that perform well and incorporate attractive Web 2.0 concepts.

The Dojo and Ajax related builders

WEF offers a multitude of Dojo and Ajax related builders. Through these builders, WEF developers can build rich interface portlets without having a deep understanding of the Dojo Toolkit or even every available Ajax technique.

The list of Dojo and Ajax related builders ranges from simple Dojo Checkbox and Tooltip builders to richer builders such as the Dojo Data Grid builder, the Dojo Accordion Container builder, and the Dojo Tree builder.

The following screenshot shows the list of these builders, which are categorized by WEF as **Rich UI builders**:

Ajax Region	Dojo Enable
Ajax Type-Ahead	Dojo Enhanced Table Modifier
Border	Dojo Form Dialog
Breadcrumbs	Dojo Hover Tab Container
Calendar Picker	Dojo Inline Edit
Client Event Handler	Dojo Lightbox
Client JavaScript	Dojo Page Element
Content Launch Action	Dojo Progress Indicator
Dojo Accordion Container	Dojo Rich Text Editor
Dojo Animation	Dojo Slider
Dojo Border Container	Dojo Tab Container
Dojo Check Box	Dojo Title Pane
Dojo Data Grid	Dojo Tooltip
Dojo Data Store	Dojo Tree
Dojo Date/Time Picker	Dynamic Validation
Dojo Drag Source	HTML Event Action
Dojo Drop Down Button	Theme
Dojo Drop Target	XML to JSON Converter

Well, at this point, we should move to build a sample to demonstrate the usage of a few Dojo builders. In addition to demonstrating the Dojo builders, you will also have the opportunity to look into a few Ajax techniques employed by WEF to build a rich portlet at the same time that we avoid full page refresh.

Actually, we will build two examples. The first example is a model, which enables users to log messages through the Dojo Rich Text Editor and submit it to be displayed at another region of the same page. This happens without a page refresh. This sample demonstrates the utilization of the following builders and techniques:

- Dojo Rich Text Editor
- Border
- The implementation of Post-Action Behavior

The following screenshot of Rich Text Editor Dojo sample depicts the first model that we will be building:

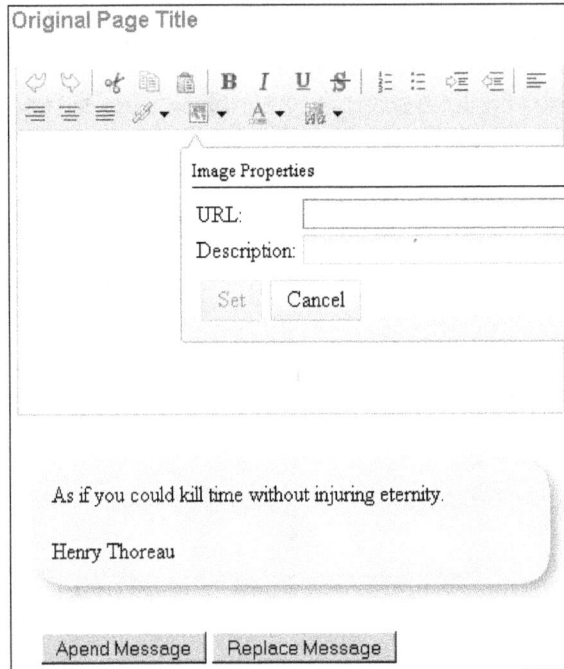

The second example we will be developing demonstrates the utilization of the Dojo Tree builder and the Client Event Handler builder to update a section of a page to avoid full page refresh.

The following screenshot of Dojo Tree sample shows the rendered content of this sample:

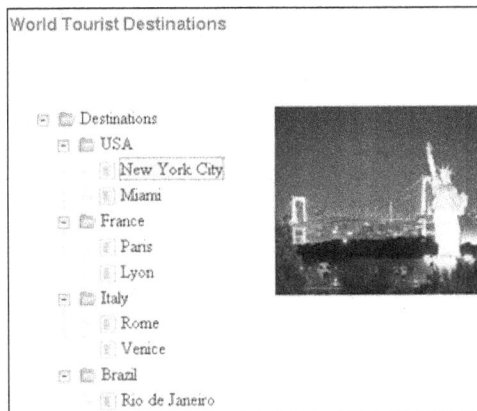

Dojo Rich Text Editor sample

Ok, we know you are eager to build your Dojo sample portlet. So, let's get started with this task.

This first portlet you will build uses the Dojo Rich Text Editor builder, the Border builder, and a few Ajax techniques. This portlet enables users to type text into the **Rich Text Editor control**, which processes this text almost like a Word Document. This text can be edited by using the rich features available in the toolbar.

The text can then be transferred to another area named the **Text control** on the page. This happens as a result of an asynchronous call that refreshes only a region of the page. Actually, it refreshes a region containing both the **Rich Text Editor control** and **Text control**. This way, the text entered into the text editor is cleared at the same time that the message is added to or replaces the content of the **Text** field. Appending a message or replacing its content with a new message is accomplished through two buttons on the page.

In addition to the features described in the preceding section, we also put a **Text** field control called the **page title** at the top of the page. This **Text** field is used to show you that the page is not being refreshed as you interact with the text area control.

Now that you know what you will be building, let's build your portlet. Your model will contain the builders, as shown in the following screenshot:

#		Name	Type
1		main	Action List
2		richText_PG	Page
⊟ 3		Variables	Comment
	4	RTEText_VAR	Variable
	5	msgEntry_VAR	Variable
	6	pgTitle_VAR	Variable
⊟ 7		Dojo Builders	Comment
	8	inputText_RTE	Dojo Rich Text ..
	9	msgBorder_BD	Border
⊟ 10		Texts	Comment
	11	msgEntry_TXT	Text
	12	title	Text
⊟ 13		Processing	Comment
	14	writeMsg_MTD	Method
	15	replace_BTN	Button
	16	append_BTN	Button

Creating the model

Please make sure that your portal server is up and running.

Open Eclipse or RAD, and then open the A2Z WEF project we have been using.

Perform the following steps to create your model:

1. Create a folder to host the models we will create in this chapter.
2. In your WEF project, under the `models` directory, create a folder named `Chapter11`.
3. Under this folder, create another folder named `UI`.
4. Inside this folder, create a new **Main and Page** model.
5. For the page type, select simple page. Name this model as **RichTextEditor**.

Adding the builders

Now let's modify the content of the Page builder. Please open the Page builder and update the current content with the following HTML code snippet:

```html
<html>
  <body>
    <form name="RTE_Form" method="post">
      <div name="PageTitle"
        style="font:12pt Arial; font-weight:
              bold;color: #336699;">
      </div><br>
        <table>
          <tr>
            <td >
              <div name="refreshMessageArea">
                <span name="inputText_RTE"></span><br>
                <div name="DjContainer">
                  <span name="messageEntry_TXT"></span>
                </div>
              </div>
            </td>
          </tr>
        </table>
```

```
    <div style="padding:20px;">
        <span name="append_BTN" ></span>
        <span name="replace_BTN" ></span>
    </div>
  </form>
 </body>
</html>
```

Rename this builder to **richText_PG**. Click on **OK** and save your model. The builder call list will display a red error symbol in the main Action List builder call, but that is ok for now.

Let's examine the preceding HTML code snippet, especially the new span and div tags:

- form: It is always a good practice to rename the form tag to something meaningful within your page context

- pageTitle: We will use this tag to associate a text field with its source in a variable to show that the page is not being fully reloaded

- refreshMessageArea: This div tag will be referenced from the Button or Action builder to indicate that after the action is performed by the button only this area will be refreshed, as opposed to the entire page

- inputText_RTE: This is where the Rich Text Editor control will be placed by WEF

- DJContainer: We will be placing a border control on this area

Now let's modify the main Action List builder so that it references our new page. Perform the following steps:

1. Open the main **Action List** builder.

2. In **ActionList**, select **richText_PG** as the new page to return. This will replace the current **page1** input value.

3. Click on **OK**. The red error symbol will go away.

4. Save your model.

5. Add a Comment builder and name it as **Variables**.

6. Click on the **OK** button.

Adding the variables

At this point, we need to create two variables, which we will be associating with the text controls on this page. Perform the following steps:

1. Add a Variable builder.
2. Name this variable as **RTEText_VAR**.
3. For **Data Type**, select **String**.
4. Click on the **OK** button.
5. Add a second Variable builder to your model.
6. Name this variable as **msgEntry_VAR**.
7. For **Data Type**, select **String**.
8. Click on **OK** in this builder.

The first variable will be associated with the Dojo Rich Text Editor. This control will read and display the content of this variable when it loads. This way, whenever we want to manipulate the content of the RTE, we can do so through this variable.

The second variable **msgEntry_VAR**, will be associated with the text control, which will capture and display the content that has been saved from the RTE. So, we will not be saving any content to any persistence mechanism. This way, we can focus on working with the Dojo controls and using Ajax techniques.

Adding the Dojo builders

Now go ahead and add another Comment builder. Name it as **Dojo Builders**. Adding the Comment builders to your model is a nice way to separate and organize your builder calls.

Next, perform the following steps to add the Dojo Rich Text Editor builder:

1. Open the **Builder Picker** dialog box.
2. In the search input files, type in **Dojo Ri**.
3. This will cause the search result list to display the **Rich Text Editor builder**. Select this builder.
4. Enter the following inputs for this builder:
   - **Name**: Leave this input blank. This way, WEF uses the tag name as the builder name.
   - **Page: richText_PG**

- ° **Tag: inputText_RTE**
- ° **Value: ${Variables/RTEText_VAR}**
- ° **Height: 200**
- ° **Minimum Height: 200**

5. Leave the check boxes set to their default values. Only the first three check boxes should be checked.

6. Click on the **OK** button, and save your model.

To make sure all is well so far, run your model. You should see only the **Rich Text Editor** control on your page.

Now let's add a Border builder to our model. The Border builder is not a Dojo builder, but is it part of the **Rich UI** category of builders. It demonstrates an example of how you can enhance the UI of your portlet with minimum effort.

Open the **Builder Picker** dialog box, and select the **Border builder**, under the **Rich UI** category.

Provide the following inputs for this builder:

- **Name: msgBorder_BD**
- **Page: richText_PG**
- **Tag: DjContainer**
- **Use Theme**: Checked
- **Attribute Modifier** – First line
  - ° **Class Identifier: .tc**
  - ° **Name: style**
  - ° **Value: width: 400**

- **Attribute Modifier** – Second line
  - ° **Class Modifier: .bc**
  - ° **Name: style**
  - ° **Value: width: 400**

> The Border builder uses two files to define its shape and styles. One is the base HTML file located at /factory/ pages/borders and it is named as border_base. html. The other file is the blue_border.css located at /factory/pages/borders. You can expose these files by unchecking the **Use Theme** option. This will enable you to select other files to be used by this builder. To modify these files, you would want to copy and rename them so that you would modify your own files. You would then modify the builder inputs to point to your own files.

Click on the **OK** button. Save and run your model. You should now see the two UI controls on the page.

Adding the Text builders

Add one more Comment builder, right after the Border builder. Name it as **Texts**.

Now let's create a text control and associate this control to the **msgEntry_VAR** variable. This control will display the messages typed into the **Rich Text Editor** control. We will place this control inside the Border control we have just created.

Add a Text builder to you model and provide the following inputs:

- **Name: msgEntry_TXT**
- **Page: richText_PG**
- **Tag: msgBorder_BD_border_data**
- **Text: ${Variables/msgEntry_VAR}**
- **Lookup Table Used: None**
- **Text Format: Allow HTML formatting of text** (Output string unmodified)
- **Replace Tag Content:** Checked

Click on the **OK** button, and save your model.

Add another Comment builder. Name it as **Processing**.

Adding the processing section

Next we add a Method builder, which contains the code to perform the action of copying the text messages from the **Rich Text Editor** area to the text control.

Add a Method builder to your model. Name it as **writeMsg_MTD**. A Method builder is similar to a method in a Java class. For those familiar with other programming languages, it can be compared to a function.

Expand the **Arguments** section and add an argument to this method. Name it as **Action**. Set **Data Type** as **String**.

Delete the complete content of **Method Body**. Type the following statements into the **Method Body** area:

```
{

    String entryMessage = webAppAccess.getRequestInputs().
                    getInputValue("inputText_RTE");

webAppAccess.getVariables().
                setString("msgEntry_VAR", entryMessage);


webAppAccess.getVariables().setString("RTEText_VAR","");

webAppAccess.processPage("richText_PG");



}
```

Let's understand this code snippet. The first statement assigns the value of the **Rich Text Editor** to the local `entryMessage` variable.

The second statement then assigns this value to the WEF `msgEntry_VAR` variable. As you recall, this variable has been associated with the **Text control** we added to the page. This means that once this region refreshes, it displays the content of this variable.

The third statement clears the content of the **Editor** so that users can type in a new message.

The last statement in this method causes the current page to be returned.

At this point, we cannot test this code yet. To do so, we need to add a button to invoke this method and have the desired action performed.

Let's add the button, which will invoke this method to copy the text messages from the **Rich Text Editor** area to the **Text control**. The button will simply replace the existing content in the **Text control** with the latest text typed into the RTE. So, add a Button builder to your model. Provide the following inputs:

- **Name**: Leave this input blank. This way WEF uses the tag name as the builder name.
- **Page**: richText_PG.
- **Tag**: replace_BTN.
- **Label**: **Replace Message**.
- **Action Type**: **Submit Form and Invoke Action**.
- **Action**: **writeMsg_MTD**.

Click on the **OK** button, and save your model.

Testing the model

Now we can test our model. Run your model. Type some text into the **Text Editor** area and click on the **Replace Message** button. The message you type in should be copied to the **Text control** inside the blue box.

Everything seems to be fine, except for a small problem. It looks like that action is performing a full page refresh. Hummmm… is it true? If so, this is not what we intended. Well, let's use a mechanism to identify whether a full page refresh is happening or not.

Add a **Text control** to the page to hold a **String** text. This text will be the page title. This text will read its value from a variable. If the title gets updated, then a full page refresh is happening.

So add one more variable to your model. Add this variable to the **Variables** section you have already created in your builder call list. To do so, right-click on the **Dojo Builders comment builder call**. Then select **Insert...** from the menu option. Now, pick a Variable builder. Name it as **pgTitle_VAR**. Set **Data Type** as **String**. Enter the text—**Original Page Title**, in the **Initial Value** area.

Now, add a Text builder to the **Texts** section of the builder calls. Provide the following inputs:

- **Name: title**
- **Page: richText_PG**

- **Tag**: PageTitle
- **Text**: ${Variables/pgTitle_VAR}
- **Lookup Table Used**: None
- **Text Format**: Display Tags as written
- **Replace Tag Contents**: Checked

Click on the **OK** button.

Let's modify the method we have created so it updates this text in the event that a full page refresh takes place. Open the **writeMsg_MTD** Method builder. Right above the last statement in **Method Body**, enter the following statement:

```
webAppAccess.getVariables().setString("pgTitle_VAR","Modified Title");
```

Click on the **OK** button, and save your model.

The builders we just added will have the following effect: when the model first loads, the page title should read **Original Page Title**. When you click on the **Replace Message** button, the **writeMsg_MTD** should be executed. If a full page refresh is happening, the title text will be changed to **Modified Title**.

So, go ahead and run your model. Confirm that the title reads **Original Page Title**.

Click on the **Replace Message** button. I am not sure what happened in your model, but on mine it happened what I feared. The page title has changed, indicating that a full page refresh is happening. Ok, no problem. Please do not panic. This is just a piece of software. Lives do not depend upon this code. So, let's address this small issue.

Implementing Post-Action for partial page refresh

Open the **replace_BTN** builder. Scroll down and expand the **Post-Action Behavior** section. Provide the following inputs in this section:

- **Post-Action Behavior**: Select **refresh specified page location after running action**
- **Page**: richText_PG
- **Tag**: refreshMessageArea

Click on the **OK** button. Save and run your model again. If your model works as expected, then the page title should not be modified when you click on the **Replace Message** button. This confirms that an Ajax call is taking place when we submit the form.

To understand what is happening, as you recall, we have created a `div` tag around **Dojo control** and **Text control** we have added. This tag is named as **refreshMessageArea**. In our Button builder, you instructed WEF to perform an extra action after the method we are invoking is executed. This action is to make an Ajax call to refresh only the page region we have specified. This way, a full page refresh is avoided and only the specified region is refreshed.

We are almost done with our sample model. Let's improve on a small detail. As you can see, you cannot append messages to your **Text control**. Every time you click on the **Replace Message** button, the existing message in the **Text control** is replaced by the new message. Let's say you want to keep the existing messages and just append the new message. Well, this is simple to implement with WEF. Let's see how to do so.

Start by adding a new Button builder to you model. Provide the following inputs to this builder:

- **Name**: Leave this input blank. This way WEF uses the tag name as the builder name.
- **Page**: richText_PG.
- **Tag**: append_BTN.
- **Label**: Append Message.
- **Action Type**: Submit Form and Invoke Action.
- **Action**: writeMsg_MTD.
- **Post-Action Behavior**: Select **refresh specified page location after running action**.
- **Page**: richText_PG.
- **Tag**: refreshMessageArea.

As you can see, this time we have already specified that **refreshMessageArea** should be refreshed when the user clicks on this button.

Before clicking on the **OK** button, please expand the **Arguments** section of this builder. Add the following arguments:

- **Name: Action**
- **Value: APPEND**

This argument will be used by the method to define the proper action course depending on the clicked button. Click on the **OK** button and save your model.

Lastly, we need to make a few changes to the Method builder. Open the **writeMsg_ MTD** Method builder.

Now update **Method Body** so that it contains the following code snippet:

```
String entryMessage = webAppAccess.getRequestInputs().
    getInputValue("inputText_RTE");

if(Action.equals("APPEND"))

        com.bowstreet.builderutilities.PageAutomationRuntime.
        assign     (webAppAccess,
        "msgEntry_VAR", "<br> "  + entryMessage, true);

    else

            webAppAccess.getVariables().
              setString("msgEntry_VAR", entryMessage);

webAppAccess.getVariables().setString("RTEText_VAR","");

    //Confirm that full page refresh is not happening


webAppAccess.getVariables().
        setString("pgTitle_VAR","Modified Title");

webAppAccess.processPage("richText_PG");
```

Click on the **OK** button. Save your model and run it. Now, you should be able to do both append and replace messages. These actions trigger an Ajax call avoiding a full page refresh.

The way it stands right now, this model is a web application that can be executed in any JEE-compliant container. It will not run on WebSphere Portal. To make this application as portlet, you need to add a Portlet Adapter builder to this model. Please do so if you want to run this application as a portlet.

Dojo Tree builder sample

Let's build another sample model to demonstrate the utilization of the Dojo Tree builder. In this sample, we will also work with the Client Event Handler builder.

In the World Tourist Destinations screenshot just before the *Dojo Rich Text Editor sample* section, you have already seen what this model looks like. Our model will feature a page with a **Dojo Tree control** on the left-hand side and an image holder area on the right-hand side of the page. The Tree builder contains a number of elements, represented by country names and city names, which fire a client event when these elements are clicked.

The click is handled by a Client Event Handler builder, which then processes the click to update the image area with the proper image.

The following screenshot shows the list of builder calls utilized in this model:

#	Name	Type
1	main	Action List
2	DJTree_PG	Page
3	destinations_TR	Dojo Tree
4	destinations_VAR	Variable
5	imgSource_VAR	Variable
6	cityImage_IMG	Image
⊟ 7	Handle Click	Comment
	treeClickHandler_CHE	Client Event Han…
	showImage_MTH	Method

Let's start building our sample model. Perform the following steps:

1. Start by creating a new model under the same UI folder where you have already created your previous model.

2. Create a new **Main and Page** model. For the page type, select simple page. Name this model as **DojoTree**.

3. Now, let's modify the content of the Page builder. Please open the Page builder and update the current content with the following HTML code snippet:

```
<html>
<body>
  <form name="DestinationsForm" method="post">
    <div style="font:12pt
    Arial;font-weight: bold;color: #336699;">
      World Tourist Destinations</div>
```

```
          <br><br>
          <table cellspacing="4" cellpadding="20">
            <tr>
              <td>
                <span name="DojoTree"></span>
              </td>
                <td valign="top">
                  <div name="refreshImage">
                  <span name="IMG"></span>
                </div>
              </td>
            </tr>
          </table>
      </form>
    </body>
  </html>
```

Rename this page to **DJTree_PG**.

4. Open the main **Action List** builder and change the only entry in the **ActionList** from **page1** to **DJTree_PG**.

5. Click on the **OK** button and save your model.

6. Add a Variable builder to your model. Name this variable as **destinations_ VAR**. For **type**, select **XML**. As this is a large XML structure, for **Initial Value**, please download the destinations_VAR.xml file from http://www. packtpub.com/support.

Here is an excerpt from this variable:

```
<Items>
    <Item>
        <ID>0</ID>
        <Name>Destinations</Name>
        <Nodes>
            <Item>
                <ID>USA.png</ID>
                <Name>USA</Name>
                <Nodes>
                    <Item>
                    <ID>NewYork.png</ID>
                    <Name>New York City</Name>
                    </Item>
                    <Item>
                    <ID>Miami.png</ID>
```

```
                <Name>Miami</Name>
              </Item>
           </Nodes>
        </Item>
     </Nodes>
```

7. Once you copy the content to the XML file to this variable, click on the **OK** button and save your model.

8. Let's add our Dojo Tree builder to our model. Please provide the following values as inputs to this builder:
   - **Name: destinations_TR**
   - **Page: DJTree_PG**
   - **Tag: DojoTree**
   - **Data: ${Variables/destinations_VAR/Items/Item}**
   - **Label Element: Name**
   - **Value Element: ID**

9. Expand the **Event Delivery** section of this builder. Check both inputs — **Use Client-side Delivery** and **Fire Event on Server**.

10. Click on the **OK** button, and save your model.

At this point, you can run your model. You should be able to see the Dojo Tree control on the page.

In this model, we use a set of images that are displayed as the user selects the tree elements. The file is named as `Chapter 11 - Destinations Images.zip`. Please download these images from `http://www.packtpub.com/support` and perform the following steps:

1. Unzip this file to a temporary folder. In your designer, switch to the **Project Explorer** tab. Create an `images` folder under `WebContent`. Inside the `images` folder, create a folder named `Chapter11`. Place the extracted images into this folder.

2. Add a Variable builder to your model. Name it as **imgSource_VAR**. For **Data Type**, select **String**. For **Initial Value**, type **/images/Chapter11/NewYork. png**. This is the image which will be displayed when the model first loads.

3. Click on the **OK** button, and save your model.

4. Add a Comment builder to you model. Name it as **Handle Click**.

5. Let's now add an Image builder to our model. Please provide the following inputs to this builder:
   - **Name: cityImage_IMG**
   - **Page: DJTree_PG**
   - **Tag: IMG**
   - **Image Source: ${Variables/imgSource_VAR}**

6. Click on the **OK** button, and save your model.

7. Now add another builder, a Method builder with the following input:
   - **Name: showImage_MTD**

8. Expand the **Arguments** section, and enter the following arguments:
   - **Name: imageSource**
   - **Data Type: String**

9. Enter the following code snippet in the **Method Body** area:

```
String path = "/images/Chapter11/";

webAppAccess.getVariables().
        setString( "imgSource_VAR", path + imageSource);

webAppAccess.processPage("DJTree_PG");
```

Client Event Handler

The preceding code snippet gets invoked by a Client Event Handler. The event is fired when the user clicks on an element of the **Tree control**.

Now, we come to our last builder in this model. Add a Client Event Handler builder to your model with the following inputs:

- **Name: treeClickHandler_CHE**
- **Location Technique: Relative to Named Tag**
- **Page: DJTree_PG**
- **Tag: DojoTree**
- **Placement: Before**

- **Event Name**: destinations_TROnClick
- **Action Type: Link To an Action**
- **Action: showImage_MTD**

Expand the **Arguments** section and provide the following arguments:

- **Name: value**
- **Value: ${JavaScript/this.value}**

Expand the **Post-Action Behavior** section and provide the following inputs:

- **Post-Action Behavior**: Select **refresh specified page locationafter running action**
- **Page**: DJTree_PG
- **Tag**: refreshImage

Click on the **OK** button, and save your model.

As you can see from the preceding inputs, one of the inputs for the Client Event Handler builder is **Event Name**. The event you have selected is an event that was created by the Dojo Tree builder. This event is related specifically to the **Event Delivery** mechanism you have selected in this builder. This event was created when you selected **Use Client Side Delivery**. You can also see that we have specified the **showImage_MTD** method as the action to be invoked when the click event is handled by the Client Event Handler.

There are two other important points that are worth mentioning in this builder — **Arguments** and **Post-Action Behavior**.

For argument, we are passing the value associated with the clicked element. In our case, this is the **ID** element of our **destinations_VAR** variable. For this **ID** node, we have defined the image filename. You can use any value for **ID**, as long as it is unique within the XML data you provide to your builder.

For **Post-Action Behavior**, we are once again specifying a region in our page to be refreshed. This is the region defined by the `div` tag, which wraps the `IMG` tag.

Run your model, and choose the destination for your next vacation.

Well, there are many more Dojo builders we would like to cover in this chapter, but while Dojo and WEF provide unlimited possibilities for UI development, we are limited by the number of pages established by our Editor!

Summary

In this chapter, you learned the advantages of using Dojo builders and Ajax techniques to improve not only the user experience but also application performance.

We looked into the Dojo builders available in WEF.

We also had the opportunity to build two sample models to demonstrate the utilization of a few Dojo builders. We also demonstrated how you can implement Ajax techniques from WEF.

In the next chapter, we will address **profiling**, which is the core of WEF technology. WEF's profiling capabilities set WEF aside from any other modeling or code generation tool.

12
WEF Profiling

In this chapter we will carry on detailed WEF profiling after its introduction in *Chapter 7, Introduction to Web Experience Factory*.

We will begin by explaining the profiling concepts and defining the related terms, followed by some of the mechanisms and techniques a developer can use to produce variability for portal applications built with WEF.

We will also develop a sample model to see how profiling concepts and techniques are utilized in an application.

The following are some of the topics we will cover in this chapter:

- Profiling
- Profile set
- Profiles
- Profile entries and profile values
- Profile set editor
- Profile selection handler
- Value setter
- Sample portlet
- Role-based profiling

Profiling

Profiling is the mechanism by which variability can be introduced into a WEF application. Through profiling, the same code base is used to produce different instances with different behaviors from the same application.

For instance, through profiling, the same application can run either on a desktop browser or on mobile device browsers. While the instance requested through a desktop can present a feature-rich experience to the user, the instance requested through a mobile device can provide a simplified and more direct experience.

The ability to use the same code base represented by a model is inherent to the core WEF technology. As a developer, you define or specify certain elements of the profiling process, such as the profiles to be used, the profile entries and their values, as well as the mechanism responsible for selecting a given profile.

It is impossible to talk about profiling in WEF without making reference to builders. As you recall, builders take input values. Besides typing in these values or specifying an indirect reference as an input, it is possible to specify that the value to be fed into a builder's input field is to come from a profile, or more accurately from a profile entry.

The following screenshot shows a Page builder and the **Profile Input** dialog box displayed when the user clicks on a builder input profile icon, indicated by an arrow here:

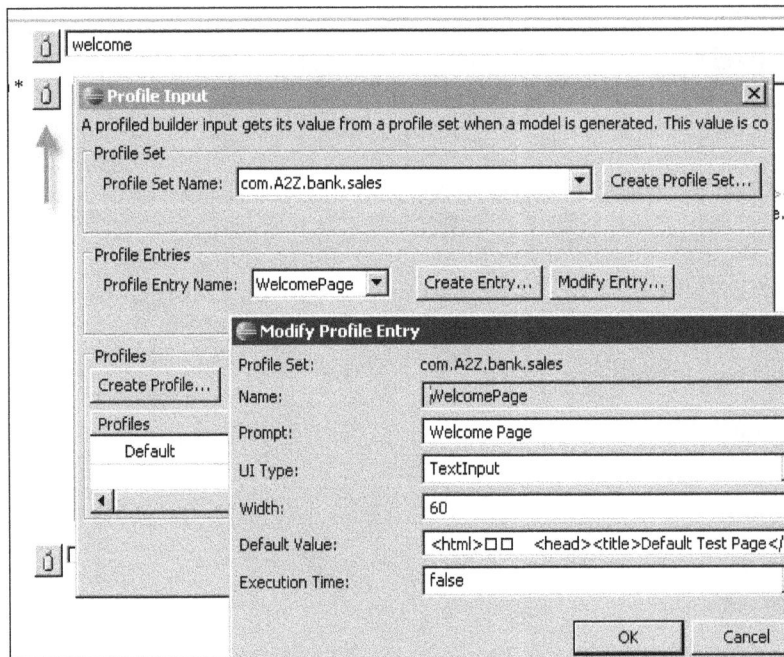

Most of the builder inputs in all builders can be profile-enabled. When a builder input can be profile-enabled, it contains the profile input button next to it, as described in the previous paragraph. So, when you see a builder input with profile input button by its side, it means that the value for that referred builder input can come from a profile.

Defining some WEF profiling terms

Let's define some profiling terms so that you have a complete understanding of what they mean:

- **Profile set**: Profile set is an XML file, which contains all the information necessary to implement profiling in WEF. Information such as profile names, their relationship, profile entries, and their respective values are defined in a profile set. The profile selection mechanism is also defined in the profile set.

- **Profile**: Profile is a means for logically grouping profile entries and their respective values.

- **Profile entry**: Profile entry identifies a single unit of variability in an application. Profile entries contain information used in the regeneration process as well as information used by the profile set editor to display meaningful and user-friendly information to developers. This information is also used by WEF to display the right UI elements when profile values are exposed in portal to end users.

- **Profile entry value**: This is the actual value assigned to a corresponding profile entry. It represents the value that is fed into the builder input at regeneration time.

Now that you have a good understanding of profiling in WEF, you must be asking yourself how a profile is selected to provide values to a model. Well, WEF has a mechanism conveniently named as profile selection handler. We will cover this mechanism in our next topic.

Profile selection handler

Once you create a profile set with all your profiles and entries, you need to define how WEF is going to select these profiles when users access your application. As we have mentioned before, this is handled by a profile selection handler mechanism.

A Profile selection handler is a set of code, which selects a profile based on predefined contexts or rules. For instance, WebSphere Portal defines access to a portal application based on roles that are directly associated to user groups. Wouldn't it be nice if WEF could tie the selection of profiles to portal user groups? This way, when a user belonging to a group, such as Executives, logs in to portal, he/she would be served with the portlet instance associated with the Executives profile. Well, that is exactly how the profile selection handler works. In fact, for this specific scenario, WEF has a profile selection handler identified as WPS Group Segment Handler.

> A profile defined in a profile set can be selected by a specific selection handler based on a predefined context.

In the same way that there is a selection handler for the portal users group, there are also several other selection handlers to select profiles in many other contexts. The following are a few of the profile section handlers provided by WEF:

- JEE Role Handler
- Locale Selection Handler
- User Attribute Handler
- WP Composite Application Role Selection Handler
- WPS Execution Model Handler
- Explicit Handler

One of the options you can choose for selection handling is the Explicit Handler. In such case, you would be delegating to users the ability to explicitly select a profile to be applied to your portlet or application.

> In addition to the selection handlers provided by WEF, users can create their own selection handlers for contexts not covered by WEF.

Now, let's cover the UI available in WEF to manage profile sets and all its related elements including, profiles, profile entries, profile values, and selection handlers.

Profile set editor

As you can infer from the topics we have covered so far in this chapter, managing profile sets is not a small task. For this task, WEF offers a profile set editor. Let's briefly examine the features of this editor.

Open your A2Z WEF project, and expand either the **Model Navigator** or the **Project Explorer** tab. Now open the `profiles` folder. Locate and double-click on the **SamplePortletAttributes.pset** profile set. This will cause the profile set editor to be opened on the right-hand side pane.

The Manage Profiles tab

The **Manage Profiles** tab is open by default. In this tab you can create, update, and delete profiles. Notice that this profile set contains four profiles named **Default**, **Hunter**, **Scarlet**, and **Violet**. As you click on the different profiles, the profile entry pane gets updated to reflect the entries defined on the selected profile.

You can also see that the three profiles defined in this profile set inherit from the **Default** profile. This means that if a profile does not define a value for a profile entry, the value is inherited from the **Default** profile.

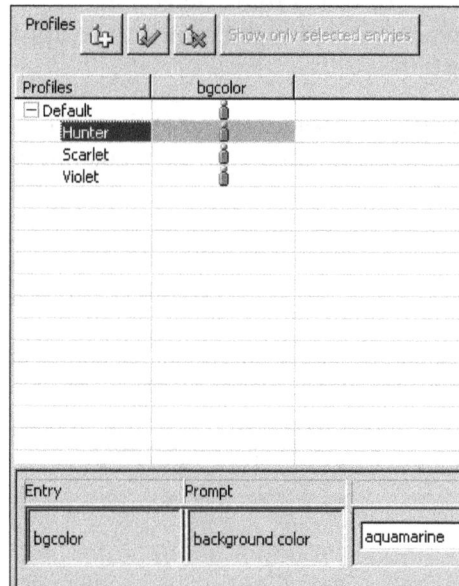

The Entries tab

The **Entries** tab enables you to manage every aspect of the profile entries. Here you can also inspect the attributes of the profile set entries, such as **Name**, **Prompt**, **UI Type**, **UI Data**, and so on.

Notice that the outline tab also lists entries containing the profile entry name and the prompt value for the entire profile set.

Notice that an entry is not associated directly with a profile. Rather, the profile entry value is what differs from profile to profile. So, a profile entry is associated with every profile defined in the profile set.

Profile Set:	SamplePortletAttributes					
Description:	profile set used in portlet adapter edit page sample					
Profile entry:	Add	Edit	Delete	Rename		

Name	Prompt	UI Type	UI Data	Default	Execution Time
bgcolor	background c...	Select	white,aquamarine,hotpi...	white	false

Select handler

The last tab in the profile set editor is **Profile Selection Handler**. This tab enables you to select the handler to be used to define the profile to be applied on the regeneration process for a given request.

On the first drop-down menu, you selected one of the existing profile selection handler mechanisms. If you have created your own custom profiles selection handler, then it would be listed here, too.

Profile Selection Settings

Profile Selection Handler: WPS Execution Mode Handler

Choose one of the profile selection handlers from the list. A profile selection handler determines the profile to apply to a specific request to a model. For more information about profile selection handlers, see the online help.

Value Setter:

This custom Java class will be used to specify a value to be used for a profile. It replaces the default mechanism. See the help for more information. Format: com.mycompany.myCustomValueClass

You can use only one profile selection handler per profile set. If you need to use more than one mechanism to select a profile, you need to create another profile set to specify the new selection handler.

You should never rename a profile set. WEF uses an internal mechanism to manage the association of profile sets with different models. When you rename a profile set, this data might get out of synchronism. This will have undesirable consequences on your profile-enabled application.

Also, if you need to copy a profile set, create a new profile set and use the "copy from" feature in the new profile set wizard.

Profiling sample

Profiling can be used in several different manners, especially with IBM WebSphere Portal. Different techniques can be applied to expose or leverage WEF's profiling capabilities. Some of the most common techniques are as follows:

- Expose profiles or profile values to portal administrators
- Role-driven profiling
- Value setter class

The first option is available only to users with portal administrative rights. In the first option, WEF exposes profiles or profile values through the **Configure** option available in each portlet. This way, when portal administrators select a profile or values associated with profile entries, the builder input values are applied to every portlet, regardless of the portal role defined for the different users. This option is valuable when you want to configure global settings to be applied to every user. Properties such as JNDI name, web services URLs, logging level, and other global properties can be easily configured through this mechanism.

For the role-driven profiling option, WEF works tightly with portal to leverage portal user groups. Through this mechanism, users are assigned a specific profile based on the portal group to which they belong.

For value setter, a Java class is designated to dynamically provide the values that can be applied to a profile-enabled model during the regeneration process. This technique enables you to define the logic of how these values will be established.

In this chapter, we will demonstrate two examples. We will create a portlet to show you how portal administrators can explicitly select either profile names or profile values in a portlet. We will also perform the required implementation so that variability to your portlet will be role driven.

Sample portlet – exposing profiles through the portal's Configure option

Throughout the next part of this chapter, we will build the portlet to be used in our profiling samples. While this exercise of building the portlet is not core to profiling, we feel that this exercise represents one more opportunity to practice and enhance your WEF expertise.

The sample code is available for download in case you need to refer to the model or to the builder inputs.

We will use the same portlet for both of our examples. First, we will expose both profile names and profile values through the **Configure** option of the portlet menu. This action will be performed by the portal administrator.

In our second profiling example, we will use the same portlet that we have built here to demonstrate how profiling can be configured to implement role-driven portal applications.

Our portlet is simple, and it will contain just one page with a table demonstrating sales figures. In addition to that, this portlet will have two elements, which will be used for the profiling purpose as follows:

- A Portlet Theme builder
- An Attribute Setter builder associated with the page title

Now that you know what we will build, let's start with the task of building the portlet first.

Please make sure that your portal server is up and running. Perform the following steps to create a new model and modify the existing HTML page:

1. Open Eclipse or RAD.
2. Open the A2Z WEF project we have been using.
3. In your WEF project, under the `models` directory, create a folder named `Chapter12`. This folder will host the model that we will create in this chapter.
4. Under the `Chapter12` folder, create another folder named `UI`.
5. Inside this folder, create a new main and page model.
6. For page type, select simple page.
7. Click on **Next**.
8. Name this model **salesFigures**.
9. Click on **Finish**.
10. Now, modify the content of the Page builder by opening the Page builder (page1) and updating the current content with the following HTML code snippet:

```
<html>
    <body>
        <form name="salesForm" method="post">
            <div>
                <div name="pageTitle"
                style="font:12pt Arial;font-weight:
                bold;color: #3333CC;"></div>
```

```
            <br>
            <span name="actualSales"></span>
        </div>
    </form>
</body>
</html>
```

11. Rename this Page builder to **sales_PG**.

12. Click on **OK**, and save your model.

Now perform the following steps to modify the main Action builder and to add a Portlet Theme builder to your model. In this section you will also add an XML variable to hold the values for the sales figures:

1. Modify the main Action List builder so that it references our new page.

2. Open this builder, and in **Action List**, select **sales_PG** as the new page to return.

3. Click on **OK**. The red error symbol should go away. Save your model.

4. Add a Comment builder as the first builder in the builder call list.

5. Name it **Portal Config**.

6. Click on the **OK** button.

7. Right-click on the **sales_PG** builder, and select **Insert...** from the menu.

8. Pick the **Theme** builder from the **Builder Picker** dialog box.

9. Name this builder **sales_TH**. We will profile-enable one of the inputs for this builder.

10. For the **Theme File** input, click on the button with the ellipses signal, and select **/WEB-INF/factory/themes/blue.uitheme**.

11. Click on **OK**.

12. Add a Variable builder to this model.

13. Name it **westSales_VAR**.

14. For type, set **XML**.

15. Enter the following code snippet for this variable:

```
<Rowset>
    <Row>
        <Name>Alice Stone</Name>
        <Goal>1,000,000</Goal>
        <Actual_Sales>750,000</Actual_Sales>
    </Row>
```

```
      <Row>
      <Name>Bryan Kimberly</Name>
      <Goal>1,000,000</Goal>
      <Actual_Sales>837,000</Actual_Sales>
   </Row>
      <Row>
      <Name>Tom Green</Name>
      <Goal>1,000,000</Goal>
      <Actual_Sales>939,000</Actual_Sales>
   </Row>
      <Row>
      <Name>James Smith</Name>
      <Goal>1,000,000</Goal>
      <Actual_Sales>231,000</Actual_Sales>
   </Row>
      <Row>
      <Name>Total</Name>
      <Goal>4,000,000</Goal>
      <Actual_Sales>2.757,000</Actual_Sales>
   </Row>
</Rowset>
```

The preceding variable will be used by the Data Page builder to create the sales table. Perform the following steps:

1. Click on **OK**, and save your model.

2. Now add a Data Page builder to your model with the following inputs:

    ○ **Name: sales_DP**

    ○ **Variable: Variables/westSales_VAR**

    ○ **Page in Model: sales_PG**

    ○ **Page Type: View Only**

    ○ **Make UI from Data**: Checked

    ○ **Location for New Tags: actualSales**

    ○ **Use Theme**: Checked

    ○ **Generate Labels**: Checked

3. Click on **OK**.

4. Save and run your model.

You should see a table representing A2Z's sales numbers for 2012, just like the one shown in the following screenshot. This table should reflect the blue theme you have defined:

Name	Goal	Actual Sales
Alice Stone	1,000,000	750,000
Bryan Kimberly	1,000,000	837,000
Tom Green	1,000,000	939,000
James Smith	1,000,000	231,000
Total	4,000,000	2.757,000

Go back to your designer and perform the following steps to add a Variable builder. This variable will hold the value to be displayed at the page title.

1. Name this variable as **pageTitle_VAR**.
2. For type set **String**.
3. For **Initial Value**, enter **Total Sales Figure for 2012**.
4. Click on **OK**.

Add another builder to this model. Select a Text builder. Provide the following inputs to this builder:

- **Name**: pageTitle_TXT
- **Page**: sales_PG
- **Tag**: pageTitle
- **Text**: Use the picker to select **${Variables/pageTitle_VAR}**
- **Lookup Table Used: None**
- **Text Format: Display Tags as written**
- **Replace Tag Contents**: Checked

Click on **OK**, and save your model.

Now that we have a Text builder to add title to the page, we are going to add a means to change the style of this title. We will accomplish this through an Attribute Setter builder.

Add another builder to your model, which is an Attribute Setter builder. Provide the following inputs:

- **Name: pageTitleStyle**
- **Page: sales_PG**
- **Tag: pageTitle**
- Attribute List
    - **Name**: Use the drop-down menu to select style
    - **Value: font:12pt Arial; font-weight: bold; color: #3333CC**
- **Overwrite Rule: Overwrite HTML Value**

Click on **OK**, and save your model.

Later on, you profile-enable this Attribute Setter builder to provide different values to it based on the selected profile.

At this point, we are done with the model. Run it and make sure it works. You should see the same table you saw last time you ran your model, but now it should have a page title.

Now that you have a working portlet, we can move on to profile-enabling this portlet so that you can understand the profiling capabilities of WEF.

Creating a profile set

Our portlet is going to use a profile set to externalize profiles to the portal administrator. So, let's create a new profile set. Perform the following steps:

1. Click on the **Model Navigator** tab. Right-click on the current project name.
2. From the menu, select **New | WebSphere Portlet Factory Profile Set**.
3. In the **New Profile Set** window, enter the following information:
    - **Project: A2Z**
    - **Name: com.A2Z.bank.salesFigures**
    - **Description: Used for Portlet Configuration**
4. Click on **Finish**.

The designer opens this profile set within the profile set editor. By default, the **Entries** tab is shown. Switch to the **Manage Profiles** tab.

Perform the following steps to create two new profiles:

1. Click on the **New Profile** button. The **New Profile** button is the first button next to the **Profiles** label on the top of the **Profile** pane. It contains a candlelight and a plus signal icon on it.

2. For the first profile, enter the following, and click on **OK**:
   - **Profile Name: Green**
   - **Parent Profile: Default**

3. Create a second profile with the following inputs, and click on **OK**:
   - **Profile Name: Blue**
   - **Parent Profile: Default**

4. Save and close this profile set. Make sure you close it; otherwise, you will get a warning message when you profile-enable your model.

Profile-enabling builder inputs

Now perform the following steps to profile-enable the builder inputs for the existing builders:

1. Open the **SalesFigures** model again.

2. Open the **sales_TH** Theme builder.

3. Click on the profiling assignment button for the **Theme File** input. This button does not have an official name; some people refer to it as the little candlelight icon or the profiling pawn, as it looks like a chess pawn.

4. The **Profile Input** dialog box opens.

5. For **Profile Set Name**, use the drop-down control to select **com.A2Z.bank. salesFigures**.

6. In the **Profile Entry** dialog box, click on the **Create Entry...** button.

7. Enter the following values in the **New Profile Entry** dialog box:
   - **Name: ThemeOption**
   - **Prompt: Select a Theme**
   - **UI Type: TextInput**
   - **Width: 60**
   - **Default Value: /WEB-INF/factory/themes/blue.uitheme**
   - **Execution Time: false**

8. Click on **OK**.

9. In the **Profile Input** window, click on **OK** again.

10. In the **Builder Editor** window, click on the **Apply** button.

You can see that the icon on the profiling assignment button becomes blue. This is to indicate that this input has been profile-enabled. That means the value for this input will be provided by a profile during the regeneration of this model.

Also notice that the input field is now disabled. Additionally, there is a label below this input indicating that the value for this input comes from a profile set named **com.A2Z.bank.salesFigures**. It also indicates that the entry associated with this input is **ThemeOption**. Save your model.

Now perform the following steps to profile-enable the second builder input, which is the Attribute Setter associated with the title text builder:

1. Open the Attribute Setter builder.

2. In **Attribute List**, click on the profiling assignment button inside the **Name Value** table, the one in front of the style entry you have created.

3. The designer will open the **Profile Row of Inputs** window.

4. Click on the **Value** button in this window. This opens the **Profile Input** dialog box.

5. Provide the inputs to this dialog box. For **Profile Set Name**, use the drop-down control to select **com.A2Z.bank.SalesFigures**.

6. In the **Profile Entry** dialog box, click on the **Create Entry...** button. Enter the following values in the **New Profile Entry** dialog box:
   - **Name: Style**
   - **Prompt: Select a Style**
   - **UI Type: TextInput**
   - **Width: 60**
   - **Default Value: font:12pt Arial; font-weight: bold; color: #3333CC**
   - **Execution Time: false**

7. Click on **OK**.

8. Click **OK** again in the **Profile Input** dialog box.

9. Lastly, click on **OK** again in the **Profile Row of Inputs** dialog box.

Notice that the **Value** input entry is now disabled. The following screenshot shows this disabled input.

Name	pageTitleStyle	
Page Location		
Location Technique: ⊙ On Named Tag ○ Relative to Named Tag ○ Advanced		
Page *	sales_PG	
Tag *	pageTitle	

Attribute List	Name	Value
	.style	font: 12pt Arial; font-weight: bold; color: #3366CC;

10. Click on **Apply** in this builder, and save your model.

Providing values to profile entries

Now that we have associated a builder input field with a profile entry, we need to provide the values to these entries for the different profiles we are using. In our example we have two profiles: **Blue** and **Green**.

In the following steps, we will assign values to be supplied at runtime for when the different profiles are selected:

1. Open the **com.A2Z.bank.salesFigures** profile set again.

2. Select the **Manage Profiles** tab.

3. Click on the **Default** profile entry. This is the first entry in the profile list.

4. The table below the profile list is updated with values for the **Default** profile. You should see the following values for the two entries we have created:
   ○ **Style: font: 12pt Arial; font-weight: bold; color: #3366CC**
   ○ **ThemeOption: /WEB-INF/factory/themes/blue.uitheme**

5. Repeat the preceding step for the **Blue** profile. You should see the same values for both **Style** and **ThemeOption**. This is because the **Blue** profile is inheriting its values from the **Default** profile.

6. Now click on the **Green** profile entry. Provide the following values for the two existing entries:
   ○ **Style: font: 12pt Arial; font-weight: bold; color: #66FF66**
   ○ **ThemeOption: /WEB-INF/factory/themes/green.uitheme**

7. Save this profile set.

Now your profile set has three profiles—**Default**, **Blue**, and **Green**. This profile set also has two profile entries—**Style** and **ThemeOption**. You have defined values to be applied to these two entries for all the three existing profiles.

Testing profiling from the designer

WEF enables you to test profiles through the **Applied Profiles** tab. This tab is available on the bottom-right-hand side of the designer.

Through this view, you can select any of the profiles or a combination of profiles you have defined and execute your model from the designer. This enables you to inspect the result of your profile-enabled application at design time.

The profile sets associated with the model you are executing are listed in this view. It also lists all the profiles defined for each profile set.

Once you select a profile or a combination of profiles and click on the **Apply** button, regeneration takes place, and the profile values defined for the selected profile will be applied to your model. You then can run the profile-enabled model in the same manner as you would run any other model from the designer.

> As you click on the **Apply** button in the **Applied Profile** view, you do not need to save your model. This confirms that the code base you have created does not change as you apply the different profiles.

If you select a profile-enabled builder and switch to the view source mode by clicking on the **Source** tab in the right-hand side pane, you can see how the profile-enabled inputs are modified to reflect the value from the selected profile.

Testing the sample portlet in the designer

Let's test our application in the designer and see how it looks like when we apply the different profiles we have created. Please perform the following steps:

1. Open the sales model. If it has been changed, and you need to save it, please do so.

2. At the bottom-right-hand side pane, you should see an **Applied Profiles** tab. Please click on this tab.

3. Your **com.A2Z.bank.salesFigures** profile set should be listed here.

4. In front of the **Profile Set Name**, there is a drop-down control.

5. Click on this control to expose all options. The three existing profiles are listed here.

6. Select the **Blue** profile. The **Apply** button should be enabled.

7. Click on the **Apply** button.

8. At this point, you can run your model. The profile values for the **Blue** profile should be applied to the builders you have profile-enabled. As a result, you should see a page with a blue page title and a blue table.

9. Now go back to the Applied Profiles pane and select the Green profile. As a result you should see a page with a green page title and a green table.

The following screenshot shows the **Applied Profiles** pane when the **com.A2Z. banks.sales** profile is selected:

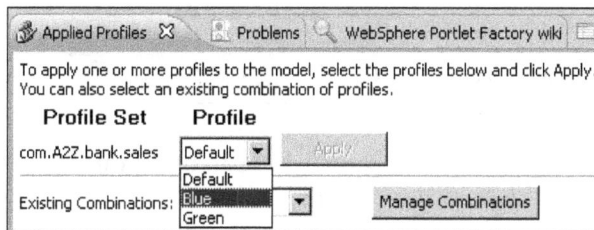

In the next section, we will expose these profiles to portal so that portal administrators can select one or another profile.

The Portlet Adapter builder

Now that we have our model and profile set, and we have profile-enabled a few builder inputs, it is time for us to specify how this profile set is to be exposed in portal.

The next step here is to add a Portlet Adapter builder to our model so that our model can run inside the portal container in WebSphere Portal.

So, go ahead and add a Portlet Adapter builder to your model. Provide the following inputs to this builder:

- **Name**: salesFigures
- **Portlet Title: Sales Figures**
- **Portlet Short Title: Sales Figures**
- **Portlet Keyword: Sales Figures**
- **Portlet Description: Sales Figures**
- **Default Locale: en**
- **User Help File**: Leave it blank

All the profile sets that have been associated with this model are being listed in the section, where it reads **Specify whether and how each Profile Set in this Model should be customized when it is in a Portal**. So, your **com.A2Z.bank.salesFigures** should be listed here.

The following screenshot shows the available options for exposing this profile set through portal:

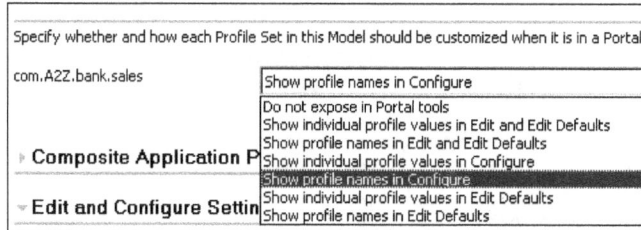

The options shown in the preceding screenshot can be summarized by what gets exposed and through which portlet options.

Regarding exposing profiles, there are two questions to be answered. The first one is the question regarding what gets exposed. The answer to this question is either profile names or profiles values. The second question is about which portlet option selects either profile names or values. The answer to this question is: **Edit**, **Edit Defaults**, or **Configure**.

Let's define each of these options, which are defined as portlet modes:

- **Edit**: The **Edit** mode relates to personalized preferences. This option provides a page for users to change their portlet settings. Changes defined through the **Edit** mode apply only to the particular user, who is performing that configuration and only on that page. With WEF, this page will enable users to choose from defined profiles or profile values. User needs to have been assigned at least the privileged user role to have access to this option through the portlet menu.

- **Edit Defaults**: This mode relates to shared preferences. When configuration is defined through this mode, then the settings defined here apply to all users who access the portlet on that given page.

- **Configure**: This mode is accessible only by portal administrators. They are directly related to the portlet definition. Settings defined through **Configure** apply to all occurrences of that portlet definition on all pages and for all users.

In this example you are building, we will expose the profile names through the **Configure** option of the portlet menu so that users with portal administration rights can modify the profile used by our portlet.

So, go ahead and select **Show profile names in Configure** from this drop-down menu.

Leave the other values in this builder to their default values. Click on **OK**, and save your model.

Now publish your portlet by right-clicking on the WEF project name and selecting the **Publish Application...** menu option. Select the proper configuration, and Click on **OK**.

Once your project is published to the portal, you need to place this portlet in a page so that you can test it.

Creating a portal page

Let's create a page and place our **Sales Figures** portlet on this page. Perform the following steps:

1. Log in to your portal with the portal administrator credentials.
2. Click on the **Administration** link.
3. In the navigation pane on the left-hand side, select **Manage Pages** under **Portal User Interface**.
4. In the **Manage Pages** portlet, click on the **Content Root** link.
5. Click on the **Home** link label.
6. On the **Home** page, click on the **New Page** button.
7. In the **Page Properties** portlet, type **Sales** for **Page Title**.
8. For unique name, type **com.a2z.sales**.
9. Click on **OK**.

Placing the portlet on the Sales page

Now that you have created the **Sales** page, place the **Sales Figures** portlet on this page.

You should be on the **Manage Pages** portlet, under the **Home** label. The last entry/link in this page should be the **Sales** link. Perform the following steps:

1. On the **Sales** row, locate and click on the **Edit Page Layout** button. The **Edit Page Layout** button has a pencil icon on it.

2. You should be taken to the **Edit Layout** portlet. Click on the **Add Portlet** button. If there is more than one **Add Portlet** button, click on the first one.

3. Portal displays a list of all available portlets.

4. In the **Search by** drop-down control, select **Title Starts With**.

5. In the **Search** input box, type **Sales**.

6. Your **Sales Figures** portlet should be listed.

7. Check it and Click on **OK**.

8. On the **Edit Layout** page, click on **Done**.

9. Portal will take you back to the **Manage Pages** portlet.

Ok, now your portlet has been added to the **Sales** page.

To examine this portlet, click on the **Home** link at the top of the current page. Now click on the **Sales** tab.

The following screenshot shows the portlet and the **Configure** option available to portal users with portal administration rights:

If you select the **Configure** option, you will be presented with a page through which you can select one of the profiles we have created. The **Default** profile is also listed here. Select the **Blue** profile, click on **OK**, and verify how the portlet changes to take on the values you have specified in the selected profile.

Exposing the individual values in portal

With WEF, it is very easy and quick to change the portlet from exposing the profile names to exposing the individual profile values.

To do so, open your Portlet Adapter builder, and change the current **Show profile names in Configure** profile set option to **Show individual profile values in Configure**.

Click on **OK**. Save your model, and publish it again to portal. You do not need to make any other changes. Log in to the portal once again, and select the **Configure** option.

Although the current input values are defined as "Text Inputs", they can be configured as "Select Controls", giving the users the ability to choose the values from a list instead of requiring them to type the values.

> Instead of accepting the default WEF model to display the configurable options in portal, you can create either an imported page or your own custom model. The custom option would then be referenced from the Portlet Adapter builder in the **Edit and Configure Settings** section of the Portlet Adapter builder.

Role-based profiling

In the previous section, you have created an example that demonstrates one of the many manners by which a profile set can be associated to a model. In this section we will describe the steps you need to perform in order to implement a role-based portal application.

In the same way you expose profile names and values to portal administrators, you can also define that portlet variability will be driven by the portal user groups. In this option, the mechanism to choose the profile to be applied to a portlet is tightly connected to the portal group a user belongs to.

The principle to serve a variation of your code base depending upon portal user groups bears many similarities to the example you just created.

Let's describe the steps you would perform to implement such an option.

Building portlet for role-based profiling

Concerning portlets, start by identifying the different groups that will be accessing your portlets. Although you do not insert the `if`, `else`, or `switch` statements to accommodate or to account for the different user groups accessing your application, you do need to have a good understand of these differences when you design your portlet applications.

Once you identify the different portal groups that will be accessing your application, they should be mapped to profiles.

After identifying the profiles, you should move on to identifying how a portlet differs from group to group or now, from profile to profile. The variable elements or aspects of your portlet can range from UI elements to presentation, to behavior, and all the way to the code execution at the most granular level. Each change should be identified as **unit of change**.

It is common for WEF modelers or developers to create a table that identifies all the units of change in a portlet and then assign values to them based on the different profiles.

The following table exemplifies an approach you can take to manage profile values according to the existing profiles:

	Profiles		
Profile entry	Platinum	Gold	Silver
Finance report link	Show	Show	Hide
Get Top Contributors button	Enabled	Disabled	Disabled
Expense radio options	Approve, create, delete, view	Create, view	View
Sales Figures Web Service operation	getTotalSales	getRegionalSales	getOfficeSales

Profile entry represents a unit of change. In your portlet it can be any element where a WEF builder provides a profiling assignment button. At the portlet level, these units of change can also be referred to as **portlet resources**, as these portlet elements are controlled by you, the WEF developer.

In possession of this table, developers would then identify the builders and the respective builder inputs, which ultimately would be mapped to the units of change.

> Although profiling can be and is used for portlet personalization, you should not build your application or provide variability to individual users.

Profile set for role-based profiling

For role-based profiling, the process of creating the profile set, the profiles, and the profile entries is similar to the one you have seen in the sample portlet we developed. However, there are two main differences as follows:

- Profile selection handler
- Mapping of profiles to portal user groups

We have already discussed the profile selection handler in this chapter. In our profiling sample, you specified that the profile would be explicitly selected by the portal administrator. For role-based profiling, you need to select a profile selection handler. This profile selection handler selects a profile, based on the portal group's context. This is specified in the profile set.

In this section, we will not develop the entire sample, but we will identify the items, which need to be addressed in order to implement WebSphere Portal role-based profiling.

Let's inspect the profile selection handler option. Open the **com.A2Z.bank. salesFigures** profile set, and switch to the **Selection Handler** tab. At the top of this pane, you will see a **Profile Selection Handlerdrop-down** control. One of the options in the **Profile Selection Handler** drop-down control is the **WPS Group Segment**. This is the option you would select to implement role-based profiling in the portal.

The second aspect you need to configure in the profile set is to map profiles to the portal groups. In the same **salesFigures** profile set, switch to the **Manage Profiles** tab. Right-click on the profile named **Blue**, and select the **Edit** option. The **Edit Profile** dialog box will open. Click on the **Advanced** label in this dialog box to expand the area to associate profiles to portal groups.

Now click on the **Add External** button. This will open a new dialog box entitle **Add External Association**. In the input box, you would specify the name of the portal group that you want to associate with the selected profile. This process needs to be repeated once for each profile you have defined in your profile set.

The following screenshot shows the dialog boxes available from the **Profile Set Editor** tab to associate profiles to portal groups:

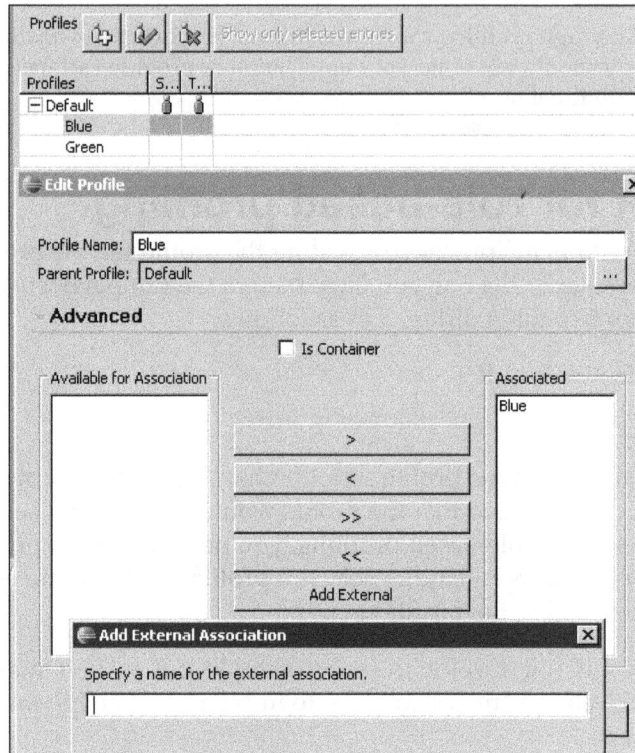

Please notice that despite the fact that in this example, we are associating the WEF **Blue** profile with the portal group of the same name, profile and portal group names do not need to be the same.

Concerning WEF, there is one last aspect you need to address. You need to specify in the Portlet Adapter builder how the existing profile set is going to be exposed in the portal. This is specified in the section labeled **Specify whether and how each Profile Set in this model should be customized when it is in a Portal**.

As you recall, we have already addressed this setting in our profiling sample. For role-based profiling, you would select the option that reads **Do not expose in Portal tools**.

Once you make the configurations listed previously, publish your WAR file, and you are done from the WEF perspective.

WebSphere Portal configuration for role-based profiling

To implement role-based profiling in portal, there is no specific configuration you need to perform. In other words, WEF does not require any special handling from the portal perspective.

There are a few aspects you need to be aware of though, so that your WEF portal application works as you intended it to work. The first one relates to the portal groups; you need to make sure that the portal group names match exactly with what you have specified when you mapped profile names to portal groups.

Another required action relates to Resource Permissions. You need to make sure that the user groups you have mapped to the profiles have access to these portlets.

Apart from the two aspects listed previously, there is nothing else you need to do in order to have role-based profiling implemented in portal.

> Although we have discussed role-based profiling within the portal context, it is important to mention that this same technique is not limited to portal. It can equally be applied to pure web applications and even applications developed to run on mobile devices.

Endless possibilities with profiling

Although we have covered only two mechanisms illustrating how profiling can be used in WEF, the possibilities and the different ways you can use profiling are really endless.

Profiling can be used for personalization and localization in portal as well as a configuration mechanism to configure models. Profiling is also used to create model-based builders.

In *Chapter 14, WEF and Mobile Web Applications*, we will explore another incredible way of using WEF profiling technology to configure models/portlets to be served as mobile web applications. WEF uses its profile selection handler capability to identify the device type, which is requesting your application. It then makes the necessary changes to render this application on a mobile device.

In summary, as far as you can think of configurable patterns, profiling can be used to achieve them.

We strongly recommend that you explore many other aspects of profiling. Having a deep understanding of profiling and its possibilities will greatly enrich your WEF skills. This will make you a more versatile developer with the ability to provide elegant, efficient, and time-saving solutions for your applications.

Summary

In this chapter we covered several aspects of the profiling technology offered by WEF.

We explained in detail how profiling works, at the same time we defined the key profiling terms used in WEF.

We also covered profile selection handlers and all the aspects of the profile set editor.

Together we built a sample model to demonstrate how a portlet can be profile-enabled not only to generate a different version of your portlet but also to learn how to expose the defined profiles in portal.

Lastly, we learned about role-based profiling in IBM WebSphere Portal.

The topics covered in this chapter do not exhaust the profiling capabilities of WEF, but the material you have read here provides a solid foundation upon which you can build and learn more advanced profiling features of WEF.

In the next chapter, we will cover the types of models available to WEF developers. We will identify and explain how the different models work independently and when they are combined with other models. We will also define WEF design patterns that efficiently take advantage of the different existing model types. Understanding these model types and how they can be combined to build your portlets will greatly improve your ability to develop efficient portlets.

13
Types of Models

Throughout the previous chapters, we discussed and worked with two types of models—service and user interface. These models perform a very specific role within the service-oriented architecture paradigm supported by WEF. However, these are not the only model types available to WEF developers. WEF developers can implement several other specialized models with different responsibilities within the application.

In this chapter we will look into these models and explain their benefits, when they should be used, as well as how to implement them. So, this chapter will discuss models from an architectural pattern perspective and how they contribute to the construction of effective applications.

The following are the model types we will cover in this chapter:

- UI models
- Service models
- Imported models
- Base models
- Configurable models
- Linked models
- Model container

One portlet, many models

A portlet might be comprised of a single or multiple models. There are no requirements, limitations, or rules specifying the number of models a portlet should contain.

We have seen that from a technical perspective, a model is a container for builder calls. Technically, there is no limit to how many builder calls a model can contain. However, this does not mean that a single model should hold all the builder calls required to construct your portlet. In fact, for commercial grade portlets, usually the best solution is accomplished through the utilization of multiple models. By doing so, builder calls can be logically organized and distributed throughout these models.

Portal and WEF architects need to consider the best patterns and architectural alternatives to efficiently identify not only the ideal number of models, but also how they relate to each other within a portlet or even the entire portal application. A well-organized model structure is crucial for the successful delivery of a reusable, robust, and scalable portal solution.

Summary of the model types

Some models are characterized by the presence of specific builders; others are characterized by their roles or responsibilities.

The following table shows the model types, and the builders or aspects, which characterize them.

Model type	Builder	Roles or Responsibilities
UI model	Service Consumer, User Interface Control	It handles user interface interaction.
Service model	Service Definition, Service Operation	It retrieves and transforms data from backend systems. It also applies business logic.
Imported models	Imported Model	It enables segregation of responsibilities and reusability. It also makes models more manageable.
Linked models	Linked Model	It enables reusability from a functional perspective.
Model container	Model Container	It places more then one model on a page. It also enables segregation of responsibilities mostly from a presentation perspective.

Model type	Builder	Roles or Responsibilities
Base model		Concept – It can be applied to imported models and configuration models.
Configuration model		It enables configurability through the utilization of profiling while importing a model.

Besides the models defined in the preceding table, you probably will see other references to models such as host model, outer model, inner model, parent model, and top-level model. The description about some of these models is as follows:

- **Host model**: Host model is employed to identify a model that contains one or more Imported Model or Linked Model builders. The same concept can be applied to define top-level model as well as parent model.

- **Outer and inner models**: Outer and Inner models are expressions commonly used throughout the WEF help documentation. Outer model refers to a model that contains one or more Model Container builders. Inner model refers to the contained model; in other words, the model running inside the model container.

- **Base model**: Unlike the other models, which can contain Imported Model, Linked Model, or Model Container builders, there is no builder named Base or Configuration. A base model can be compared to a base Java class. It contains base functionality or elements, which can be defined once and imported into several other models.

- **Configuration model**: A configuration model is not a model, which contains a Configuration builder, but a model that can be configured through the profiling capability of WEF. We will cover the base and configuration models in more details.

> Base model and configuration model are conceptual terms.

From the preceding table, you can see that WEF makes available several model types. Developers need to understand how these models can be employed and combined in an efficient manner to build efficient portlets and overall portal solutions.

Model types demystified

Let's dive into the details of each model type so that you understand what they are. By understanding their definition and concepts, you will have the foundation knowledge to make educated decision to build your solution efficiently.

User interface models

The user interface models embody the presentation layer on the two-tiered paradigm supported by WEF.

While in the service-oriented architecture supported by WEF, most focus is given to the Service builders used on the service provider models; we cannot diminish the importance of the presentation layer within this architecture.

In the previous chapters you have already been exposed to user interface models. As we saw, within the WEF service-oriented architecture, a UI model is easily identifiable by the virtue of containing a Service Consumer builder call.

Depending upon the complexity of the solution, UI models might require multiple Service Consumer builders. Conversely, some portlets might not implement any service, although this is unusual. In this case, the UI model would not have a Service Consumer builder. When the UI models do not contain a Service Consumer builder, we can define the UI model by being the model which holds the UI builder calls such as pages, HTML controls, Dojo controls, JSP, images, JavaScript, and other UI-related builders.

Also, some models might implement complex UI display and navigation patterns. Such models might require numerous UI builders. For such a scenario, it is recommended that you split these builders into other smaller and more manageable models.

The Rule of 50

In the preceding section we mentioned the possibility of splitting a model due to the large number of builders in a single model. You might be asking yourself about the recommended number of builders a model should contain. To answer this question, we need to refer to the document entitled, *Best practices for model development with IBM WebSphere Portlet Factory*. You can find a copy of this document at `http://www.ibm.com/developerworks/websphere/library/techarticles/0606_odonnell/0606_odonnell.html#download`.

This document contains valuable recommendations every developer should follow. In this document you will find an entry entitled, *Keep model size under 50 Builders*. The main focus of this entry is manageability of models. This recommendation does not refer to a portlet, but rather to a model, as a portlet might be comprised of multiple models.

Keep in mind that this is just a recommendation and not a technical limitation. Experienced WEF developer can easily organize and manage models with 60, 70, or even more builders. Sometimes it does not make sense to split models just for the sake of meeting recommendations. As a developer, you make the call on what makes or what does not make sense in your application.

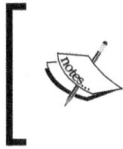

> Concerning memory consumption and performance, a single model containing 100 builders performs equally well when compared to the approach where these same 100 builders are split into two 50-builder models.

The Portlet Adapter builder

Only one Portlet Adapter builder is added to the presentation layer, even if your portlet contains multiple presentation models. Usually you add the Portlet Adapter builder to the same model, which contains the main method or main Action List builder call.

Service models

We have already covered service provider models or just service models as sometimes they are described.

Here we reference the service models as one of the model types, which should be implemented whenever backend data access is required. The WEF best practices document mentioned previously also recommends the utilization of the service models to concentrate all the data retrieval, data manipulation, and business logic in the service models.

The implementation of service models brings flexibility to service-driven applications, at the same time, it provides numerous features to make it easy and faster to develop against any backend system.

It is not difficult to understand the numerous advantages of using service models whenever backend data access is involved. A few of these advantages are included in the following list:

- Concentrates backend activities in specialized models
- Enables presentation layer to work when disconnected from the backend systems
- Provides a standard way to expose backend data regardless of the backend system
- Provides testing support without the need for a presentation layer
- Provides reusability when backend systems are swapped

> The communication between the presentation and the service layers is done through in-memory Java calls. This does not add any perceptible overhead to the service-oriented architecture paradigm when compared against the option of not using this paradigm.

IBM has published a rich, best practices document for service-oriented model development. We recommend you read this document before implementing your service models. The document is entitled, *Best practices for service-oriented model development with IBM WebSphere Portlet Factory software*. This document can be found at `ftp://ftp.software.ibm.com/ftp/lotusweb/websphere/portletfactory/BP_SOA_wp_hr.pdf`.

Imported models

Imported models are vastly used in any project developed with WEF.

Imported model is the mechanism by which a model is included into another model. The model, which imports another model is referred to as **host model**.

The following are some of the benefits of using imported models for application development:

- Support modular development
- Keep models manageable
- Enable reusability
- Enable the utilization of configurable components

Overall, importing another model is similar to adding all the builder calls existing in another model into your model with one small difference—the builder inputs from the imported model cannot be modified by the host model.

In order to import another model, or to bring in the builder call list from another model, the host model adds the Imported Model builder to its builder call list. By doing so, the host model has access to all the artifacts created by the model being imported.

The following screenshot shows the **Imported Model** builder:

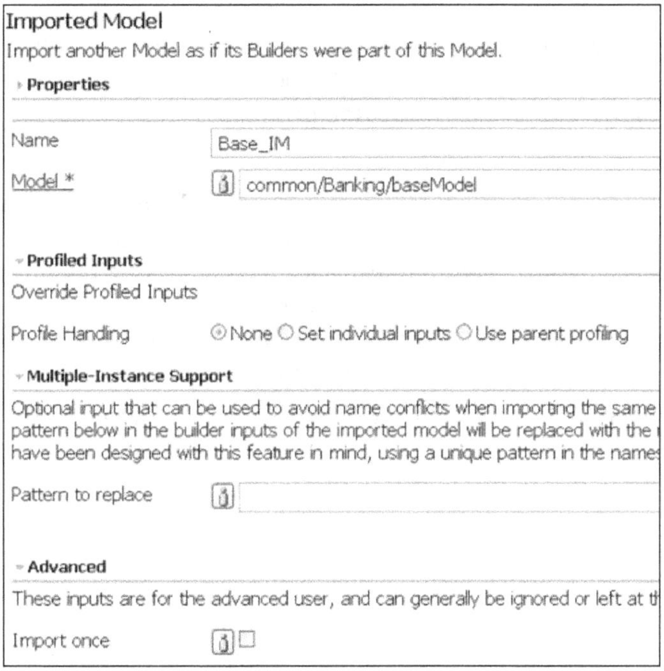

Let's look at the inputs available for the **Imported Model** builder, as shown in the preceding screenshot:

- **Name**: Builder call name
- **Model**: This indicates the model to be imported. Only models existing in the same project can be imported.

- **Override Profiled Inputs**: **Profile Handling**: This refers to builder inputs that have been profile-enabled in the model being imported. There are three options as it follows:

    ◦ **None**: If any builder input is profiled in the model being imported, these values are not handled by the host model. Regeneration will take place using the default values for these inputs.

    ◦ **Set individual inputs**: The profile-enabled inputs in the imported model will be exposed in a section of the **Imported Model** builder's interface in the builder editor. Through this option, users can override the default values of profiled input values.

    ◦ **Use parent profiling**: This applies one or more profiles defined in the host model to the imported model. Both host model and imported model need to use the same profile set.

- **Multiple-Instance Support**

    ◦ **Pattern to replace**: This is used to handle the scenario where a model is imported more than once into the same host model. This is designed to avoid namespace collision among the imported models. If this scenario is applicable to the development of your solution, you should plan ahead and implement a naming convention to apply to the imported model when you are creating it.

- **Import once**: This is used to avoid importing similar artifacts more than once into the same host model.

> When you are building a model to be imported into another model, consider establishing a naming convention approach to avoid naming conflicts. The host model and the imported model cannot have builder calls with the same name.

Once you understand the benefits of imported model and the different ways in which you can use it, imported model will become one of your best friends in the WEF world.

Sample scenario for imported model

To demonstrate the utilization of imported models, let's look at a simple scenario.

Consider a scenario where you need to develop a portlet to manage A2Z user accounts. The following is a brief description of the requirements to develop such portlet:

- Portlet needs to enable A2Z branch associates to create, update, delete, and list bank accounts.

- Managers should be able to add or link features and products to the accounts. Features and products include vault, special rates, credit card, and other financial products.

- Portlet should log auditing information for each operation listed here.

Technically, you could create all of these features in one single model. However, such a model would be difficult to maintain and to reuse. Moreover, there are several pieces of functionality that could be easily segregated. To start addressing this issue, let's look at the most obvious separation. You need to separate the models to handle presentation and backend system access. The service consumer/provider architecture is the clear choice for this task. Backend system access is done through web services. We will not address the service side of the implementation. Instead, let's focus on the presentation layer, where we will have the opportunity to explore imported models.

As we will be focusing on the presentation layer, we should group and identify the functionality we need to address. Functionality can be grouped as follows:

- Create, update, delete, and list users

- List and manage features and products for a given account

- Handle exceptions

- Capture user information and log auditing information

Now let's see the models we could create to accommodate the functionality grouping that we mentioned in the preceding list. The following are the models we can consider:

- Common functionality model

- Create account model

- Update account model

- Delete account model

- Manage features and products for accounts

The common functionality model should handle aspects that are used by all models. This includes, but it is not limited to:

- Exception handling

- Building an object or an XML variable to capture information about the currently logged in user

- Performing auditing tasks

The creation of individual models for Create, Update, and Delete activities is justified by the complexity of managing these individual operations.

Lastly, the activities for managing account features and products also require a model of its own.

The following diagram shows a graphical representation of these models, which captures their relationship inside the user management portlet:

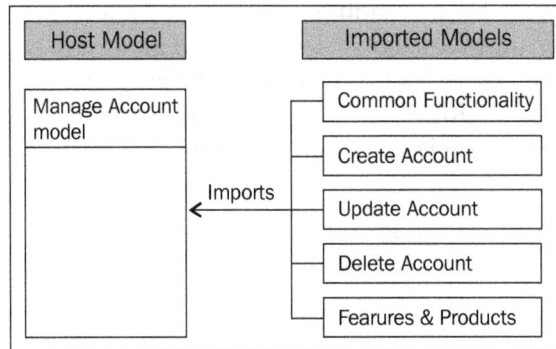

The Manage Account model is our host model. It contains all Imported Model builders. It also holds the Portlet Adapter builder.

By implementing the imported model technique, we can split the different pieces of functionality across several different models. We then import these models and make the host model behave as if it were one single model. We will do all of this without any special handling.

The following screenshot shows what the builder call list for our **AccountManagement** model would look like:

Please notice that builder call number **5, baseModel_IM**, holds the functionality we have defined as common functionality. Well, this gives us the opportunity to introduce the concept of base models.

Base models

Base model is a concept commonly used in WEF projects. It is a WEF solution design concept. As such, WEF does not provide a builder named Base Model builder. Instead, this concept is enabled through the utilization of the Imported Model builder.

Let's use the preceding sample scenario to describe how the implementation of base models can help you in your WEF project. In the previous section we listed a couple of common functionality items, such as exception handling and logging audit events. All the imported models we have identified in our sample scenario need to perform the tasks implemented in our common model. Instead of copying the builders that implement this functionality into each model, we implement all the common functionality in a single model. Then we import this model whenever we need the desired functionality. Most likely, we will import this model into each portlet in our solution.

> Although WEF provides the Error Handler builder, which handles exceptions, in this section we refer to exception handling as a small framework. This small framework can be implemented as a group of Java classes, the Error Handler builder, and messages, which gracefully handle business and system exceptions in a standard manner throughout the entire application.

Configuring imported models through profiling

One of the advantages of using imported models is their reusability. We can save valuable efforts and resources when we reuse existing models. However, many times the model being imported needs to be modified to adjust to our development needs. WEF provides such capability through profiling.

We have already covered profiling, but this is another way of employing profiling by which you can create configurable models. The configurable elements (builder inputs) are exposed when these models are imported into a host model. In other words, you can define a single model to behave differently depending upon the inputs you set in the host models.

If you refer back to the **Profiled Inputs** section of the **Imported Model** builder interface, you will notice that one of the options in this section is **Set individual inputs**. If you select this option when you are importing a model that has profile-enabled inputs, the Imported Model builder automatically displays these input fields. The input name is the text you have defined as the prompt value in the profile entry.

In the example we are describing in this section, assume that our base model includes a Theme builder. As a good WEF developer you are, you would want to give other developers the ability to configure the look and feel of your base model when they import it. That being the case, you would profile-enable at least the **Theme File** input of the Theme builder.

The following screenshot shows the **Profiled Inputs** section of an Imported Model builder. This builder imports a model that has profile-enabled the **Theme File** input field:

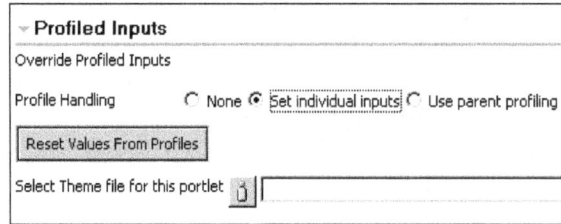

Model container

Another resource available for managing models in portlets is the Model Container builder. **Model container** is another powerful mechanism, which enables reusability at the same time that it makes the construction of complex portlets easily manageable. It also enables collaboration, where developers can develop different sections of the portlet in parallel.

The Model Container builder enables you to load one or multiple models into a specified location on your JSP page. Through the Model Container builder, you point to another model that can be loaded at the specified tag on your JSP page.

It is possible to load one or multiple models into a single container. When the Model Container builder is used to load a single model, the model is referenced at design time. When multiple models are meant to be loaded into a single container, then you can invoke the methods, which enable you to select, initialize, and load any existing presentation model in your WEF project. These methods are made available in the web application when a Model Container builder is added to a model. If a model container is implemented to contain multiple models, then only one model can be active at a time per model container.

To illustrate the utilization of the Model Container builder, we can revisit the same portlet we discussed in the *Imported models* section of this chapter, but this time considering the model container's implementation instead of imported models.

The following diagram illustrates the user interface of our A2Z Account Management portlet and the concept of model container:

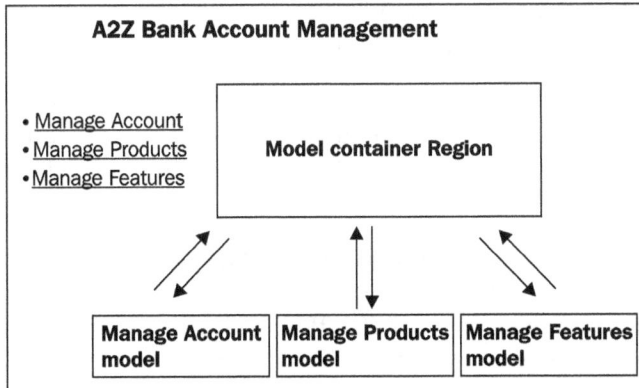

The area defined as **Model Container Region** in the preceding diagram is represented by a named tag in our JSP page. This tag works as a placeholder for the content to be placed by the Model Container builder.

In this example, the Account Management portlet is comprised of a host or outer model, a model container builder, and three other models. The outer model also contains other UI elements, such as the links and the welcome page, the main action, and the Portlet Adapter builder. The code to swap the models inside the container at runtime also resides on the outer model.

With this implementation, when a user clicks one of the links, we invoke the method to load the desired model into the container. In doing so, we bring into the welcome page the presentation of other model and keep a single shell for this model. This operation is done seamlessly without any indication that models are being swapped in the model container region.

When the model is first loaded into the container, the model container calls the main action of the contained model. This will enable the initialization of the contained model in a standard manner.

> The Model Container builder enables container hierarchy. You can use the Model Container builder in a model that is already contained by an outer model.

Linked models

Linked model is another mechanism by which WEF developers can reuse functionality residing in different models. Just like imported model and model container, linked models also represent a means to better manage multiple models in a portlet.

A model can be linked to another model through the utilization of the Linked Model builder. This builder exposes methods, action lists, public LJO methods, and pages from the linked model.

Unlike the Imported Model builder, this builder does not cause the artifacts of the linked model to be added to the WebApp object of the host model. Instead, it adds to the host model just an identifier (or a slot), which enables you to reference the methods and pages defined in the linked model.

The linked model needs to be present in the same WEF project as the models referencing it.

The linked model is ideal for scenarios where you want to reuse functionality developed in other models, as opposed to presentation elements. To enhance the reusability of functionality developed in other models, the Linked Model builder allows the creation of either multiple instances of the model being linked in or a single instance model, also known as **Session Singleton**.

> It is important to notice that the model types defined in this chapter can be combined in many different ways according to the portlet and portal solution design needs. In another words, they are not mutually exclusive.

Summary

In this chapter you had the opportunity to learn about the different model types available to WEF developers to build portlets and other applications.

The different model types can be identified explicitly by the builders they contain, such as Imported Model, Model Container, and Linked Model builders, or they can also be identified by the concept that they represent, such as the base model and configurable models.

The availability of different model types assists WEF developers concerning reusability, manageability, and maintenance of complex portlets. In addition to that, parallel development can be accomplished through the simultaneous construction of similar or different model types by multiple developers.

A portlet memory footprint can also be reduced by efficiently employing the appropriate model types.

The efficient construction of complex portlets that use multiple models depends upon the understanding of the working mechanism of each model type available in WEF.

In the next chapter we will explore the mobile space to demonstrate how WEF can address reusability and reduce costs by enabling a single application to run on multiple devices, including mobile devices.

14
WEF and Mobile Web Applications

In the recent years, we have been experiencing an explosion in the mobile devices' market. Cellular phones and tablets have become integral part of everyone's life. In many countries, the number of mobile devices has surpassed their population. Such growth should not come as a surprise to any one aware of the benefits provided by the mobile technology.

The applications running on these devices play a major role in this space. In the mobile arena web applications continue being of crucial importance for corporations. Currently, almost every corporation wants to enable its customers to access its existing web applications over mobile devices.

WEF has expanded its capability to enable the development of web applications capable of being rendered in mobile devices. IBM refers to this newly added capability as an expansion to support the development of multichannel applications.

In this chapter we will look into the solution provided by WEF to enable developers to develop web applications with such capabilities. We will not only discuss the resources available in WEF for such development, but we will also develop a web application sample model, which is capable of being rendered on both desktops and mobile devices.

The following are the topics we will cover in this chapter:

- The mobile device space
- Mobile web applications
- Requirements for mobile web applications

- WEF capabilities and features for developing mobile web applications
  - New builders
  - New UI themes
- Sample application

Mobile devices

The mobile device space represents such a huge segment that encompasses numerous vendors and numerous different device types. It is not the intent of this chapter to discuss all the nuances of this segment. Instead, for the purpose of this chapter, we will focus on what we believe to be the biggest and most prominent segment within the mobile space—smartphones and tablets.

From a software perspective, there are two categories of applications, which enable interaction with these devices—native device applications and web applications.

Native device applications are developed utilizing the specific **software development kit (SDK)** created and supported by the vendors of such devices. These applications are extremely rich and utilize the full set of features available in each of these devices. Some of these features include still camera, video recording, GPS locator device, voice activated applications, and so on.

Mobile devices also render web applications. For running web applications on their mobile devices, vendors ship their devices with browsers that meet their mobile requirements. From the core perspective, all the browsers are built upon one or another type of web engine. Most of the smartphone browsers utilize the WebKit web browser engine. The WebKit engine is used in browsers such as Google Chrome and Apple Safari. It is also the basis for the default browser in the iOS, Android, and webOS mobile operating systems.

Web applications designed to be rendered in mobile devices need to take into account the characteristics and peculiarities of these devices. Two important characteristics to keep in mind are screen size and the speed of the internet connection.

In addition to the two categories we have just mentioned, you could consider a third category, although it is actually a combination of these two categories. Through this combination, web applications can access certain features of the devices on which the web application is running. For instance, a web application can access the still camera or dial out a phone number from the device.

Desktop applications versus mobile web applications

In the previous topic, we mentioned mobile web applications. In order to enable you to develop mobile web applications, you need to understand the similarities and the differences between applications designed to run on browsers installed in desktops or laptops and applications designed to run on mobile devices, especially smartphones and tablets.

Let's start with the similarities. The most significant similarity is that both the desktop and mobile web applications use the same UI technologies, such as HTML, JavaScript, and CSS styling to render content in the browser. This is an immense common denominator, which enables reutilization and cost reduction.

On the other hand, there are a few differences between these two categories of devices. A few of them, which we need to keep in mind from the web development perspective are as follows:

- **Screen size**: While desktops have plenty of real estate to show content, mobile devices have limited real estate.

- **Internet connection speed**: While most of desktops access the internet through a high-speed connection, the mobile devices still have limited data speed.

- **Subtle differences in the behavior of the UI controls**: The UI controls might behave differently when running on a mobile device. This is mostly due to the fact that the browsers developed upon the WebKit engine are less robust than other engines used to create browsers that target desktops.

- **Navigation pattern**: While desktop-targeted web applications have a multitude of navigation patterns, mobile web applications need to implement a navigation pattern, which is more limited and suited for small screens.

In summary, despite the fact that the same UI technology is used to develop web applications for both device categories, the differences listed previously place some constraints on the application development effort and require developers to be sensitive to these differences.

WEF handling of mobile web applications

Now that we have briefly covered several aspects of mobile web applications, we can transition to look into the capabilities and features provided by WEF for developing mobile web applications.

Support for mobile web application came into picture in August of 2011 with the release of WEF 7.0.1. This support is added in the form of a WEF feature set named Mobile. You need to add this feature set in order to have access to the builders, themes, profile selection handler, UI themes, base profile sets, and other artifacts available to build mobile web applications.

WEF does not require you to learn new mobile technology or advanced mobile techniques in order to develop mobile web applications. In fact, WEF leverages and takes advantage of the same model-driven design approach with which you are already familiar. Models, builders, and profiling represent a well-suited combination to handle the differences between devices at the same time that it preserves the commonalities represented by the utilization of the HTML, JavaScript, and CSS technologies.

WEF 7.0.1 offers a set of new builders to handle the differences and features of mobile web applications. The list of these new builders is as follows:

- **Data Layout builder**: This builder enables a model to specify numerous characteristics related to the display of listed data. Developers can choose from a variety of layout templates at the same time that they can create their own layout templates.

- **Geolocation builder**: This builder enables a model to obtain the information about geographical location if the device supports this feature. This is done through the geolocation API specification.

- **Page navigation**: This builder enables a model to specify the page navigation format to be implemented. The options available include formats which are geared towards mobile devices.

In addition to the builders we have just listed, WEF mobile capabilities include a wizard, which creates a mobile web application. This is the Mobile List and Detail Service Consumer wizard. This wizard creates a model, which includes builders suited for developing mobile web applications.

To support the development of mobile web applications, WEF also provides a multitude of mobile UI themes to be used with the already existing Theme builder.

Profiling has also been used to enable the development of mobile web applications. WEF has created a special profile selection handler, which identifies the type of device from which the request is coming. With this component, developers can profile-enable their models to serve content tailored to specific devices.

While the features listed in the preceding section demonstrate the enhancements provided by WEF to enable the development of mobile web applications, it does not represent any deviation from the standard way in which WEF utilizes its core technology of models, builders, and profiling. In the end, such support is made possible through the model-driven approach implemented by WEF.

Mobile web application sample

We have spent the last few pages discussing about the characteristics and the WEF support for development of mobile web applications. While we could spend several more pages further discussing these topics, we would like to transition into the development of a sample model. This way, you will have the opportunity to see some of these builders and artifacts in action as well as the technique WEF employs to detect the device type on each request.

While we will not be developing an extensive application, we will have the opportunity to use and discuss the most important elements in the WEF mobile web application arena.

A2Z web mobile strategy

You have been asked to participate in a secret meeting where A2Z unveils its new strategy for the credit card division. In this meeting everything is going as usual. You are almost falling asleep due to the multitude of PPT slides they are throwing at the audience and you are looking forward to the coffee break. However, all of a sudden you hear an expression that catches your attention—multichannel web applications.

The Program Director explains that in order to reduce costs and do more with less, the A2Z IT department needs to be able to develop a single web application capable of running on desktop browsers, smartphones, and tablets. A2Z cannot afford to have three different development teams developing one version for each device type.

At this point, most of the participants express their skepticism, and one of them even voices his/her concern—it is impossible to do so.

But, since you know WEF capabilities, you confidently state that you can implement such strategy. You convince the Program Director to let you lead the development of a **Proof of Concept** (**POC**) to demonstrate how this can be accomplished.

The Program Director agrees with you and describes the high-level requirements, which are listed in the following section.

Requirements

The multichannel web application should be written once and could be invoked from different device types. The three main device types with which you should be concerned are desktops, smartphones, and tablets.

The welcome page should display a list of the credit card options as follows:

- Account details
- Transactions
- Rewards
- Customer support

Upon clicking on each link, the credit card user would be taken to the corresponding page. Each page needs to take into account the characteristics of each device. The smartphone version needs to make accommodations to use the limited real estate efficiently at the same time that it provides a native look and feel that is common in smartphones.

You think to yourself—this challenge is not for the faint of heart. But then you recall you have seen such an example in the book *IBM WebSphere Portal 8: Web Experience Factory and the Cloud*.

So, you start feeling pretty confident that you can do a fantastic job with this POC and maybe get even closer to that well-deserved promotion. You are right. You should be pretty confident, because we will help you with this task.

Expected outcome

The following screenshot shows what the application should look like when it is invoked from a desktop browser:

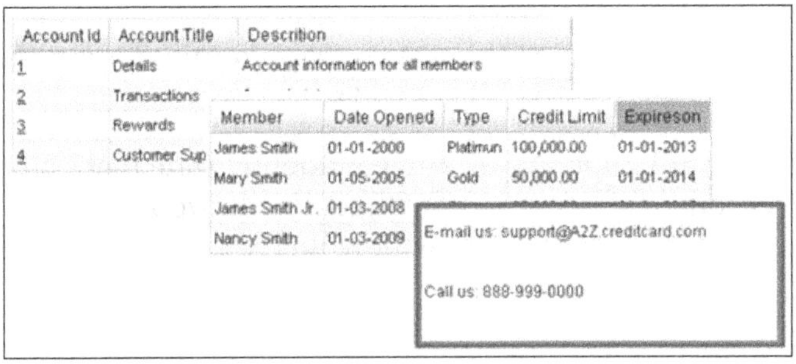

And the following screenshot shows what the application should look like when it is invoked from a smartphone device:

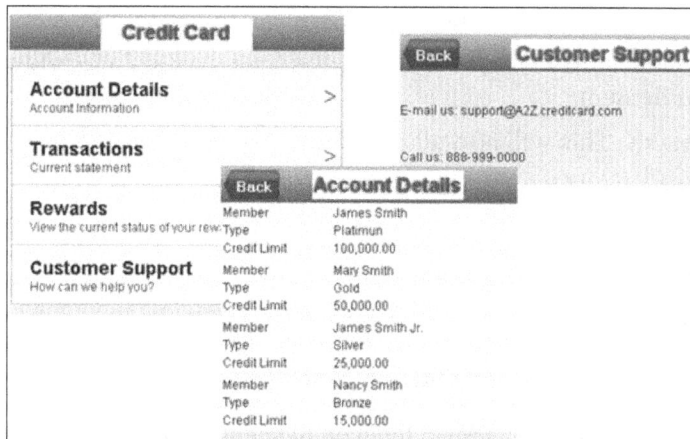

Multichannel web application sample

This section shows how we are going to develop this POC.

In this POC we will be using the following builders:

- The Theme builder with the new mobile themes
- The Page Navigation builder with the new mobile layout templates
- The Data Layout builder with the new mobile layout templates

In addition to the builders we have just listed, we will use the new Mobile Device Type profile selection handler.

> Please notice that the new mobile features are available through the Mobile feature set. This feature set is available only in Version 7.0.1 and higher versions.

Let's start our sample. Open Eclipse or RAD, and then open the A2Z WEF project we have been using.

Before we create our model, we need to add the Mobile feature set to this project so that we can have access to the new mobile builders and artifacts. Perform the following steps to do so:

1. Right-click on the project's root—the **A2Z** folder.
2. From the context menu, select **Properties**.
3. Expand the **WebSphere Portlet Factory Project Properties** in the left-hand side pane.

4. Click on the **Feature** Info node.

5. In the **Feature Info** window, expand the User Interface folder, and check the **Mobile** item.

6. Click on **OK**. This will add all the mobile elements we need.

7. Create a new folder under the models folder.

8. Name it chapter14.

9. Inside this folder, create a new empty model named creditCard.

10. Click on **Finish**.

Once the model opens, access the **Outline** panel, and perform the following steps:

1. In the **Outline** panel, click on the icon to open the **Builder Picker** dialog box.

2. From the **Category Name** panel, click on the **Mobile** category.

3. From the **Builder** panel, select the Theme builder.

4. Provide the following inputs:

    ° **Name: mobile_THM**

    ° **Theme File: /WEF-INF/Factory/themes/mobile/mobile_slide.uitheme**

5. Click on **OK**, and save your model.

This theme file contains style entries to enable the slide-in effect common in smartphones.

> Please notice that the theme that you have added here refers to the WEF portlet or application theme. This is different from the mobile-oriented portal themes offered by IBM WebSphere Portal.

Adding variables to your application

Next, perform the following steps to create the variables for holding the list of credit card options valid for a given A2Z customer.

We provide the content of these variables in an XML file, which can be downloaded from http://www.packtpub.com/support. The files are named Options.xml and ListDetails.xml.

1. Add a Variable builder to your model.

2. Enter the following inputs for this variable:

    ° **Name: ccList_VAR**

    ° **Type: XML**

○ **Initial Value**:

```
<CCList>
    <Account>
        <Account_ID>1</Account_ID>
        <Account_Title>Details</Account_Title>
        <Descrition>Account information for all
            members</Description>
    </Account>
    <Account>
        <Account_ID>2</Account_ID>
        <Account_Title>Transactions</Account_Title>
        <Descrition>Current statement</Description>
    </Account>
    <Account>
        <Account_ID>3</Account_ID>
        <Account_Title>Rewards</Account_Title>
        <Descrition>View the current status of your reward
            account</Description>
    </Account>
    <Account>
        <Account_ID>4</Account_ID>
        <Account_Title>Customer Support</Account_Title>
        <Descrition>How can we help you?</Description>
    </Account>
</CCList>
```

3. Click on **OK**, and save your model.

4. Add one more variable with the following inputs:

    ○ **Name: ccdetails_VAR**

    ○ **Type: XML**

    ○ **Initial Value**:

```
<Details>
    <Detail>
        <Member>James Smith</Member>
        <Date_Opened>01-01-2000</Date_Opened>
        <Type>Platimun</Type>
        <Credit_Limit>100,000.00</Credit_Limit>
        <Expires_on>01-01-2013</Expires_on>
    </Detail>
    <Detail>
        <Member>Mary Smith</Member>
        <Date_Opened>01-05-2005</Date_Opened>
        <Type>Gold</Type>
```

```
            <Credit_Limit>50,000.00</Credit_Limit>
            <Expires_on>01-01-2014</Expires_on>
        </Detail>
        <Detail>
            <Member>James Smith Jr.</Member>
            <Date_Opened>01-03-2008</Date_Opened>
            <Type>Silver</Type>
            <Credit_Limit>25,000.00</Credit_Limit>
            <Expires_on>01-01-2015</Expires_on>
        </Detail>
        <Detail>
            <Member>Nancy Smith</Member>
            <Date_Opened>01-03-2009</Date_Opened>
            <Type>Bronze</Type>
            <Credit_Limit>15,000.00</Credit_Limit>
            <Expires_on>01-01-2016</Expires_on>
        </Detail>
    </Details>
```

5. Click on **OK**, and save your model.

Now that we have created the variables, which will emulate the data returned by web service calls, we can move on to adding the pages required in this application.

Adding pages to your application

In total, we will add six pages to our model. We provide the content for these Page builders in a file named Chapter 14 - html files.txt. This file has six sections, one for each builder. This file can be downloaded from http://www.packtpub.com/support.

So, add one Page builder for each page listed in the following section.

- **Name: cc_home_dstp_PG**
- **Page Contents (HTML):**

```
<html>
        <body>
            <div name="ccMenuOptions"></div>
        </body>
</html>
```

- **Name: cc_home_mobile_PG**
- **Page Contents (HTML):**

```
<html>
    <body>
```

```
        <div align="center" name="page_header"
            class="wpfMobilePageHeader">
        <div name="page_header_text"
            class="wpfMobilePageHeaderText"></div>
        </div>
            <form name="cc_form" method="POST">
                    <div name="ccMenuOptions"></div>
            </form>

    </body>
</html>
```

- **Name: account_details_PG**
- **Page Contents (HTML):**

```
<html>
  <body>
    <div name="page_wrapper" class="wpfMobilePage">
      <div align="center" name="page_header"
          class="wpfMobilePageHeader">
        <span name="back_button" class="wpfMobileBackButton">
      </span>
    <div name="page_header_text"
        class="wpfMobilePageHeaderText">
    </div>
    </div>
  <span name="cc_details"> </span>
  </div>

  </body>
</html>
```

- **Name: rewards_PG**
- **Page Contents (HTML):**

```
<html>
 <body>
  <div name="page_wrapper" class="wpfMobilePage">
   <div align="center" name="page_header"
    class="wpfMobilePageHeader">
    <span name="back_button"
    class="wpfMobileBackButton"></span>
    <div name="page_header_text"
    class="wpfMobilePageHeaderText">
    </div>
   </div>
```

```
    <BR><BR>
    <div  class="wpfMobilePageHeader">
      A world of rewards is waiting for you... </div>
    </div>
  </body>
</html>
```

- **Name: customerSupport_PG**
- **Page Contents (HTML):**

```
<html>
 <body>
  <div name="page_wrapper" class="wpfMobilePage">
   <div align="center" name="page_header"
       class="wpfMobilePageHeader">
   <span name="back_button" class="wpfMobileBackButton"></span>
   <div name="page_header_text"
       class="wpfMobilePageHeaderText"></div>
  </div>
   <BR><BR>
   E-mail us: support@A2Z.creditcard.com  <BR><BR><BR>
   Call us: 888-999-0000
   </div>
  </body>
</html>
```

- **Name: transactions_PG**
- **Page Contents (HTML):**

```
<html>
 <body>
  <div name="page_wrapper" class="wpfMobilePage">
   <div align="center" name="page_header"
       class="wpfMobilePageHeader">
   <span name="back_button" class="wpfMobileBackButton"></span>
   <div name="page_header_text"
       class="wpfMobilePageHeaderText"></div>
  </div>
  </div>
   <BR><BR>
   <div  class="wpfMobilePageHeader">
   No transactions this month. ... </div>
  </body>
</html>
```

Perfect. Now that you have added all the HTML pages that we will need to build our multichannel application, save your model.

Adding profile set to your application

Our next step is to add a profile set to provide the proper builder inputs depending upon the device type invoking our application. In addition to providing the inputs, our profile set will also enable us to specify the profile selection handler to be used with our model. For our multichannel application, we will use the device type profile selection handler.

Please perform the following steps to handle the profile set section of your application:

1. From your **Project Explorer**, right-click on the root of our project, and select **New | WebSphere Portlet Factory Profile Set**.

2. Select the **A2Z** project, and provide the following inputs:
    - Name: com.A2Z.creditCard.mobile
    - Description: Profile set for A2Z credit card multichannel application
    - Choose a Profile Set to duplicate: mobile_devicetype_base

3. Click on **Finish**.

WEF creates a profile set, which is a copy of the existing profile set used for multichannel applications. This profile set contains four entries related to mobile devices. Also, if you click on the **Select Handler** tab of this profile set, you will see that **Profile Selection Handler** has been set to **Mobile Device Type Handler**. This is a new profile selection handler, which has been developed to identify the device type making the page request. By knowing the device type from which the user is requesting the application, this selection handler can convey this information to WEF, which can serve the corresponding profiled instance of your application.

Now, let's continue our steps to add one entry to this profile set so that it will have five entries that will be available to our model:

1. Click on the **Entries** tab of the profile set you just created.

2. Click on the **Add** button for the profile entry.

3. The **New Profile Entry** widow is displayed.

4. Enter the following values in this window:
    - Name: initialPage
    - Prompt: Select initial page to load
    - UI type: TextInput
    - Width: 60

- ○ **Default Value:**
- ○ **Execution Time: false**

Notice that we are leaving the **Default Value** input field blank.

5. Click on **OK**, and save this profile set.

6. Let's add one more entry to this profile set. Provide the following inputs to this new entry:
    - ○ **Name: enableTheme**
    - ○ **Prompt: Enable Theme?**
    - ○ **UI type: TextInput**
    - ○ **Width: 60**
    - ○ **Default Value:**
    - ○ **Execution Time: false**

7. Click on **OK** to close the **New Profile Entry** window.

8. Save and close this profile set file, and let's go back to our model.

9. Add another builder to this model — an Action List builder.

10. Name it **main**, and for return type, leave it set to **Object**.

Now, here is where we will use our profile set to profile-enable an input on this builder to indicate that the value for this input will be provided by a profile to be selected at regeneration time.

In front of the **Actions** input, there is an **ActionList** box. Inside this box (not outside), on the first line there is a profile icon and the profiling assignment button, which looks like a chess pawn or a little golden candle.

The following screenshot shows the profiling assignment button, which needs to be clicked in order to open the profile window for this input:

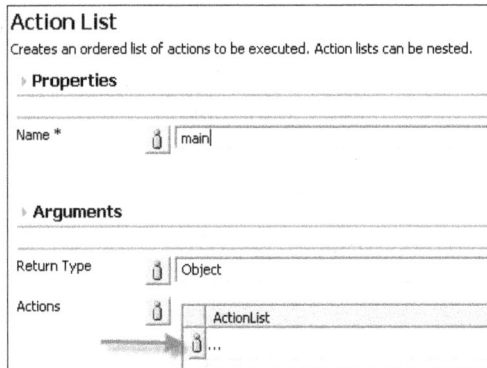

Let's light this candle then. Click on the icon indicated in the preceding screenshot to open the **Profile Row of Inputs** dialog box. Inside this dialog box, there is an icon in front of the **Action List** label. Click on this icon to open the **Profile Input** dialog box. For **Profile Set Name**, select the profile you just created—**com.A2Z.creditCard. mobile**. For **Profile Entry Name**, select **intialPage**.

Now let's provide the values for each profile. Perform the following steps to do so:

1. Under the **Profiles** column, the first entry is the **Default** profile. On the right-hand side, at the end of this row, there is a pencil icon. Click on this icon to open the **Modify Profile Value** dialog box.

2. In this box, click on the button with the three dots.

3. From the **Pages** node, select **cc_home_mobile_PG**. Click on **OK** to confirm your input for this window and for the **Modify Profile Value** window. This will cause all the other entries to be populated with this value.

4. Modify the **Browser** entry and instead of **cc_home_mobile_PG**, select **cc_ home_dstp_PG**.

   Your **Profile Input** window should look like the following screenshot:

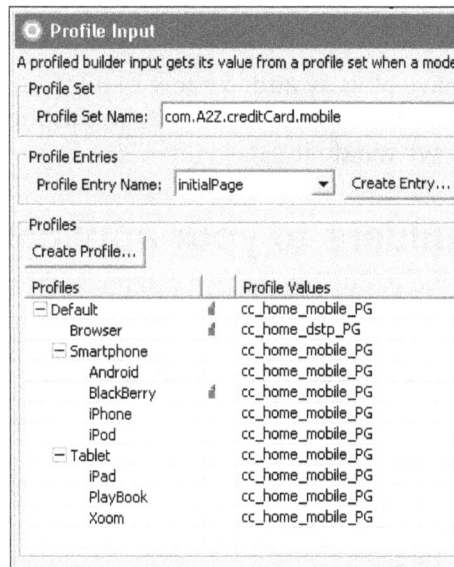

5. Click on **OK** on the dialog boxes and on the main Action List builder call.

6. Save your model.

At this point, we still cannot test our application. We still need to add a few more builders to our model. Before testing what we have built so far, let's profile-enable one more builder input:

1. Open the Theme builder you have added to your model.

2. Expand the **Properties** section of this builder.

3. Click on the **Profile Assignment** icon in front of the **Enable Builder** label. This action opens the **Profile Input** dialog box.

4. For **Profile Set Name**, select the profile you just created — **com.A2Z. creditCard.mobile**.

5. For **Profile Entry Name**, select **enableTheme**.

6. On this same dialog box, locate the **Profiles** section.

7. In this section, click on the pencil icon in the first row — the **Default** profile.

8. From **Modify Profile Value**, select **true**. This causes all the profile values to be populated with the value of **true**.

9. Modify the entry for the **Browser** profile, and set it to **false**.

10. Click on **OK** in the **Profile Input** dialog box and on the Theme builder**.**

11. Save your model.

Despite the fact that we have already added a few builders to our model, we still cannot show any content in the browser when we run this model. We need to add a few more builders before we can do it.

Adding more builders to your application

So, let's continue adding the builder so that we can reach the point where we can test our model.

The next builder we will add is Data Page with the following inputs:

- **Name: home_dskt_DP**
- **Variable: Variables/ccList_VAR/CCList**
- **Page in Model: cc_home_dstp_PG**
- **Page Type: View Only**
- **Make UI from Data**: Checked
- **Location for new tags: ccMenu Options**
- **Use Theme**: Checked
- **Generate Label**: Checked

Click on **OK**, and save your model.

Let's add one more builder before we run our first test. Add a Page Navigation builder to your model.

Supply the following inputs to this builder:

- **Name: menuOptions_PN**
- **Page: cc_home_mobile_PG**
- **Tag: ccMenuOptions**
- **Layout Template: Mobile Navigation List**
- **Style Sheet File: /factory/data_layout_templates/mobile_navigation_ border_list.css**
- For the **Navigation** inputs, enter the values, as shown in the following screenshot:

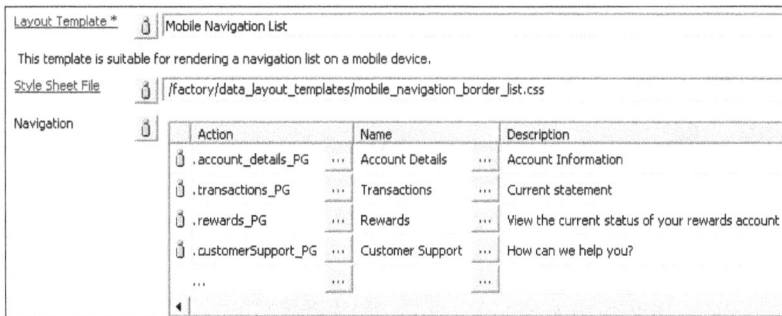

Click on **OK**, and save your model.

Testing your application

Finally, now we can run this model to see what it currently looks like on the browser. This will also give us the opportunity to see how profiling is defining the display of the application, depending upon the device type requesting our application.

At the bottom pane on the right-hand side of the designer, select the **Applied Profiles** tab. For **Profile Set**, this tab should be showing **com.A2Z.creditCard. mobile**. In the drop-down menu, you should see several options including **Browser**, **Smartphone**, and **Tablet**. As we have discussed when we covered profiling, this pane gives us the opportunity to apply the different profiles from the designer, thus emulating the profile to be applied at runtime. In other words, while at runtime, the profile selection handler will select the profile based on the device; here we explicitly select the profiles to be applied so that we can test our model.

So select **Browser** from the **Profiles** drop-down menu. Click on the **Apply** button. Now, run your model. You should see a regular table with three columns. This is what will be presented to users when they invoke this application from a desktop or a laptop device.

Now let's see what would be presented to users when they invoke the application from a smartphone device. Change the **Profiles** drop-down option in the **Applied Profile** pane to **Smartphone**. Click on the **Apply** button. The browser should render the smartphone version of your application, which takes into account the characteristics of smartphones, including screen with limited real estate. This version also presents a native looking smartphone, which matches the device type.

Adding header and links

OK. Now that we have confirmed that the application is working as we expected, and that we can apply profile to render the profiled version that matches the device, we can continue expanding our application towards the final version.

Add one more builder to your model. This time add a Text builder with the following inputs:

- **Name: page_header_TXT**
- **Page: cc_home_mobile_PG**
- **Tag: page_header_text**
- **Text: Credit Card Menu**
- Leave the other inputs to their default values.

Click on **OK**, and save your model again.

This Text builder will add the header only to the mobile pages.

Now we need to add the link, which will take the user from the home page with the list of credit card options to the selected page. This link will be added to the **Account** page with the selected option. We will add this link only to the browser version, because the mobile version will utilize a different navigation mechanism. Add a Link builder to your model. Supply the following inputs to this builder:

- **Name: account_LKN**
- **Page: cc_home_dstp_PG**
- **Tag: Account_ID**

- **Link text:**
- **Action Type: Link to an action**
- **Action:**

Click on **OK**, and save your model.

Notice that both the **Link text** and **Action** inputs are left blank. The reason we left the **Action** field blank is because we still have not created the method that determines which page will be returned when the user clicks on the link in the table for the browser version of our application.

Ok then, let's add a Method builder to our model with the following inputs:

- **Name: returnRightPage**
- **Arguments:**
    - ○ **Name: AccountID**
    - ○ **Data Type: int**
    - ○ **Return Type: void**
    - ○ **Method body:**

```
{
      int page = AccountID;
      String pageStr ="";

            switch (page) {
            case 1:   pageStr = "account_details_PG";
                    break;
            case 2:   pageStr = "transactions_PG";
                    break;
            case 3:   pageStr = "rewards_PG";
                    break;
            case 4:   pageStr = "customerSupport_PG";
                    break;

            }

      webAppAccess.getVariables().setString(
            "menuOptions_PNPreviousPage", "cc_home_dstp_
PG");
      webAppAccess.processPage(pageStr);
}
```

Click on **OK**, and save your model.

The preceding method will select the corresponding page when the user clicks on the link. As you recall, when we added the Link builder, we specified an argument in that builder. That argument is **Account Id**, which will be passed to this method. This method in turn will determine the page that should be returned upon clicking on the **Account Id** link.

Now that we have created this method, we can go back to the Link builder and provide the input for the **Action** input field, which currently is blank. So, open the Link builder you have added in the previous step, and select the **returnRightPage** input for the **Action** input field.

Click on **OK**, and save your model.

Adding the Data Page and Data Layout builders to your application

We are almost done with our multichannel mobile web application. We need to add only three more builders. Now add a Data Page builder with the following inputs:

- **Name: detail_DP**
- **Variable: Variables/ccDetails_VAR/Details**
- **Page in Model: account_details_PG**
- **Page Type: View Only**
- **Make UI from data**: Checked
- **Location for New Tags: cc_details**
- **Use Theme**: Checked
- **Generate Labels**: Checked

Click on **OK** and save your model.

Now, let's add two more builders, which will modify the data page layout depending upon the device type. The Data Page Layout builder is a great enhancement to WEF. It enables users to select from a multitude of pre-existing layout templates to be applied to the content created by a Data Page builder. In addition to using the pre-existing layout templates, you can create your own templates.

OK, let's move on. Add a Data Layout builder with the following inputs:

- **Name: details_sm_DL**
- **Container Field: [account_details_PG]Detail_DP/Details/Detail**
- **Layout Template: Multi-Line List**

- **Style Sheet File:**
- In the **Data Layout** table, select the following values for the already existing names:
    - ° **left_top**: Member_LABEL
    - ° **left_middle**: Type_LABEL
    - ° **left_bottom**: Credit_Limit_LABEL
    - ° **center_top**: Member
    - ° **center_middle**: Type
    - ° **center_bottom**: Credit_Limit

Leave the other values in this table blank. Before saving this builder, there is one more thing we need to do. That is to profile-enable an input in this builder. Through profiling, we will apply the page layout created by this builder to requests coming from smartphone devices. To do so, scroll all the way down to the top of this builder and expand the **Properties** section of this builder. Click on the **Profile Input** icon of the **Enable Builder** input. This action will open the **Profile Input** dialog box. Choose the following inputs:

- **Profile Set Name**: com.A2Z.creditCard.mobile
- **Profile Entry Name**: SmartPhoneDevice
- In the **Profiles** table, check the following checkboxes in the **Profile Values** column:
    - ° Smartphone
    - ° Android
    - ° BlackBerry
    - ° iPhone
    - ° iPod

Click on **OK** in this dialog box and then on the builder, and save this model.

Now, let's add the last builder to this model. We will add another Data Layout builder with the following inputs:

- **Name: details_tablet_DL**
- **Container Field: [account_details_PG]Detail/Details/Detail**
- **Layout Template: Thumbnail 2 Column Multi-Line List**
- **Style Sheet File:**

- In the **Data Layout** table, select the following values for the already existing names:
  - ◦ **left_image: Member**
  - ◦ **center_top: Type_LABEL**
  - ◦ **center_middle: Credit_Limit_LABEL**
  - ◦ **center_bottom: Expires_on_LABEL**
  - ◦ **right_top: Type**
  - ◦ **right_middle: Credit_Limit**
  - ◦ **right_bottom: Expires_on**

We will also profile-enable an input in this builder. This time we will enable this builder only when the request comes from tablet devices. Once again, scroll all the way up to the top of this builder and expand the **Properties** section of this builder. Click on the **Profile Input** icon of the **Enable Builder** input. This action will open the **Profile Input** dialog box. Choose the following inputs:

- **Profile Set Name: com.A2Z.creditCard.mobile**
- **Profile Entry Name: TabletDevice**

In the **Profiles** table, select the following checkboxes in the **Profile Values** column:

- **Tablet**
- **iPad**
- **PlayBook**
- **Xoom**

Click on **OK** in this dialog box, then click on **OK** on the builder, and save this model.

Testing the final version of your application

Now we can test our model and see how the application will be displayed on each device type.

We have already seen how WEF renders both desktop and smartphone profiled versions. Now, let's see how our application is presented on a tablet mobile device versus a smartphone. In your designer, select the **Applied Profile** tab in the bottom-right pane. For **Profiles**, select **Smartphone**. Click on **Apply**, and run your model.

You should see the native looking smartphone welcome page of our credit card application. Now, click on the **Account Details** section of this page. Our application invokes the credit card details page to be rendered by a smartphone device, as shown in the following screenshot:

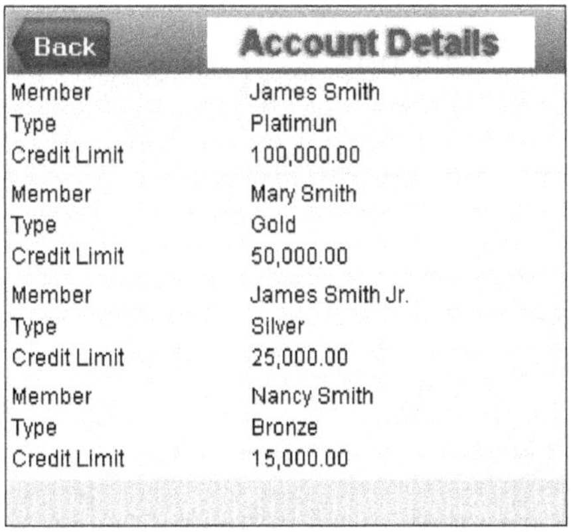

Now, let's take a look at the same page when the **Tablet** profile is applied. Once again, this is the version that will be served when our application detects that the request is coming from a device member of the **Tablet** family. In the **Applied Profile** pane, select the **Tablet** profile, and click on **Apply**.

As tablets have much more real estate to display web pages, the application will render the tablet version of our credit card account details page, as shown in the following screenshot:

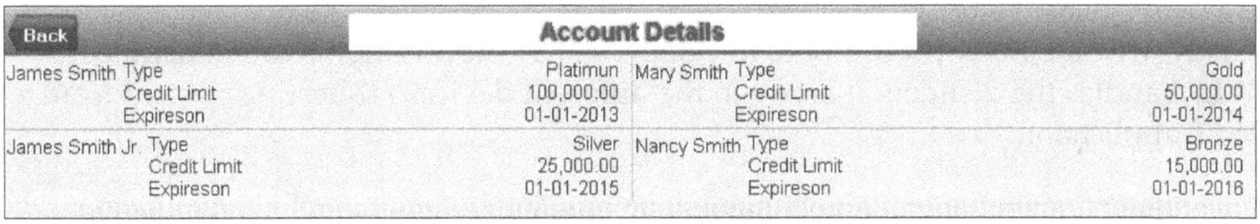

Testing your application on an iPhone simulator

While testing your profile-enabled application to render on iPhone, you might want to see what your application looks like and how it behaves on an iPhone. For this purpose, developers can use the iPhone emulator application offered by Genuitec. You can download a free trial version from `http://www.genuitec.com/mobile/`.

Expanding the sample model

The sample model we have just created can be expanded to implement the hybrid mode where our current model could access and interact with features of mobile devices. WEF does provide builders and other artifacts to implement such development model. The Geolocation builder and the Mobile Rich Data Definition base file are two examples in this category.

While we will not be able to cover these features in this book, we strongly encourage you to investigate these features of WEF, as it will greatly enrich the user experience of your applications.

Summary

The mobile space is an exciting field, which has exponentially expanded lately, especially with the advent of smartphones and tablet devices. In this chapter we have just scratched the surface of what WEF can offer in terms of developing multichannel applications.

Despite the fact that there are many more items to discuss about the development of multichannel applications using WEF, you have been exposed to various important features of WEF for this space.

We looked at how the model-driven approach can be a feasible approach, not only from the technical perspective, but also from the financial perspective, as it cuts cost by developing one single application that can be invoked by multiple devices.

We also looked at the builders and artifacts that comprise the WEF Mobile feature set. This feature set has been created specifically to address the mobile aspect of multichannel applications.

Lastly, we had the opportunity to develop a sample application to demonstrate how WEF handles the distinction between the different devices requesting content from a WEF application.

15
How to Implement a Successful Portal Project with WEF

Throughout the last eight chapters, we have covered several important aspects of developing portal applications utilizing WEF. From introduction to WEF to developing Dojo and multichannel web applications, you have learned a great deal about WEF.

You are ready and well qualified to start your next portal project utilizing the power and the flexibility of WEF. However, there are a few important portal project-related topics we would like to convey to you so that you can apply them to your next project.

Throughout the years, we have learned what works and what does not work from an overall project perspective. We have also identified a few important areas that are usually overlooked or addressed at a late time in the project. So, in this chapter we want to pass on to you the lessons we have learned from numerous portal projects we have participated in and point out the areas that are overlooked.

We want to make sure that when you use WEF as the development tool for your portal project, you are well equipped to complete your project successfully. With this goal in mind, in this chapter we will cover the following topics:

- Required skills for developing portlet with WEF
- Training and mentoring
- Development environment
- Source control with WEF

- XMLAccess scripts
- Roles, permissions, access level
- Development of POCs or prototypes
- WEF project folder structure

Planning for success

Success is not achieved by chance. To achieve success, meticulous planning needs to take place from the very beginning of the project. This truth is also applicable to any project, and WEF portal project is not an exception.

As WEF consultants, we have been invited to help portal projects that found themselves in a less than desirable situation. The following list sums up the most common points we identified on these projects:

- Lack of clear and solid project planning.
- Failing to notice important areas, which causes serious problems as the project progresses.
- When proper planning is not implemented from the beginning of any portal project, it is very difficult and expensive to correct the problems and put the project back on the right track.
- Sometimes, pressure from the project sponsors leads to aggressive and unrealistic schedule to deliver the first portal application release. Some IT departments try to meet the initial deadlines by eliminating several important initial phases of the project to deliver a few portlets quickly.

Sadly, the shortcuts taken at the beginning of the project result in several problems such as poor quality of the code, high number of defects, difficulty in maintaining code, and an application that does not meet the requirements. Ironically, the required investment in time and resources to fix these issues is usually greater than the time and resources it would have taken if the project had been well planned from the beginning.

So, in the next sections we will look at some items that should never be overlooked when using WEF as the Rapid Application Development tool in your portal project. Furthermore, most of these tasks should be implemented at the beginning of the project.

Required skills for developing a portlet with WEF

WEF is a portlet development tool, which not only enables fast portlet development, but it also insulates developers from the complexity of developing portlets. While WEF makes the development task easier, it does not mean that development should be performed by resources without any experience with the tool. It also does not mean that your project does not need a portal architect and experienced WEF Developers.

Many organizations implementing their first portal project have a strong JEE background. These organizations rightly want to leverage and reuse the JEE knowledge and resources, which had been used on previous JEE projects. There is nothing wrong with this approach. However, the following are a few important points that need to be taken into account when this is the case:

- Difference between a portal project and a JEE project
- Requirement of experienced WEF Developers for WEF development
- Training and mentoring
- Hiring or contracting an experienced portal architect/WEF developer

Let's dissect these four statements.

Difference between a portal project and a JEE project

When organizations move from JEE projects to their first portal project, they do not have a clear understanding of the differences between both technologies. We will not cover these differences in detail, but it is important to notice that while many of the JEE skills and knowledge can be reused, it is necessary formal and detailed "gap analysis" program to identify the differences and properly train or hire resources with the right portal skills to fill these gaps. Existing JEE experience will play a big role in the vital requirement of understanding the portal framework and its APIs.

It is equally important to understand that skill gaps happen on all levels of the project and not only at the development level. Resources such as Project Managers, Development Managers, Business Analysts, and Infrastructure Professionals, all need to be trained to understand not only the challenges, but also the benefits and opportunities that portal technologies bring to the project.

We are not going to comment on all of these resources, but take the Business Analyst role for instance. In most of the cases, these resources are completely left out of training and discussions on the portal technology.

The Business Analysts are asked to provide the business requirements for a solution, which is going to run on a new platform with which they are completely unfamiliar. In order to complete their required deliverables, they draw from their JEE experience and perspective, not taking into account any of the portal features. This results in requirements that are suitable to run on a JEE environment, but that will behave poorly in a portal environment.

Successful WEF project requires experienced WEF developers

WEF provides significant benefits over traditional development tools, but the ability to be successfully used by untrained and inexperienced developers is not one of them.

To develop portal projects successfully with WEF, an organization needs to augment its in-house skills with experienced WEF leads.

Sometimes WEF can be a complex tool. Productivity can be very low if not utilized by someone who fully understands the intricacies of the tool.

Training and mentoring

IBM and IBM Business Partners do provide excellent WEF training. Money spent on training is a valuable investment, and it will save you money in the long run.

Developers have an incredible ability to learn new technologies by themselves. While it is perfectly possible to learn WEF by oneself, it is more productive if a developer attends a formal class with good material and good instructors. Formal training will help you think like a WEF Developer, and at the same time it will teach you how to avoid pitfalls and costly mistakes.

In addition to training, implementing an approach where your developers work with an experienced mentor can be very helpful to the success of your project.

An experienced mentor helps at the beginning of the project when important decisions need to be taken. Your developers can learn as they work on the project under the guidance of an experienced mentor. This will certainly avoid costly mistakes, but at the same time you make sure the proper foundation is established for your whole project.

Hiring or contracting an experienced portal architect/WEF developer

Having the right resource in your project is the key to the success of your project. Any portal project, even the smallest ones, should have at least one portal architect. In addition to that, one or more Senior WEF Developers would greatly increase your chance for success.

These resources should be brought at the very beginning of the project so that they can participate on the most crucial phases of the project. Not bringing experienced resources at the beginning of the project can also be a costly mistake.

Development environment

At the beginning of a portal project that will utilize WEF as the portal application development tool, companies have some questions regarding the configuration of the development environment.

This is not a complex matter, but the availability of documentation involving this topic is somehow more limited and many companies are not sure how to set up their development environment for the first time.

So, in this section we will discuss the configuration of a typical WEF development environment.

In most projects, development is performed on desktops running the Windows system. So, in our example we will represent the development environment for a Windows machine.

WebSphere Portal Server installation

The configuration of a WEF development environment can start with the installation of the IBM Websphere Portal Server. WEF Developers will need to have an instance of IBM WebSphere Portal Server running on their local machine to test their portlets during the development phase of the project.

Any member of the portal server family of products can be used in the development environment. Please notice that if you want to develop against **Web Content Management (WCM)**, then you need WebSphere Portal versions that include WCM.

WebSphere Portal runs on top of IBM WebSphere Application Server. These two servers can be installed as a part of a two-step process, or you can install both servers as a part of the same installation process.

For development purposes, you do not need to configure the portal to authenticate users against **Lightweight Directory Access Protocol (LDAP)**. You also do not need to configure the database to use an external database system, such as DB2 or Oracle. The standard installation with derby suffices.

During installation, you can choose to configure portal to run in development mode. This is a good option if you do not need to perform every administrative task on your machine.

> If you intend to create virtual portals on your local machine, you cannot specify the development mode. The components to create and maintain virtual portals are not available in development mode.

WebSphere Portal Server Community Edition – WAS CE

The standard installation of WEF installs the **WebSphere Application Server Community Edition** or **(WAS CE)** on your machine. WAS CE has a reduced startup time and it is very light in terms of memory consumption. This server enables beginner developers to deploy and test their WEF applications quickly from the designer. While WAS CE has its advantages, we recommend that you use it with caution and sparely during the development of your portlets especially for testing UI components. That is because many UI features might not work in the portal in the same way they work when executed from WAS. It is not unusual to see UI components that work perfectly well when executed from WAS CE, but do not work at all in the portal.

Development IDE

Once portal server has been installed, you will move on to install your choice of development IDE. WEF is a plugin which can be installed either on the Eclipse IDE or on RAD. As both IDEs are very robust and mature, WEF behaves equally well on both of them.

WEF on Eclipse

You do not need to download your own version of Eclipse. WEF already ships with installable Eclipse. By default, during the installation process, WEF automatically installs the right Eclipse version for the current WEF version you are installing.

It is recommended that you let WEF install the Eclipse version that ships with WEF. This will avoid any possible issue due to version conflicts.

WEF on RAD

If RAD is the development IDE of your choice, then you will install WEF on an existing RAD instance.

During the installation of RAD, you need to select the portal development toolkit. By doing so, you can have access to the portal development features offered by RAD.

Whether you already have RAD installed on your machine or if you are installing a new instance of RAD, you need to indicate that you want to install the WEF plugin on an existing instance of RAD. This is done by choosing the **Custom Installation** option in the third step of the installation process. This will give you the opportunity to point to the location where your RAD has been installed. Actually, to be more precise, WEF installer detects the presence of one or more instances of RAD on your machine and allows you to choose the instance in which WEF should install its plugin.

> Once you install WEF, you should install the latest fix packs for the current WEF version you have installed on your system. To obtain the latest fix packs, you should access IBM "Fix Central" site and provide the proper information for your current product. The URL to IBM Fix Central page is http://www-933.ibm.com/support/fixcentral.

The following image demonstrates what a typical WEF development environment would look like. We have included in this image a reference to a source control plugin, which is part of a typical WEF development environment. We will discuss source control with WEF in the next section.

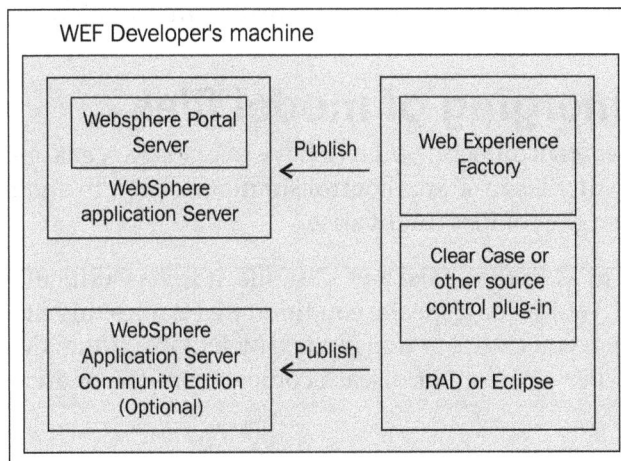

Source control with WEF

Configuring your environment to perform source control with WEF is not a complex task, but sometimes people do not have a clear picture of what needs to be done to have a WEF project checked in to a source control system.

Regardless of the source control system your company uses, the approach is the same—check in to the source control system only the artifacts that developers add to the project. In other words, do not check in your entire project. The entire project contains files such as HTML templates, JavaScript, CSS, Java, and JAR files, which are added to every project when a WEF project is created in your workspace. So, you do not want to add these files to your source control system.

By default, WEF already maintains a list of folders and files to be excluded from source control. To inspect this list from your IDE, select **Window | Preferences | Team | Ignored Resources**. By default, entries that start with `*/WebContent` are provided by WEF and are ignored by the source control system. Through your IDE, you can edit this list to include other files or folders you want to ignore. It is important to notice that the `.project` file is not on this list, but you should include it, because you do not want to check this file in to your source control. This is an example of a file that is added to every project by WEF.

The files to be added to the source control system include files from both servable and nonservable content that you create.

This chapter contains a section entitled *WEF project folder structure*. In that section, we have listed folders that should be created in your project and added to a source control system. Please refer to this section for further information on this topic.

Avoiding merging of model files

In a multideveloper environment, you will have to manage scenarios where developers might edit files in source control simultaneously. In another words, the need to manage merging of files might arise.

Models are stored in XML files. Like any XML file, it is very difficult to do a merge in such file format. WEF adds a special condition that makes this situation even more difficult. When you compare two models by looking at the XML files, it is very difficult to know when to accept or discard content from one or another model.

While WEF now offers a tool that makes merging of model files easier, you should avoid situations where a merge of these files would be required. As we have already seen, WEF offers several mechanisms by which developers can work on separate models in the same project. Segregation, such as service provider and service consumer layers, imported model and model container enables developers to split the workload in a logical manner, which avoids the need for two developers to work on the same file concurrently.

XMLAccess scripts

Let's start this section by defining XMLAccess. **XMLAccess** is an extremely useful batch-processing utility, which can be executed from a command line. Through XML Access scripts, you can perform most of the tasks which are normally performed through the portal administration page. XMLAccess enables WEF developers and portal administrators to capture and execute from files the repetitive and tedious steps performed through the portal administration page.

XMLAccess scripts provide a huge help to the deployment process of your project. This benefit is even more noticeable if you need to deploy your project to multiple environments across your organization. The larger the number of environments to which you need to deploy your project, the higher the productivity gains you will experience.

In this sense, you should create the XMLAccess scripts as early as possible in the development cycle of your project.

The following are a few tasks that can be accomplished with XMLAccess scripts:

- Deploying portlet to portal
- Creating portal pages
- Placing portlets on the page
- Granting access to portal resources
- Configuring wiring between portal pages
- Deleting pages to prepare for reinstallations of a portal application

From the preceding list, you can see how beneficial the creation of XMLAccess scripts can be, especially when they are created at the early stage of a project.

The following image shows a sample XMLAccess script. This simple script is used to delete pages and labels from the portal. Such script is very helpful when configuration from one environment needs to be propagated to other environments. The utilization of such script not only increases productivity but also reduces errors across environments.

```
- <request xsi:A2ZSchemaLoc="PortalConfig_1.4.xsd" type="update" create-oids="true">
    <!-- Delete pages and lables-->
  - <portal action="locate">
      <content-node action="delete" uniquename="com.A2Z.customer.label"> </content-node>
      <content-node action="delete" uniquename="com.A2Z.accounts.label"> </content-node>
      <content-node action="delete" uniquename="com.A2Z.credit_cards.page"> </content-node>
      <content-node action="delete" uniquename="com.A2Z.auto_pay.page"> </content-node>
      <content-node action="delete" uniquename="com.A2Z.investments.page"> </content-node>
    </portal>
  </request>
```

For further information on XMLAccess, please consult IBM Portal Info Center through the following link: http://publib.boulder.ibm.com/infocenter/wpdoc/v6r0/index.jsp?topic=/com.ibm.wp.ent.doc/wps/admxmlai.html.

Roles, permissions, access level

Another important aspect of a portal project relates to user access control. In this section we will discuss this topic from two perspectives—access to portal and portlet resources.

We found it important to discuss this topic in this chapter, because this is an area that you should address early in the design phase of your portal solution. The sooner you define how different users will be accessing your application, the better. In fact, this aspect of a portal application comes into play even before the solution design phase. This subject needs to be first addressed when the business analysis team writes the requirements and use cases for the entire solution.

In this section we will not discuss the role of the business analysis team in the overall project, but it is suffice to say that Business Analysts need to understand and clearly convey the defined roles, their access level to portal resources, and how the application is supposed to behave when a given role has access to portlet resources.

When companies are transitioning from developing JEE applications to portal applications, portal architects should work more closely with the business analysis team to make sure they understand the differences between these two technologies. Furthermore, during this collaborative work, Portal Architects will have the opportunity to influence and validate the role and access model for the solution.

Access level and the behavior of the application depending on roles or groups is a subject that permeates the entire application. As such, it needs to be addressed as part of the entire portal solution.

Authentication versus authorization

Security, roles, permissions, access level, and other similar terms are broadly used to refer to the authentication and authorization mechanism implemented by WebSphere Portal.

Authentication involves configuration of portal to authenticate users directly against a supported user directory or through a policy-based authentication system, for example SiteMinder.

Authorization comes into play after a user is authenticated. Basically, authorization is the process by which portal checks to verify and grant access to portal resources to the logged in user. Through the authorization mechanism, portal maintains controls over a multitude of portal resources. To stay focused and keep it simple, we will discuss authorization control involving only two portal resources — Portal pages and portlets.

Portal resources versus portlet resources

Access to portal resources is controlled differently from the way by which access to portlet resources is controlled. By portlet resources, we mean portlet pages, UI elements, execution flow, and everything that resides and happens inside the portlet.

Let's briefly look at the driving factor behind portal authorization. Authorization, and consequently, access to portal resources is strictly tied to LDAP groups. LDAP groups can be defined as a collection of users that are listed under a specific label in any users' directory. Groups can be defined as static, dynamic, hybrid, and so on.

Whenever the topic of LDAP groups is discussed, LDAP roles are also brought into the discussion. While LDAP roles refer to a conceptual complement to groups, in the portal security schema, portal resources are not tied to LDAP roles. They are directly tied to the LDAP groups.

If access to a page or a portlet on a page is granted to a certain group through portal, then when a user member of that group logs in to portal, he/she will have access to these resources.

The following screenshot shows the list of portal resources controlled by WebSphere Portal. This screenshot is a screen capture of the **Resources Permission** page of the portal administration page:

Resource Types
Pages
PSE Sources
Policies
Policy Root
Portlet Applications
Portlets
Application Templates
Application Template Categories
URL Mapping Contexts
User Groups

While access to portal resources is controlled by the authentication mechanism of portal, access to resources and the behavior of content inside the portlet is controlled by the Portlet Developer. Developers cannot plug in to the portal security schema to control or differentiate how users access or execute their portlets.

Through the assignment of portal roles, user can have access not only to portlets but also to different features of a portlet, such as edit menu and configuration menu.

Portlet resources and WEF

In the previous section we stated that the portal authorization mechanism cannot be leveraged to control access inside the portlet. You must be asking yourself, well, then what if I need to extend the same framework to the content inside the portlet? No worries—enter the WEF profiling mechanism.

With the WEF profiling mechanism, you can define how content inside the portlets can be accessed by different LDAP groups in the same way it has been defined for the portal resources.

Inside the portlet, WEF profiling capabilities can control not only the access to UI components of a portlet, but also their state (enabled or disabled) and other aspects, for example the execution flow of your portlet.

To illustrate the preceding concept, we have created a table that demonstrates the relationship between portlet resources and LDAP groups. To understand this table, imagine a portlet designed for the sales organization. This portlet contains a page with several links leading to different reports on other pages. These reports, however, are not to be accessible to all users.

Through WEF profiling, we can control the visibility of these links, depending upon the LDAP group to which a user belongs. As you know, portal already leverages these groups.

In our example, these LDAP groups are Sales Directors, Sales Managers, and Sales Reps. Each of these groups is mapped to equivalent WEF profiles defined in a WEF profile set. For instance, the LDAP Sales Directors group would have an equivalent Sales Directors profile in WEF. The same would be true for the other LDAP groups.

The table in the following image defines the groups that have access to the different links:

Portlet Resource Type	Label	Sales Directors	Sales Managers	Sales Reps
Link	Total Sales	Yes	No	No
Link	Trends	Yes	No	No
Link	Sales Indicators	Yes	Yes	No
Link	Promotions	Yes	Yes	No
Link	Products	Yes	Yes	Yes
Link	Expenses	Yes	Yes	Yes

The following image helps us understand how portlet resources (such as UI elements, pages, and methods), profiles, and LDAP groups are connected to each other.

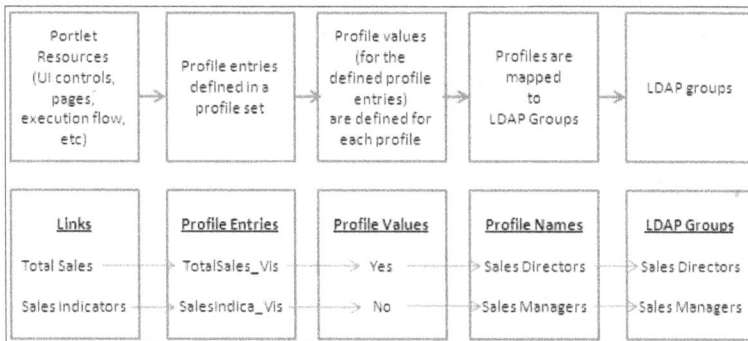

Please notice that the visibility of the links defined in this examples is controlled by the Visibility Setter builders. In this sense, the Visibility Setter builders are associated to profile entries (profile-enabled) instead of the links itself. In the preceding image, this is denoted by the box entitled Profile Entries.

> In this example, the profile names and LDAP groups have the same name, but this is not a requirement. They can have completely different names, as long as their association is properly done through profile set manager in WEF.

In summary, inside the portlet you can leverage WEF profiling capability, which plays a major role in providing variability to your portlets. As you already know, profiling can be tied to the LDAP groups and can provide a valuable means to enable you to extend the same structure you use to map access level to portal resources.

Development of POCs or prototypes

Portal projects can greatly benefit from WEF's ability to quickly put together models or portlets to demonstrate or to help you define several aspects of a portal solution.

We have been successfully using the approach of developing modest **Proof of Concepts (POCs)** or prototypes for many years now. The benefits yielded by this approach can be easily quantified and they can represent gains to every area of the project.

For discussion purposes, these benefits can be broadly grouped into two categories according to the teams to which they cater.On one hand the development of small models or portlets would be geared to the product management and business analysis teams. These groups would refer to this effort as prototyping. So, in this sense we would be extending the regular usage of WEF to prototyping.

The following list indicates how the product management and business analysis teams can utilize WEF prototypes to assist them with their goals:

- Determine the feasibility of implementing advanced requirements
- Demonstrate how features would look like once they are implemented
- Help the product management team in making decisions

The other teams that can benefit from the approach of creating modest models or portlets would be the portal architecture team, the development team, and even the testing team. The benefit to the testing team comes in the form of improved quality of the final product by reducing the number of defects.

The benefits of this approach to these teams can be listed as follows:

- It helps guide design decisions
- It helps developers with the implementation of complex features

While the benefit of extending WEF to developing POCs or prototypes can be segregated and mapped to two significant groups in the project, truly the benefit is extended to the entire portal project.

Let's briefly discuss how the two major groups we have listed previously can benefit from employing prototyping or POCs as a part of their regular activities. Let's look first at the benefits provided to the product management and business analysis teams.

Benefits to the product management and business analysis teams

The benefit of demonstrating what a feature would look like once it is implemented goes hand in hand with the benefit of helping the product management team in their decisions regarding which features and how these features blend into the product.

The benefits we discuss in this section can be more closely correlated to prototyping than to POC. In the technical sense, prototyping mostly serves to demonstrate what a product or a feature would look like, as opposed to prove that it can be done.

As part of their daily activities, Product Managers want to implement new ideas or concepts that flow out of their creative minds. Prototyping with WEF can help them capture and translate their abstract ideas and concepts to a format that can be visualized and manipulated.

The ability to manipulate and interact with what the final product would look like enables them not only to validate their ideas, but also to visualize and expand their ideas to other possibilities and dimensions, not considered before. As the WEF prototype gets form and shape, it provides a fertile soil to Product Managers to germinate even more ideas and new concepts.

Benefits to the portal architecture and development teams

WebSphere Portal has been used in the most diverse industries. Many of the portal projects are cutting-edged projects, which push the limit of the technology. Companies not only want to use the latest technologies, but also need new ways of representing or executing new concepts.

In order to investigate whether the implementation of complex features are feasible or not, architects and developers can resort to the development of small POCs to validate their approach.

The development of POCs helps the project not only at the design phase, but also at the development phase.

In the design phase, through the development of modest POCs, many unforeseen problems can be identified and can be brought into discussion at early phases of the project.

In the development phase, developers will have higher success rates if they can refer to a working POC or prototype during the construction phase, as opposed to solely stare at angry and dry requirement documents.

Depending on whether a feature or concept proves to be possible or not to implement as portlets, it translates into gains to the entire project. If the prototype or POC proves that the feature cannot be implemented, then it saves numerous hours of the Business Analysts, Portal Architects, and WEF Developers by avoiding spending time on implementing something that cannot be accomplished. If the POC proves that it can be done, then the resulting POC can be used by all teams to accomplish their tasks with less effort and more accuracy.

Regardless of how this effort is named, the end result is the same — increased quality and productivity gains across the entire project.

In summary, the regular practice of developing POCs or prototypes, utilizing WEF can yield great benefits for a portal project.

Depending on the magnitude of your project, you can even have one or more WEF resources dedicated to work closely with the product management team, the business analysis team, the portal architecture team, and the development team to develop, maintain, and manage POCs or prototypes.

WEF project folder structure

A WEF project has a folder structure similar to a JEE project. It contains the servable and the nonservable content sections, with the servable content being directly under the WebContent folder and the nonservable content directly under the WEB-INF folder.

When you create a WEF project, WEF creates the folder structure containing all the files that a standard WEF project needs. If you add extra feature sets, such as Dojo, SAP, or Domino Extensions, then WEF automatically adds all the folders and files associated with those feature sets.

In addition to the folders and files created by WEF, your project also needs to contain the files created by you and your development team. These files are the files that will be controlled by a source control system, such as ClearCase, CVS, or any other source control system you use. As we have mentioned previously, files created by WEF are not added to any source control system.

In this section, we will discuss the structure of the folders that host the files you create during the development of your project.

We want to bring to your attention that the folder structure to host these files should be clearly defined and shared among all the developers so that your project will be consistent across the entire development team. This definition needs to be developed before the project development starts.

Developers set up their individual projects on their own development machines. However, the project folder structure needs to be defined at the project level. In addition to that, every developer needs to adhere to this project folder structure. This folder structure is enforced by the structure created in the source control system. So, whenever a developer starts a new project and gets the folders and files from your source control, he/she will have this defined folder structure added to his/her local project.

Each project might have the need for a specific folder structure, and it might be slightly different from project to project, but your project will have some common folders that most likely all your projects will have.

Here is what you need to do before you create your project. Define the folder structure for both servable and nonservable content that you will create in your project.

Folder structure for the servable content

While WEF can create a set of similar folders at the time when the project is created, we still have the preference of creating our own folders. This approach gives us the opportunity not only to create as many folders as we want, but also to name them according to the corporate naming convention if one exists.

It is important to notice that when you take the approach of creating your own custom folders, you should not check the **Create default folders** option when you create your WEF project. If you do check this option, then WEF will create a set of default folders, which then you will have to delete later.

The following screenshot shows the inputs for the **Project Name** dialog box, which captures the information about the creation of default folders when you are creating your WEF project. Notice that the **Create default folders** option is unchecked:

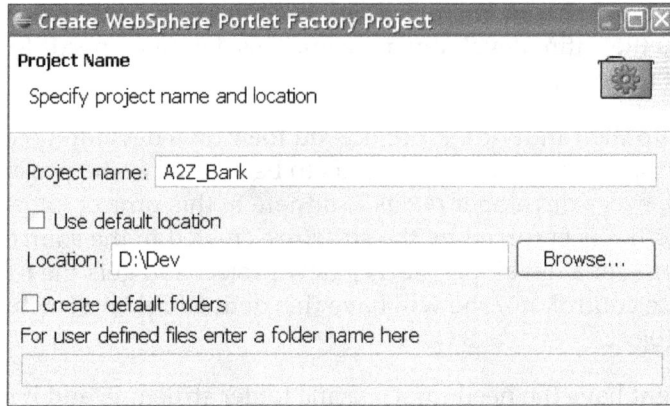

> The **Project Name** dialog box is the same regardless of the IDE you are using, be it Eclipse or RAD.

Let's start by defining the folders that should be created at the servable content level. You will need to create five folders at this level. However, instead of creating them directly under the **WebContent** folder, create them under a single folder that represents the nature of your project. This will make it easier to maintain these folders. We will take the example of the project we created for the Credit Card division of our A2Z Bank.

For the Credit Card project we created a folder named **creditCard** under the **WebContent** folder. Once this folder had been created, we added the five folders we need inside this folder.

The following list shows the folders you need to create:

- **css**
- **html**
- **images**
- **scripts**
- **templates**

The following screenshot shows what the folder structure looks like for the servable content of our Credit Card project:

Now, the **creditCard** directory along with its subfolders are the folders that need to be added to the source controls system.

All the folder names are self explanatory about the content they should contain. The **templates** folder will contain WEF HTML templates created to customize the layout of the forms or tables created by the Data Page builder.

Folder structure for the nonservable content

Let's identify the folders you need to create for the nonservable content part of your project to hold the files that your team creates.

For the nonservable content we will take similar approach, which we took in the previous section. We will create a folder named **creditCard** directly under the **WEB-INF** folder.

Under this **creditCard** folder, we will create the following folders:

- **portletTheme**
- **properties**
- **rdd**
- **wsdl**
- **xml**

The following screenshot shows what the folder structure looks like for the nonservable content of our Credit Card project:

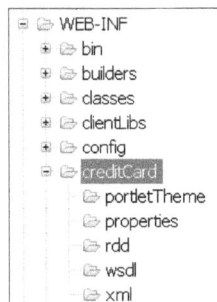

For this section, all the folder names are also self explanatory about the content they should contain. `rdd` stands for Rich Data Definition. If you are using WEF the way it should be used, you will have at least a couple of these files in your project. The `wsdl` folder is to host the WSDL files your project uses, but if your project is not accessing backend data through web service calls, you do not need this folder.

Similar to the `creditCard` folder in the servable content section, this `creditCard` folder and its subfolders also need to be added to you source control system.

Lastly, it is recommended that you add one more folder under the `models` folder so that you can group all your models under a single folder that is easily managed through your source control system. In our sample project for the Credit Card division, we would creatively name it `creditCard`. Under the `models\creditCard` folder, you have the option to add two more folders for `data` and `UI`, or you can add more subfolders and then inside these folders make the distinction between UI and service models, creating one folder for each of these categories.

Summary

In this chapter, we wanted to convey to you a little bit of our years of experience implementing portal projects utilizing Web Experience Factory as a Rapid Application Development tool.

We know that there is no substitute for experience. In this sense, you will have to gain your own experience and grow in knowledge and confidence as you work more extensively with WEF. However, it is our deepest hope that the few topics we have discussed here will enable you to take the right decisions early in the project and lead it to complete success.

We have a strong conviction that if you observe and follow the guidelines and approaches defined in this chapter, you will have better chance to succeed in your portal project regardless of the magnitude of your project.

This chapter also marks the end of the WEF chapters. By choice we have not covered every nuance of WEF. This task cannot be accomplished in one single book, let alone in only nine chapters. However, we have made a choice of covering topics, which have not been covered by any other WEF book out there. Some of these examples are as follows:

- The Data Service User Interface builder, the Design pane, and the explanation on how WEF builds the User Interface in *Chapter 10, Building the Application User Interface*

- The manner in which we covered the Dojo topics in *Chapter 11, The Dojo Builders and Ajax*

- The focus we have given and how we have presented the model types a WEF developer can use in *Chapter 13, Types of Models*

- The development of mobile web applications with WEF in *Chapter 14, WEF and Mobile Web Applications*

- And lastly, the way we shared our field experience in this chapter

At the same time, we have decided not to give too much focus to other areas which have already got a good amount of coverage through other WEF books or other media elements.

It is our desire that these WEF chapters not only help you expand your knowledge of WEF, but that they should also be an instrument to help you progress in your WEF career.

16
Portlet and Portal Testing

The next four chapters go hand in hand in synergy. Testing, monitoring (reporting), troubleshooting, and tuning are different efforts and disciplines within the same overall quality control workflow. This chapter covers some of the best practices in portal and portlet testing. The test-driven approach is discussed, along with some of the techniques for validating the compliance to a portal, functional and nonfunctional goals via testing. By the end of this chapter, we will have looked at:

- Test strategy and plan
- Functional/nonfunctional test tools and automation
- Test environments and test data
- Test automation
- Test metrics
- Portal testing
- Portlet testing
- WEF testing
- Security testing

Test strategy and plan

This entire transformation effort was supported by an interconnected and Jazz-enabled set of runtimes supporting many testing roles within the lifecycle of the project. It adopted **Collaborative Application Lifecycle Management (CALM)** traceability with Rational Requirements Composer, Rational Quality Manager, Rational Team Concert, and Rational Change. For those new to Jazz, it is a brand new platform, which is used for collaborative development purposes. It is designed to help in making development more productive and agile. It integrates people, processes, and runtimes.

For more information on the Jazz platform, please see the video at the following link:

`http://www-01.ibm.com/software/rational/jazz/jazz-plattform-video.html`.

A2Z further implemented the testing stack with Rational Performance Tester for the execution of automated test cases and the validation against the nonfunctional requirements for those test cases. Rational Functional Tester was used on the other hand to automate and facilitate the testing of all the functions documented in the test cases for both A2Z banking and call center domains. Remember that there is a common denominator in the testing effort—the testing goals and the requirements used as input for those goals. It is important to keep the traceability of project artifacts in synchronization. So, use cases (or stories) will drive test cases, which will drive scripts to be executed to generate metrics and produce results. It will generate defects that will go back into the development cycle for remediation.

Now, we will look at how we are enabling the testing framework via several testing roles that support the lifecycle of the A2Z portal application. The following image demonstrates the roles involved in the testing effort for the portal assets, artifacts, extensions, and integrated portal interfaces. Consider, there are possible overlaps in these roles, or that some roles are done by the same human resource; but in a nutshell, they would be represented somehow in a portal team.

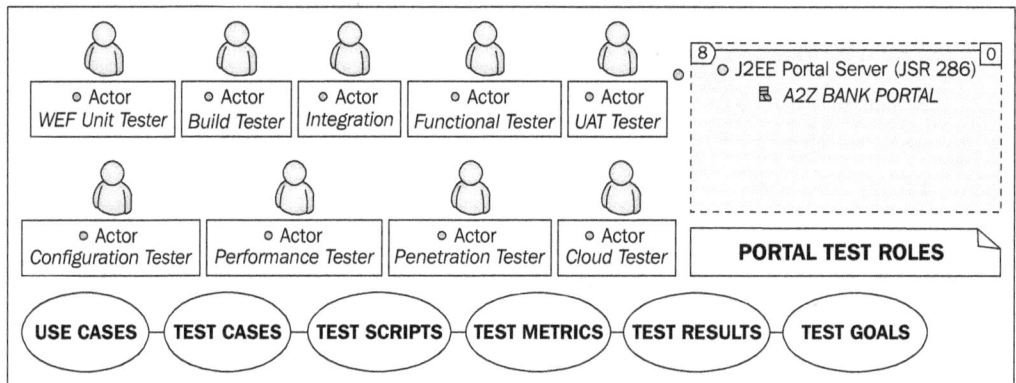

The following list shows the roles involved in the testing effort:

- WEF specialists develop, do unit testing, and post the tested code to CVS.
- Build testers build and test the build quality of that code.
- Portal administrators or cloud infrastructure testers deploy, promote, and test deployable units to target environments. They may also perform regression tests.

- Configuration or integration testers test integration points invoked by the code (telephony, data power, and so on). They may also perform regression tests.

- Functional testers and user acceptance testers test based on functional test cases. They oftentimes also test for nonfunctional requirements related to aesthetics, accessibility, trainability, and so on. They may also perform regression tests.

- Performance testers test for nonfunctional requirements related to performance, scalability, failover, disaster recovery, and capacity.

- Penetration testers test for the security of portal applications.

- Cloud testers test deployed cloud patterns and cloud applications.

Functional/nonfunctional test tools and automation

Portal test cases are oftentimes represented in many scripts at the implementation and execution level. Automation is the key for creating repeatable test harnesses with the appropriate test data mapped in the form of test data pools. A **test data pool** is a way to store data that is going to be used and/or replaced at runtime during a test execution. They can contain user credentials, form variables, and so on. A2Z automated both of its functional and nonfunctional performance testing. Other types of nonfunctional testing were executed manually or in semi-automated way, for example security. For functional testing, IBM Rational Functional Tester was utilized to cover the functional test cases for A2Z core banking and call center portals. It provided significant value by allowing testers to record the scripts and play them back, based on the defined success criteria. It also allowed test data to be collected and shared. It provided precise reporting and integrated with the Jazz platform.

For performance testing, IBM Rational Performance Tester was the chosen tool for load test. It provides much-needed automation, combination of tests cases via scheduling, sophisticated data correlation for its virtual users, and much more. Personally, we have worked with this tool since its inception and highly recommend it for portal application. It can be used to benchmark portal with the intended workload. It also provides significant value in the case of longevity tests, which are long-running load tests with stable loads that try to uncover memory leaks.

Functional Testing Automation

The scope of functional testing differs from the nonfunctional one in terms of the target functionality to be tested to meet the established functional requirements. The concept of having a test plan and a test strategy applies to any type of formal testing. As mentioned previously, A2Z Bullion Bank used automation of functional testing via the Rational Functional Tester scripts for both the core bullion bank and call center test cases. Some of the advantages of this integrated tool approach are the capability of test results reporting and immediate validation of performance goals with pass/fail status; the automated defect tracking and alert to the owner of the component if action is required based on a defect; streamlined testing, reporting, tracking flow with proactive alerting with the functional testing lifecycle. One way to automate your portal testing efforts is to use IBM Rational Functional Tester, which is available at the following URL:

```
http://www.ibm.com/developerworks/downloads/r/rft/
```

Additionally, please learn more about how to record and play back functional tests and how to manage requirements, results, and defects with IBM Rational Quality Manager.

> **Interactive time – learn IBM Education Assistant for Rational Functional Tester and Quality Manager**
>
> Please check the following URLs:
>
> ```
> http://publib.boulder.ibm.com/infocenter/ieduasst/
> rtnv1r0/index.jsp?topic=/com.ibm.iea.rft/rft/
> RFTv70_Topic.html
> ```
>
> ```
> http://publib.boulder.ibm.com/infocenter/ieduasst/
> rtnv1r0/index.jsp?topic=/com.ibm.iea.rqm/rqm/1.0/
> Overview/Introduction_RQM/player.html
> ```

The only exception to using the tool for functional testing was the ability for human testers to use the test cloud during **User Acceptance Testing (UAT)** to execute business functions, which in this case was all manual work and did not involve the tool itself.

Nonfunctional testing

The scope of nonfunctional testing is also based on the complexity and granularity of the nonfunctional requirements. For portal applications, there are a few areas of interest. It spans, foundationally speaking, from security to accessibility to capacity to scalability and performance. The performance test is based on the nonfunctional requirements goals and the workload model developed during analysis and design.

One of the main important aspects for achieving quality results in performance testing is the repeatability factor (can the same load tests be rerun with the same unique test data?), and the quality of the test data and the test environment themselves. Along with that is the question of how well one can capture real systems and user requirements to the point of being able to be loyal when reproducing these test case scenarios via systematically automated repeatable test runs. The following are some key questions to be asked for portal projects around performance engineering:

- **Portal users**: How many users should the portal support? Average and peak loads, and user types? How long do they have to stay logged in?

- **Portal user think-time**: What is the average think-time of the portal user?

- **Portal user arrival rate**: At which rate do users log in? Can that ramp-up be reproduced in test so it represents real usage patterns without artificial bottlenecks?

- **Transactional response**: What response time is required by the portal page or the portlet? How well are dependent service calls or backend calls performing outside of portal?

- **Transaction volume**: What is the volume in average **transaction per second** (**TPS**), peak times, or percentile business transactions?

- **Transactional mix**: How well do the performance test scripts represent load in terms of the 80-20 percent rule of most frequently used business transactions?

- **Throughput**: What is the maximum throughput objective? Can it be generated via load test in an environment other than production? Can we test for capacity and scalability based on the nonfunctional requirements or actual realized demand?

- **Response time**: What is the expected response time? Can it be achieved with and without **Parallel Portlet Rendering** (**PPR**)?

- **Utilization**: What are the thresholds for utilization on portal servers, related servers, and services?

- **Availability**: What are the SLAs, service windows, meantime between failure, meantime time to repair?

- **Modeling assumptions validation**: Testing is a way to confirm the model projections and forecasts concerning response time, utilization, scalability.

A2Z Bank utilized all the best practices in the design of its applications. It realizes the following things upfront:

- Performance problems are rarely manifested and diagnosed as silver bullet items, but generally as "death by a thousand cuts", where many small problems accumulate to a degraded portal experience
- Finding fundamental problems during testing is much more expensive to the project than during design or even development

Performance testing needs to be executed according to the performance test plan and strategy along with its test cases; but performance engineering for the A2Z portal started long ago when nonfunctional requirements' gathering started. During the design phase, performance was taken into account, and a test-driven approach was executed for each WEF component, dependent services, and backend-related calls. Performance engineering has to do with the entire engineering approach that encompasses the lifecycle of a project concerning performance. How the development methodology accounts for these activities, how the project plan at the program level accounts for them in the project plans, how tools and human skills are able to support a process around performance, these are all contributing factors to how successful the performance testing discipline will be when applied to your project needs. The test strategy has to be one of the deliverables by the performance and overall test engineering effort. A nice flow of correlated and traceable items map each other from functional and nonfunctional requirements to test cases to test scripts, test executions, test reports, and defect tracking.

Besides the normal testing routines based on the performance engineering efforts, there may be some specific testing done due to some performance bottleneck or constraint found during the normal performance tests. In these cases, there are certain test cases to be developed, depending on the nature of the testing that is needed. There are ways to create new test cases based on the demand. There are two main sources of information that can shed light on the possible test cases based on the results and conclusions from your particular test environment as follows:

- *IBM WebSphere Portal Performance Troubleshooting Guide* at `https://www-304.ibm.com/support/docview.wss?uid=swg27007059`
- *IBM WebSphere Portal V7.0 Performance Tuning Guide* at `http://www-10.lotus.com/ldd/portalwiki.nsf/dx/WebSphere_Portal_Tun`

They should always be consulted as guidelines for what to examine. Here, we will use some of the potential scenarios that would merit certain performance test cases to be created based on demand. They come from the *IBM WebSphere Portal Performance Troubleshooting Guide*:

- Poor response time under light load
- Poor response time at light load for most or all users
- Slow page retrieval at low load
- Slow page rendering
- Poor response time at light load for certain users
- Inability to utilize full system capacity
- Poor response time for specific operations
- Poor login response time
- Poor response time for certain pages
- Poor response time for most or all operations

So, testing for performance has to have some fluidity to it in terms of being able to control portal changes for tuning and testing efforts within:

- An acceptable turnout time on requests for environment changes
- An acceptable turnout time on defect remediation
- An acceptable turnout time on request for test data restaging

The testing and validation of nonfunctional requirements require a set of skills and tools to test all the potential aspects of this in reality. Let's look at some other nonfunctional aspects tested by A2Z Bank:

- **Aesthetics**: For the call center and core banking portal applications, users tested against GUI-related requirements.
- **Accessibility**: This is tested for compliance based on NFRs.
- **Accuracy**: WEF specialist in core transactions tested the accuracy level of output provided by portlet. The functional and UAT testers further validated them.
- **Availability**: Because of the production cloud's elasticity and its proper hosting capabilities for highly available applications, A2Z tested for all the failover and disaster recovery scenarios.
- **Consistency**: This requirement is aligned with portal capabilities and tested under other test cases.
- **Efficiency**: This is another requirement fulfilled by the use of a cloud-enabled execution environment.
- **Usability**: Usability is a key portal capability, which is well aligned with this requirement and the business goals.

- **Mobility**: This requirement is fulfilled by the Mobile Accelerator and architecture implementation. Brokers had the application on the iPhone.

- **Reliability**: One of the great combinations to fulfill this requirement, architecturally speaking, is the use of the cloud.

- **Recoverability**: The cloud provides the proper resilience for recovery, but full recoverability still needs to be planned and tested thoroughly.

- **Security**: Cloud-suitable security model and **Single Sign-On (SSO)** are implemented along with corporate and IT guidelines, and business requirements. We could write a whole book on the security implementation itself. Due to limited page constraints, we will fully cover it in another edition along with **Business Process Management (BPM)** and **Web Services for Remote Portlets (WSRP)**.

Test environment and test data

The combination of these composite quality elements shown in the following list will determine the level of success and potentiality for achieving testing and business goals:

- Quality of the test environment (for functional and nonfunctional testing)

- Quality of the test data having a direct impact on the result's quality

- Quality of the recorded test scenarios and its automation to mimic real usage patterns of transactions workload and volumetric

- Quality of monitoring and reporting

- Quality and maturity level of the processes, which need to support the lifecycle of these activities in a repeatable way

- Quality of testing and service level provided by other components that interface with portal

In case of A2Z portal the test environment was very well controlled and administered in the test cloud. The test case itself was well managed and maintained via a data governance process created to identify, extract, sanitize, provision, reset or restage test data based on the test data criteria. Portal projects really benefit from this rigid process by guaranteeing the level of quality and reliability in the test results.

Overall test metrics

Understanding which metrics to examine goes together with instrumenting those metrics with monitoring and then validating if the customer's and system's nonfunctional requirements are met once repeatable tests are executed. Some of the most obvious metrics to be examined are given in the following table. This table comes from a great IBM paper entitled *Performance Implications of Cloud Computing* by Lydia Duijvestijn, Avin Fernandes, Pamela Isom, Dave Jewell, Martin Jowett, Elisabeth Stahl, and Todd R Stockslager. It serves as a starting point for overall metrics, definitions, and respective units of measurement that can be applied to cloud-enabled portal applications or traditionally deployed portal applications and other systems connected to portal applications:

Service level	KPI	Definition	Unit of measurement
category			
Availability	Service window	Time window within which KPIs are measured	Time range
	Service/system availability	Percentage of time for which service or system is available	Percentage
	MTBF	Mean time between failure	Time units
	MTTR	Mean time to repair	Time units
Performance	Response time	Response time for composite or atomic service	Seconds
	Elapsed time	Completion time for a batch or background task	Time units
	Throughput	Number of transactions or requests processed per specified unit of time	Transaction or request count

Service level	KPI	Definition	Unit of measurement
Capacity	Bandwidth	Bandwidth of the connection supporting a service	bps
	Processor speed	Clock speed of a processor (CPU)	MHz
	Storage capacity	Capacity of a temporary or persistent storage medium, such as RAM, SAN, disk, tape	GB
Reliability	Service/system reliability	Probability that service or system is working flawlessly over time	Percentage
Scalability	Service/system scalability	Degree to which the service or system is capable of supporting a defined growth scenario	Yes/no, or description of scalability's upper limit

There are other interesting metrics for portal applications in particular. They are listed and described in the next sections.

Response time

The response time metric is particularly interesting for portal applications as, unlike J2EE applications, it is not only the page response time the user perceives, but also each individual portlet's load response time on the portal page. Then there is real server, system component, and user-perceived response time. Other than that, there are other portal and J2EE specific metrics to be monitored. There are free tools to look at the page load time that can be beneficial to WEF and WebSphere Portal specialists to use during development. Most of systematic monitoring is enabled in higher environments, such as staging, performance, and production.

As mentioned previously, IBM Rational Performance Tester can generate load and also provide the entire page load and other performance statistics, but IBM Page Detailer is another great tool to use for sanity checks on portal's page load time only when doing single manual checks. You can check this tool at `https://www14.software.ibm.com/webapp/iwm/web/preLogin.do?source=AW-0BR`.

Java Virtual Machine

Every code written and compiled in Java runs inside a **Java Virtual Machine (JVM)** and resides mostly in heap memory. The bit level of the operating system determines the threshold for the maximum size of the heap. Depending on the operating system and the vendor-implemented JVM flavor, the JVM will have different ways to deal with generational data, but they all comply with the JVM specification. Turning on garbage collection and having a garbage collection log generated allows for some basic level of monitoring and reporting. So, in sum, there are a few metrics to examine when looking at health state and performance of portal applications as follows:

- **Overall heap size**: Minimum and maximum sizes
- Collection mode and its performance based on the portal application goals
  - `-Xgcpolicy:optthruput`
  - `-Xgcpolicy:optavgpause`
  - `-Xgcpolicy:gencon`
  - `-Xgcpolicy:balanced` (only WebSphere Application Server v8 and above; Garbage collection in Application Server v8 uses generational collection as default policy
- **Generational size**: Young, tenure generations and survival ratio sizes can be evaluated by looking at patterns and root causes of minor and major garbage collections, and allocation failures, fragmentation, and out of memory conditions
- For AIX operating systems, large object area and small object area, and pinned and non-pinned objects' configuration play a role in the overall heap memory's health state.

JDBC pool

JDBC pools need to be adjusted and tuned based on the portal workload demand. They can easily become a bottleneck in the portal application.

Thread pool

Likewise, thread pools need to be adjusted and tuned based on the portal workload demand. Particularly, the **Simple Object Access Protocol (SOAP)** and WebContainer pools need to be closely monitored and tuned for optimal performance.

The following screenshot shows how **WebSphere Performance Monitoring Infrastructure (PMI)** can be used to monitor the thread and JDBC pools among other metrics. This is a free out-of-the-box functionality.

Session size

The size of the session object has a direct impact on how the portal will scale. There is a direct correlation between the session size and footprint of a single user (considering different user types) and how many users to whom certain clusters would be able to support based on the maximum sizes of the JVMs in the cluster(s) and total number of users with that certain memory footprint. As virtual memory mapping depends on the capabilities of the operating system bit level itself, it is true that 64-bit OS provides much more room to accommodate a larger memory footprint, but there is always a trade-off with pros and cons for deciding to go with 32- or 64-bit for portal applications.

Elapsed time

Outside of the user-perceived response time and portal component response time, there is an overall elapsed time for an end-to-end transaction in which portal is also a participant. It is important to be able to distinguish between time is spent on portal versus the time spent outside of portal within the same business transaction.

CPU

Portal applications are memory bound, but in high volume processing or intensive I/O scenarios, they can be more CPU bound. nmon is a great tool for Linux and AIX systems when nothing else is available for CPU monitoring.

> nmon can be freely downloaded from `http://www.ibm.com/developerworks/wikis/display/WikiPtype/nmon`.

Parallel Portlet Rendering

Visit the WebSphere Portal Information Center to confirm how to turn on PPR. However, after that enablement, you will need to look at the "before and after" PPR picture of performance numbers to decide whether PPR is beneficial to your portal application. That is, by considering your portlets as PPR candidates, you can use our simple testbed for deciding PPR's value:

1. Generate one user's transaction flow to baseline the page performance.
2. Capture current page load without PPR (Use IBM Page Detailer).
3. Capture CPU activity without PPR (Use something like nmon).
4. Capture thread pool activity (WebSphere PMI).

Once that is documented repeat the previous steps with stable load of x users (10, 100, and 1000; 100 being ideal):

1. Generate one user's transaction to baseline the page performance.
2. Capture current page load with PPR (IBM Page Detailer).
3. Capture CPU activity with PPR (nmon).
4. Capture portlet timer (screenshot – it can be turned on via property files).
5. Capture thread pool activity (WebSphere PMI).

Use your results to evaluate whether PPR is beneficial or not to your portal applications. PPR has direct implications to CPU usage. Watch CPU metrics carefully as you ramp up the load in your test cases for PPR.

Caching

Yet another set of metrics to be carefully watched in a portal application are the caches in general, from the browser level to the portal server engine, application server engine to databases and active control lists. There is much to be watched, monitored, and tuned to make sure caches are delivering the value they are expected to deliver.

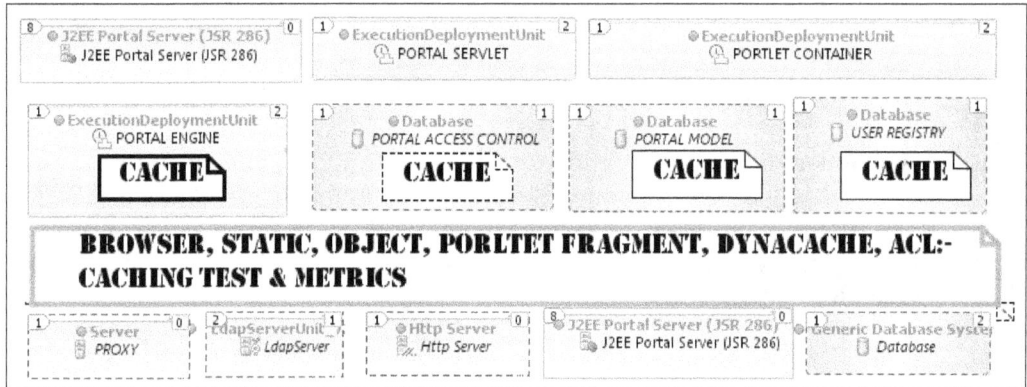

IBM Extended Cache Monitor for WebSphere is a great out-of-the-box bonus, which provides extra functionality over the traditional application server's cache monitor. It can also display the content of object cache instances, as well as the dynamic cache MBean statistics for all the instrumented cached instances.

> IBM Extended Cache Monitor can be downloaded from http://www.ibm.com/developerworks/websphere/downloads/cache_monitor.html.

The portal server also has internal caches that cannot be monitored via dynacache monitor. These are internal to portal and can be used to improve portal application performance. It is important to check limits on number of entries, cleanup frequency, flushing and delay offload policies, replication and invalidation support among other items. With this particular cache viewer, the following items can be seen:

* Cache name
* Current number of entries
* Observed entries
* High water mark

- Configured maximum size
- Access information
- Discard information
- Notes
- Hit rate

> From the link mentioned in preface, you can download the deployable WAR file that can be used to look at internal portal caches.

After installing, the following portlet should render:

This portlet provides indispensable and granular-level information on portal internal caches.

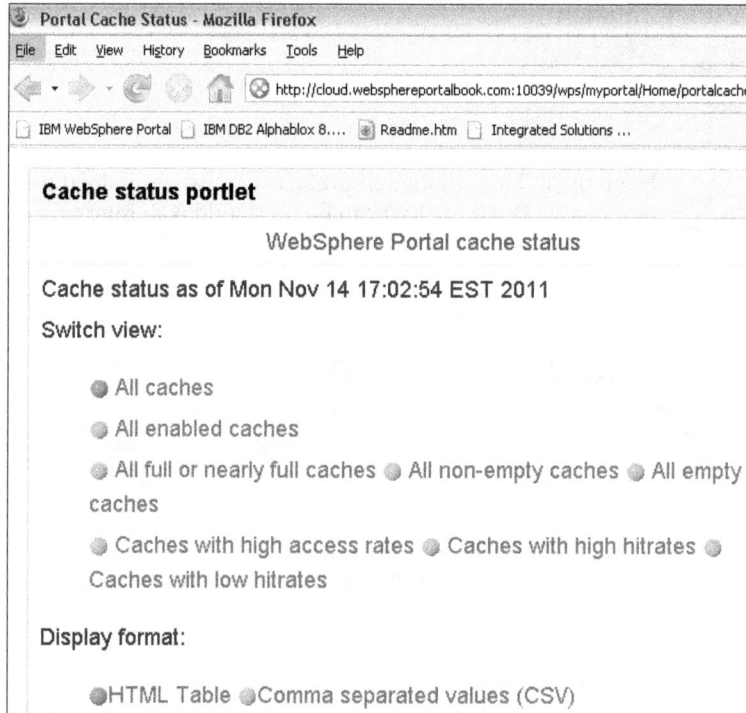

Finally a table should display all the cache information for all portal-related caches. To illustrate, we name a few of them here as follows:

- `DigestCache.cache`
- `PortletMenuCache`
- `com.ibm.lotus.search.cache.dynacache.CacheServiceImp`
- `com.ibm.lotus.search.siapi.search.imp.propertiesScope`
- `com.ibm.portal.rest.userprofile.PagingCache`
- `wsrp.cache.wsrp.portlet`
- `wsrp.cache.producer.user`
- `wsrp.cache.producer.objects`
- `wsrp.cache.deleted.portlets`
- `wps.mappingurl.LookupCache`
- `wps.mappingurl.ContextsCache`

Portal testing

Portal testing is one of the most fundamental phases to validate the portal functionality and performance among other nonfunctional aspects.

- **Performance**: Performance validates if the implemented portal meets the nonfunctional requirements criteria. Performance tests can have slightly different tangents such as load, stress, longevity (endurance)
- **Operational**: Operational tests validate how the implemented portal would operate under a failover and disaster recovery scenario
  - ° **Failover**: Failover validates if the session data would fail over to another node or cluster in case when a cluster or node goes down while maintaining the expected level of SLA
  - ° **Disaster recovery**: Disaster recovery validates how portal would recover from backups and large-scale failover situations
- **Security**: Security validates how portal is behaving based on the expected authorization and authentication architecture. It also validates whether portal is not vulnerable to malicious attacks.

Benchmarking portal – validating NFRs via load testing

Benchmarking an application is normally associated with an activity around pre- and post-production release's rollout. While it is true that benchmarking is essential prior to and after production, it is a best practice to start benchmarking your portal application as soon as possible. While there are standard benchmarks available for Java and application servers (by **Standard Performance Evaluation Corporation (SPEC)**), it is normally left to portal customers to decide on the standards for benchmarking their own portal.

There are different ways to decide on a methodology for portal benchmarking. However, some of these items are almost standard. We will look at some of them now. Consider the best practices on having a production benchmarking and a performance (staging) benchmarking. This exercise should be an iterative one where pre- and post-results are analyzed, and one scenario is tested at a time with controlled and documented changes. Start small and create repeatable process to reset the test data in order to use the same test data set for all test runs. Baseline portal for the following:

- Maximum throughput (page/requests per second – hits per second – GC – CPU cost per page – I/O – response time)
- Concurrent users and think time (virtual users' load based on expected workload then on extrapolation for benchmarking purposes)

- **Longevity test**: Stable load for long period to observe how memory and other resources perform to test system stability
- **Time based**: Fixed time for test run
- **Low load**: Stable load for each test run

As the A2Z portal architecture team took into account performance during design and WEF specialists tested their code throughout the component development, testing started with a more stable code set and not a lot of surprises. There are ways to benchmark portal with single user transactions (another multiple of 10), and say 10, 100, 1000 users and with load, stress, saturation, and longevity tests. Finding saturation points for portal applications is relevant to determining its scalability, providing insight into capacity planning activities. Another fundamental test for portal applications is the longevity test. This is a long-running test (eight hours for instance) with stable load that is intended to uncover memory leaks in the portal application. It can reveal memory leaks, exhaustion, fragmentation, or memory growth patterns that can be used as an input to tuning to optimize the portal application's performance. Generating repeatable load is fundamental to the portal testing efforts.

The multimedia presentation in the *Interactive click and learn* tip given ahead shows step by step how to record an HTTP test. This can be used by senior WEF or portal architects, testers, or specialists to provide a baseline of each major portal build before it is promoted and deployed to higher environments. IBM Rational Performance Tester can be downloaded for free, and it comes with a default five virtual user license that is also free of charge. It is just about one of the best load testing tools out there, which is also Eclipse based and very user friendly; so WEF users will feel at home. During development phase and then officially during the test phase, the following items were test cases for the validation of the performance-oriented architecture:

- **I/O operations**: Consolidate frequently used queries results and getting the right granularity for the call.
- **Data size**: Fetch more data than the portlet's needs.
- **Backend call**: Minimize number of backend calls via lazy loading and caching.
- **Portal session**: Use the session as transient storage. Keep session object size as small as possible. Use Java Serialization for session failover purposes. Avoid allowing anonymous pages to have session turned on, and try to check if a session already exists. Turn off the creation of sessions in JSPs by default and keep render parameters small.

There is, however, a more systematic way to test for each bottleneck identified in the first battery of testing and identify the performance metrics for each of the preceding items and others not mentioned here, as follows:

1. Determine the current system capacity with a stress test.

2. Find the factor, which currently limits system capacity.

3. Resolve that capacity limit by tuning and/or adding resources.

4. Repeat these steps until the nonfunctional goals are reached.

So, for instance, if your constraint is memory, you want to test the JVM saturation, as follows:

1. Ramp a single portal JVM to saturation.

2. Determine the bottleneck(s) that exist at that saturation point.

3. Resolve the bottleneck(s) by tuning and/or adding resources.

4. If system capacity does not meet nonfunctional goals, go back to step 1 and find the next bottleneck or constraint.

> **Interactive click and learn**
>
> Install IBM Rational Performance Tester from `http://www.ibm.com/developerworks/downloads/r/rpt/`.
>
> Learn IBM Education Assistant – IBM Rational Performance Tester – Recording an HTTP performance test at `http://publib.boulder.ibm.com/infocenter/ieduasst/rtnv1r0/index.jsp?topic=/com.ibm.iea.rpt/rpt/8.0/Operations.html`.

Portlet testing – time to walk the walk

To perform portlet testing, test the following:

- **PPR**: Portlets by default will render sequentially. The WebSphere Portal Information Center can provide more information on how to turn PPR on to provide the ability for portlets to render in parallel. But, besides its activation at portlet and server levels, it is necessary to look at PPR from strategic perspective where the criteria for testing, deciding its benefit for a certain page is determined, as mentioned in the overall metrics session in the *Overall test metrics* section. At a high level, we can affirm that in order to be able to decide on PPR benefits, it s necessary to test them.

- **Themes and skins**: Set aside some time to test themes and skins for performance. Test themes and skins for performance, cache as much as possible, but also test themes for security, as there could be some exposed security vulnerability via the themes.

- **Custom code (portlets and servlets)**: Be extra diligent on the testing of custom code. Test the 80-20 percent rules, (20 percent of the code executed 80 percent of the time). Apply the same rigor to the testing of these artifacts to keep quality control in check.

WEF testing

WEF's Model Action Tracing allows WEF specialists to test their code with tracing to look at the application flow, find problem, and execute some level of debugging. It helps them identify slow methods and code response. Besides, it also performs the following:

- It looks at actions and subactions for every portlet request

- It looks at time spent in each subaction for every portlet request

- It is triggered with a property or within WEF designer perspective using the Run command

- It is recommended for use only during development

- It looks at a single-user test case executed manually or automatically

- It is saved in the Web Experience Factory WAR folder for each WAR file, for example modelActions.txt in text format at WEB-INF/logs

WEF performance best practices are as follows:

- Use runtime and schema caching whenever plausible and cache across users.

- Consider the scope of variables (request, read-only, read/write) while avoiding the use of request scope for large XML variables with high usage patterns. Avoid large data sets and large variables.

- Consider the right level of logging.

- Use the serverStats.txt log file that is constantly capturing statistics about server usage and performance metrics. It is located at WEB-INF/logs in the deployed WAR format.

- Avoid excessively large WAR files. Consider caching that can't be shared across WAR files.

- Baseline the performance impact of personalization and WEF profiling.

Remember that entries in the properties file determine what information is logged. The `logging.serverStats` section of the `WEB-INF/config/logging.properties` file can have any number of entries. Each entry begins with `log.serverStats.criterion` and has the attributes that are listed in the next sections to determine what is logged. The sample of such an item is `log.serverStats.criterion.tooManySessions.item=Sessions`.

Comparator

This setting sets the configuration for the mathematical comparison operator as follows:

- `>=`: This sets threshold to greater than or equal to x value
- `>`: This sets threshold to greater than x value
- `=`: This sets threshold equal to x value
- `<`: This sets threshold to less than x value
- `<=`: This sets threshold to less than or equal to x value

An example of the `comparator` attribute is as follows:

```
log.serverStats.criterion.tooManySessions.comparator=>
```

Threshold

This setting sets a threshold as a value defining an upper or lower limit for the item seen in the preceding table. An example of the `threshold` item is as follows:

```
log.serverStats.criterion.tooManySessions.threshold=50
```

Message

This setting mandates a message in text strings, which displays the logged event. An example of such `message` item is as follows:

```
log.serverStats.criterion.tooManySessions.message="Session
threshold reached"
```

flushImmediately

This setting mandates an immediate flush to the log, instead of queuing it for later output. An example of `flushImmediately` is as follows:

```
log.serverStats.criterion.tooManySessions.flushImmediately
```

Let's now take a closer look at what this `serverStats` file provides. Let's examine a real sample from the A2Z Bank's WEF development environment. Keep these metrics in mind, because they will be the baseline to evaluate how WEF's executed code is performing. These are the metrics used during tuning, and after testing, they can used to validate based on test results if tuning changes have caused expected improvements. The key is to look for red flags in this file to find WEF-related performance bottlenecks. The sooner you are able to find these potential performance bottlenecks during development (and even prior to that at the design level), the better off the team is in finding less critical items during formal performance testing. What one will look for here is how model variables' executions are performing along with schemas, backend calls, SQL statements, cache activity, and memory consumption. Note that these metrics given in the table just after the following code snippet are related only to WEF components as the portal server will also have a set of caches and other server metrics to be examined. It is advisable to have this log file pointed outside of the filesystems or simply control its growth by the `Log File Max Size` setting in the `logging.properties` file. Log entries prefixed with `log.serverStat` have information concerning `serverStatus` logging. During performance testing, expect it to grow exponentially, so having control of the file itself helps to capture the right amount of metrics. Let's take a look at the unit testing version of a log containing such items just to be familiarized with the metrics:

```
*-- TIME: [2011-11-01 19:17:50,188] --*
Category: bowstreet.system.server.logging.serverStats.default
Priority: INFO
Thread:   WebSphere Portlet Factory (server stats logging)
Msg:      Sessions: 1
RestoredSessions: 0
ModelCacheRegenEntries: 2
Regens: 6
RegensFromCache: 2
OutputCacheHits: 0
OutputCacheMisses: 0
MemTotal: 639958528
MemFree: 281910736
MemInUse: 358047792
ErrorsLogged: 0
SevereErrorsLogged: 0
WarningsLogged: 0
PeakSessions: 1
ParallelModelRequests: 0
```

```
WebAppRequests: 2 Latency: 8523 Max: 13937
WebAppRequests/Chapter11/UI/DBInvestor: 2 Latency: 8523 Max: 13937
WebAppRequests/Chapter11/UI/DBInvestor/main: 2 Latency: 8523 Max:
13937
WebAppSOAPRequests: 0
WebAppMethodClassWritten: 1
WebAppJSPSourceWritten: 2
WebAppsInstantiated: 4
SchemaCacheHits: 148
SchemaCacheMisses: 6
SchemaCacheEntries: 6
ProfileCacheHits: 0
ProfileCacheMisses: 0
ProfileSetCacheHits: 0
ProfileSetCacheMisses: 0
ModelXmlCacheEntries: 38
ModelXmlCacheHits: 2
ModelXmlCacheMisses: 6
VariableProcessor: 0
SqlDataSource: 5
SqlDataSource/Investors_STCDataSource: 5
SqlDataSource/Investors_STCDataSource/JndiLookup: 1
SqlDataSource/Investors_STCDataSource/Release: 2
SqlDataSource/Investors_STCDataSource/Acquire: 2
SqlStatement: 2 Latency: 15 Max: 31
SqlStatement/Investors_STCListStatement: 2 Latency: 15 Max: 31
SqlStatement/Investors_STCListStatement/Create: 2 Latency: 15 Max: 31
SqlTransformToXml: 2
SqlTransformToXml/Investors_STCListTransform: 2
SqlTransformToXml/Investors_STCListTransform/Execute: 2
DiscardableVariableCacheHits: 0
DiscardableVariableCacheMisses: 0
DiscardableVariableRefetches: 0
```

Let's now see which metrics are captured, defined, and how they relate to the A2Z portal application sample:

Metric	Description	A2Z action item
ActiveSessions	Number of sessions that were accessed since the last update—Snapshot.	It investigates how many portlet sessions are in use. User session is the result of portlet sessions (X) divided by number of portlets in use (Y). In this case, it was just a single user.
ErrorsLogged	Logs cumulative number of error-level events generated. The error details are normally recorded in the event log.	It investigate top offenders for every test case run. In this sample, there were zero errors logged.
MemFree	Logs free heap memory in bytes.	It assesses heap health looking at garbage collection activity as well with Verbose GC. It was 281910736 bytes in this sample.
MemInUse	Logs in-use heap in bytes.	It assesses heap health looking at garbage collection activity as well with Verbose GC. It was 358047792 bytes in this sample.
MemTotal	Logs Java heap size in bytes.	It assesses heap health looking at garbage collection activity as well with Verbose GC. It was 639958528 bytes in this sample.
ModelCacheEntries	Logs present number of models in cache.	It ensures that models are not excessive.
ModelCacheRegenEntries	Logs present number of concurrent regenerated web applications in cache.	Default cache size is bowstreet.cache.model.size=2000. For each profile in memory, there is a corresponding entry. It was two in this sample.

Metric	Description	A2Z action item
OutputCacheHits	Logs cumulative number of hits to cached output data or when the Cache Control builder is triggered.	It shows number of requests a schema executed to source. It was zero in this sample.
OutputCacheMisses	Logs number of misses to cached output or how many times output data was written to cache.	It shows how many of those requests above would have come from cache control when it is turned on. It was zero in this sample.
PeakSessions	Logs maximum number of sessions in memory since IBM® WebSphere® Experience Factory servlet started — Accumulated.	Typically, this value equates to sessions. It was one in this sample.
Regens	Logs cumulative total number of requests for regenerated models for a session. Not actual number of regenerations.	Actual number of regenerations is (RegensX − RegensFromCacheY). It was six in this sample.
RegensFromCache	Logs total cumulative number of regenerations that came from cache.	Metric should be monitored to ensure it is close to the Regens value. It was two in this sample.
RestoredSessions	Logs total number of sessions recovered from a session failover.	None in this case.
Sessions	Logs concurrent number of user sessions in memory.	One
SevereErrorsLogged	Logs cumulative number of severe-level events created.	Zero

Metric	Description	A2Z action item
WarningsLogged	Logs cumulative number of warning-level logs created.	Zero
WebAppJSPSourceWritten	Logs cumulative total number of times a generated JSP source page is written to disk.	Two
WebAppMethodClassWritten	Logs cumulative number of times a generated method class for a web application is written (to the genjava folder) and compiled.	One
WebAppRequests	Logs final number of requests to web application models.	It was two in this sample. Note latency metrics—8523 and maximum of 13937 in milliseconds. This can be a candidate for tuning and should be flagged so performance testers have a test case for it.
WebAppsInSessions	Logs total cumulative number of model instances instantiated then mapped to and stored in all sessions in the Java Virtual Memory.	Four
WebAppSOAPRequests	Logs number of incoming SOAP requests	None in this sample

In addition to the metrics given in the preceding table, note that the file also contains three other sets of important metrics:

```
SchemaCacheHits: 148
SchemaCacheMisses: 6
SchemaCacheEntries: 6
```

The schema cache-related metrics along with more of the model cache data are as follows:

```
ModelXmlCacheEntries: 38
ModelXmlCacheHits: 2
ModelXmlCacheMisses: 6
```

Finally, SQL-related performance metrics are displayed, as follows:

```
SqlDataSource: 5
SqlDataSource/Investors_STCDataSource: 5
SqlDataSource/Investors_STCDataSource/JndiLookup: 1
SqlDataSource/Investors_STCDataSource/Release: 2
SqlDataSource/Investors_STCDataSource/Acquire: 2
SqlStatement: 2 Latency: 15 Max: 31
SqlStatement/Investors_STCListStatement: 2 Latency: 15 Max: 31
SqlStatement/Investors_STCListStatement/Create: 2 Latency: 15 Max: 31
SqlTransformToXml: 2
SqlTransformToXml/Investors_STCListTransform: 2
SqlTransformToXml/Investors_STCListTransform/Execute: 2
```

Security testing

Like any other application, portal applications should be tested for penetration and other malicious attacks. The following are some of the items to be looked at via a penetration test strategy and robust exploit framework:

- XSS cross scripting vulnerabilities at themes, WCM, portlet, JavaScript, and JSP levels
- SQL injection and other SQL-related vulnerabilities
- Basic authentication, impersonation and **Trust Association Interceptor (TAI)** hijacking
- Denial of service via remote requests
- XMLAccess vulnerabilities
- DNS poisoning
- Man-in-the-middle attack
- Attack vectors for administrative or any other group or user role
- Ajax, SOAP, REST, and web services vulnerabilities

Performance anti-patterns

Keep the anti-patterns in check from the time of design, before development starts. But, during development and testing if any anti-patterns are found, there are ways to tune it out of them in most cases. In some cases redesign or new architectural decisions may need to be made. So, good examples of them are too many portlets on a page; **access control lists (ACLs)** via deeply nested LDAP groups; poor caching configuration and poor cache control policies; excessive I/O operations; and client/server round-trips, wrong scope for WEF variables, poor usage of models and builders. On the other hand, if we consider the best practices in performance patterns, we will find caching benefits being realized and planned for; tested and tuned; consolidated I/O via optimization of queries or service calls; proper transaction isolation level; smaller session object; smaller render parameters; proper use of Ajax and REST; proper use of variable scope and caching in WEF.

Summary

We started this chapter by looking at some basic performance engineering strategy that is much needed for the final success of the testing effort. We then looked at testing goals' definition along with test tools, automation and metrics. We finally looked at some of the portal, portlet, and WEF testing specifics, and finally looked at some real samples. We finished off briefly looking at security. Because testing, monitoring, troubleshooting, tuning, and fixing is an interactive process, the following chapters are interrelated layers within the same process flow. They all complement each other.

Other references:

- `http://www-10.lotus.com/ldd/pfwiki.nsf/dx/`
  `performance-best-practices`

17
Portal and Portlet Performance Monitoring

This chapter covers the subject of monitoring, which allows one to measure the success of portal based on established criteria. Both business and technical monitoring are much needed capabilities to ensure the right visibility that allows for the tracking of goals and KPIs. Monitoring facilities are available out of the box in the WebSphere Application Server via PMI and via analytics for the portal server. They can be utilized to monitor portlet, services and related portal server performance, and user metrics. We will also cover other monitoring capabilities that are available for purchase, and use **IBM Tivoli Composite Application Manager (ITCAM)** as an example, and cover some web analytics capabilities; but for the purpose and scope of this chapter we will look at:

- Business and technology monitoring
- APM as a discipline
- Server and application infrastructure monitoring with ITCAM
- PMI as your best friend
- Web analytics
- Cloud monitoring
- Green Data Center monitoring

Before getting into the chapter itself, we would like to highlight a site that offers a plethora of options and new techniques related to WebSphere Portal performance and monitoring. Check WebSphere portal performance wiki at `http://www-10.lotus.com/ldd/portalwiki.nsf/xpViewCategories.xsp?lookupName=Performance`.

Business and technology monitoring

Performance is a concept that applies to both the technical and business domains. In business terms, it really means to keep track of the KPIs defined as success criteria for the business goals. For the technical domain, it means to keep track of events and metrics at the seven different layers to validate that they comply with the expected **service-level agreements** (**SLAs**) and nonfunctional requirements. There are different types and dimensional aspects to monitoring. We will discuss some of them and how A2Z Bank utilized them as follows:

- **A2Z resource monitoring**: This monitors all types of resources associated with a device or an application, such as CPU utilization, storage, and memory

- **A2Z availability monitoring**: This monitors the availability of portal applications, related systems, and other IT infrastructural elements

- **A2Z transaction/response time monitoring**: This monitors across the managed resources to present a more end user-focused metric

- **A2Z service monitoring**: This monitors the response time of its loosely-coupled application including monitoring and managing service flows within an Enterprise Service Bus, DataPower, and the overall SOA layer

- **A2Z Business Monitoring**: Dashboard for applications with correlated data from multiple sources are critical to the banking bullion business with KPIs

APM as a discipline – choose your weapons

It is crucial that in the **Application Performance Monitoring** (**APM**) discipline, there is a matching in the capabilities of the tooling with mature repeatable processes around its operationalization. APM implementations can initially focus more on the monitoring aspects. However, it can evolve and focus on the full-fledged lifecycle encompassing process of application performance. According to Gartner research group, APM is comprised of five distinct functional dimensions as follows:

- **End user experience monitoring**: This refers to the capture of data about how end-to-end application availability, latency, execution correctness, and quality appear to the end user.

- **Application runtime architecture discovery and modeling**: This refers to the discovery of the software and hardware components involved in application execution and the array of possible paths across which these components could communicate to enable that involvement.

- **User-defined transaction profiling**: This is also called "Business Transaction Management". It refers to the tracing of logical unit of work events, as they occur among the components or objects as they move across the paths discovered in the second dimension. A user transaction profile is generated in response to a user's attempt to cause the application to execute what the user regards as a logical unit of work.

- **Application component deep-dive monitoring**: This refers to fine-grained monitoring of resources consumed by events occurring within the components discovered in the second dimension

- **Application data analytics**: This refers to the marshaling of techniques, including behavior learning engines, **Complex Event Processing** (**CEP**) platforms, log analysis, and multidimensional database analysis to discover meaningful and actionable patterns in the typically large data sets generated by the first four dimensions of APM.

Gartner continues defining APM as a process with (at least) five elements:

- It tracks in real time the execution of the algorithms that constitute an application

- It measures and reports on low or scarce (hardware and software) resources that are consumed as the algorithms execute

- It determines whether the application has executed successfully

- It records the latencies associated with some of the execution step sequences

- It determines why an application has failed to execute successfully or why resource consumption and latency levels have departed from expectations

The stronger the APM discipline is in the organization where portal is being implemented as an enterprise-level solution, the stronger will be the visibility for problem management and likelihood for customer satisfaction. In the case of A2Z Bullion Bank, the financial domain imposes some compliance requirements, and full APM is not an option but must have a discipline, aligned with the portal program and **Project Management Office** (**PMO**) strategies. The reality is that in many cases for other portal domains, the monitoring value is underestimated; and in some instances there is no proper budget for the proper solution. Sometimes, one is forced to start monitoring with out-of-the-box or open-source tools. In the next section, we will cover in more detail one purchased APM solution, which would cover some major aspects of the APM dimensions.

Portal server monitoring with ITCAM for WebSphere

This is an excellent tool that provides comprehensive problem determination and diagnostics for the Subject Matter Expert to handle. Its capabilities include:

- Root cause analysis
- Performance measured down to Java method level
- Portal application-related memory leaks diagnostics
- Three monitoring levels to increase visibility and be switched on the fly
- Ability to correlate and trace J2EE transactions from WebSphere
- Ability to provide performance information in real time at the instance level

The following are some interesting links for you to explore:

- *Evaluate: Tivoli Monitoring* at `http://www.ibm.com/developerworks/downloads/tiv/tivolimonitoring/cloud.html`
- Great basic YouTube demo on foundational aspects of ITCAM for WebSphere by Brian Fisher at `http://www.youtube.com/watch?v=cp6jCfZxrRk`

Problem determination – memory diagnostics

Additionally to the preceding YouTube demo, we would like to share some of the actual extra capabilities of ITCAM for WebSphere.

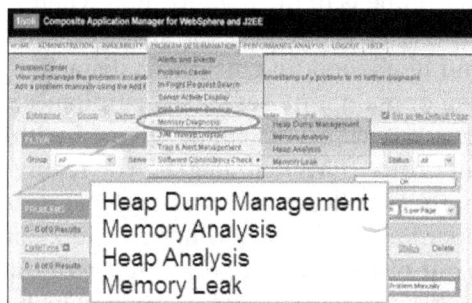

The capabilities of ITCAM for WebSphere are as follows:

- **Number of GCs versus JVM CPUs:** How much is the portal transaction response time impacted by frequent garbage collection calls?

- **Number of GCs versus average response time**: How much is portal transaction throughput impacted by frequent garbage collection calls?

- **Number of GCs versus number of requests**: Does portal JVM garbage collection occur due to high heap usage?

- **Number of GCs versus JVM heap size**: How much of portal JVM garbage collections delay a factor in long transaction response times?

- **Total GC time versus average response time**: How is throughput impacted by garbage collection delay?

- **Total GC time versus number of requests**: How much is heap usage contributing to garbage collection delay?

- **Total GC time versus JVM heap size**: How is long garbage collection delay related to the system paging rate?

- **Total GC time versus system paging rate**: How is the operating system paging rate related to the total GC time?

The Memory Leak Diagnosis view

Portal applications, for example other Java-based applications, have to deal with potential memory leaks and other memory-related issues not easily detected without proper tooling. For that matter, ITCAM provides a robust portal solution where leak candidates are identified and diagnostics can be presented.

The Server view

The **Server** view provides a one-stop shop for response time, throughput, session size and user metrics, JVM allocation, and CPU by JVM to name a few. It provides further proactive alerts based on performance thresholds that can be configured for the portal application.

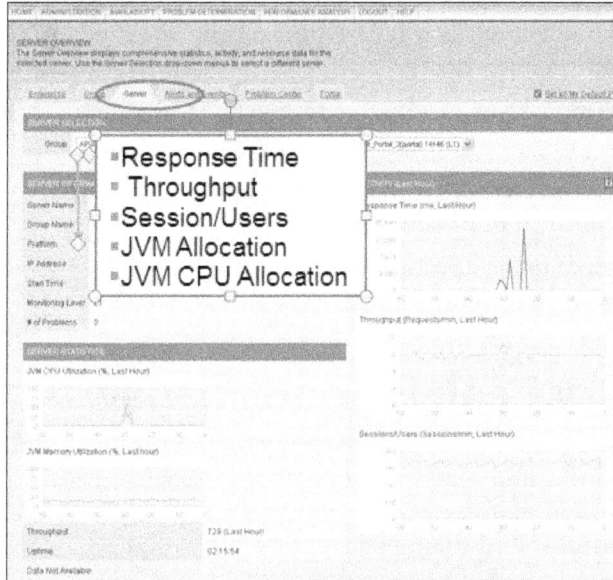

The Portal view

The **Portal** view provides substantial value for portal-related metrics. It looks at model building time, authentication, authorization, portlet- and page-level performance metrics.

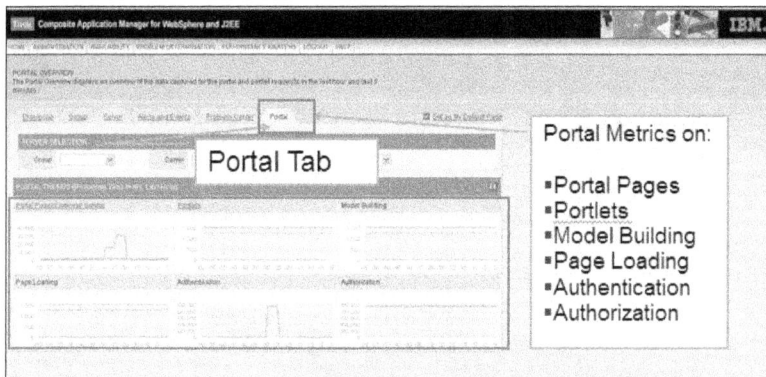

Monitoring slowest portlets

It further provides another view into the slowest portlets. This is an easy way to see which portlets are slow, and to go back to other views to see why they are slow.

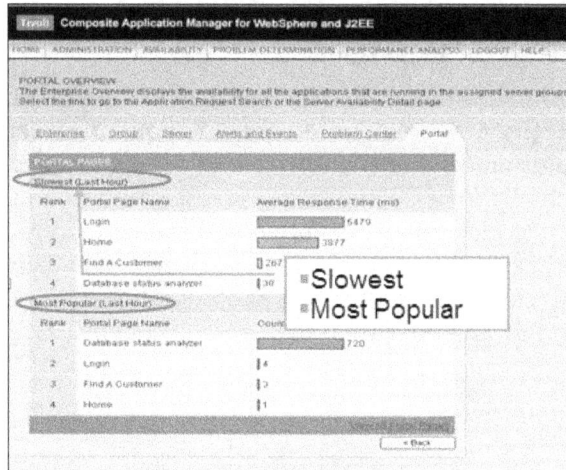

Monitoring contentions and locks

Everybody involved in Java development has dealt at one point or another with thread locks and other contentions at the thread pool, class loader, or object levels. ITCAM provides a way to diagnose and drill down into the portlet requests in specific time (as opposed to JDBC, Servlet, SOAP, EJB, CICS, and so on) in real time. This is another amazing feature, and this allows for a fast turnaround time for diagnostics and resolution planning.

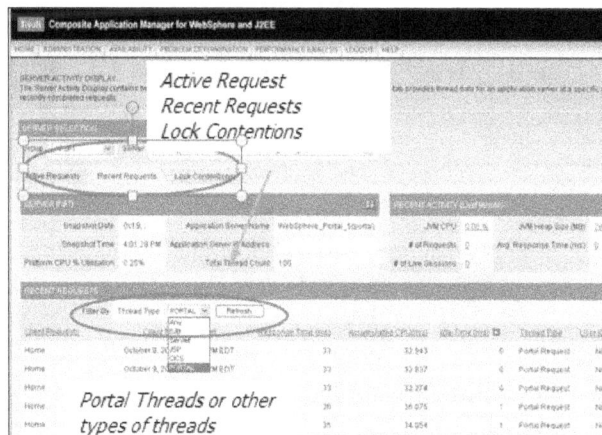

The preceding screenshot illustrates **Active Requests**, **Recent Requests**, and **Lock Contentions** filtered according to **Thread Type**.

Setting traps and alerts based on performance thresholds

Performance monitoring can be reactive or proactive in the case of application traps. In the case of ITCAM, it provides a highly configurable interface for setting performance thresholds on different resources and managed objects. You can set a threshold that is actually lower than the worst-case scenario, thus allowing for problem management to kick off its resolution and mitigation processes around an identified, isolated performance problem. This is especially beneficial during production, so portal/cloud Administrators and operational people can act based on information presented by an application trap.

STEP 1 - TRAP TYPE SELECTION
On this page, select your trap type, and the target type. Click Next to define the target type.

TRAP TYPE

Trap Type   ○ Server Resource Trap   ⊙ Application Trap

Target Type   Occurrence

Occurrence
CPU Time
Resident Time -- Completed
Wait Time
Resident Time -- In-Flight
Uncaught Exceptions
Lock Acquisition Time -- In-Flight
Lock Acquisition Time -- Completed

TRAP ALERT SETTINGS

Condition   Number of time(s) the Trap Definition occurs 1

Severity   High ▾

Alert Action(s)   ☐ Send Email (comma separated)

       ☐ Send SNMP Message

Data Action(s)   ☑ Collect Component/Method Trace

                                        Add

The preceding screenshots illustrate application trap capabilities.

Code performance monitoring via Java profiling

Method profiling is a very powerful way to go into the details of a Java execution stack. As one says, the devil is in the details — method profiling is able to provide insight into the total CPU time, elapsed time — for each java method executed. A filter can be created to exclude any methods and drill down into specific classes based on captured method-level performance evidence. It is a level of detail that is sometimes much needed during development, testing, and ideally before a portal application hits production. As part of portal performance engineering best practices, A2Z Bullion Bank decided to profile its code for major releases throughout the development lifecycle. It provided more insight to the development team on areas of improvement and allowed for almost the elimination of performance surprises of this nature in testing or production.

The preceding screenshot illustrates method profiling capabilities.

PMI is your best friend

When you are in development mode and/or there are no other tools, WebSphere Application Server PMI should be used. We showed you an image of PMI in *Chapter 16, Portlet and Portal Testing*.

Portlets, servlets, JSP, and method-level metrics should be looked at via PMI. Thread pools along with JDBC pools should always be checked at each release baseline.

In the tuning chapter, we will show how to use the out-of-the-box PMI during development to start tuning and optimizing code generated by the WEF in a proactive way. Performance testing should never come at the end of the project. When implemented during the development process, it can be extremely efficient in promoting code with higher quality standards.

Web analytics

The term **web analytics** refers to gathering, assembling, and measuring portal usage information via a standardized log format and turning it into knowledge. It is not about performance or purely system logs, but about understanding how portal is being used from a user and customer perspective. Remember there is a distinction on the collection method between active analytics (based on tagging) and passive analytics (based on logging).

> IBM has been supporting the **User Experience Optimization Initiative** (**UEOI**) that enables WebSphere Portal customers to capture and measure portal user usage and activity patterns easily to allow more targeted and better adjustment to opportunities and changing demands.

Ideally every portal project is able to budget for a web analytics solution. In a great IBM developerWorks article, Steffen Uhlig and Stefan Liesche show how to use open-source tools for WebSphere Portal analytics.

> Check *IBM WebSphere Developer Technical Journal: Using portal analytics with open-source reporting tools* at http://www.ibm.com/developerworks/websphere/techjournal/0609_liesche/0609_liesche.html.
>
> Also check *Site analytic support in IBM WebSphere Portal 6.1.5*, which is well presented in a white paper format at http://www.ibm.com/developerworks/websphere/zones/portal/proddoc/dw-w-siteanalytics/index.html.

The versions for the software mentioned previously have changed, but overall the strategy can still be applied. There are some great packaged web analytics tools available for portal analytics that are not open source. Regardless of the tool, there are some architectural items to be decided on when injecting and collecting portal analytics from portal users. There is the client and server portal analytics "way of doing things". Let's take a look at some of the implementation discrepancies by server- and client-side instrumentation:

Server side	Client side
Portal server logs user activity and meta data to server-hosted log files.	JavaScript communicates with analytics server with user activity data.
Log files can be available offline for later processing as they are stored.	Online data is collected by analytics system and resides outside of the portal server and browser.

Server side	Client side
Analytics systems parse log files for analytics data.	Injection capability is provided out of the box in WebSphere Portal 8.
Only direct portal server instantiations are recorded, excluding cache-based instantiations.	Injected JavaScript defines which data will be captured and recorded. Events with cached data can also be captured.
Activation is via configuration in the portal server. No special coding for page- and portlet-based reports is needed.	Activation is via JavaScript injection on themes and skins. Portlet markup can also contain JavaScript providing reports on page and portlet views.
Specialized functionality is available via portal analytics logs API.	Specialized functionality is available via portal analytics client injection.

Activation is done, depending on the instrumentation mechanism, via client or server side. Overall, on the server side, there is a generic setting allowed by both JSR 168 and JSR 286 portlets specified in Portlet Statistics Event Logging API. Portal server provides a configuration service (SiteAnalyserLogService), which determines the type of data to be collected for site analysis. It can include events such as page management (CRUD lifecycle), requests of pages, portlets, login and logout by user, and other user management CRUD actions.

Once this feature is enabled, the outcome is created in the format of a log compliant to the **National Center for Supercomputing Applications (NCSA)** combined industry standard. It allows for data gathering of custom business events at the portlet level for a more sophisticated and customized portal usage analytics intelligence. Portal has three main configuration services to enable this feature as follows:

- com.ibm.portal.portlet.service.siteanalyzer. PortletSiteAnalyzerLoggingServiceHome: This is a JNDI-based service exposing a method to provide insight into the request type (ActionRequest, RenderRequest, EventRequest, and ResourceRequest)

- com.ibm.portal.portlet.service.siteanalyzer. PortletSiteAnalyzerLogger: This service queries logger space and writes entries to the log

- com.ibm.portal.portlet.service.siteanalyzer. ParameterNamesProcessor: This allows the site analyzer service interface to call site analytics framework prior to the assembly of the query string section of the request URI, based on the encoding of the request parameter

As a sample, this can be enabled in the following way:

```
Activate the SiteAnalyzerJSRPortletLogger logger
SiteAnalyzerJSRPortletLogger.isLogging = true
Use the SiteAnalyzerJSRPortletLogger within your JSR Portlet
    (JSR168 + JSR286)
saLogger.log("Bullion Vault business event");
```

For step-by-step details on how to enable analytics collection on WebSphere Portal, please see the following *Fix readme* paper on *Logging custom details of business events for site analysis* available at http://www-01.ibm.com/support/docview. wss?uid=swg21372892.

WebSphere Portal as an evolving product has been increasingly adding support for web analytics. There are many choices and vendor solutions out there. All of them have pros and cons and it is really up to each portal program/project team to evaluate what works best for their portal solutions based on many factors including budget, vendor relationship history, and defined technology roadmap. Some of them are as follows:

- **Coremetrics**: In May 2011, IBM announced new Cloud Analytics Software, which you can find at http://www-01.ibm.com/software/marketing-solutions/coremetrics/.

- **Webtrends**: This has thousands of success stories in the portal space. You can find it at http://webtrends.com/.

- **Adobe SiteCatalyst**: Previously known as Omniture, it provides great ROI. You can find it at http://www.omniture.com/en/products/tours.

As for A2Z Bullion Bank, it decided on a tool named IBM Unica NetInsight. It adopted the tool because it allowed for the creation of custom questions in plain English to be formulated and answered based on captured portal-user interaction data. A sample of which types of questions can be formulated and responded by the analytics engine is shown in the following screenshot:

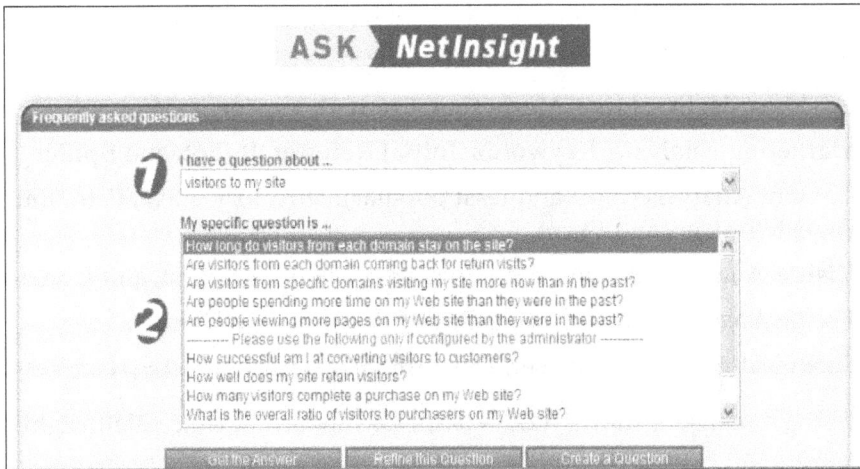

Unica NetInsight also has a very rich and intuitive dashboard interface with the proper user metrics' classification. It is highly configurable and provides the right level of details and granularity for each of its dashboards domains, as shown in the following screenshot:

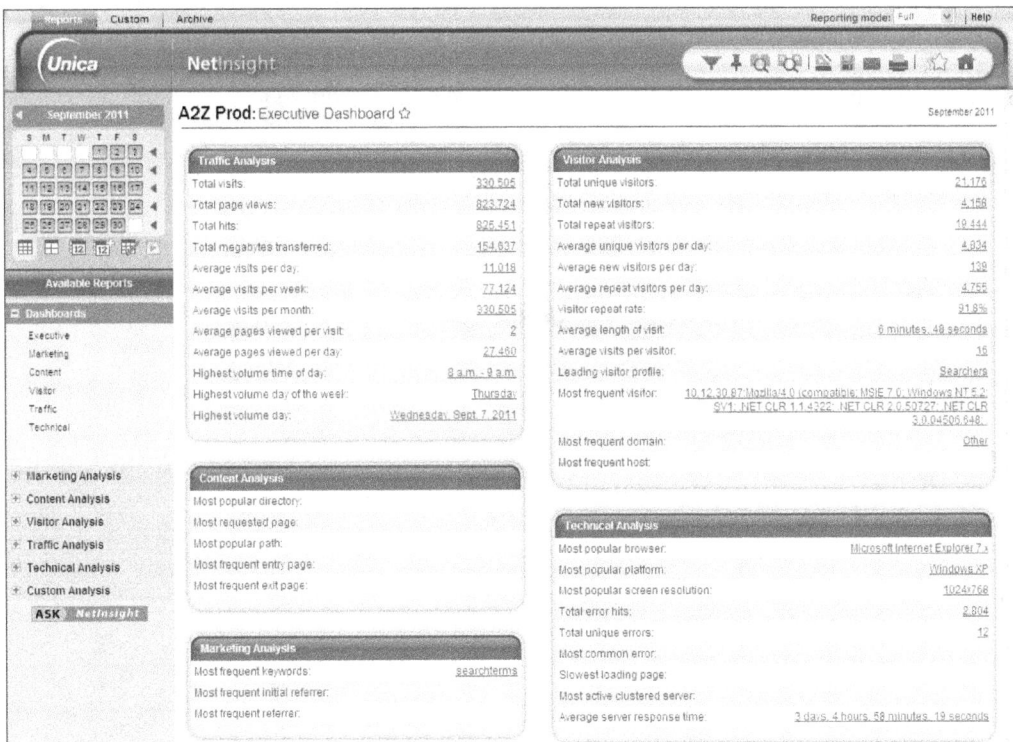

The dashboards are fully customizable, but are separated and represented out of the box as follows:

- **Dashboards: Executive, Marketing, Content, Visitor, Traffic,** and **Technical**
- **Marketing Analysis: Keywords, Initial Referrer, Robot,** and **Spider**
- **Content Analysis** (most and least popular): **Directory, Page, Path, Entry Page, Exit Page,** and **Event**
- **Visitor Analysis: Profile, Visit Duration, Retention, Host,** and **Domain**
- **Traffic Analysis: Traffic, Date, Day of the Week,** and **Time**
- **Technical Analysis: Browser, Platform, Error, Server,** and **Screen Resolution**

The following screenshot shows **A2Z: Visitor Dashboard** in Unica NetInsight:

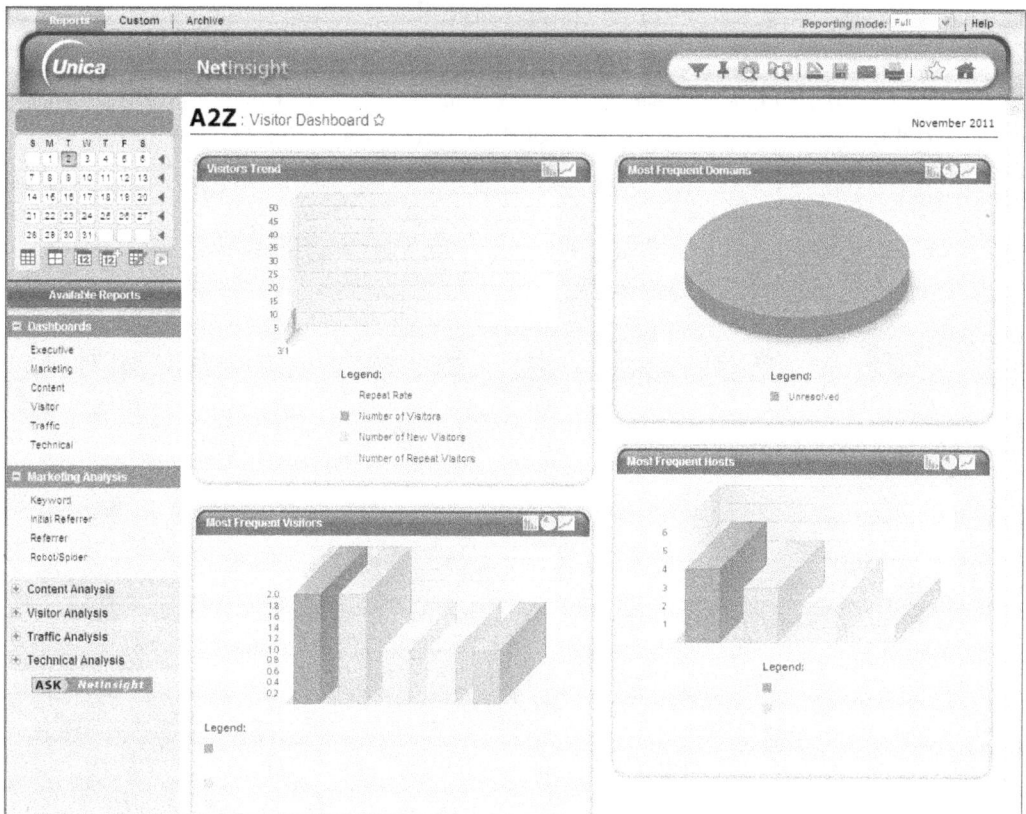

Cloud monitoring

Depending on the cloud provider, you have many options for monitoring full APM lifecycle that goes along with the capabilities of each provider. It is based on vendor trust, cost, and reliability. The level or granularity at which you need to monitor is also based on the APM dimensions mentioned in *Chapter 16, Portlet and Portal Testing*. Let's now look at some monitoring samples from three of the most prominent cloud service providers as follows:

- **IBM Cloud monitoring**: A great article — *Monitor services in the cloud* goes into details of monitoring with Tivoli, which is available at `http://www.ibm.com/developerworks/cloud/library/cl-monitorcloudservices/index.html`.

- **Amazon monitoring with BMC**: If your portal solution uses Amazon Cloud, it is being monitored by another great software maker, BMC. To learn more, go to `http://www.bmc.com/videos/Amazon.html`, where Amazon's CTO talks about BMC Cloud monitoring.

- **VMware Cloud monitoring**: VMware vFabric Hyperic is a great option for monitoring virtualized infrastructure by the lead in the virtualization space. You can find a great product demo at `http://www.youtube.com/hyperichq`.

Green Data Center monitoring

In today's world, the effort to become more sustainable and greener is also in the A2Z Bank technological roadmap and strategic goals. Data center efficiency becomes even a more critical component in a socially responsible portal implementation. It is a win-win situation. We will consider not only tax incentives for more conscious enterprises and huge savings, but also energy reduction, and last but not least, efficiency as the key element to build a greener IT. For those interested in exploring these possibilities, please check out the following link:

`http://www14.software.ibm.com/webapp/download/demo.jsp?id=Green+IT+-+Datacenter+Efficiency+Dec08.`

Summary

We started this chapter looking at some basic monitoring concepts and types. We looked at APM as a discipline. We used ITCAM as a sample for a robust portal monitoring solution. We finished off looking at web analytics and cloud monitoring.

In the next chapter, we will explore how to troubleshoot problems one may find while monitoring its portal environments.

18
Portal Troubleshooting

This chapter covers the main approaches for classifying, isolating, and resolving portal problems via troubleshooting and problem determination. It also covers tooling and the best practices. By the end of this chapter, we will have looked at the following:

- Problem determination and troubleshooting
- Divide and conquer
- **IBM Support Assistant (ISA)** – general tools
- Splunk tool

Problem determination and troubleshooting

In order for problem determination, troubleshooting, and remediation to work together, there is a lot of preparation that needs to be done upfront to get the proper processes established. Problem determination actually starts before something undesired happens. It includes problem prevention best practices along with the problem detection, monitoring, and alerts to avoid problems going undetected for any period of time. Let's start this section by prefacing what problem determination is not:

- It is not an exact science. It is an evolving process subject to other influences.
- It is not an isolated process, but collaborative among organizations and experts to organize the investigation and characterize the problem set at hand.

One of main ingredients in the recipe to be successful in the operational aspects of a portal is to have a consistent yet flexible strategy. At a high level we can say there are steps and best practices for problem determination, and root case identification to be followed. We need to be able to do the following:

- Understand a problem based on the reported behavior
- Devise a plan of action based on the severity of the problem
- Carry out the plan to recreate, isolate, diagnose, and fix the problem
- Examine the solution and monitor its efficacy to track progress

Once a problem is diagnosed and has a known fix or workaround, a multidisciplinary troubleshooting and change effort should encompass a plan that allows it to be:

- Implemented consistently across environments
- Based on pre/post production and run the business operational processes
- More automated with proactive regression testing
- Error prevention aware and well documented for future reference

Divide and conquer

There are different layers and standard operational procedures within these layers for problem determination and management.

Project lifecycle interdisciplines

On one side we have an interdisciplinary approach to managing problems throughout the development lifecycle and across environments including production, based on reported incidents. These foundational and intertwined disciplines are within the domains of incident management, change management (including configuration and release management), and problem management. On the other side we have quality management and the APM dimensions. They all play a fundamental role in helping portal applications to behave and perform as planned and have operational excellence.

In the case of the A2Z Bank, an effective workflow for portal operational processes around problem and incident management were implemented. At a high level, without taking into account specific roles and all the plethora of tools, let's take a look at how A2Z Bank implemented this workflow, which serves both banking and call center help desk domains.

Use case

We have the abstract use case of an A2Z Bank customer having a problem with the portal application. It makes a call to support and has an incident case created with the proper priority assigned. After some research the portal help desk person decides whether impersonation is needed. **Impersonation** is a feature introduced in portal since version 6.1.5, which allows a support analyst or portal administrator to login as a user and have the same experience as the real user. It then decides if that is enough to allow help desk to recreate, resolve, and close the case. If that is true, a solution is provided and the incident is closed. If that does not solve the problem, then incident control creates a profile of the case based on help desk and customer's problem description. Once the diagnostics portion of the workflow starts, it is when an arsenal of available tools is used to drive the problem to isolation, remediation, and resolution. If a change is required then change management gets a task in the workflow to look into the request and follow the related workflows with development, IBM support, third parties, and whatever action item is needed to drive it to completion. The request flow is prioritized based on impact analysis criteria and results. Based on those factors, a change plan is put in place to schedule the remediation deployment, test, and implementation for the required change. Once it is implemented successfully it is then communicated, documented accordingly, and tracked for quality assurance. The following diagram summarizes this process flow at a high level:

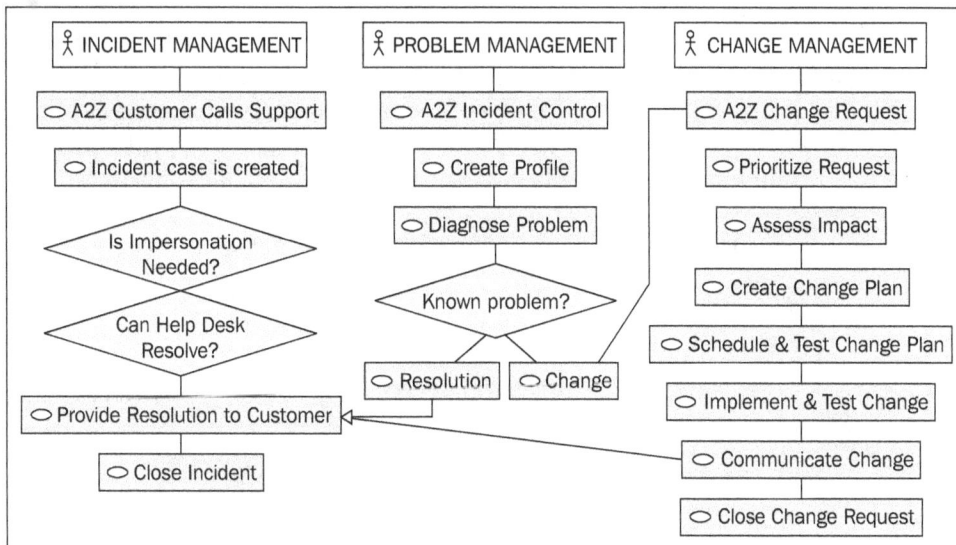

Skills and tools level

Within these disciplines there are a set of tools and skill sets required to operate, execute, and interpret results with the help of these tools to the point of recommending a solution to a given problem. There are several monitoring tools with diagnostics and troubleshooting features within reach as we saw in *Chapter 5, Portal Gold and Cloud Architecture*. Aside from those within the APM domain, we will look at three major tools selected by A2Z Bank for troubleshooting and support purposes alone, as follows:

- **IBM Support Assistant (ISA)**
- IBM Support Assistant Lite for WebSphere Portal
- Splunk

Let's now take a look at these options and see what value they bring to the table. The tools listed previously represent the ones selected by A2Z Bank for the purpose of supporting new portal initiative. The great beauty about these ISA tools is that they allow one to gather, trace, and log information in an automated way; diagnose and interpret the problem; open a PMR case with IBM and send pertinent data to IBM support. Normally some portal shops that do not have ISA implemented have a turnout time of a few days to gather and provide IBM support with data to work on.

IBM Support Assistant – general tools

For updated information on new tools and products add-ons to the ISA tool, please visit the add-on page at `http://www-01.ibm.com/support/docview.wss?uid=swg27012689`. The same capabilities for finding, analyzing problem sets, collecting and sending Data to IBM support are available for all add-ons here.

> You can listen to the on the go MP3 files at the following URLs:
> - ISA part 1 – customize ISA and find information at `ftp://public.dhe.ibm.com/software/websphere/techexchange/ISA_Part1.mp3`
> - ISA part 2 – automated data collection and problem determination capabilities at `ftp://public.dhe.ibm.com/software/websphere/techexchange/ISA_Part2.mp3`
> - ISA part 3 – problem determination tooling, troubleshooting tools, and data collection options at `ftp://public.dhe.ibm.com/software/websphere/techexchange/ISA_Part3.mp`

Depending on the types of software stack or different problem types, such as JVM related, configuration, specific tools for CICS and Lotus, for example, are available to fit your physical topology and software runtime, as follows:

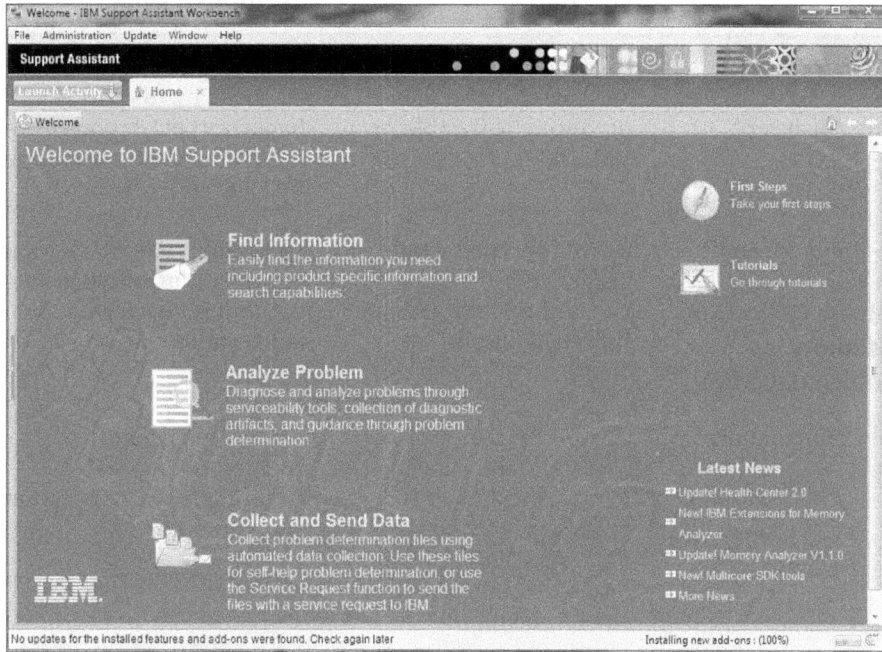

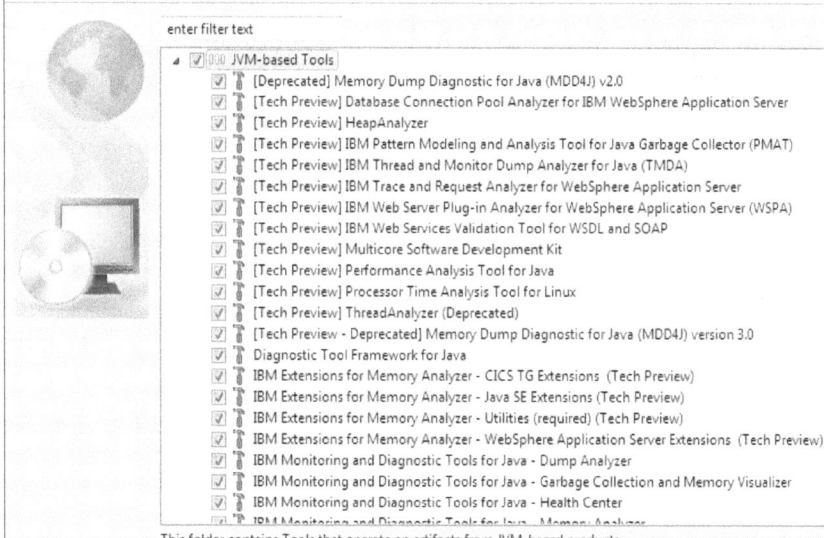

The following table shows which tools were selected by A2Z teams to support the operational aspects of portal as well as the development lifecycle:

ISA tool name	Description	Use for A2Z Bank
IBM Monitoring and Diagnostic Tools for Java – Dump Analyzer	Executes automated analysis of dump files produced by the IBM Java VM.	Analyzing system dumps produced by IBM JVMs to diagnose typical problems such as out of memory, deadlocks, JVM and JNI crashes.
IBM Monitoring and Diagnostic Tools for Java **– Garbage Collection** and **Memory Visualizer (GCMV)**	GCMV provides great insight analysis and views of verbose garbage collection output.	Analyzing Verbose GC logs the -Xtgc output native memory logs (output from ps, svmon, and perfmon).
Visual Configuration Explorer	Compares configuration snapshots and allows for visualization of configuration values for different environments or release tracks within an environment.	Visually analyzing, troubleshooting, and exploring cross-IBM product configuration.
Assist On-site	Provides remote desktop capabilities for IBM live support.	Collection of data and problem determination.
IBM Web Server Plug-in Analyzer for WebSphere Application Server	Looks at HTTP plugin configuration, logs, and traces.	Detecting configuration problems at the HTTP request level.

ISA for WebSphere Portal

ISA is a great tool for the many IBM stacks used by the A2Z Bank runtime architecture. It includes capabilities for portal troubleshooting. ISA Lite for WebSphere Portal is an evolution of an IBM internal portal problem determination tool, which only focuses on WebSphere Portal. It is very light, being appropriate for all environments. One of the reasons for having this tool in your troubleshooting arsenal is because it can be easily installed in development and integration environments, allowing for efficient early isolation and diagnostics. It is also a great tool to have in the staging and production environments. Even in your own unit-testing environment, this tool can be beneficial. If you refer to the preceding workflow screenshot, this tool and its processes fall under the Diagnose Problem use case. ISA should be set up right, because the environments become ready for use. This should not be delayed until problems are manifested. Let's now take a look at some of the spefificics.

DIR – Download, install, and run

First thing to do is to download it, install it, and run it. Then, have some information handy such as portal and application server administrative credentials, as they will be needed. The **Data Collection Options** option on the menu offers the main WebSphere Portal categories.

> **Click and download**
>
> IBM ISA Lite For WebSphere Portal at http://www-01.ibm.com/support/docview.wss?uid=swg24008662
>
> Split-Second User's Guide at http://www-01.ibm.com/support/docview.wss?rs=688&uid=swg27008317

The first option is to direct the data collection mechanism to isolate a problem to one of the domains, if possible. The **General** tab would help in cases where there is no other domain that matches the problem set at hand:

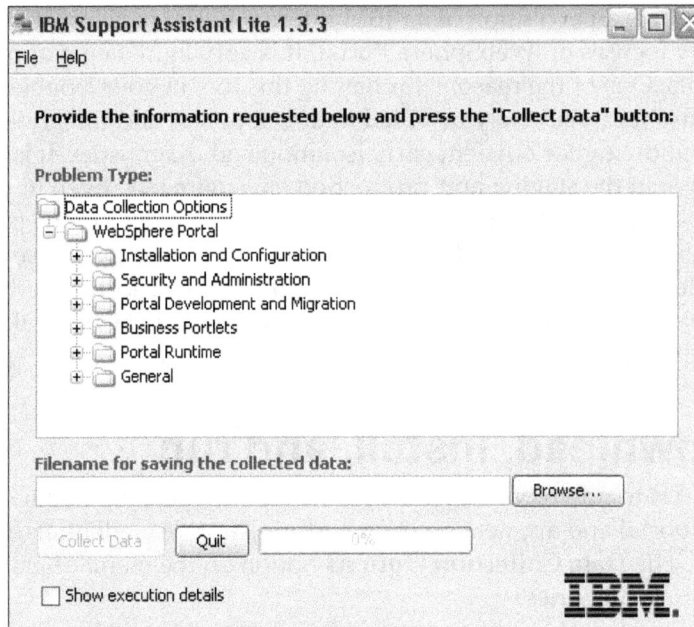

Choose Problem Type

The next step is to drill down into the particular subcategories under each main **Problem Type** category. Once that is determined, it is a matter of allowing the tool to run and collect data from the target nodes and clusters.

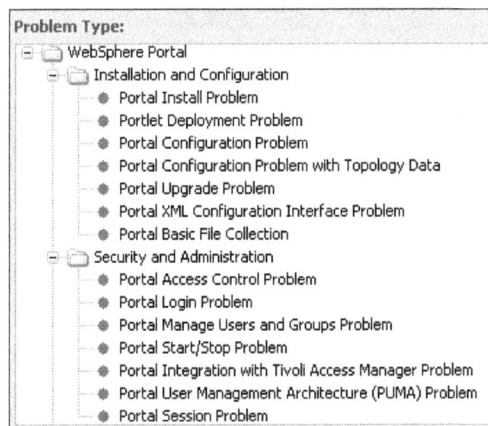

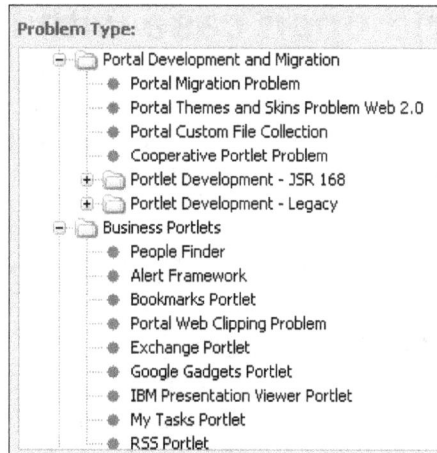

Enable Split-Second (if needed)

If the problem is performance related and it is manifested in an environment that needs quick resolution, Split-Second can be turned on. Once enabled, Split-Second will allow for diagnosis for any of the following problem areas:

- Overall portal performance
- Overall WCM performance
- **Java Content Repository (JCR)** performance
- Portal database performance
- Portal access control performance
- User registry and authentication performance
- Portlet performance
- **Personalization (PZN)** performance

The following screenshot shows the **Enable Split-Second** option under **General**:

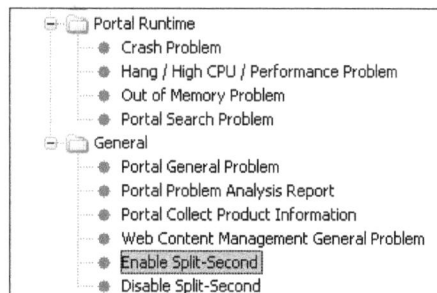

View output and open case with IBM

Here is one of the best features, the capability of opening a PMR case with IBM support from the tool itself. It allows for fast and consistent vendor engagement during problem management incidents. In some situations, it becomes critical to engage IBM support in the troubleshooting and solution efforts.

Troubleshooting in WebSphere Application Server v8

WebSphere Application Server comes equipped with some out-of-the-box troubleshooting tools. Under the administrative console, the **Troubleshooting** option provides simple ways to increase trace and log verbosity levels, look at configuration and runtime errors. Additionally, it allows one to consume various logs such as JVM, Verbose GC, system out/error, native standard logs, and look at class loader-related errors. As a new feature in Version 8 and above, there is a way to generate heap and Java dumps quickly via the GUI.

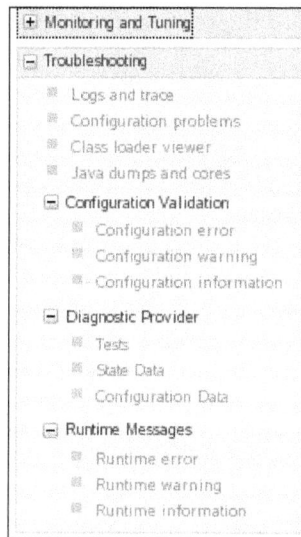

Cell=wp8betaCell, Profile=wp_profile

Java dumps and cores   ? –

Java dumps and cores

Use this panel to generate heap dumps, Java cores or system dumps for a running process. The files resulting
from these operations are placed on the local file system.

⊞ Preferences

| Heap dump | Java core | System dump |

Select	Server ◊	Node ◊	Host Name ◊	Version ◊	Type ◊
You can administer the following resources:					
☐	WebSphere_Portal	wp8betaNode	localhost.cloud.websphereportalbook.com	ND 8.0.0.0	servers
☐	server1	wp8betaNode	localhost.cloud.websphereportalbook.com	ND 8.0.0.0	servers
Total 2					

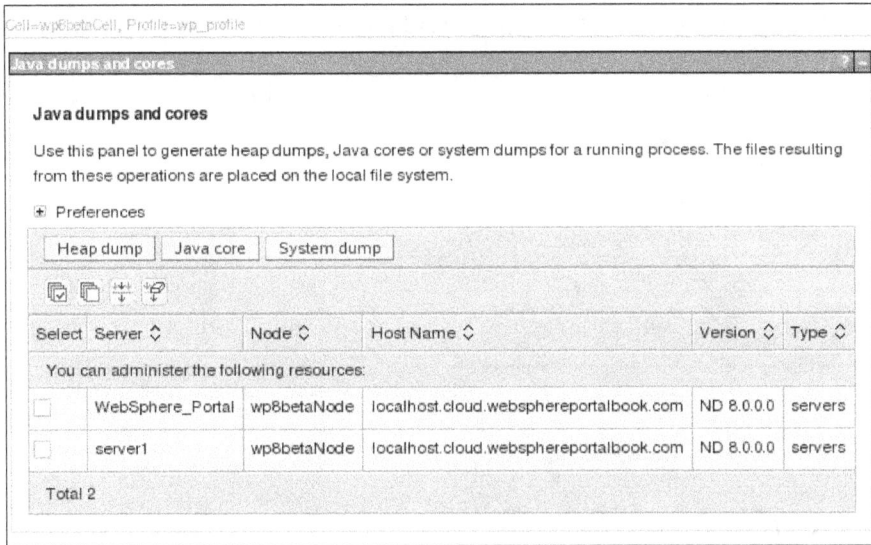

Another feature that is particular to Version 8 and above is that HPEL mode
is available. **HPEL** stands for **High Performance Extensible Logging**. Based
on literature provided by the product's information center, the following table
represents how to view basic versus HPEL mode functions:

Source	Basic mode files	HPEL mode files	How to view the HPEL files
System.out	SystemOut.log, trace.log (when trace enabled)	logdata/*.wbl, TextLog_<timestamp>. log (when text log enabled)	LogViewer to view logdata + filtering + logdata as readable text. Any text editor TextLog – any text editor
System.err	SystemErr.log	Same as System.out	Same as System.out
java.util. logging (levels DETAIL and above)	SystemOut.log activity.log trace.log (when trace enabled)	Same as System.out	Same as System.out

Source	Basic mode files	HPEL mode files	How to view the HPEL files
`java.util.logging` (levels below DETAIL)	`trace.log`	`tracedata/*.wbl` `TextLog_<timestamp>.log` (when text log enabled)	Same as `System.out`
`native cout`	`native_stdout.log`	`native_stdout.log`	Any text editor
`native cerr`	`native_stderr.log`	`native_stderr.log`	Any text editor

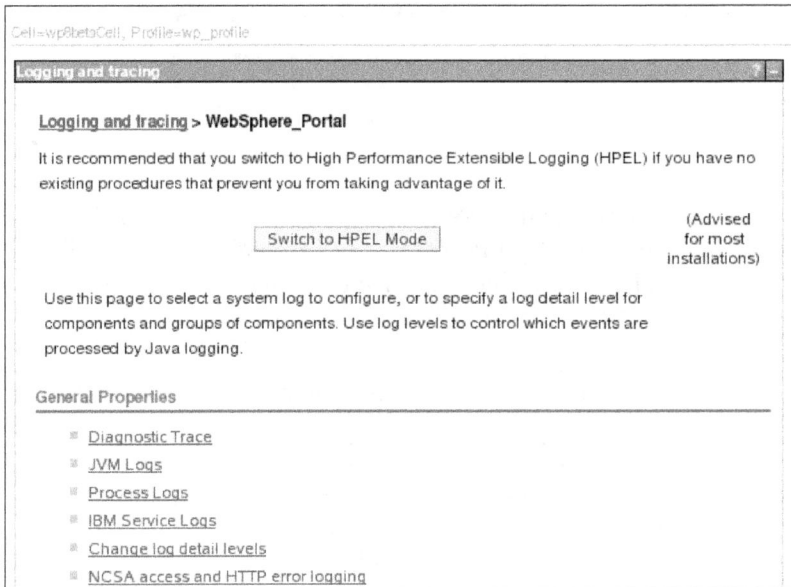

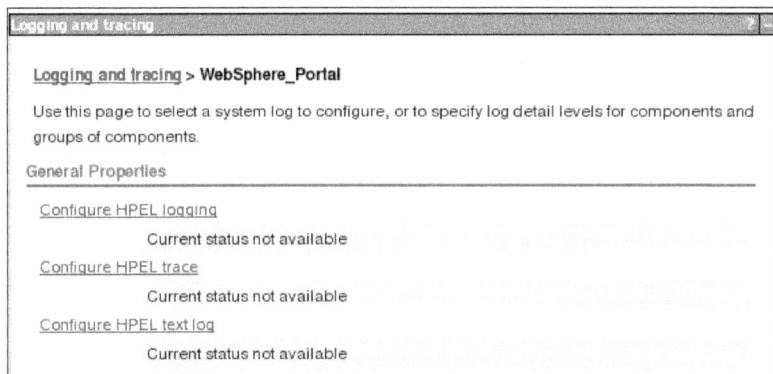

Cell=wp8betaCell, Profile=wp_profile

Logging and tracing

Logging and tracing > **WebSphere_Portal**

It is recommended that you switch to High Performance Extensible Logging (HPEL) if you have no existing procedures that prevent you from taking advantage of it.

Switch to HPEL Mode

(Advised for most installations)

Use this page to select a system log to configure, or to specify a log detail level for components and groups of components. Use log levels to control which events are processed by Java logging.

General Properties

- Diagnostic Trace
- JVM Logs
- Process Logs
- IBM Service Logs
- Change log detail levels
- NCSA access and HTTP error logging

Logging and tracing

Logging and tracing > **WebSphere_Portal**

Use this page to select a system log to configure, or to specify log detail levels for components and groups of components.

General Properties

Configure HPEL logging
　　　　　Current status not available
Configure HPEL trace
　　　　　Current status not available
Configure HPEL text log
　　　　　Current status not available

Trace level – debug with ARM turned on

There are times when one must rely on out-of-the-box capabilities. Request metrics is a tool feature based on the **Application Response Measurement (ARM)** standard, which in this case allows tracking of each individual transaction in WebSphere Application Server. It basically records the end-to-end response time from the Application Server to any other component. Use this menu on the administrative console to enable request metrics. It is easy to select target components types, which would be instrumented by WAS request metrics. Optionally, you can set trace levels for different components types to be instrumented or insert your own custom ARM implementation class. It can be enabled either by command line using **Java Management Extensions (JMX)** API interfaces or via the GUI using the administrative console.

Once enabled, the request metrics data will be written to the systemOut.log file. It can be easily consumed by an AS-IS tool (except for z/os) created by Sebastian Faulhaber from the IBM ISSW Lab in Germany to consume these logs. The ARM log entries would look like something like this:

```
HTTP request /broker/scenario ------------------------> 82 ms
Portlet/broker/scenario -----------------------------> 180 ms
Portlet/call to A2Z back-end system ---------------> 58 ms
```

Splunk engine

Splunk is another exceptional toolset that has significant advantages as far as being easy to use and cost aware. It is essentially a very smart machine data engine that can correlate data from all seven layers, and build views into a transaction flow. It works for data moving between servers, devices, and applications running physically, logically, or virtually in the cloud. It allows for proactive monitoring across all tiers, and provides search and dashboard capabilities for root cause analysis and problem determination. This is a tool that we personally highly recommend because its value is provided in minutes. The same DIR principle applies. Download, install, and run.

You can find a demonstration on Splunk engine for machine data at http://www.splunk.com/view/SP-CAAAEZY.

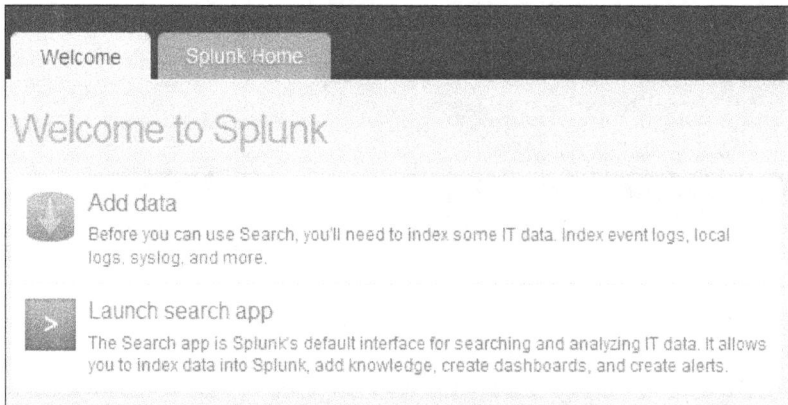

Then, the next step is to add the data type needed to be monitored that is part of the Incident case. Splunk has out-of-the-box capabilities to look at the lifecycle of a business transaction via its sophisticated data engine, and build a view of the problem. This is a very valuable tool that has a small footprint, and is very intuitive to use. We recommend even development workstations and unit testing using WEF to be powered by Splunk.

The following screenshot shows the **Splunk Manager** page:

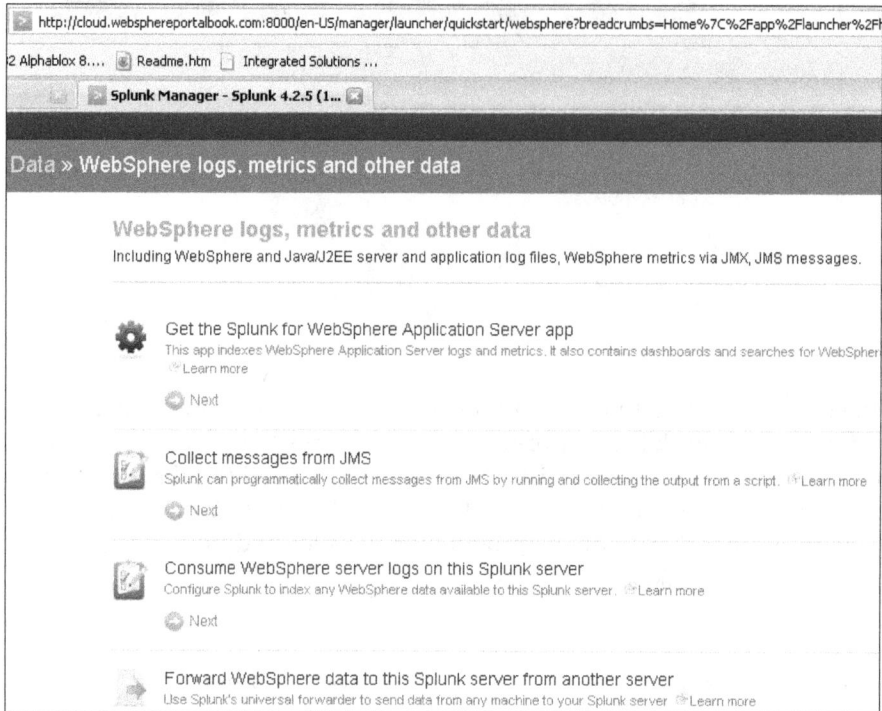

Finally, the magic happens right before your eyes. Lots of valuable information is captured and presented to allow a quick isolation for diagnostics of a given problem. Instrumenting data from network devices to middleware to backend systems is a click away. In the case of A2Z Bank, all the environments (physical, virtual, and cloud enabled) were monitored with Splunk. In the case below, A2Z is proactively looking at its portal and other logs. But in the case where quick diagnostics are needed, it is equipped to do so. It makes isolation and detection of issues more efficient, and requires little to no ramp-up time to the tooling itself.

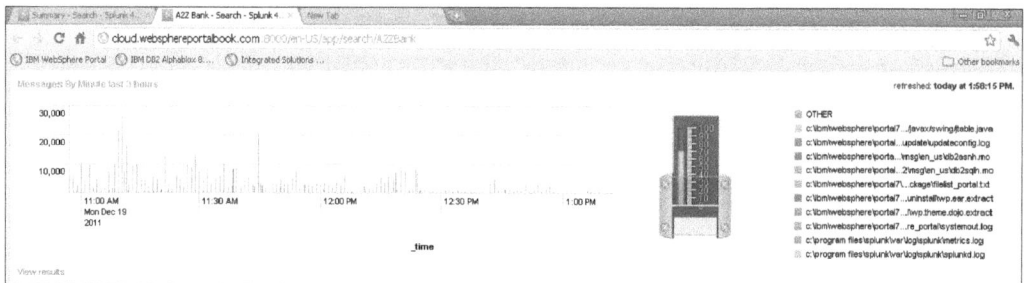

Summary

We started the chapter looking at the overall high-level integrated processes for incident, problem, and change management. We talked about a strategy that can be repeatable and proactive in troubleshooting efforts. We talked about some of the available tools to be used during troubleshooting tasks in any of the given environments where a problem is manifested. We covered ISA, ISA for portal advantages of connecting WebSphere Portal problems to IBM support. We also looked at some WebSphere Application Server Version 8 features and at the great Splunk engine. As we have pointed out, these disciplines of monitoring, testing, troubleshooting, and tuning go hand in hand. Troubleshooting and root cause identification is a multidisciplinary effort. Even with the right set of tools, it can still be challenging at times. It is the combination of the right technical expertise, environment, application knowledge with repeatable tools and processes supporting root cause identification and remediation, which increases the likelihood for operational success.

19
Portal, WEF, and Portlet Tuning

This chapter deals with the tuning aspects of portal and portlets. Tuning is an essential, iterative activity that must occur before portal applications go into production. We will take a look at some of the performance metrics, best practices, and how WEF and portal tuning candidates can be identified and improved. By the end of this chapter, we should have covered the following:

- Tuning strategy
- Tuning lifecycle
- Tuning candidates and sanity checklist
- Tuning test cases
- WEF performance tuning – A deep dive into WEF

Tuning – strategy and knowledge

Another whole book could be written on tuning alone, so what we present here is just a sample of what needs to be done. The key takeaway lesson is to apply a proven and validated methodology to any endeavor—discipline and repeatability on how to identify, isolate, and tune bottlenecks. Even though tuning is a highly technical endeavor, it needs to be supported by a repeatable strategy and specialized knowledge in the many areas a portal application can touch. So, there is a process around tuning that goes along with the monitoring, test, and change management processes. In terms of how soon to start tuning is a matter of how the overall development and testing strategies tackle it. Traditionally, it is in the performance test or staging environments that testing and tuning exercises are executed and then applied to production. There are other possible test-driven methodologies that force tuning to occur much earlier in the lifecycle.

Regardless of how soon testing and tuning starts, an encompassing tuning strategy needs to consider the following items in its dependent processes:

- Mature process around sensing, isolation, testing, and tuning
- Environment isolation for reproducing conditions
- APM monitoring to provide visibility into a tuning checklist
- Multidisciplinary know-how in the several technology stacks portal touches
- Clear RACI chart indicating roles and responsibilities of all parties involved
- Project plans accounting for tuning activities necessary

Tuning lifecycle

All portal projects need tuning at different phases in their lifecycles. Considering lower-level environments are tuned, tuning is then applied to production. There are many layers of tuning for a portal environment. One needs to peel the onion in order to drill down into the exercise and understand what needs to be done and where. The first thing to know is what compelling evidence exists to justify parameter, component, application, server, or any other tuning. All systems need tuning at one point or another. Once portal server is installed, everything is installed with out-of-the-box default values for the most part. From the operating system to the network layer to the application layer on portal, to the backend layer, there are many opportunities for improving the quality of service via tuning. The tuning exercise is based on a system-level agreement goal or on an undesirable response time and end user experience (during performance testing) or combined functionality that does not meet its nonfunctional performance requirements. Having clear goals and evidence based on captured performance metrics helps to set and implement the tuning lifecycle according to the chosen tuning strategy and supporting processes around it.

Tuning, (along with monitoring, testing, performance, and capacity planning) has a lifecycle of its own integrated and intertwined into the lifecycle of the other IT disciplines. As we just mentioned, tuning can start at any point in the SDLC. It also depends on what kind of tuning is needed right away. It could be as simple as tuning a development workstation (cloud or non-cloud based) for faster start up development purposes. Tuning does not end the when application goes into production. There is tuning done prior to an application going to production, which is mostly the case, but there are cases where things are found in production, and tuning or replication of the problem is needed in a performance or staging environment. After an assessment of changes that need to be done, a pass or fail verdict is determined. It is necessary start by asking the following questions and taking some actions based on the responses:

- Classifying and prioritizing the performance problem.

- Collecting information about the problem.

- Identify the environment(s) with the performance problem.

- Has the problem always been present in development environments?

- Has the environment been configured for high performance?

- Is the problem affecting a specific set of users, portlet, pages, services, or transactions?

- How reproducible is the problem likely to be?

- What other transactions are affected?

- How is the problem observed?

- What other symptoms are being seen?

- Can the monitoring tools detect these metrics and are these valid measurements?

- What conclusions can be drawn from the test results and test run analysis?

- How soon can a plan of action and remediation be implemented?

Any tuning lifecycle activity, which is normally part of the performance engineering and testing lifecycle (along with release management, problem management, and so on) will account for some of the preceding questions and will be better prepared to face the performance problems portal applications face sometimes inside the portal runtime, sometimes outside of the portal but integrated to it. Because portal is integration at the glass, many times it can seem that it is the portal server, which has the bottleneck. There is an essential guide provided by IBM Redbooks, which should always be used to understand which parameters to look at and consider during tuning efforts. You can find *IBM WebSphere Portal V 7.0 Performance Tuning Guide* at `http://www-10.lotus.com/ldd/portalwiki.nsf/dx/WebSphere_Portal_Tun`.

The following are three points to always keep in mind and reinforce to leading teams as needed:

- Use the tuning guide as a reference for all the basic portal interconnected containers, such as LDAP, Database and tune one item (parameter) per time. It is not written to be adopted blindly, but as a reference for what to examine, and then make changes based on environment and expected load for example.

- Tuning needs to be holistic and applied to all interfaces connected to portal that are part of a bad performance transaction, or portlet or portal page.

- **Repeatability and consistency**: Use the same techniques for testing and troubleshooting when tuning in terms of test scenario, test data, and so on for each tuning exercise. Never underestimate how test data can affect or skew performance metrics. So, using the same load, same test data (as much as possible), same environment and application code base, will increase the chances of successful repeatability and better tuning control over the items to be addressed.

There is tuning that occurs early when an environment is set up. For example, there is operating system or network tuning that can be done in advance, based on the technology blend and requirements at hand. What to tune and which parameters to change should be isolated and documented in a test case based on performance metrics or nonfunctional requirement goals. Ideally, once tuning candidates are identified, the same rigor for performance testing — the same test data set, test harness, and test strategy — is applied to tuning efforts. Before tuning, one must prioritize what needs tuning first, as follows:

- Assess the A2Z portal system throughput and response times against a predefined set of performance goals

- Allow APM to sense, isolate, identify the bottlenecks or underperforming portions of the system or the portal transaction in any of the seven layers

- Execute tuning steps in repeatable and identical testing scenarios to bring overall satisfactory performance results

- Use the tuning guide as a guide to identify possible parameters

Tuning candidates and test cases

We start the test cases based on the evidence that a certain component or function is not performing as expected. The bottlenecks and limiting factors can exist on the portal runtime itself or on any of the other systems integrated into portal. Because they are getting ready to decide on tuning exercises (for performance, availability, security, and so on), A2Z found a need to start tuning for response time and throughput. In the tuning cases given next, the IBM Rational Performance Tester Suite was used to create the test harness, with the proper user ramp up and the expected throughput, and to valid test results against the documented nonfunctional requirements concerning both response time and throughput.

Ramp up and think time are very important for the reproduction of a realistic user load scenario in the load tool. **Ramp up** means the rate at which virtual users will be added to the portal load and login. It must be done based on reality, and not left for the tester to figure out. So, for example, if users login at a rate of 60 per minute during peak hours, the test scenario should take it into account when reproducing a portal load test. The **think time** indicates in average how long a user stays on a page (or portlet) before taking another action. These two factors can negatively influence a test result if they are not in sync with reality.

However, prior to getting to the stage of tuning portal system itself, there were several prerequisites, which also needed to be tuned accordingly. A basic checklist needs to be identified along with a defined criteria basis to validate these common items are taken care of by the performance engineering teams. Along with that, via the monitoring facilities, there needs to be a detail-oriented validation that there are no other portal-specific tuning candidates that can help in achieving the technical and business goals. It is not something that can be done without the SMEs in performance monitoring, and the container domains and application SMEs collaboration and team work.

A2Z performance testing and engineering teams also created a basic set of checklists to see if there was a need to tune the following portal-specific tuning. They always consulted the WebSphere Tuning Guide for further details and to use as a guideline.

They looked at the lowest hanging fruits first, starting with basic questions, as follows:

- Has the portal infrastructure and application been benchmarked?
- What is the portal **transactions per second** (**TPS**) point of saturation per JVM (per node, cluster, and so on)?
- What are the response times for key transactions (80/20 rule)?
- What are the average response times?
- How many users can be supported at peak time?
- What is the portlet session size?
- Have JVMs been tuned (JVM sizes, collection modes, generational tuning)?

Then look for tuning opportunities in other areas beyond portal. The following diagram shows a huge list of such potential candidates to systems directly integrated into the portal system:

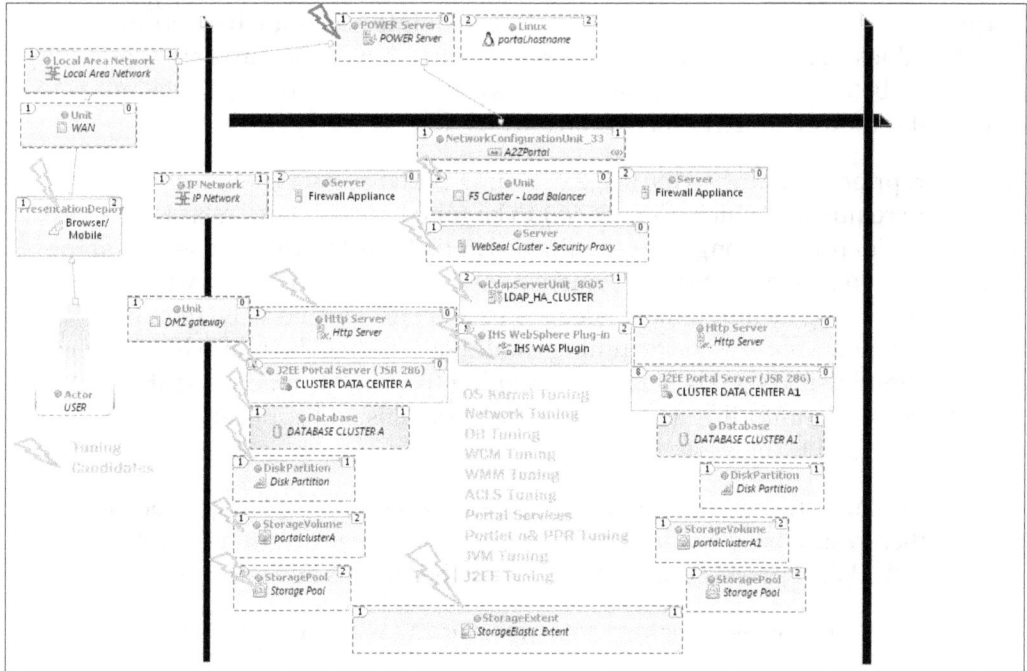

The following is a list of potential non-portal systems that can impact overall performance:

- **LTPA tuning**: It is a costly operation and set of transactions to calculate the cryptographic signature for LTPA tokens.

- **VMM Context Pool tuning**: To optimize concurrent access to LDAP servers.

- **Portlet caching for client side rendering and themes**: Check whether portlet fragments can be cached via `portlet.xml`

- **Portal services**: Based on how your portal application uses portal services, there are sets of them that can be tuned at granular levels.

- **Navigator services**: This handles how the content model is presented and reloaded to authenticated and unauthenticated users. It also correlates to HTTP cache control header's lifetime.

- **Registration services**: The portal server container keeps track of resource types in its database, and uses memory to memory to replicate some of its resources for performance reasons. It can be tuned as to how often changes are picked up.

- **Cache services**: Similar to registration but with a more dynamic nature in terms of change, these services also use memory-to-memory replication but each type has its own cache for that type. Number of objects and lifetime timeframe can be tuned per cache.

- **PZN tuning**: If personalization rules on portlets and pages are not going to be used it can be turned off for performance optimization.

- **WEF**

  - Session size
  - Variable scope

Still, based on the results from the performance tests for both the A2Z core banking and call center portal application releases, some tuning candidates became very obvious. The ones not passing the performance goals were selected for further investigation.

For the A2Z core banking domain, there were performance bottlenecks with two broker services in particular, which would prevent A2Z to go into production – broker registration services and vault lease rates. We will now look at them.

Bottleneck 1 – broker services – registration services – 7 seconds of response time results with a 4-second max goal to achieve

This means that the actual user perceived response time for this portal page is 7 seconds. The service-level agreement and expected response time, based on nonfunctional requirements, is 4 seconds maximum.

The portlet itself and the first set of results are illustrated, as follows:

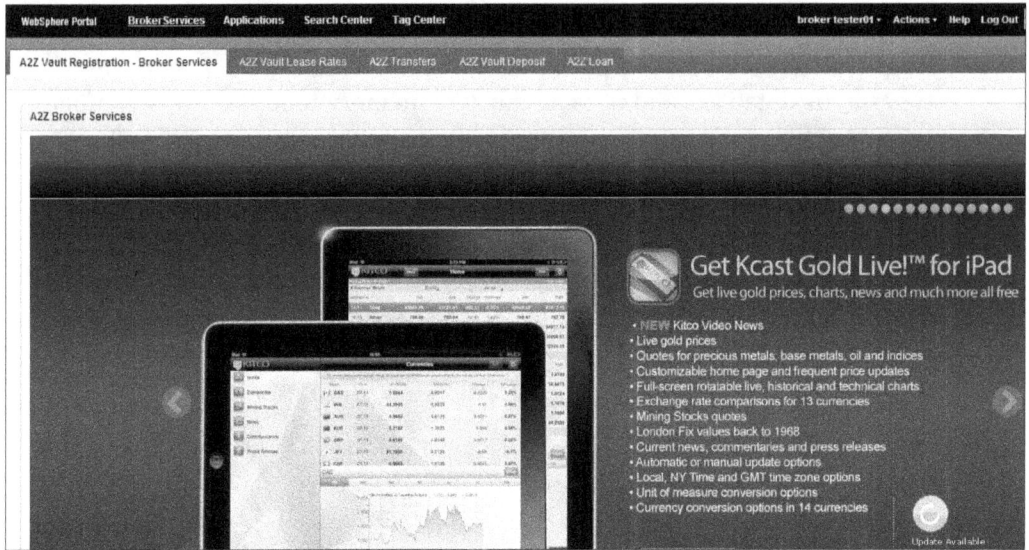

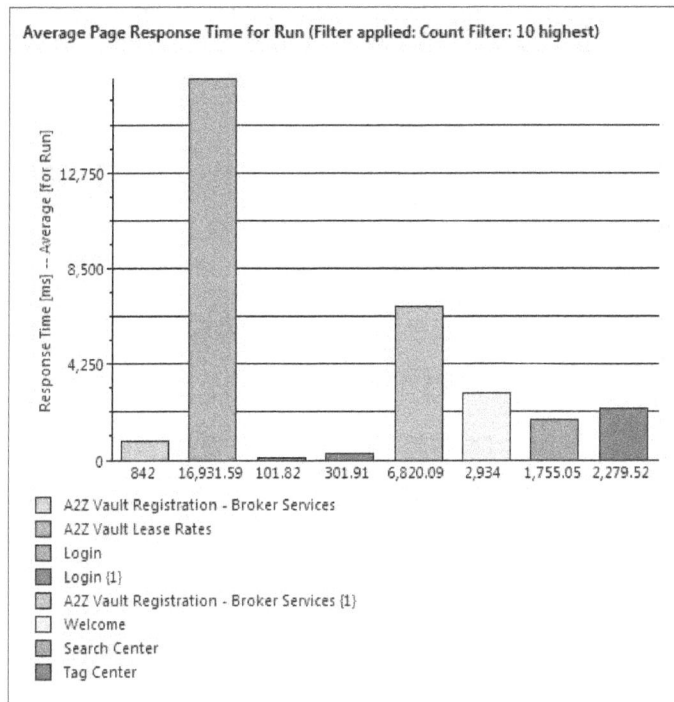

Then the confirmation of the problem as the testing progressed is further documented. You can see in the following graph that the broker services registration page had a high response time of 17 seconds. The vault service registration page also had a high response time of 7 seconds, thus violating the expected performance goal of 4 seconds response time.

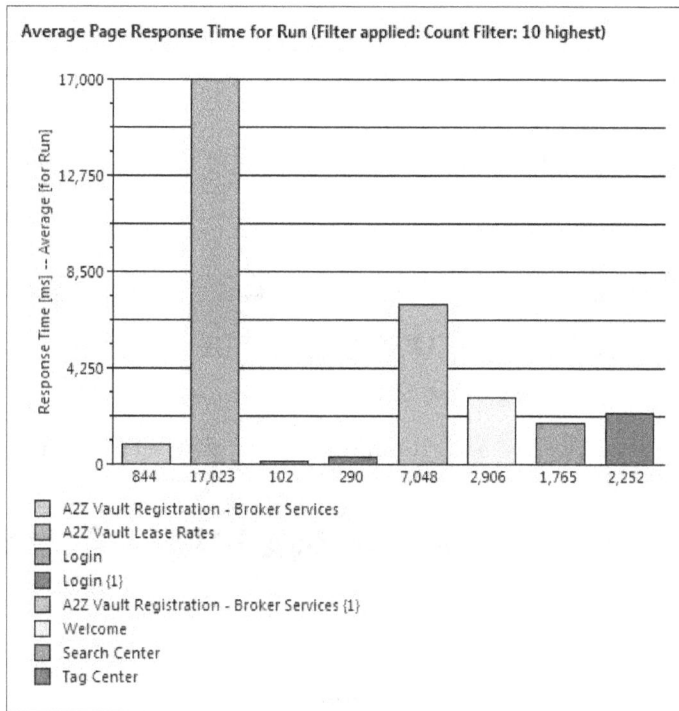

The functional characteristic of these portlets on this page was to present the broker with a Swiss army knife of bullion services. When one registers a vault or a customer, this transaction is database intensive as an account and customer will be tied to a vault; there is a lot of data creation and database activity in terms of CRUD. Because this is not a read-only data or a purely static data that can be a caching candidate, the alternatives had to be analyzed and understood. There is also a lot of decision-making when it comes to artificial intelligence-based recommendations to future vault lease terms or metal types. In our tests it was important to discern if this was a problem related to the number of concurrent users or not. This would also rule out scalability as a concern. Tests were created using Rational Performance Tester to create test cases and scripts with data pools with 1, 10, 100, and 1000 of concurrent virtual users.

The SQL query indirectly used by the portlet, invoked via services, was indeed very intensive. But, the tests results revealed that the response times for all tests were about the same, 6 to 8 seconds. The service-level agreement and nonfunctional requirements for this portal page spelled for 4 seconds (for all portlets on this page). What these results indicated is that this was not a scalability issue that would be impacting the A2Z vault registration performance as users were added, vaults created and related to existing account or customers. This was in fact something that was common to all users, regardless if one user was using it or 100. So, the registration web service itself was behaving under milliseconds, the database pool was not exhausted in any of the test cases executed, and the users were accessing from the same network. **Parallel Portlet Rendering (PPR)** was tested and the results continued to be the same.

Bottleneck 2 – broker services – lease rate services – tuning for response time

This means 16.9 seconds of response time with a 5-second max goal to achieve.

The following screenshot shows portlet itself and the first set of performance test results:

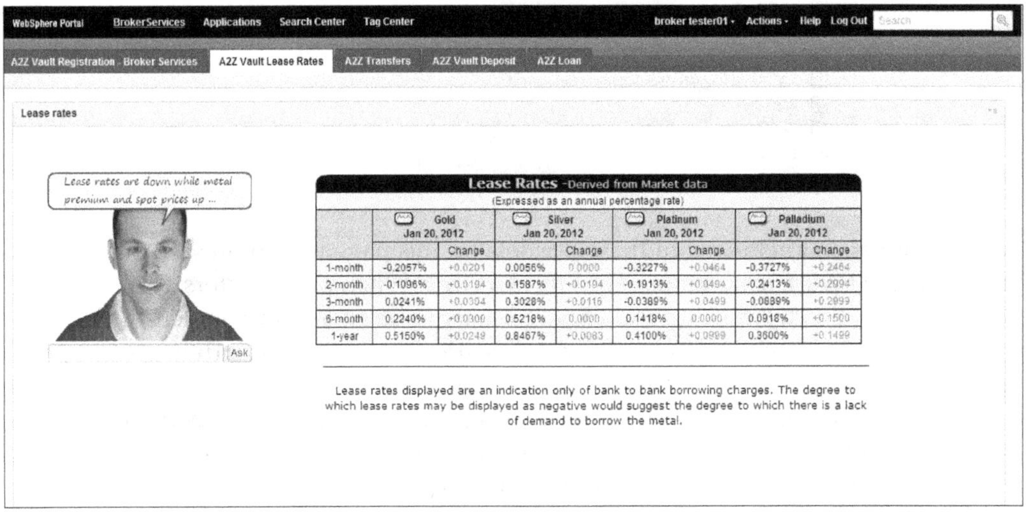

Additionally, the portal page would load the other wired portlets and pages such as **Deposit** and **Loan**, as shown in the following screenshots:

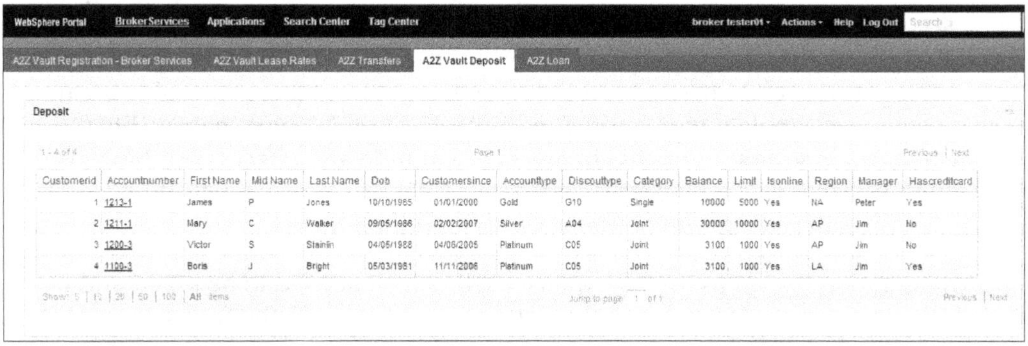

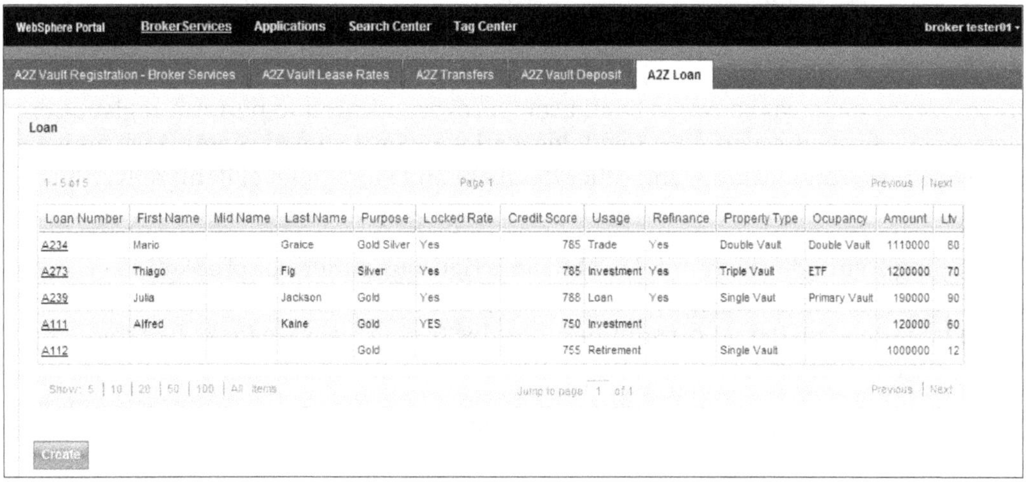

The characteristic of these portlets on this page was to perform high level of decision making and some level of reporting. In terms of decision making, it matches Bullion lease rates (future profit) for the vaults based on several factors, including type of bullion, quantity, lease term, metal spot price rate, and customer risk tolerance among others. It then uses a decision brain (an algorithm) to evaluate the associated market variables, future simulations it would recommend vault operations based on the forecast result done in artificial intelligence and present it in the portlet. As a composite service, it would have operations in the backend, in the SOA layer, and in the portal server itself. So in simple terms, it looks at how much the vault value itself changes based on contracts, market changes, and locks, and based on forecast recommendation it would implement a certain vault transaction.

Let's say an A2Z Bullion broker has a client that has a vault with 10,000 ounces of silver and 640 ounces of gold. Based on the longevity of the lease contract, and how the market changes the store of value and spot prices, that vault value is changing every second the sport price changes in any of the open markets (New York, London, Honk Kong, and Australia). That means this is a highly transactional page bound to CPU activity as it is I/O intensive. At the same time, it is memory intensive because it keeps some session data in memory, and because of its dynamic nature, little caching can be done as spot prices change every minute and affect everything else related to this primary data piece affected by it. CPU and garbage collection logs metrics were analyzed, and no bottleneck was identified there.

The investigation turned to the SQL query itself, which needed to be tuned and new table indexing was needed to make the performance goals. As the web service had impeccable performance, the SQL tuning and table indexing was enough to bring the response time of the page and the registration portlet (which heavily depended on this SQL and its counterpart web service) under 4 seconds of response time. Because each registration would create a new set of tables to be related to vaults and leases, the impact was common to all users (brokers allowed to perform registration) regardless of concurrency. Updated table statics and automated reorgs, SQL and table optimization indexing, and other database and storage-level items solved the bottleneck.

The tuning solution was multifold. The same rigorous pattern of problem determination is done, along with monitoring in order to be able to identify tuning candidates. In sum, the report summary for this tuning test case looks like the following at a high level:

- **Problem determination to classify the problem**: 7 to 18 seconds response time
- **Recreate the problem**: Yes
- **Identify engines and components parts of the end-to-end transaction, along with metrics and potential tuning parameters candidates based on monitoring**: DB2 tuning, elastic (Fast VP) storage pool, and SQL tuning
- Create test cases, scripts to simulate a performance test based on specific needs
- **Schedule and Implement**: SQL tuning as the best "bang for the buck" result
- Test changes and verify results until goals are achieved
- Promote and release to other environments

In the end, after tuning, the following results were achieved:

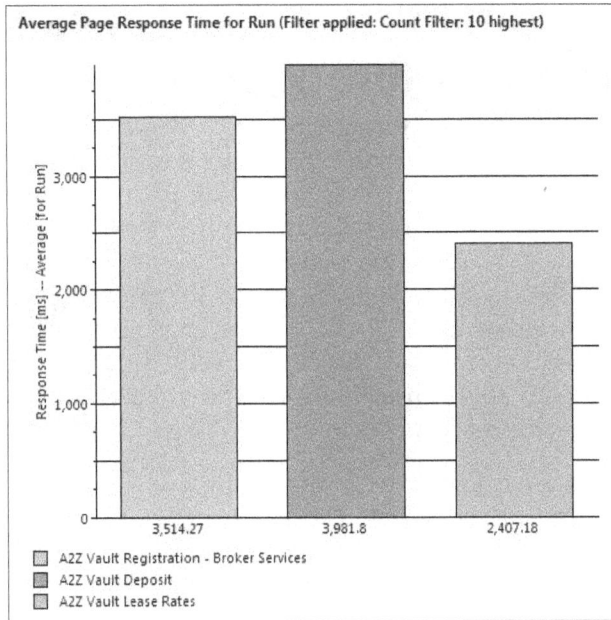

To confirm and sign off on the resolution, another official set of load tests (performance and stress) were executed with the same positive results, as follows:

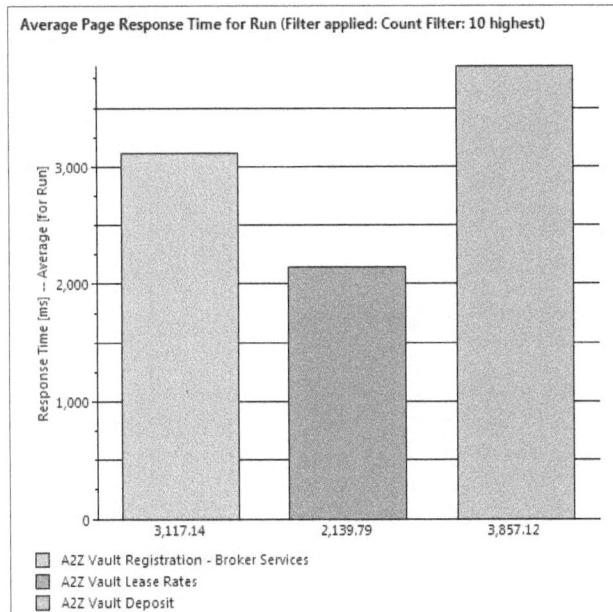

Bottleneck 3 – call center services – softphone incoming call and live call portal – tuning for throughput

The top CSR transaction (`a2zcsr_global`), which carried a unique identifier used in call center operations to track the number of transactions associated to a call historically, had to handle a transfer rate of at least 500 bytes received per invocation in order to achieve the intended throughput for the related nonfunctional performance requirements. These were basically synchronous calls to the voice server so that it would act as a broker or dispatcher for incoming calls. The softphone phone portlet, the incoming call, live call, customer, account, and vault information populatated on the **360 View** page directly depended on this initial global transaction. Tuning this transaction would have a positive cascading effect on everything else that depends on it.

The following graph shows that:

- `A2z_csr_global` had a transfer rate throughput of 62 to 220 bytes
- `A2z_csr_global` had a transfer rate goal of 500 bytes

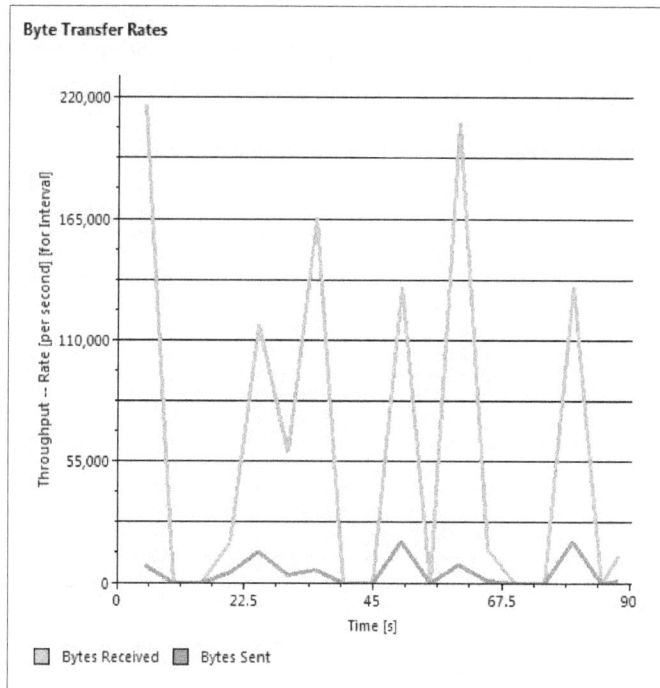

Synchronous transactions integrated into portal but with poor throughput performance can have a direct impact on response times for portlets and portal pages waiting for results from those transactions. There are times when poor response times are not related to throughput. In some cases like this one the relationship is direct.

- **Softphone incoming call**: 16.6 **response time (RT)** – goal of 1 second max to achieve

- **Softphone live call**: 36.1 RT – goal of 2 seconds max to achieve

- **360 View**: Goal of 5 seconds max to achieve

The following graph shows the problem identification based on performance test results:

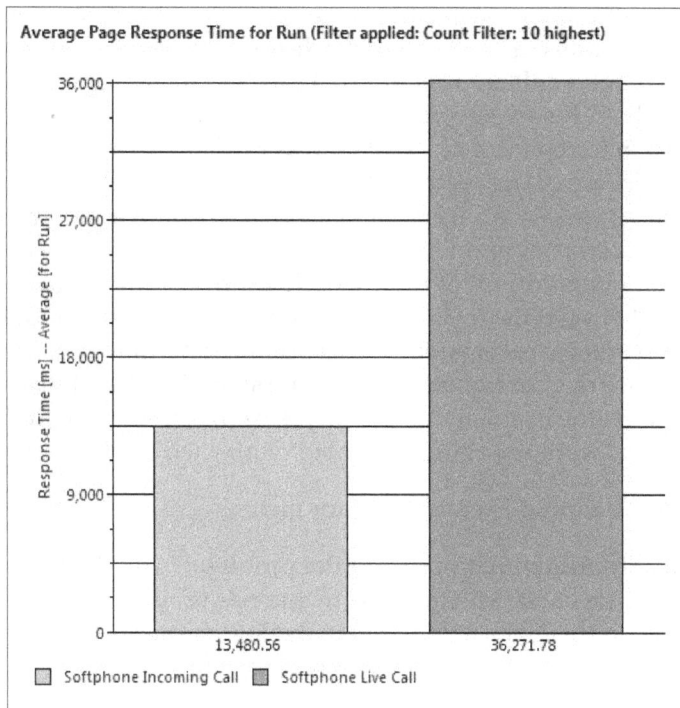

The banking modernization also had its tuning exercises in the call center domain. In terms of total end-to-end transactions coming to the call center, it needed to support 20,000 per second, which translated in each customer service representative receiving up to 6 calls per hour. Above all, it needed to be under a second for the call transfer and softphone initialization to be compliant with 4 seconds of max response time requirement for the **360 View** page, user perceived total response time. It became clear during performance tests that the voice servers were only able to support 60 bytes of transfer rate per initial global transaction, when the goal was to get to 500 bytes of transfer rate. It was noted that this call routing was essential; it was an operational business device and had lots of support from banking and call center senior management to be implemented during this very first portal release. So a bank customer would call 1800 that would trigger an interactive voice response server infrastructure. That telephony infrastructure would pass on calls to the voice server infrastructure, which initiated an SIP session, transferring the call data to the portal CSR user. The user (equipped with a CSR headset) would be alerted by the softphone portlet, which would transfer the incoming call and populate the entire portal page with that customer and vault account information. The incoming call represents the transfer from the IVR server infrastructure and an SIP session initiation into the portal clusters in the cloud. The problem was further confirmed and the tuning exercise started. Because of the complexity of these portlets and the services associated to them, it was necessary to tune them in isolation in order to know what is affecting what. In terms of problem isolation, network traces were looked at along with full end-to-end monitoring. The bottleneck for the incoming call was identified and manifested in between the traffic from the voice server to the portal session integration. Portlet and global session size inspection determined the session was not bloated and the best practices were used to create small JRS 286 global session objects to be shared based on the customer or primary account number. So, network traces determined packages were not being truncated or affected by the transport layer.

The following are the tuning Exercise Drill for incoming call:

- **Problem determination to classify the problem**: 62-kB to 200-kB transfer rate, with goals of 500 kB and 15 to 18 seconds of response time for pages depending on this transaction, due to the low throughput from the voice servers

- **Recreate the problem: Yes**

- Create test cases, scripts to simulate a performance test based on specific needs

- **Identify engines and components parts of the end-to-end transaction, along with metrics and potential tuning parameters**: Server, interactive voice response server

- **Schedule and implement**: Changed voice server pool size, increased thread pool size, increased SIP session size, and additional virtual nodes to the cluster
- Test changes and verify results until goals are achieved
- Promote and release to other environments

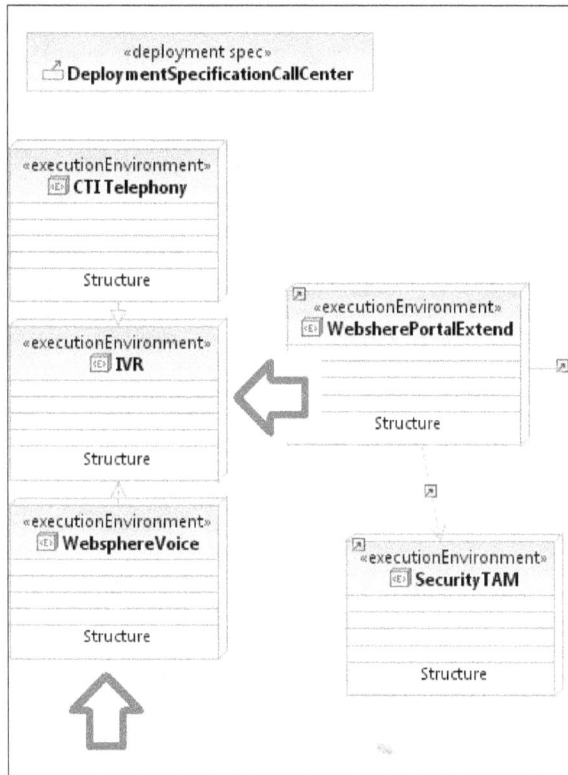

Via isolated tests, the tuning had to be done at each main portlet transaction level. It allowed each of the bottlenecks to be resolved in isolation due to the complexity of their related services and end-to-end transaction view.

The bottleneck was determined to be in the voice server, because it needed to support the incoming calls and hand it over to the call center portal. Because the voice server was not able to keep up with throughput, the other portal components parts of the same end-to-end transaction would have timed out, tried to reconnect, lost session context, therefore shown a long response time.

Let's look at how the throughput and response time correlation performed after isolation was done and tuning was applied:

Byte Transfer Rates

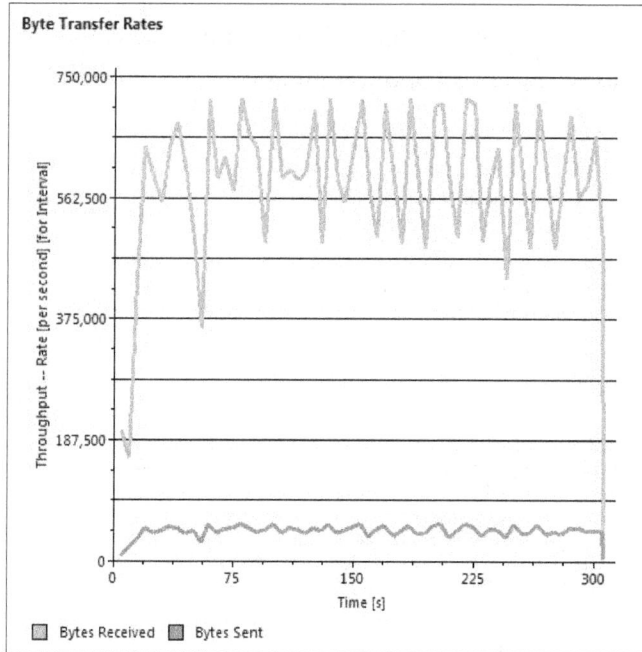

Average Page Response Time for Run (Filter applied: Count Filter: 10 highest)

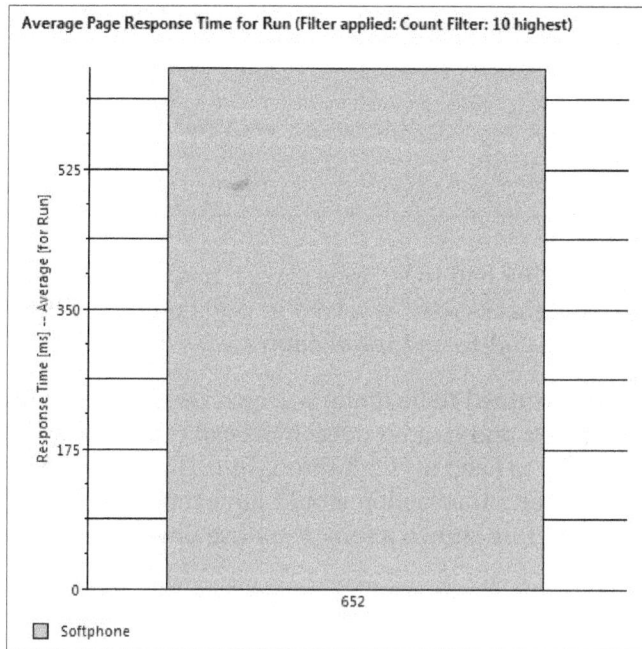

Along the same lines of bad performance the response time of the live call portal business transaction was unacceptable. Live call is a transaction that represents the time of softphone portlet population itself along with the voice activation. That would trigger the 360 View to be fully populated with recent calls, transactions, futures, and some other data pertinent to that customer or account including future leases, basic vault information. All of them had to be tuned in isolation to keep separation of concerns and track of improvements. at the following graphs show the test results and how they passed the NFR performance goals:

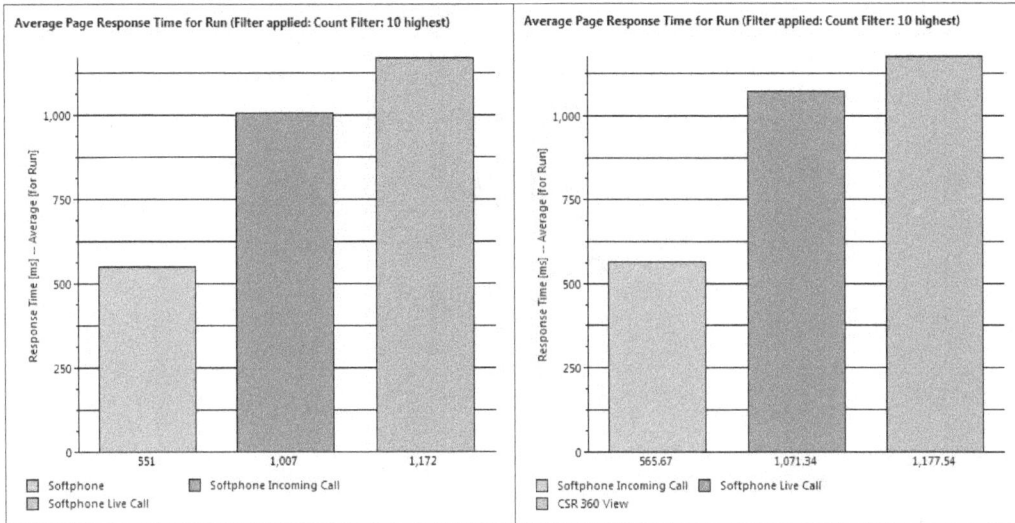

To sign off finally on the resolution and tuning results, a final battery of stress tests ramping up to 200 percent load were executed to confirm the positive results, as follows:

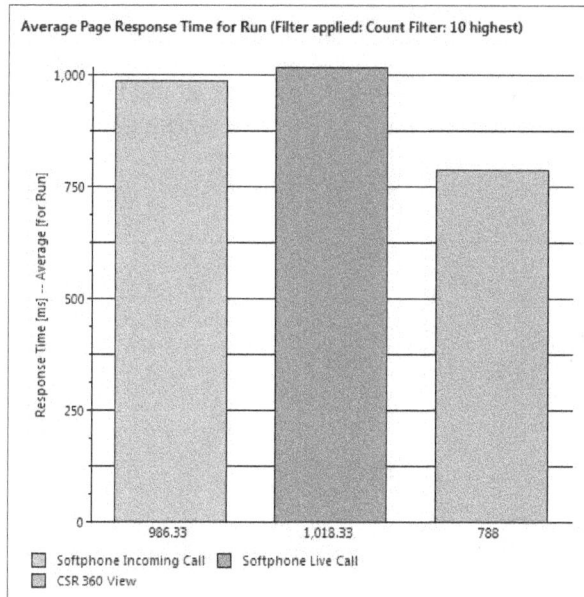

Performance tuning — a deep dive into WEF

While WEF does a great job helping developers to create portlets, developers and portal architects still need to be mindful about performance aspects of their portal solutions.

In this section dedicated to performance aspects of portlets created using WEF, we will cover topics that every developer should be aware of when using WEF as the Rapid Application Development tool for creating portlets. Some of the topics we will cover include the following:

- Performance best practices
- Addressing memory consumption
- Size of result sets
- Paging data
- Cache Control builder and caching strategy
- Log and tracing files

Before getting into the specifics of each topic, we would like to emphasize the importance of having at least one experienced WEF developer and a portal architect to implement your project. Performance is a crucial area where these experienced resources play an important role.

Performance best practices

Some schools of thought believe that developers should not give much attention to performance at the beginning of the development cycle. Such school of thought believes that developers should postpone the performance-related matters to the phase after the application is built. We strongly disagree with this approach, and we advocate that performance considerations should be taken into account early in the design of the portlets. In fact, we have seen that projects which do not give the due attention to performance matters early in the project, pay a high price in the form of redesign and code changes to bring the applications within the service-level agreement. So, our first recommendation as part of performance best practices is, "Take performance into account when you design your portlet and write all the code always having performance in mind."

In addition to reading the sections covered in this chapter, you should also read at least two other performance-related documents published by IBM, as follows:

- *Performance Best Practices*: This article is available on the IBM Web Experience Factory wiki. This document contains a multitude of performance best practices that should be taken into account when a WEF application is designed and developed. The following is the link to this document:

  ```
  http://www-10.lotus.com/ldd/pfwiki.nsf/dx/performance-best-
  practices
  ```

- *Techniques to enhance WebSphere Portlet Factory application performance*: WebSphere Portlet Factory has been renamed as WEF. This technote is available at the IBM support site. It contains a multitude of tips and recommendations that should not be neglected while you design and develop your WEF application. The following is the link to this technote:

  ```
  http://www-01.ibm.com/support/docview.wss?rs=3044&conte
  xt=SSRUWN&dc=%C3%9B520&uid=swg21268497&loc=en_US&cs=UTF-
  8&lang=en&rss=ct3044websphere
  ```

The next topics we cover will help you identify some of the specific elements of development you will need to address and monitor throughout the development lifecycle of your project.

Addressing memory consumption

Memory consumption should be at the forefront of your considerations when you design and code you portlets using WEF. To avoid high memory consumption and dreadful "out-of-memory" exceptions, WEF developers need to manage the utilization of XML content in WEF efficiently.

Because most of transactional data in a WEF model is manipulated as XML objects, the memory consumption can grow rapidly if these XML objects are not used properly across the several models that comprise a portlet.

XML data can be stored in XML variables created by developers by adding the Variable builders and setting their type to XML. XML variables are also created by builders that manipulate XML data. A few examples of builders that create XML variables are the builders in the service category, such as Web Service Call and SQL Call. These service builders create several XML variables, but the most important concerning memory utilization are the XML variables created to store the result set resulting from the call to the backend system.

The following screenshot shows the variables created by a SQL Table Create builder named **loans_SCT**. You can see that the **retrieveLoans_SCTResults** variable is created to store the result of the SQL call in the XML format:

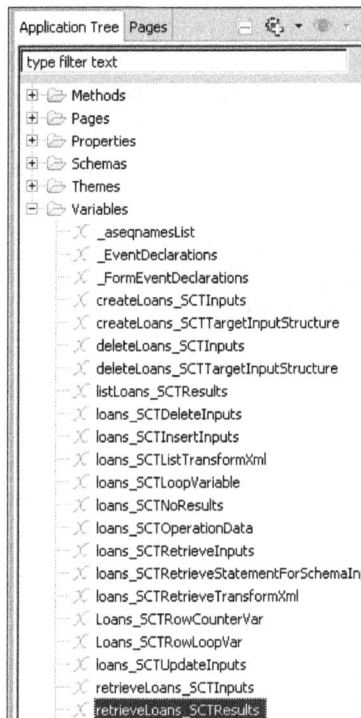

While developers cannot control the number of variables created by WEF, they do need to control aspects such as the size of the result set that is retrieved as well as the scope of the variables.

Size of result sets

In order to reduce memory consumption of portal applications, you should reduce the size of the result sets you retrieve from the backend system. Regardless of the type of backend system to which you are connecting, be it directly to databases and enterprise systems or through web services, there is always way to retrieve only the required set of data for each operation. Efficient SQL statements and efficient web service operations are critical to avoid large result sets.

Stateless services

When you create the Service Provider models through the Service Definition builder, whenever possible, you should always set **Service State** to **Stateless: fresh model instance for each call**. This input available in the Service Definition builder marks the Service Provider model to be destroyed after a service call is complete. In doing so, the Service Provider models do not hold on to the result sets retrieved from the backend.

Paging data

Any result set larger than a couple of hundred records should be paged. Some builders provide paging implementations by default while others do not. The SQL Call and Domino builders that retrieve data from the backend do provide such features. Also the Service Operation builder provides an input to enable paging.

For other builders that retrieve data from other backend systems including Web Service Call builder, you should implement a customer data retriever class, which would enable you to implement paging. We will not cover Customer Data Retriever, but WEF does provide information through the help documentation, which can be used as a sample to build your Customer Data Retriever.

Cache Control builder and caching strategy

WEF provides a builder named Cache Control builder, which enables modelers to cache data. Caching reduces the number of trips to backend systems, thus improving performance. To be more precise, the Cache Control builder caches the output of a method or action.

The Cache Control builder provides three main inputs to enable your WEF portal application to cache the output of a method or action, as follows:

- **Action to Cache**: This specifies the method or action, whose output is to be cached.

- **Refresh Intervals**: This specifies the period of time when the output of the defined method or action will be cached. This time is defined in seconds.

- **Keys**: When the output of the method or action you are caching can vary, you can use the key input to identify the possible different results with a key value. When WEF invokes a method, whose output is supposed to be cached, it first evaluates the key being passed. If the result for corresponding key already exists in cache, then that value is retrieved from cache. If it does not exist, then a new call is made to the backend system, the output is cached, and this output is associated with the new key.

Caching strategy

When using the Cache Control builder, you should develop a caching strategy to make sure your application maximizes the benefit of caching. To develop your caching strategy, you should take into account the following points:

- **Single user versus cross-users**: If the output of a service is unique to individual users, then you should not cache such data. You should cache only data that is commonly used by multiple users. Usually, look up data is a good candidate for caching, because in most of the cases it is the same for all users.

- **How often the data changes**: If data is used across multiple users but it changes often, say every minute, then you should not cache such data because your server will have some overhead to maintain this data and caching will not provide any benefit to you.

- **How often the data is accessed**: If the data you are considering to cache is accessed very infrequently even though it might be accessed across multiple users, you should not cache it. This is even more evident if the output you are dealing with is a large data set. Caching such data will consume valuable memory resources, although it will provide minimal performance benefit.

- **Profiling**: When cashing is defined for a model/portlet that is profile-enabled, you need to take into account that each profile gets its own copy of the data in cache. This scenario can cause undesirable results if your WEF portal application contains multiple profiles and the result can be associated with multiple keys. In such case, you can end up with a large variable set of data in cache. Such scenario will consume valuable memory resources with a small number of retrievals from cache.

In the next section we will cover performance-related log files. One of the files we will discuss is `Server Stats`. This file contains an entry, which indicates the number of times the output of methods or actions are retrieved from cache. The entry is named `OutputCacheHits`. In addition to that, another entry named `OutputCacheMisses` indicates the number of times the application did not retrieve the output of a method or action from the cache.

You should use the information provided by these entries to define your caching strategy.

Performance-related log files

WEF provides a large number of log files to help you analyze and troubleshoot your application. Out of these files, the three most important files for performance-related matters are as follows:

- `Model Actions`
- `Server Stats`
- `Session Size`

Model Actions log file

The `Model Actions` log file is an excellent starting point to learn about performance aspects of your application. This file lists all the WEF actions that take place when the user interacts with your portlet. By analyzing this file you can extract important information about the time each action takes to execute. Such data should easily identify slow performing actions in any portlet. The analysis should be performed on individual portlets for each individual user interaction.

The `Model Actions` log file is entitled `modelActions.txt`. It is located in the `WEB-INF\logs` directory of your WAR file. By default, the logging action to this file is disabled. To enable logging of actions and their respective times, you need to open the `log4j.properties` file through the designer. In your project, this file is located under `WEB-INF/config`. Open this file and locate the `log4j.logger.bowstreet.system.modelActions=WARN,ModelActions` entry. Set this entry to `log4j.logger.bowstreet.system.modelActions=DEBUG,ModelActions`. There is no need to restart the portal server for this setting to take effect.

Once `Model Actions` logging is enabled, every action the user performs on your portlet will be logged into this file. The following screenshot shows the list of actions that are performed when a portlet named **transfer** is first loaded into portal:

```
*-- TIME: [2012-08-27 19:59:23,119] --*
Category: bowstreet.system.modelActions.ui_chapter19_transfer
Priority: INFO
Thread:   webContainer : 6
Msg:
   Session:    3685v8N_oHf15enwwSWbPOL
   Model:      ui/chapter19/transfer
   User Name:  wpsadmin
       0     906     Start Request: webAppRunner.doRequest
       0       0     [ui/chapter19/transfer]
      16     359     Instantiate: ui/chapter19/transfer
     203     203     .Regen: No profile
     140     140     .Compile: Methods Class
       0     547     Method: main
       0       0     .Method: Account_SCListCustomer_STC
       0       0     ..Method: Account_SC.executeOperation
       0       0     ...Method: Account_SC_createHelper
       0       0     ...[data/chapter19/DBCustomersPr]
       0       0     ...Instantiate: data/chapter19/DBCustomersPr
       0       0     ...Method: listCustomer_STCExecute
       0       0     ....Method: customer_STCListInvoke
       0       0     .....Method: customer_STCListInvokeBase
       0       0     ......Method: customer_STCDataSource_createHelper
       0       0     .......Method: customer_STCDataSource_refreshHelper
       0       0     ......Method: customer_STCListStatement_createHelper
       0       0     .......Method: customer_STCListStatement_refreshHelper
       0       0     ......Method: customer_STCListTransform_createHelper
       0       0     .......Method: customer_STCListTransform_refreshHelper
       0       0     ......Method: customer_STCListTransform.executeForCaching
       0       0     .......Method: customer_STCListTransform_refreshHelper
       0       0     ......Method: customer_STCDataSource_refreshHelper
       0       0     .......Method: customer_STCListStatement_refreshHelper
       0       0     .Method: Customer_STCRowHandlePageLoad
       0       0     ..Method: Customer_STCRow_createHelper
       0       0     ...Method: Customer_STCRow_createRetriever
       0       0     ..Method: Customer_STCRow.getUpdatedData
       0       0     ...Method: Customer_STCRow_createRetriever
     219     547     .Page: Account_PG
      94      94     ..Page: splitPagerTopPage
       0       0     ..Method: Customer_STCRow.getFirstDisplayRow
     234     234     ..Page: splitPagerBottomPage
```

This file shows that the entire action of rendering this portlet took **906** milliseconds, as indicated by the **Start Request: webAppRunner.doRequest** entry, which is the first entry in this section. Most of the time was spent performing the **main** action, **547** milliseconds. The main action is comprised of several children actions. Most of these actions were performed in less than one millisecond. That is why you see numerous entries with the value of **0**. On the left-hand side of this file, there are two columns. The leftmost column lists the amount of time in milliseconds that it took to perform that specific action. The other column lists the accumulated value for the parent action.

To demonstrate the parent/child relationship depicted in the `Model Actions` log file, consider the example demonstrated in the preceding screenshot. For instance, the **main** action (**Method: main**) is parent to all the other actions that follow it and start with one or more dots. The dots represent the hierarchical relationship between these entries (actions).

The preceding screenshot shows that the **.Page: Account_PG** is child to **Method: main** and it is comprised of three children actions, the three last ones. The **.Page: Account_PG** action took **547** milliseconds, which is the sum of the time its three children actions took to be executed.

For further information on how to interpret the entries written to the `modelActions.txt` file, please refer to the WEF help documentation.

Server Stats log file

The `Server Stats` is another important file, which should be examined when you need to do performance analysis. The file is named `serverStats.txt`, and is also located in the `WEB-INF/logs` directory of your WAR file. This file collects all the information related to the requests made by a WEF application.

The information logged into this file is extremely helpful when you want to analyze the behavior of your application under a certain load either in a testing environment or even in production. This information is logged every 5 minutes.

This file is enabled by default in your WAR file. This file contains a multitude of important performance indicators that can help you analyze and tune your application.

Some of the indicators available through the **Server Stats** file include the following:

- `OutputCacheHits`
- `OutputCacheMissses`
- `ErrorsLogged`
- `PeakSessions`
- `ParallelModelRequests`

Chapter 16, Portlet and Portal Testing provides a table with the description of each indicator logged into the `Server Stats` file. Please refer to the *Portlet testing – time to walk the walk* section.

> IBM Web Experience Factory wiki makes available a nifty model, which displays the information from the Server Stats log file on a browser. The information is nicely formatted and the model even provides the ability to collapse and expand the entries. This model can be downloaded from `http://www-10.lotus.com/ldd/pfwiki.nsf/dx/Server_Stats_Viewer_Model`.

Session Size log file

While developing your application, you certainly want to keep track of the session size concerning memory utilization. The number and size of variables in your models are major contributors to memory size increases. If you do not efficiently control the size and the number of variables your application stores in memory, you might significantly reduce the number of concurrent users your application could support.

Although variables are not stored directly in session, they do consume memory because they are contained in an instance data object, which itself is stored in the session.

WEF provides a log file, which collects information on session size. Throughout the application development lifecycle, you should enable and analyze the logging of such information.

The session size information is logged into a file conveniently named `sessionsize.csv`. This file is stored in the `WEF-INF/logs` directory of your WAR file.

Enabling session size tracing

In order to enable session size tracing, you need to perform a few extra steps compared to the steps required to enable other log files. The following section describes the steps you need to take to enable session size tracing:

1. Open your project in the designer.
2. Open the `Bowstreet.Properties` file. This file is located under the `WEF-INF/Config` directory.
3. Locate the `bowstreet.diagnostic.trace.enabled` entry and set it to `true`.
4. Locate the `bowstreet.diagnostic.trace.sessionSize.interval` entry, and set its value to `60`. Also uncomment this entry. This means that trace output will be written to this file each 60 seconds.
5. Locate the `bowstreet.diagnostic.trace.sessionSize.userName` entry, and provide the user ID for the portal user whose session size information you will be collecting. Also uncomment this entry.
6. Save and close this file.

In order for these settings to take effect you need to restart the portal server.

Analyzing the session size log file

Once your portal server restarts, log in to portal using the credentials you have provided for the `bowstreet.diagnostic.trace.sessionSize.userName` entry. Make sure no other user is simultaneously logged in to portal. You want to collect the session size information for a single user only.

Navigate to your application in the same way that this user would do. 60 seconds after you have logged in, open the `sessionsize.csv` file. The size of the objects stored in session at that time will be logged into this file.

To read the information from this file more easily, open this file with an Excel application.

The `sessionsize.csv` file displays the following information for each variable:

- `Model`: Name of the model which creates the variable
- `Name`: Name of the variable as defined by the developer or by WEF if it is a WEF-created variable
- `Type`: Variable type as defined either by the developer or by WEF for WEF-created variables
- `Scope`: Scope of the variable
- `Size`: Total number of bytes for objects which implement serialization
- `toString()`: Number of characters an object contains as returned by the `toString()` method.

The `Session Size` log file shows two values, `size` and `toString()`, because sometimes serialization can fail. In that case the size column will show `-1`, as the value for that object. In that case, `toString()` is a better estimate for that object. You should pay special attention to non-serializable objects because they interfere with failover and session migration.

Please be aware that in some cases, for non-serializable objects, the `toString()` method can be accurate, but in some cases it can be way off. For instance, if a LJO which holds large amounts of data does not implement `toString()` properly, this could cause the session size tracing file to report a very small size for this object.

WEF uses the techniques described previously, because Java does not provide a simple way to accurately capture the size of different object types residing in memory.

The following screenshot shows an excerpt of the `sessionsize.csv` file for one of the portlets we have created for covering performance-related topics:

60	*-- 2012-08-30 20:11:40,906 --*				
61	Session Size Info for user wpsadmin				
62	Model	Name			
63	ui/chapter19/deposit	Account_SCListCustomer_STCResults			
64	ui/chapter19/deposit	Account_SC			
65	ui/chapter19/deposit	deposits_VAR			
66	ui/chapter19/deposit	StandardFormatter			
67	ui/chapter19/deposit	RowData			
68	ui/chapter19/deposit	Customer_STCRow			
69	ui/chapter19/deposit	Customer_STCRowData			
70	ui/chapter19/deposit	Customer_STCRowRetriever			
71	ui/chapter19/deposit	account_PBResourcesInfo			
72	ui/chapter19/deposit	bowstreet.method.class			

62	Type	Scope	Size	StringSize
63	com.bowstreet.services.base.TaggedData	Session	201902	48448
64	com.bowstreet.builders.webapp.ServiceCo	Session	0	65
65	com.bowstreet.services.base.TaggedData	Session	878	260
66	com.bowstreet.builders.webapp.pageautor	Session	0	71
67	com.bowstreet.services.base.TaggedData	Session	842	196
68	com.bowstreet.builders.webapp.methods.I	Session	35239	61
69	com.bowstreet.services.base.TaggedData	Session	20240	4862
70	com.bowstreet.builders.webapp.methods.)	Session	0	63
71	com.bowstreet.services.base.TaggedData	Session	526	181
72	genjava.ui.chapter19._deposit	Session	0	38

The preceding screenshot shows the session size information for a portlet named **deposit**. We had to split this screenshot in two sections because of the horizontal length of the rows. However, these two sections represent continuous rows. Please refer to the row number to link the rows from each section of the screenshot.

This portlet contains both variables and objects created by both, the WEF modeler as well as by WEF itself. For instance, the variable named **depositis_VAR** is a variable created by the modeler. Also the data type reported by this log file is **com.bowstreet. services.base.TaggedData**, even though the actual type we have defined when we created this variable is XML. In fact, this variable is a schema-typed XML variable. However, WEF reports its base type.

By analyzing the session size entries reported by the `sessionsize.csv` file, we can quickly identify the largest variable in this portlet, which is **Account_SCListCustomer_STCResults**. This is understandable, because this variable holds the result of the service call we make to get a list of customers. The fact that we have identified this variable as the largest one in this model, is not necessarily an indication that this is a problem. This shows us that architects and developers need to understand their application and use the session size tracing file as the helping tool to identify abusive or unnecessarily large objects in a session.

The last item we want to bring to your attention regarding session size is that at the end of each snap shot, the `sessionsize.csv` file shows a summary of all the models for which it is reporting objects size. This summary is a good starting point when you start looking into memory usage, because you can identify the models with the largest numbers, and then start your analysis by looking the details about these models.

The following screenshot shows a summary of the A2Z portlets we have created for the purpose of investigating performance-related matters:

Model	SessionScopeTotal
ui/chapter19/customer	262589
ui/chapter19/deposit	259627
ui/chapter19/loan	204460
ui/chapter19/transfer	258785
Total	985461

Summary

We started this chapter looking at some of the basic governance preceding tuning activities to define its strategy, lifecycle, processes, and human resources. We reminded the importance of consulting tuning guides for portal and portal components, but also for other runtimes integrated to portal that can be part of a performance bottleneck. We then looked at some basic problems with response time, throughput. Finally, we looked at WEF-specific tuning test cases.

20
Portal Post-production

This chapter covers some aspects that should be considered after a portal application is cut over to production, and also covers some important pointers in managing a live portal. Portal production main areas of APM, training, impersonation, and the potential benefits of a cloud-based solution will be covered. By the end of this chapter, we will have looked at the following:

- A2Z business and technical monitoring
- Measuring portal and cloud success
- Training and support
- Governance support and APM
- Reusable portal enterprise-wide operational assets
- Capacity planning and performance engineering

A2Z Bank business and technical monitoring

There is a considerable amount of post-production work involved once portal releases go live. It is crucial to understand how portal is performing based on the required and expected service-level agreements. For this, we have two disciplines to rely on — APM for technical monitoring and analytics for business monitoring. The two combined disciplines will provide understanding from a system as well as user metrics perspective. Along with these disciplines for producing, knowledge, problem management, and operational support are of extreme importance. They help to ensure portal continues to be operational and are structured to identify, prioritize, and solve issues to be able to continue to meet its nonfunctional requirements.

For any enterprise-level application, both business metrics as well as technical metrics should be monitored, reported, validated, and consumed by its audience. On the business side, it is important to keep track of **key performance indicators (KPIs)** (in relation to an SLA or a certain business target) related to a business process for the core banking self-service portal application or to the call center. Business monitoring aggregates data based on human-centric or data changes, and business transaction paths provided by the portal application. Near-time monitoring (as opposed to real-time monitoring) is applied to business monitoring and focuses on aggregated business data. Even though there are clear distinctions between business monitoring and technical monitoring, in certain cases, even business data can overlap with technical data.

Technical monitoring is focused on the events and real-time monitoring for IT. The concept of **Application Performance Monitoring (APM)** should go beyond monitoring and expand to the overall problem and release management aspects of the development lifecycle during and after it goes live, with the adoption of mature and repeatable standard operational procedures. Why is APM so fundamental for a portal project specifically? Portal topologies touch many other systems. Oftentimes, the portal application is blamed for performance or other aspects that are really beyond the control of the portal server runtime itself. By having a strong APM practice, you enable the visibility and processes around portal performance to be managed in a more cohesive manner.

APM provides you with the technical side of the portal performance during the entire lifecycle, while analytics give you the usage patterns after production. If these organizational components are strong in the portal initiatives in the realms of governance, APM, and analytics chances are increased for a smooth development and post-delivery phase transition to operational teams. It also applies to subsequent business release phases that will also be developed and go into production. We got a good idea of portal and portlet monitoring in *Chapter 17, Portal and Portlet Performance Monitoring,* and then how troubleshooting and tuning play an important and continuously supporting role in the pre- and post-production versions of portal releases in the subsequent chapters. So both business and technical continuous monitoring sets the stage for having the right set of tools to measure portal success.

Measuring portal and cloud success

When the portal project is first envisioned, there is a set of success criteria that is set from the start at a governance level. It applies to the entire program and also to each individual project level.

Check points for measuring these aspects should be set around as follows:

- Operational performance
- Compliance adherence
- Risk management

Besides these items, the need to measure **return on investment** (**ROI**) in the cloud and portal technologies is evident for validation to be done based on expected ROI.

Training users and support

How the people supporting portal operations also need to be trained and part of the overall portal success should not be underestimated. Training is essential not only for business users but also for the project people supporting future releases from a development and support role perspective. Business users need to be content with how the application functions and performs, and during their training these two items will be scrutinized. They will need to understand how portal pages and portlets work for them. Development staff (which is sometimes migrated to another team once a portal goes live to support future releases), need to pick up the work for future workstreams for the same initiative.

Many levels of training are essential for the knowledge transfer to be successful. Support staff needs to be trained in the many features available to them to troubleshoot and expedite the processes around problem determination, isolation, and resolution. Among many, we will cite one portal feature in particular, which is an awesome asset to support efforts.

Enabling impersonation

A great feature of portal support is the impersonation feature. We do remember the times portal did not have this much desired feature, and some creativity was needed to achieve it.

The impersonation feature allows a user, for example a support specialist, to access another user's system to test out a new page, portlet, and so on; and to see any issues as they occur on the end user system. **Portal Access Control** (**PAC**) controls the ability to impersonate another user. To enable impersonation, perform the steps given ahead.

A2Z portal support folks performed the following steps to enable user impersonation:

1. Log on to the WebSphere Application Server Integrated Solutions Console or Network Deployment Administration Console.

2. Navigate to **Resources | Resource Environment | Resource Environment Providers | WP Authentication Service | Custom Properties**.

3. Click on **New**.

4. Enter **logout.explicit.filterchain** in the **Name** field.

5. Enter **com.ibm.wps.auth.impersonation.impl.ImpersonationLogoutFilter** in the **Value** field.

6. Click on **Apply**, and then click on **Save** to save the changes directly to the master configuration.

7. Navigate to **Resources | Resource Environment | Resource Environment Providers | WP PortletServiceRegistryService | Custom Properties**.

8. Click on **New**.

9. Enter **jndi.com.ibm.portal.portlet.service.impersonation. ImpersonationService** in the **Name** field.

10. Enter **com.ibm.wps.portletservice.impersonation.impl. ImpersonationServiceImpl** in the **Value** field.

11. Click on **Apply**, and then click on **Save** to save the changes directly to the master configuration.

12. Stop and restart the **WebSphere_Portal** server.

Perform the following steps to assign the Delegator role to a user:

1. Log on to WebSphere Portal as the administrator.

2. Click on **Administration**.

3. Click on **Access | User and Group Permissions**.

4. Click on **Users**.

5. Search for the user you want to assign as Delegator.

6. Click on the **Select Resource Type** icon for the required user.

7. Navigate to the page that contains the **Virtual Resources** option by using the **Page Next** button and clicking on that link.

8. Navigate to the page that contains the **USERS** option, and click on the **Assign Access** icon.

9. Select the **Explicitly Assign** checkbox for the Delegator role.

10. Click on **OK**.

11. Verify that the required user now has User and Delegator access.

12. The user(s) with the Delegator role can now impersonate another user.

A2Z portal support team can fully explore this feature along with other support tools to better troubleshoot your end user experience problems. Impersonation can also be used for functional problems, not only performance related. There are differences between performance issues and potential issues faced by a specific user or role. For example, what if performance is great, but users are seeing the wrong data or no data? This is where impersonation comes in handy as well.

Summary

In this journey, we have looked at the entire lifecycle for a portal engagement. A more **Business Driven Development** (**BDD**)approach is important for anyone involved in a portal initiative to be aware of the business drivers and the forces around the portal-related decisions. Engage the right people at the right level upfront and be fully covered with all the best practices provided in this book. From the first portal assessment, to the POV to architecture and development and production—build a great foundation for your initiative and have a successful portal experience.

Index

Symbols

.excludeFromServer file
 about 121, 122
 using 121
/nodeploy/ directory
 about 121
 using 122
.pset extention 146
<<States>> enumeration 66

A

A2Z 330
A2Z availability monitoring 358
A2Z Bank
 layers 87, 88
A2Z Bank business
 and technical monitoring 423, 424
A2Z Banking Reference
 and Portal Application Architecture 73
A2Z Bullion Bank 60
A2Z Business Monitoring 358
A2Z Call Center Reference
 and Portal Application Architecture 74
A2Z resource monitoring 358
A2Z service monitoring 358
A2Z transaction/response time monitoring 358
A2Z web mobile strategy
 about 287
 expected outcome 288
 requisites 288
access control lists (ACLs) 356
access-level control lists (ACLs) 113
access levels 317

Action List 160
ActiveSessions metric 352
Add External button 263
Adobe SiteCatalyst 368
Advanced section, Web Service
 Call builder 179
Ajax
 about 219, 220
 related builders 221, 222
Ajax, and Dojo in Portal development
 benefits 220
alerts
 setting, based on performance thresholds 364
Amazon Cloud
 about 12
 portlets, publishing to remote AMI instance 128
Amazon EC2
 about 104
 cloud approach 21-23
Amazon Elastic Compute Cloud. See Amazon EC2
Amazon Machine Image (AMI) 21, 128
Amazon monitoring, with BMC 371
Amazon Monthly Calculator 104
Ant task 127
Apple Safari 284
Application Architect 80
application component deep-dive monitoring 359
application data analytics 359
Application Performance Management (APM) 19, 96

[PACKT] enterprise
PUBLISHING
professional expertise distilled

Thank you for buying
IBM Websphere Portal 8: Web Experience Factory and the Cloud

About Packt Publishing

Packt, pronounced 'packed', published its first book "Mastering phpMyAdmin for Effective MySQL Management" in April 2004 and subsequently continued to specialize in publishing highly focused books on specific technologies and solutions.

Our books and publications share the experiences of your fellow IT professionals in adapting and customizing today's systems, applications, and frameworks. Our solution based books give you the knowledge and power to customize the software and technologies you're using to get the job done. Packt books are more specific and less general than the IT books you have seen in the past. Our unique business model allows us to bring you more focused information, giving you more of what you need to know, and less of what you don't.

Packt is a modern, yet unique publishing company, which focuses on producing quality, cutting-edge books for communities of developers, administrators, and newbies alike. For more information, please visit our website: www.packtpub.com.

About Packt Enterprise

In 2010, Packt launched two new brands, Packt Enterprise and Packt Open Source, in order to continue its focus on specialization. This book is part of the Packt Enterprise brand, home to books published on enterprise software – software created by major vendors, including (but not limited to) IBM, Microsoft and Oracle, often for use in other corporations. Its titles will offer information relevant to a range of users of this software, including administrators, developers, architects, and end users.

Writing for Packt

We welcome all inquiries from people who are interested in authoring. Book proposals should be sent to author@packtpub.com. If your book idea is still at an early stage and you would like to discuss it first before writing a formal book proposal, contact us; one of our commissioning editors will get in touch with you.

We're not just looking for published authors; if you have strong technical skills but no writing experience, our experienced editors can help you develop a writing career, or simply get some additional reward for your expertise.

IBM WebSphere Application Server v7.0 Security

ISBN: 978-1-84968-148-3   Paperback: 312 pages

Secure your WebSphere applications with Java EE and JAAS security standards

1. Discover the salient and new security features offered by WebSphere Application Server version 7.0 to create secure installations

2. Explore and learn how to secure Application Servers, Java Applications, and EJB Applications along with setting up user authentication and authorization

3. With the help of extensive hands-on exercises and mini-projects, explore the various aspects needed to produce secure IBM WebSphere Application Server Network Deployment v7.0 infrastructures

IBM WebSphere Application Server v7.0 Security

Secure your WebSphere applications with Java EE and JAAS security standards

Omar Siliceo   [PACKT] enterprise ⊞

IBM WebSphere Application Server 8.0 Administration Guide

ISBN: 978-1-84968-398-2   Paperback: 496 pages

Learn to administer a reliable, secure, and scalable environment for running applications and IBM WebSphere Application Server 8.0

1. A significant update of Packt Publishing's WebSphere Application Server 7.0 Administration Guide with 30% new content for v8.0

2. Get to grips with the new WebSphere installer, managed deployments, MQ Link, HPEL Logging, and more in this book and e-book

3. A step by step administration guide with a variety of real-world examples

IBM WebSphere Application Server 8.0 Administration Guide

Learn to administer a reliable, secure, and scalable environment for running applications with IBM WebSphere Application Server 8.0

Steve Robinson   [PACKT] enterprise ⊞

Please check **www.PacktPub.com** for information on our titles

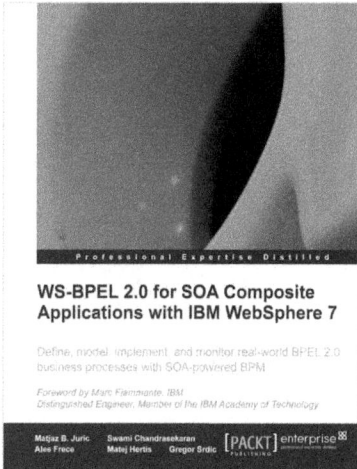

WS-BPEL 2.0 for SOA Composite Applications with IBM WebSphere 7

ISBN: 978-1-84968-046-2   Paperback: 644 pages

Define, model, implement, and moniter real-world BPEL 2.0 business processes with SOA-powered BPM

1. Develop BPEL and SOA composite solutions with IBM's WebSphere SOA platform

2. Automate business processes with WS-BPEL 2.0 and develop SOA composite applications efficiently

3. Detailed explanation of advanced topics, such as security, transactions, human workflow, dynamic processes, fault handling, and more — enabling you to work smarter

WS-BPEL 2.0 for SOA Composite Applications with IBM WebSphere 7

Define, model, implement, and monitor real-world BPEL 2.0 business processes with SOA-powered BPM

Foreword by Marc Fiammante, IBM
Distinguished Engineer, Member of the IBM Academy of Technology

Matjaz B. Juric   Swami Chandrasekaran
Ales Frece   Matej Hertis   Gregor Srdic   [PACKT] enterprise

Application Development for IBM WebSphere Process Server 7 and Enterprise Service Bus 7

ISBN: 978-1-847198-28-0   Paperback: 548 pages

Build SOA-based flexible, economical, and efficient applications

1. Develop SOA applications using the WebSphere Process Server (WPS) and WebSphere Enterprise Service Bus (WESB)

2. Analyze business requirements and rationalize your thoughts to see if an SOA approach is appropriate for your project

3. Quickly build an SOA-based Order Management application by using some fundamental concepts and functions of WPS and WESB

Application Development for IBM WebSphere Process Server 7 and Enterprise Service Bus 7

Build SOA-based flexible, economical, and efficient applications

Swami Chandrasekaran   Salil Ahuja   [PACKT] enterprise

Please check **www.PacktPub.com** for information on our titles